FULL CREEL

FULL CREEL

A Nick Lyons Reader

Nick Lyons

Illustrations by Mari Lyons

Foreword by Thomas McGuane

ATLANTIC MONTHLY PRESS
NEW YORK

Published simultaneously in Canada
Printed in the United States of America

FIRST EDITION

Library of Congress Cataloging-in-Publication Data
Lyons, Nick.
    Full creel : a Nick Lyons reader / Nick Lyons ; with illustrations by Mari Lyons.
        p. cm.
    ISBN 0-87113-813-1
    1. Fishing.   2. Fly fishing.   I. Title.
SH441.L942 2000
799.1'2—dc21   00-030636

Design by Laura Hammond Hough

Atlantic Monthly Press
841 Broadway
New York, NY 10003

00 01 02 03   10 9 8 7 6 5 4 3 2 1

Contents

Foreword by Thomas McGuane

Nick Lyons lives a life much like the lives of most fishermen but it is unlike the life of most people who write about fishing and who seem to exist in a gravity-free state alongside their obsession, accompanied only by their "beloved" fishing tackle. Lyons lives a harried, domestic, urban life of hard work and insufficient recreation. Yet he has persisted over many years in wringing angling opportunity from arid circumstances, a man of excursions. He reminds me of the men who used to train fine bird dogs in Central Park with which they wiped the eyes of local grouse hunters in Maine and New Brunswick each fall; or the owner of a fine Crocker ketch who made a beautiful set of sails in his East Side apartment with which he drove his wooden ship to the West Indies every year. Wife and children have not been abandoned on the cutting-room floor; indeed it is difficult to imagine many of these tales without the presence of Mari Lyons, wife and companion, and her airy refusal to ever quite twig to the goings-on of fly fishermen, whose general dottiness is backlit by her amiable good sense. Lyons is mostly loyal to his hometown of New York, that Gorgon's mouth into which much of the nation's industry is poured to emerge rouged and painted as "retail." On the few occasions he illuminates its dark side, he does so with a vengeance and the reader is chilled by the things Lyons sees every day. When he stoops to help a woman who has collapsed on a winter street, a passing lawyer advises him to keep his distance. No wonder he fishes, we think, but why does he ever go back? He goes back because he loves New York. Here is a life, an actual life, and his essays even contain characters other than himself, surprising in a genre that is customarily the haunt of the tightly focused autobiographer. Above all, here is fishing and despite Lyons's breeziness and humility, it shines forth in its genuine, if hard to explain, glory.

Fishing literature is a bit like pornography in that it serves to not only remind us of past achievements, in detail, but to rekindle our urges for a hopeful and immediate future. Jim Harrison has called fishing the world's most overscrutinized activity. Blithely, we anglers agree with him. Same goes for sex though we couldn't *quite* say of angling, as we could of sex, that it is all that nature seems to care about. Anyway, we are indifferent to criticism, as are all who have given up explaining themselves.

Actually, Lyons is especially good at explaining us. He is a civilized, indeed a cultivated, man and goes to great and eloquent courtesies to lift our passion to fish from its matrix in the unconscious for a critical audience we can never please. I am reminded of an old farmer in my wife's hometown in Alabama who was selling chickens from a roadside stand. An elegant woman drove up in a big sedan, got out, examined the chickens, and taking one in her hands, spread the drumsticks and sniffed the interior. "It's not fresh," she declared. "*Lady*," said the old farmer, "Marilyn Monroe couldn't pass *that* test." Unable to adequately account for ourselves to frowning inquisitors, we cling to our illusions, casting through memory for a sunny day creekside with a grandfather who's been gone for fifty years or a limestone pool like one of Charlie Fox's, now poked into a culvert to make way for a most elaborate cloverleaf that can fling automobiles in four directions without them hitting each other.

I have had more than a few instances of deflation while propping up the idyll of angling. Most recently, I was intoning a trout rhapsody to a receptive audience of book and fishing people in Milwaukee. After my reading, I invited commentary and questions from the floor. A young man still in his fishing clothes said that he had been fishing in a river that ran through town that very evening. There were salmon spawning in the river and three young louts bitten by the fishing bug were casting lures at a sedate old spawner. When she refused to move off her redd to bite the spinner, the most avid of the three sports drew out his revolver and began shooting. The interlocutor wanted to know what I made of this event, vis-à-vis angling today. As this was the first time I had contemplated someone pulling a gun *on a fish*, I prevaricated on grounds that a meaningful reply would require further thought. Further thought suggests that hightailing it in the face of our rapidly evolving national destiny might be just what the doctor ordered. Anglers have some of this in them, this heading out for the territory. Lyons celebrates the desperate need for *some* portion of our lives which cannot be logically accounted for. To the skeptic who points out that our streams and brooks are a rather effete version of the territory ahead, we reply that any water in the hands of God, with its fish and birds and insects, aquatic plants and sheltering trees, its lute-curves of bank, its altering speeds and swelling temperatures is *absolutely the territory ahead* even if, as in one of Lyons's stories, it is the Hudson at Riverside Park. Incidentally, it is a testament to Lyons's skill as a writer that the Hudson is one of the few rivers whose name he gives away freely.

Most New Yorkers have a veteran's pride in surviving New York. They go to places of renewal trailing the trauma of life in their chosen city like tattered flags. They go away to recover and when they feel a bit better, they rush back to New York—baffling to the rest of us who gaze upon them as though we were anthropologists. In the course of this compendious book, we observe the widening gyre of a convinced New Yorker and there are times when it appears that the center won't hold and Lyons will, with his most tolerant Mari, build his wattled hut on some savage Montana streamside. Certainly there are times when his paeans to Old Gotham seem like whistling in the dark, especially when they follow descriptions of motorists beating each other's cars with hammers or off-duty policemen dismembered by pimps and divided among numerous trash cans. He sees the city fairly clearly as a place of arrogance, hatred, and politics. And yet it is the tension, the uncertainty, this counting of trade-offs that gives his writing its considerable vitality, the tang of irony, and separates it from so much sporting literature that seems based on *Superman* comics. When one of his expeditions of escape ends with him being pelted with rocks on the Esopus by leering, rural louts, no place seems reliably safe. There is little room on a trout stream for normal people anyway; here fish are kissed, waters saluted, and the birds of daybreak awakened by our own songs. Such people are bound to be misunderstood.

Above all, Nick Lyons is a married man, a family man, and a wonderful indirect portrait emerges of his wife Mari who is a serious painter and fantastically patient with a husband who, like all anglers, is a hair's breadth away from common mindlessness. I have tried with no success to picture my own wife reading in the car while I fished; so, Mari gets an A in Dutiful in my book while maintaining a wise distance from her husband's enthusiasms through the loftiest incomprehension. She gets an A plus for riding shotgun while he hurtles down the shore road in Martha's Vineyard chasing bait and birds. And his children are delightfully chaotic. Watching Lyons try to fish on a Father's Day trip to Vermont and upstate New York is like watching someone practice the violin in a soccer riot. Still, we cheer when Lyons, back in New York, pleasantly elbows the old lady on the subway who bumps his sunburn.

He is an enthusiast: there are parts of this book where the word "trout" could be replaced by the word "heroin" without so disturbing the text that a philologist would cavil. He makes clear that even the writing we have here in hand is part of his fishing. I find this exceedingly familiar: it's not enough to experience fishing in one dimension. It must be multiplied into at least one other medium. A general public choking on anglers' newsletters and fishpix might be unmoved by this explanation but it's true, honest. And unique: the pressure of today's life is toward novelty and the avoidance of repetition. The angler loves rhythm and recurrence, the similarities in seasons. He is not happy when he returns to his waters and finds them changed. The rest of the world wants to change them, to change everything. Anglers like it the way it is, or used to be. Moreover, they are on Parsifalian quests.

Lyons reserves a special admiration for certain anglers who are masters of repose. He seems to reproach himself as a kind of eager beaver, trying too hard, falling in the water, accidentally spraying fly dope in his eyes, snagging things while the admired masters, such as the aging Catskills trout Samurai "Hawkes," lazily reserve all effort until the gossamer moment arrives, whereupon they arise and lay waste. There's a sharp little portrait of Art Flick where, for the first time, we can really see this great fisherman at work. Lyons even admires the unqualified delusions of some of his companions, like the one who plans to stock the fountains of New York with trout. When he talks of his blunders—a cavalcade of pratfalls—they are deep, persuasive, and thoroughly embarrassing, and not some sort of amiable posturing. Like all anglers of a certain age, Lyons has seen some storied rivers simply vanish before the spread of man, a further urgency. Still, he goes on searching for privacy, pleasure, and freedom in a context he best understands. His standards are increasingly democratic and as time goes by his fish begin to come from warmer waters. He amiably accepts that any status he might have acquired from his numerous accomplishments in the off-stream world are as naught in the eyes of some rustic who knows his way around an old outboard motor. He understands that the modest man finding his way into the world's most sequestered angling opportunities is often a guileful and well-oiled poacher who prefers gentle access to forcing his way up a half-drained culvert in the dark of night. He is an angler.

Here, then, is a generous serving of Nick Lyons's lifelong pleasures afield, the ruminations of an unpretentious and intelligent angler discovering such treasure in the richness of the natural world that there is no need whatsoever to claim it as art or religion. Like all the best angling writers the biggest part of his job is the expression of gratitude.

Preface

The creel in the title of this collection is metaphoric, of course, since I have not carried a wicker container for my catch since I was a teenager. Call this one the repository of memories and stories caught over a long lifetime of fishing, and in this sense the creel is full to bursting.

I always loved those wicker creels. I liked the look of them and the feel of them on my shoulder, held by sturdy harness and growing heavier as a fishing day lengthened. I liked their unique shape, larger at the bottom, and the way the interwoven strips let in air. I liked the way they were lightly stained, often fitted with leather corners and edges and a leather hasp, and I liked the little square hole at the top, through which you were supposed to slip your fish, though I cannot remember ever using it. In my teens, in the 1940s, I rarely returned a fish to the water and always measured a day's success in terms of that weight hanging at my left side. I liked the smell of the creel, too, with its blending of grasses and fish slime, and sometimes some of what was in a sandwich, mingled with a half-dried garden worm or two. And I like creels now and collect but do not use them.

When I stopped carrying a creel, I also stopped measuring a day at all; instead, I wanted to fill it with memorable moments—some or many, quick images or fully orchestrated events, beginning at dawn and sometimes lasting until after midnight. And in my mid-thirties, prodded by an itch to write—about what I did not at first know—I began to transform those inchoate memories into words, mostly essays and narratives. I was teaching literature then and was mad for it, and I think the words and people in what I taught mingled carelessly and naturally with my fishing memories.

Writing about fishing promptly multiplied the pleasure I'd always taken from fishing: I now had the thing itself and then the thing I'd made on paper. Of course, like any sensible fisherman I knew how to tell a lie, though in my case I usually understated my successes and made my mishaps a bit more clownish than they were. If carefully done, I saw immediately, writing could give some fixed form to the fluid stream of experiences—taking from a long day or a week or a season of fishing an essential moment or two worth saving. The moments accumulated. I wrote more and more exclusively about fishing, in a variety of different ways, over a period of thirty years, put together seven full books about my passion, and now have had the experience of reading through all of it together, in the order in which I wrote the pieces, to select the contents of *Full Creel.*

Though its sections have been plucked from perhaps three times as much work as I have here, this is still an ample book. At least for me, there is a pattern to it all—from the innocent enthusiasms of *The Seasonable Angler* to the more philosophic, sometimes darker, more brooding work that characterizes what I have written in the last half dozen years. It troubled me not at all to let certain parts of those seven books stay where they were, but what did hurt now and then was to pull a piece from its home in a book I'd been at some pains to make a coherent whole. Those pieces seemed to come to a bit more in their original context—and I can only hope that a section or two from, say, *Spring Creek* will send a few readers to that book itself, for which the excerpts were originally written.

But I am very happy to see this collection in existence. The stories and essays were a great pleasure to write and now, culled and collected, I see that they make a full and hefty creel, one I'm proud to carry.

Nick Lyons
New York City
December 1999

Acknowledgments

My warm thanks to Don Zahner, for giving me "The Seasonable Angler" column in *Fly Fisherman* magazine nearly thirty years ago; to Emile Capouya, for asking me to write "a melange of poetry and technology," which became my first fishing book, *The Seasonable Angler;* to John Randolph and Philip Hanyok of *Fly Fisherman,* for first publishing so many of the sections in this book, and for always publishing them the way I had written them; to Lamar Underwood, for publishing sections of this book in *Sports Afield* and *Outdoor Life,* when he was a great editor for those magazines, and for always offering such intelligent support; to Duncan Barnes and Slaton White of *Field & Stream,* who always published what I sent them, some of it herein; to Carl Navarre, for publishing and editing *Spring Creek,* and to Morgan Entrekin, Eric Price, and Andrew Miller for wanting to republish all of my fishing books and especially this full anthology. I am especially grateful to Bonnie Thompson, who has copy-edited all of my recent books, and this huge one, so deftly.

Finally, I'm thankful for all the good work my daughter and agent, Jennifer Lyons, has done on my behalf.

from

The Seasonable Angler

(1970)

PREFACE TO *THE SEASONABLE ANGLER*

A generous fish . . . he also has seasons.
—*Izaak Walton*

There is a rhythm to the angler's life and a rhythm to his year.

If, as Father Walton says, "angling is somewhat like poetry, men are to be born so," then most anglers, like myself, will have begun at an age before memory—with stout cord, bamboo pole, long, level leader, bait hook, and worm. Others, who come to it late, often have the sensation of having found a deep and abiding love, there all the while, like fire in the straw, that required only the proper wind to fan it forth. So it is with a talent, a genius even, for music, painting, writing; so it is, especially, with trout fishing—which "may be said to be so like the Mathematics that it can never be fully learnt."

There is, or should be, a rhythmic evolution to the fisherman's life (there is so little rhythm today in so many lives). At first glance it may seem merely that from barefoot boy with garden hackle to fly fisherman with all the delicious paraphernalia that makes trout fishing a consummate ritual, an enticing and inexhaustible mystery, a perpetual delight. But the evolution runs deeper, and incorporates at least at one level an increasing respect for the "event" of fishing (I would not even call it "sport") and of nature, and a diminishing of much necessary interest in the fat creel.

But while the man evolves—and it is the trouter, quite as much as the trout, that concerns me—each year has its own rhythm. The season begins in the dark brooding of winter, brightened by innumerable memories and preparatory tasks; it bursts out with raw action in

April, rough-hewn and chill; it is filled with infinite variety and constant expectation and change throughout midspring; in June it reaches its rich culmination in the ecstatic major hatches; in summer it is sparer, more demanding, more leisurely, more philosophic; and in autumn, the season of "mellow fruitfulness," it is ripe and fulfilled.

And then it all begins again. And again.

I am a lover of angling, an aficionado—even an addict. My experiences on the streams have been intense and varied, and they have been compounded by the countless times I have relived them in my imagination. Like most fishermen, I have an abnormal imagination— or, more bluntly, I have been known to lie through my teeth. Perhaps it comes "with the territory." Though I have been rigorous with myself in this book, some parts of it may still seem unbelievable. Believe them. By now I do. And why quibble? For this is man's play, angling, and as the world becomes more and more desperate, I further respect its values as a tonic and as an antidote—on the stream and in the imagination—and as a virtue in itself.

These then are the confessions of an angling addict—an addict with a "rage for order," a penchant for stretchers, and a quiet desire to allow the seasons to live through him and to instruct him.

WINTER DREAMS AND WAKENING

The gods do not deduct from man's allotted span the hours spent in fishing.
—*Babylonian Proverb*

When do I angle?
Always.

Angling is always in season for me. In all seasons I fish or think fish; each season makes its unique contribution, and there is no season of the year when I am not angling. If indeed the gods do not deduct, then surely I will be a Struldbrug.

Yet sometimes in October I do not think angling. The lawful season has recently ended, I have neglected my far too numerous affairs grossly, my four children have begun school and are already cutting up, my wife trots out her winter repair list. It is a busy, mindless time.

But it is good that my secret trouting life lie fallow—after one season, before another. I welcome the rest. Sometimes this period in October lasts as long as seven or even eight days.

But by late October, never later than the twenty-third or twenty-fourth, the new season commences—humbly perhaps, but then there it is.

Perhaps the office calendar will inaugurate the new year this year. Casually I may, on a blustery late-October afternoon, notice that there are only sixty-eight days left to the year: which means since the next is not a leap year, that there are exactly one hundred and fifty-eight days left until Opening Day. I have long since tabulated the exact ninety days from January first until April first. It is not the sort of fact one forgets.

Or a catalog may arrive from one of the scores of mail-order houses that have me on their lists. I leave it on the corner of my desk for a day, two days, a full business week, and then one lunch hour chance to ruffle through its pages, looking at the fine bamboo rods with hallowed names like Orvis, Pezon et Michel, Payne, the Hardy and Farlow reels, the latest promises in fly lines, the interminable lists of flies, the sporting clothes.

Yes, perhaps this year I shall buy me a Pezon et Michel instead of that tweedy suit my wife assures me I need, or a pair of russet suede brogues with cleated heels and fine felt soles.

In my mind I buy the rod and receive it in the long oblong wooden box, unhouse it for the first time, flex it carefully in my living room. Then I am on the Willowemoc or the West Branch and I thread the line and affix the fly and the line is sailing out behind me and then looping frontward, and then it lies down softly and leader-straight on the water, inches from the steadily opening circles of a good brown steadily rising.

Yes, there is every reason why I should buy a Pezon et Michel this year. And a pair of brogues.

Or perhaps one evening after I have lit the fire, my wife may be talking wisely about one of the supreme themes of art, love, shopping, or politics, and she will notice that I am not there.

"You're not at all interested in what I have to say about Baroque interiors," she says.

"You know I am, Mari. I couldn't be more interested."

"You didn't hear a word I said."

"Frankly, I was thinking of something else. Something rather important, as a matter of fact."

My wife looks at me for a long time. She is an artist, finely trained and acutely sensitive to appearances. Then she says, with benign solicitude—for herself or me, I cannot tell—"But it's only October."

"My mind drifted," I say.

"Not the Beaverkill! *Already?*"

"No. To be absolutely truthful, I was not on the Beaverkill."

"The West Branch of the Croydon? Fishing with Horse Coachmen?"

"Croton. Hair Coachmen. Actually," (I mumble) "actually, I was on the Schoharie, and it was the time of the Hendricksons, and . . ."

And then she knows and I know and soon all my four children—who know everything—know, and then the fever smokes, ignites, and begins to flame forth with frightening intensity.

I take every piece of equipment I own from my fishing closets. I unhouse and then wipe down my wispy Thomas and my study old Granger carefully. I check each guide for rust. I look for nicks in the finish. I line up the sections and note a slight set in the Thomas, which perhaps I can hang out by attaching to it one of my children's blocks and suspending them from the shower rod. (My children watch—amused or frightened.) I rub dirt out of the reel seat of the Thomas. I take apart my Hardy reel and oil it lightly. I toss out frayed and rotted tippet spools. I sit with my Granger for a half hour and think of the fifteen-inch brown I took with it on the Amawalk, with a marabou streamer fished deep into a riffled pool the previous April.

From the bedroom my wife calls. I grumble unintelligibly and she calls again. I grumble again and continue my work: I rub clean the male ferrule of my Thomas and whistle into its mate.

Then I dump all the thousands of my flies into a shoe box, all of them, and begin plucking them out one by one and checking for rust or bent wings or bruised tails; I hone points, weed out defectives, relacquer a few frayed head knots, and then place the survivors into new containers. I have numberless plastic boxes and metal boxes and aluminum boxes—some tiny, some vest-pocket size, some huge storage boxes. Each year I arrange my flies differently, seeking the best logic for their placement. Is the Coachman more valuable next to the Adams? Will I use the Quill Gordon more next year? Should all the midge flies go together? Only three Hendricksons left. Strange. I'll have to tie up a dozen. And some Red Quills. And four more No. 16 Hairwing Coachmen. And perhaps that parachute fly, in case I make the Battenkill with Frank.

There is little genuine custom in the world today, and this is a consummate ritual: the feel of a Payne rod, its difference in firm backbone from a Leonard or a parabolic Pezon et Michel; the feel of a particular felt or tweed hat; those suede brogues with cleated heels and fine felt soles; the magic words "Beaverkill," "Willowemoc," "Au Sable," "Big Bend," and "trout" itself; the tying and repairing; the familiar technical talk, the stories. Fishing is not for wealthy men but for dreamers.

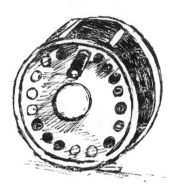

Have I always had so serious a case? Practically. That is the safest answer I can give. Practically. I cannot remember a time when I was not tinkering with my equipment; I cannot remember a time when I did not think about fishing.

And each item of tackle is charged with memories, which return each winter in triumphant clarity out of the opaque past: a particular fly recalls a matched hatch on the translucent Little Beaverkill near Lew Beach; a nick in my Thomas recalls a disastrous Father's Day weekend evening on the East Branch when I almost lost the rod and forfeited my married life. And the mangled handle on my Hardy reel summons that nightmarish fire that raged in on the crest of furious winds during the dead of winter, buffaloing up out of the stone church next door and doing its work quick and voracious as a fox on a chicken raid.

I remember the policeman's light flicking through my little study. My fly-tying table—with all the hooks and hackles, threads, and bobbins—had been decimated. I had raced to the closet, its door seared through. With the borrowed flashlight I searched into the hollowed-out section of the wall. My vest, in which I had most of my working tackle, hung loosely from a wire hanger. It was almost burned away. On one side, several plastic boxes had been chewed through: the flies were all singed or destroyed; nothing could be saved there. Little items—like tippet spools, leader sink, fly dope, clippers, penlite, and extra leaders—could be replaced easily enough: they were all gone. My waders were a lump of melted rubber; my old wicker creel was a small black skeleton on a rear nail; an ancient felt hat was a mere bit of rag; several glass rods without cases had gone up; a fine old net that had always been there at the crucial moments was only a charred curved stick; and a whole shelf of storied angling knick-knacks had collapsed and lost itself in the wet, black debris on the floor. In a corner, the aluminum rod cases were roasted black (Frank Mele later got Jim Payne to check them out: they are no doubt the better for it). And in the debris I found the Hardy reel, its chamois case burned away, the fine floating line devoured, the plastic handle mutilated.

And every Carlisle hook I ever see—long and impractical—recalls my first trout, my first fishing lie.

My first angling experiences were in the lake that bordered the property my grandfather owned when the Laurel House in Haines Falls, New York, was his. At first no one gave me instruction or encouragement, I had no fishing buddies, and most adults in my world only attempted to dissuade me: they could only be considered the enemy.

It was a small, heavily padded lake, little larger than a pond, and it contained only perch, shiners, punkinseeds, and pickerel. No bass. No trout. Invariably I fished with a long cane pole, cork bobber, string or length of gut, and snelled hook. Worms were my standby, though after a huge pickerel swiped at a small shiner I was diddling with, I used shiners for bait also, and caught a good number of reputable pickerel. One went a full four pounds and nearly caused my Aunt Blanche to leap into the lake when, after a momentous tug, it flopped near her feet; she was wearing open sandals. She screeched and I leaped toward her—to protect my fish.

I also caught pickerel as they lay still in the quiet water below the dam and spillway. It was not beneath me to use devious methods; I was in those days cunning and resourceful and would lean far over the concrete dam to snare the pickerel with piano-wire loops. It took keen discipline to lower the wire at the end of a broomstick or willow sapling, down into the water behind the sticklike fish, slip it abruptly (or with impeccable slowness) forward to the gills, and yank.

After the water spilled over at the dam it formed several pools in which I sometimes caught small perch, and then it meandered through swamp and woods until it met a clear spring creek; together they formed a rather sizable stream, which washed over the famous Kaaterskill Falls behind the Laurel House and down into the awesome cleft.

Often I would hunt for crayfish, frogs, and newts, in one or another of the sections of the creek—and use them for such delightful purposes as frightening the deliciously frightenable little girls, some of whom were blood (if not spiritual) relations. One summer a comedian who later achieved some reputation as a double-talker elicited my aid in supplying him with small frogs and crayfish; it was the custom to have the cups turned down at the table settings in the huge dining room, and he would place my little creatures under the cups of those who would react most noticeably. They did. Chiefly, though, I released what I caught in a day or so, taking my best pleasure in the catching itself, in cupping my hand down quickly on a small stream frog, grasping a bullfrog firmly around its plump midsection, or trapping the elusive backdancers as they scuttered from under upturned rocks in the creek bed.

Barefoot in the creek, I often saw small brightly colored fish no more than four inches long, darting here and there. Their spots—bright red and gold and purple—and their soft bodies intrigued me, but they were too difficult to catch and too small to be worth my time.

That is, until I saw the big one under the log in the long pool beneath a neglected wooden bridge far back in the woods. From his shape and coloration, the fish seemed to be of the same species, and was easily sixteen or seventeen inches long. It was my eighth summer, and that fish changed my life.

In August of that summer, one of the guests at the hotel was a trout fisherman named Dr. Hertz. He was a bald, burly, jovial man, well

over six foot three, with kneecap difficulties that kept him from traveling very far by foot without severe pains. He was obviously an enthusiast: he had a whole car trunkful of fly-fishing gear and was, of course, immediately referred to me, the resident expert on matters piscatorial.

But he was an adult, so we at once had an incident between us: he refused, absolutely refused, to believe I had taken a four-pound pickerel from "that duck pond," and when he did acknowledge the catch, his attitude was condescending, unconvinced.

I bristled. Wasn't my word unimpeachable? Had I ever lied about what I caught? What reason would I have to lie?

Yet there was no evidence, since the cooks had dispatched the monster—and could not speak English. Nor could I find anyone at the hotel to verify the catch authoritatively. Aunt Blanche, when I recalled that fish to her in Dr. Hertz's presence, only groaned "Ughhh!"—and thus lost my respect forever.

Bass there might be in that padded pond, the knowledgeable man assured me: pickerel, never. So we wasted a full week while I first supplied him with dozens of crayfish and he then fished them for bass. Naturally, he didn't even catch a punkinseed.

But it was the stream—in which there were obviously no fish at all—that most intrigued him, and he frequently hobbled down to a convenient spot behind the hotel and scanned the water for long moments. "No reason why there shouldn't be trout in it, boy," he'd say. "Water's like flowing crystal and there's good stream life. See. See those flies coming off the water."

I had to admit that, yes, I did see little bugs coming off the water, but they probably bit like the devil and were too tiny to use for bait anyway. How could you get them on the hook? About the presence of trout—whatever they might be—I was not convinced.

And I told him so.

But old Dr. Hertz got out his long bamboo rod and tried tiny feathered flies that floated and tiny flies that sank in the deep pools where the creek gathered before rushing over the falls and down into the cleft.

Naturally, he caught nothing.

He never even got a nibble—or a look, or a flash. I was not surprised. If there *were* trout in the creek, or anywhere for that matter, worms were the only logical bait. And I told him so. Worms and shiners were the only baits that would take *any* fish, I firmly announced, and shiners had their limitations.

But I enjoyed going with him, standing by his left side as he cast his long yellow line gracefully back and forth until he dropped a fly noiselessly upon the deep clear pools and then twitched it back and forth or let it rest motionless, perched high and proud. If you could actually catch fish, any fish, this way, I could see its advantages. And the man unquestionably had his skill—though I had not seen him catch a fish, even a sunny, in more than week.

And that mattered.

As for me, I regularly rose a good deal earlier than even the cooks and slipped down to the lake for a little fishing by the shore. I had never been able to persuade the boat-boy, who did not fish, to leave a boat unchained for me; unquestionably, though he was only fourteen, he had already capitulated to the adults and their narrow, unimaginative morality. One morning in the middle of Dr. Hertz's second, and last, week, I grew bored with the few sunfish and shiners and midget perch available from the dock and followed the creek down through the woods until I came to the little wooden bridge.

I lay on it, stretching myself out full length, feeling the rough weathered boards scrape against my belly and thighs, and peered down into the clear water.

A few tiny dace flittered here and there. I spied a small bullfrog squatting in the mud and rushes on the far left bank—and decided it was not worth my time to take him. Several pebbles slipped through the boards and plunked loudly into the pool. A kingfisher twitted in some nearby oak branches, and another swept low along the stream's alley and seemed to catch some unseen insect in flight. A small punkinseed zigzagged across my sight. Several tiny whirling bugs spun and danced around the surface of the water. The shadows wavered, auburn and dark, along the sandy bottom of the creek; I watched my own shimmering shadow among them.

And then I saw him.

Or rather, saw just his nose. For the fish was resting, absolutely still, beneath the log-bottom brace of the bridge, with only a trifle more than his rounded snout showing. It was not a punkinseed or a pickerel; shiners would not remain so quiet; it was scarcely a large perch.

And then I saw all of him, for he emerged all at once from beneath the log, moved with long swift gestures—not the streak of the pickerel or the zigzag of the sunfish—and rose to the surface right below my head, no more than two feet below me, breaking the water in a neat little dimple, turning so I could see him, massy, brilliantly colored, sleek and long. And then he returned to beneath the log.

It all happened in a moment: but I knew.

Something dramatic, miraculous, had occurred, and I still feel a quickening of my heart when I conjure up the scene. There was nobility in his movements, a swift surety, a sense of purpose—even of intelligence. Here was a quarry worthy of all a young boy's skill and ingenuity. Here, clearly, was the fish Dr. Hertz pursued with all his elaborate equipment. And I knew that, no matter what, I had to take that trout.

I debated for several hours whether to tell Dr. Hertz about the fish and finally decided that, since I had discovered him, he should be mine. All that day he lay beneath a log in my mind, while I tried to find some way out of certain unpleasant chores, certain social obligations like entertaining a visiting nephew my age—who simply hated the water. In desperation, I took him to my huge compost pile under the back porch and frightened the living devil out of him with some huge night crawlers—for which I was sent to my room. At dinner I learned that Dr. Hertz had gone off shopping and then to a movie with his wife; good thing, I suppose, for I would surely have spilled it all that evening.

That night I prepared my simple equipment, chose a dozen of my best worms from the compost pile, and tried to sleep.

I could not.

Over and over the massive trout rose in my mind, turned, and returned to beneath the log. I must have stayed awake so long that, out of tiredness, I got up late the next morning—about six.

I slipped quickly out of the deathly still hotel, too preoccupied to nod even to my friend the night clerk, and half ran through the woods to the old wooden bridge.

He was still there! He was still in the same spot beneath the log!

First I went directly upstream of the bridge and floated a worm down to him six or seven times.

Not a budge. Not a look. Was it possible?

I had expected to take him, without fail, on the first drift—which would have been the case were he a perch or huge punkinseed—and then march proudly back to the Laurel House in time to display my prize to Dr. Hertz at breakfast.

I paused and surveyed the situation. Surely trout must eat worms, I speculated. And the morning is always the best time to fish. Something must be wrong with the way the bait is coming to him. That was it.

I drifted the worm down again and noted with satisfaction that it dangled a full four or five inches above his head. Not daring to get closer, I tried casting across stream and allowing the worm to swing around in front of him; but this still did not drop the bait sufficiently. Then I tried letting it drift past him, so that I could suddenly lower the bamboo pole and provide slack line and thus force the worm to drop near him. This almost worked, but, standing on my tiptoes, I could see that it was still too high.

Sinkers? Perhaps *that* was the answer.

I rummaged around in my pockets, and then turned them out onto a flat rock: penknife, dirty handkerchief, two dried worms, extra snelled hooks wrapped in cellophane, two wine-bottle corks, eleven cents, a couple of keys, two rubber bands, dirt, a crayfish's paw—but no sinkers, not even a washer or a nut or a screw. I hadn't used split shot in a full month, not since I had discovered that a freely drifting worm would do much better in the lake and would get quite deep enough in its own sweet time if you had patience.

Which I was long on.

I scoured the shore for a tiny pebble or flat rock and came up with several promising bits of slate; but I could not, with my trembling fingers, adequately fashion them to stay tied to the line. And by now I was sorely hungry, so I decided to get some split shot in town and come back later. That old trout would still be there. He had not budged in all the time I'd fished over him.

I tried for that trout each of the remaining days that week. I fished for him early in the morning and during the afternoon and immediately after supper. I fished for him right up until dark, and twice frightened my mother by returning to the hotel about nine-thirty. I did not tell her about the trout, either.

Would they understand?

And the old monster? He was always there, always beneath the log except for one or two of those sure yet leisurely sweeps to the surface of the crystal stream, haunting, tantalizing.

I brooded about whether to tell Dr. Hertz after all and let him have a go at my trout with his fancy paraphernalia. But it had become a private challenge of wits between that trout and me. He was not like the huge pickerel that haunted the channels between the pads in the lake. Those I would have been glad to share. This was my fish: he was not in the public domain. And anyway, I reasoned, old Dr. Hertz could not possibly walk through the tangled, pathless woods with his bum leg.

On Sunday, the day Dr. Hertz was to leave, I rose especially early—before light had broken—packed every last bit of equipment I owned into a canvas bag, and trekked quickly through the wet woods to the familiar wooden bridge. As I had done each morning that week, I first crept out along the bridge, hearing only the sprinkling of several pebbles that fell between the boards down into the creek, and the twitting of the stream birds, and the bass horn of the bullfrog. Water had stopped coming over the dam at the lake the day before, and I noticed that the stream level had dropped a full six inches. A few dace dimpled the surface, and a few small sunfish meandered here and there.

The trout was still beneath the log.

I tried for him in all the usual ways—upstream, downstream, and from high above him on the bridge. I had by now, with the help of the split shot, managed to get my worm within a millimeter of his nose, regularly; in fact, I several times that morning actually bumped his rounded snout with my worm. The old trout did not seem to mind. He would sort of nudge it away, or ignore it, or shift his position deftly. Clearly he considered me no threat. It was humbling, humiliating.

I worked exceptionally hard for about three hours, missed breakfast, and kept fishing on into late morning on a growling stomach. I even tried floating grasshoppers down to the fish, and then a newt, even a little sunfish I caught upstream, several dace I trapped, and finally a crayfish.

Nothing would budge the monster.

At last I went back to my little canvas pack and began to gather my scattered equipment. I was beaten. And I was starved. I'd tell Dr. Hertz about the fish and if he felt up to it he could try for him.

Despondently, I shoved my gear back into the pack.

And then it happened!

I pricked my finger sorely with a huge Carlisle hook, snelled, which I used for the largest pickerel. I sat down on a rock and looked at it for a moment, pressing the blood out to avoid infection, washing my finger in the spring-cold stream, and then wrapping it with a bit of shirt I tore off—which I'd get hell for. But who cared.

The Carlisle hook! Perhaps, I thought. Perhaps.

I had more than once thought of snaring that trout with piano wire lowered from the bridge, but too little of his nose was exposed. It simply would not have worked.

But the Carlisle hook.

Carefully I tied the snelled hook directly onto the end of my ten-foot bamboo pole, leaving about two inches of firm gut trailing from the end. I pulled it to make sure it was firmly attached, found that it wasn't, and wrapped a few more feet of gut around the end of the pole to secure it.

Then, taking the pole in my right hand, I lay on my belly and began to crawl with painful slowness along the bottom logs of the bridge so that I would eventually pass directly above the trout. It took a full ten minutes. Finally, I was there, no more than a foot from the nose of my quarry, directly over him.

I scrutinized him closely for a long moment, lowering my head until my nose twitched the surface of the low water but a few inches from his nose.

He did not move.

I did not move.

I watched the gills dilate slowly; I followed the length of him as far back beneath the log as I could; I could have counted his speckles. And I trembled.

Then I began to lower the end of the rod slowly, slowly into the water, slightly upstream, moving the long bare Carlisle hook closer and closer to his nose.

The trout opened and closed its mouth just a trifle every few seconds.

Now the hook was fractions of an inch from its mouth. Should I jerk hard? Try for the under lip? No, it might slip away—and there would be only one chance. Instead, I meticulously slipped the bare hook directly toward the slight slit that was his mouth, guiding it down, into, and behind the curve of his lip.

He did not budge. I did not breathe.

And then I jerked up!

The fish lurched. I yanked. The bamboo rod splintered but held. The trout flipped up out of his element and into mine and flopped against the buttresses of the bridge. I pounced on him with both hands, and it was all over. It had taken no more than a few seconds.

Back at the hotel I headed immediately for Dr. Hertz's room, the seventeen-inch trout casually hanging from a forked stick in my right hand. To my immense disappointment, he had gone.

I wrote to him that very afternoon, lying in my teeth.

Dear Doctor Hertz:

I caught a great big trout on a worm this morning and brought it to your room but you had gone home already. I have put into this letter a diagram of the fish that I drew. I caught him on a worm.

I *could* have caught him on a worm, eventually, and anyway I wanted to rub it in that he'd nearly wasted two weeks of my time and would never catch anything on those feathers. It would be a valuable lesson for him.

Several days later I received the letter below, which I found some months ago in one of my three closets crammed with fly boxes, waders, fly-tying tools and materials, delicate fly rods, and the rest of that equipment needed for an art no less exhaustible than the "Mathematics."

Dear Nicky:

I am glad you caught a big trout. But after fishing that creek hard I am convinced that there just weren't any trout in it. Are you sure it wasn't a perch? Your amusing picture looked like it. I wish you'd sent me a photograph instead, so I could be sure. Perhaps next year we can fish a real trout stream together.

Your friend,
Thos. Hertz, M.D.

Real? Was that unnamed creek not the realest I have ever fished? And "*your friend.*" How could he say that?

But let him doubt: I had, by hook and by crook, caught my first trout.

And when I have dreamed that first trout a thousand times, it is time to think of the present. For the new year has turned.

Then, inside me, the spring trout begin to stir: I feel them deep in their thawing streams—lethargic, slow. I begin to feel the coverts gouged out of the stream floors, the tangled roots and waterlogged branches, the whitened riffles and soft sod banks. Yes, the year has turned. And has not Frank written me: "There are forty-three days left until the season opens, Nick—and you had better give some serious thought to your tying." And he encloses a spritely barred rock neck and, on the spot, I tie up three Spent-wing Adamses.

And then it is time to lay down Schwiebert and Jennings, to set aside Halford and Marinaro, to put up my Walton with those well-underlined passages. I begin to frequent the tackle stores during lunch hour; I stop off at Abercrombie's on my way to work to flex a Payne rod (for what day is not blessed by having first flexed a Payne); I write out an elaborate order to Orvis—but realize it is far beyond my means and whittle it down; a bit of wood duck, an impala tail, floss, assorted necks, two spools of fine silk threat arrive from the economical Herter's. And then, in the evenings—all the tugs and tightenings of the day dissolved—I sit down at my vise and begin to tie.

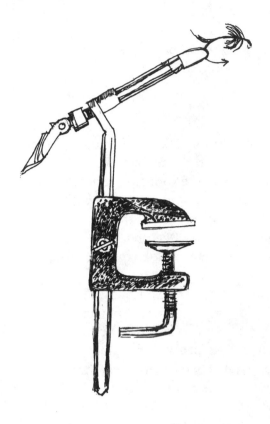

In my salad days, February and March were filled with action. To wet an early line, I would travel to Steeplechase pier at Coney Island and stand, near-frozen, with other hardy souls on a windy day casting lead and spearing down for ugly hackleheads, skates, and miniature porgies. Later I would practice fly-casting on the snow—or in gymnasiums. And as March grew I would wade the tidal flats for winter flounder and that strange grab bag of the seas found at the Long Island shore.

But now I am older and can wait less anxiously. Sometimes. I try to remember that the season will come in its own good time. It cannot be rushed.

My hands are busy at the vise; I use the back of a match to seal and varnish a last guide or two; I send for travel folders I cannot afford to use; I remember a huge trout rising in a small unnamed creek, a little boy slipping a bare Carlisle hook up into its mouth—and then, with a momentous yank, the new season has begun.

THE LURE OF OPENING DAY

Who so that first to mille comth, first grynt.
—*Geoffrey Chaucer, Prologue to "The Wife of Bath's Tale"*

The whole madness of Opening Day fever is quite beyond me: it deserves the complexities of a Jung or a Kafka, for it is archetypal and rampant with ambiguity. And still you would not have it.

Is it simply the beginning of a new season, after months of winter dreams?

That it is *one* day—like a special parade, with clowns and trumpets—that is bound by short time, unpredictable weather, habit, ritual?

That it is some massive endurance test?

Or the fact that the usually overfished streams are as virgin as they'll ever be?

That there are big fish astream—for you have caught your largest on this day?

Masochism—pure and simple?

A submergence syndrome?

That you are the first of the year—or hope to be? And will "first grynt"?

I don't know. I simply cannot explain it. When I am wise and strong enough (or bludgeoned enough), I know I shall resist even thinking of it. I know for sure only that March is the cruelest month— for trout fishermen. And that the weakest succumb, while even the strongest must consciously avoid the pernicious lure of Opening Day.

On approximately March fourth, give or take a day—I get up from my desk year after year and industriously slip into the reference room, where I spend hours busily studying the *Encyclopaedia Britannica*, Volume I, under "Angling": looking at pictures of fat brook trout being taken from the Nipigon River, impossible Atlantic salmon bent heavy in a ghillie's net, reading about Halford and Skues and the immaculate Gordon and some fool in Macedonia who perhaps started it all.

Then on lunch hours I'll head like a rainbow trout, upstream, to the Angler's Cove or the Roost or the ninth floor at Abercrombie's—sidle up to groups rehashing trips to the Miramichi, the Dennys, the Madison, the Au Sable, the Beaverkill, and "this lovely little river filled with nothing smaller than two-pounders, and every one of 'em dupes for a number twenty-six Rube Winger."

It is hell.

I listen intently, unobtrusively, as each trout is caught, make allowances for the inescapable fancy, and then spend the rest of the day at my desk scheming for this year's trips and doodling new fly patterns on manuscripts I am supposed to be editing. Or some days I'll head downstream, and study the long counter of luscious flies under glass at the elegant William Mills', hunting for new patterns to tie during the last March flurry of vise activity.

It is a vice—all of it: the dreaming, the reading, the talking, the scant hours (in proportion to all else) of fishing itself. How many days in March I try to get a decent afternoon's work done, only to be plagued, bruited and beaten, by images of browns rising steadily to Light Cahills on the Amawalk, manic Green Drake hatches on the big Beaverkill, with dozens of fat fish sharking down the ample duns in slow water. I fish a dozen remembered streams, two dozen from my reading, a dozen times each, every riffle and eddy and run and rip and pool of them, every March in my mind. I become quite convinced that I am going mad. Downright berserk. Fantasy becomes reality. I will be reading at my desk and my body will suddenly stiffen, lurch back from the strike; I will see, actually see, four, five, six trout rolling and flouncing under the alder branch near my dictionary, glutting on leaf rollers—or a long dark shadow under a far ledge of books, emerging, dimpling the surface, returning to its feeding post.

My desk does not help. I have it filled with every conceivable aid to such fantasies. *Matching the Hatch*, Art Flick's *Streamside*

Guide, The Dry Fly and Fast Water reside safely behind brown paper covers—always available. There are six or seven catalogs of fly-fishing equipment—from Orvis and Norm Thompson and Dan Bailey and Herter's and Mills'; travel folders from Maine, Idaho, Quebec, Colorado—all with unmentionable photos of gigantic trout and salmon on them; I have four Sulfur Duns that Jim Mulligan dropped off on a visit—that I *could* bring home; and there is even a small box of No. 16 Mustad dry-fly hooks and some yellow-green wool, from which I can tie up a few heretical leafrollers periodically, hooking the barb into a soft part of the end of the desk, and working furtively, so no one will catch me and think me quite so troutsick mad as I am.

But no. It is no good. I will not make it this year. I cannot wait until mid-May. Even then there will be difficulty abandoning Mari and my children (still under trouting size) for merely a day's outing.

And yet for many years there was this dilemma: after years of deadly worming and spinning, I became for a time a rabid purist, shunning even streamers and wet flies. How could I fish Opening Day with dries? It was ludicrous. It was nearly fatal.

But it was not always so.

I can remember vividly my first Opening Day, and I can remember, individually, each of the ten that succeeded it, once at the expense of the college-entrance examinations, once when I went AWOL from Fort Dix, and once . . . well . . . when I was in love.

A worm dangled from a nine-foot steel telescopic rod took my second trout. He was only a stocked brown of about nine inches, and I took him after three hours of fishing below the Brewster bridge of the East Branch of the Croton; I was just thirteen and it was the height of the summer.

On Opening Days you can always see pictures of the spot in the New York papers. Draped men, like manikins, pose near the falls upstream; and Joe X of 54-32 Seventy-third Avenue is standing proudly with his four mummy buddies, displaying his fat sixteen-inch holdover brown, the prize of the day; a buddy has ten—are they smelt? You do not die of loneliness on the East Branch of the Croton these days.

Probably it was always like that. But memory is maverick: the crowds are not what I remember about the East Branch—not, certainly, what I remember about my first day.

In the five years since I had caught my first trout, I had fished often for largemouth bass, pickerel, perch, sunfish, catfish, crappies, and even shiners—always with live bait, usually with worms, always in lakes or ponds. Once, when my mother tried to interest me in horseback riding, I paused at a creek along the trail, dismounted, and spent an hour fishing with a pocket rig I always carried.

It could not have been the nine-inch hollow- and gray-bellied brown that intrigued me all that winter. Perhaps it was the moving water of the stream, the heightened complexity of this kind of fishing. Perhaps it was the great mystery of moving water. What does Hesse's Siddhartha see in the river? "He saw that the water continually flowed and flowed and yet it was always there; it was always the same and yet every moment it was new." He saw, I suppose, men, and ages, and civilizations, and the natural processes.

Whatever the cause, the stream hooked me, too. All that winter I planned for my first Opening Day. There were periodic trips to the tackle stores on Nassau Street, near my stepfather's office; intermi-

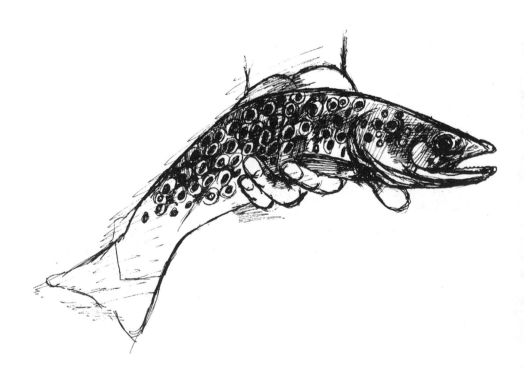

nable lists of necessary equipment; constant and thorough study of all the outdoor magazines, which I would pounce on the day they reached the stands.

My parents were out of town the weekend the season was to open, and my old grandmother was staying with me. My plan was to make the five forty-five milk train out of Grand Central and arrive in Brewster, alone, about eight. My trip had been approved.

I arose, scarcely having slept, at two-thirty by the alarm and went directly to the cellar, where all my gear had been carefully laid out. For a full ten days.

I had my steel fly rod neatly tied in its canvas case, a hundred and fifty worms (so that I would not be caught short), seventy-five No. 10 Eagle Claw hooks (for the same reason), two jackknives (in case I lost one), an extra spool of level fly line, two sweaters (to go with the sweatshirt, sweater, and woolen shirt I already wore under my mackinaw), a rain cape, four cans of Heinz pork and beans, a whole box of kitchen matches in a rubber bag (one of the sporting magazines had recommended this), a small frying pan, a large frying pan, a spoon, three forks, three extra pairs of woolen socks, two pairs of underwear, three extra T-shirts, an article from one of the magazines on "Early Season Angling" (which I had plucked from my burgeoning files), two tin cups, a bottle of Coca-Cola, a pair of corduroy trousers, a stringer, about a pound a half of split shot, seven hand-tied leaders, my bait-casting reel, my fly reel, and nine slices of rye bread. Since I had brought it down to the cellar several days earlier, the rye bread was stale.

All of this went (as I knew it would, since I had packed four times, for practice) into my upper pack. To it I attached a slightly smaller, lower pack, into which I had already put my hip boots, two cans of Sterno, two pairs of shoes, and a gigantic thermos of hot chocolate (by then cold).

Once the two packs were fastened tightly, I tied my rod across the top (so that my hands would be free), flopped my felt hat down hard on my head, and began to mount my cross.

Unfortunately, my arms would not bend sufficiently beneath the mackinaw, the sweater, the woolen shirt, and the sweatshirt—I had not planned on this—and I could not get my left arm through the arm-strap.

My old grandmother had risen to see me off with a good hot breakfast, and hearing me moan and struggle, came down to be of help.

She was of enormous help.

She got behind me, right down on the floor, on my instructions, in the dimly lit basement at three in the morning, and pushed up. I pushed down.

After a few moments I could feel the canvas strap.

"Just a little further, Grandma," I said. "Uhhh. A . . . litt . . . ul . . . more."

She pushed and pushed, groaning now nearly as loudly as I was, and then I said, "NOW!" quite loudly and the good old lady leaped and pushed up with all her might and I pushed down and my fingers were inside the strap and in another moment the momentous double pack was on my back.

I looked thankfully at my grandmother standing (with her huge breasts half out of her nightgown) beneath the hanging light bulb. She looked bushed. After a short round of congratulations, I told her to go up the narrow stairs first. Wisely she advised otherwise, and I began the ascent. But after two steps I remembered that I hadn't taken my creel, which happened to contain three apples, two bananas, my toothbrush, a half pound of raisins, and two newly made salami sandwiches.

Since it would be a trifle difficult to turn around, and I was too much out of breath to talk, I simply motioned to her to hand me the creel from the table. She did so, and I laboriously strapped it around my body, running the straps, with Grandma's help, under the pack.

Then I took a step. And then another. I could not take the third. My steel fly rod, flanged out at the sides, had gotten wedged into the narrow stairwell. In fact, since I had moved upstairs with some determination, it was jammed tightly between the two-by-four banister and the bottom of the ceiling.

It was a terrifying moment. I *could* be there all day. For weeks.

And then I'd miss Opening Day.

Which I'd planned all that winter.

I pulled. Grandma pushed. We got nowhere. But then, in her wisdom, she found the solution: remove the rod. She soon did so, and I sailed up the stairs at one a minute.

A few moment later I was at the door. "I'll . . . have . . . to hurry," I panted. It's three thirty-five . . . already."

She nodded and patted me on the hump. As I trudged out into the icy night. I heard her say, "Such a pack! Such a little man!"

The walk to the subway was only seventeen blocks, and I made it despite the lower pack smacking painfully at each step against my rump. I dared not get out of my packs in the subway, so I stood all the way to Grand Central, in near-empty cars, glared at by two bums, one high-school couple returning from a dress dance, and several early workers who appeared to have seen worse.

The five forty-five milk train left on time, and I was on it. I unhitched my packs (which I did not—could not—replace all that long day, and thus carried by hand), and tried to sleep. But I could not: I never sleep before I fish.

The train arrived at eight, and I went directly to the flooding East Branch and rigged up. It was cold as a witch's nose, and the line kept freezing at the guides. I'd suck out the ice, cast twice, and find ice caked at the guides again. After a few moments at a pool, I'd pick up all my gear, cradling it in my arms, and push on for another likely spot. Four hours later I had still not gotten my first nibble.

Then a sleety sort of rain began, which slowly penetrated through all my many layers of clothing right to the marrowbone. But by four o'clock my luck had begun to change. For one good thing, I had managed to lose my lower pack and thus, after a few frantic moments of searching, realized that I was much less weighted down. For another, it had stopped raining and the temperature had risen to slightly above freezing. And finally, I had reached a little feeder creek and had begun to catch fish steadily. One, then another, and then two more in quick succession.

They weren't trout, but a plump greenish fish that I could not identify. They certainly weren't yellow perch or the grayish largemouth bass I had caught. But they were about twelve to fourteen inches long and gave quite an account of themselves after they took my night crawler and the red-and-white bobber bounced underwater.

They stripped line from my fly reel, jumped two or three times, and would not be brought to net without an impressive struggle.

Could they be green perch? Whatever they were, I was pleased with myself and had strung four of them onto my stringer and just

lofted out another night crawler when a genial man with green trousers and a short green jacket approached.

"How're you doin', son?" he asked.

"Very well," I said, without turning around. I didn't want to miss that bobber going under.

"Trout?"

"Nope. Not sure what they are. Are there green perch in this stream?"

"Green perch?"

Just then the bobber went under abruptly and I struck back and was into another fine fish. I played him with particular care for my audience and in a few moments brought him, belly up, to the net.

The gentleman in back of me had stepped close. "Better release him right in the water, son; won't hurt him that way."

"I guess I'll keep this one, too," I said, raising the fish high in the net. It was a beautiful fish—all shining green and fat and still flopping in the black meshes of the net. I was thrilled. Especially since I'd had an audience.

"Better return him now," the man said, a bit more firmly. "Bass season doesn't start until July first."

"Bass?"

"You've got a nice smallmouth there. They come up this creek every spring to spawn. Did'ya say you'd caught some more?"

I knew the bass season didn't start until July. Anybody with half a brain knew that. So when the man in green said it was a bass I disengaged the hook quickly and slipped the fish carefully back into the water.

"I'm a warden, son," the man said. "Did you say you'd caught s'more of these bass?"

"Yes," I said, beginning to shake. It was still very cold and the sun had begun to drop. "Four."

"Kill them?" he asked sternly.

"They're on my stringer," I said, and proceeded to walk the few yards upstream to where the four fish, threaded through the gills, were fanning the cold water slowly.

"Certainly hope those fish aren't dead," said the warden.

I did not take the stringer out of the icy water but, with all the grace and sensitivity I could possibly muster, and with shaking hands, began to slip the fish off and into the current. The first floated out and immediately began to swim off slowly; so did the other two— each a bit more slowly. The fourth had been on the stringer for about fifteen minutes. I had my doubts. Carefully I slipped the cord through his gills and pushed him out, too.

He floated downstream, belly up, for a few moments.

"Hmmm," murmured the warden.

"His tail moved; I'm sure it did," I said.

"Don't think this one will make it."

Together we walked downstream, following the fish intently. Every now and then it would turn ever so slowly, fan its tail, and flop back belly up again. There was no hope. Down the current it floated, feeble, mangled by an outright poacher, a near goner. When it reached the end of the feeder creek and was about to enter the main water, it swirled listlessly in a small eddy, tangled in the reeds, and was dead still for a long moment.

But then it made a momentous effort, taking its will from my will perhaps, and its green back was up and it was wriggling and its green back stayed up and I nearly jumped ten feet with joy.

"Guess he'll make it," said the warden.

"Guess so," I said, matter-of-factly.

"Don't take any more of those green perch now, will you?" he said, poker-faced, as he turned and walked back up the hill. "And get a good identification book!"

I breathed heavily, smiled, and realized that my feet were almost frozen solid. So I began to fold in my rod, gather together my various remaining goods—almost all unused—and prepare to leave. I cradled my pack in my arms and trudged up the hill to the railway station, glad I'd taken some fish, glad the fish had lived.

It was ten o'clock that night when I returned. Somehow I stumbled up the stairs and, with a brave whistle, kissed my grandmother on the cheek. She did not look like she would survive the shock of me. Then, without a word, I collapsed.

FAMILY INTERLUDES

He that views the ancient ecclesiastical canons shall find hunting to be
forbidden to churchmen, and being a toilsome, perplexing recreation; and
shall find angling allowed to clergymen, as being a harmless recreation, a
recreation that invites them to contemplation and quietness.

—*Izaak Walton*

Though the relationship of an avid fisherman to his family may
be said to have no season, or to be always "in season," it reaches
the peak of its intensity—or aggravation—in the very height of the
trouter's year.

There are, I am sure, innumerable arcane and esoteric reasons
for this.

But the safe pragmatic reason is simply this: the trout fisher is at
his moment of greatest self- and trout-absorption—and least resistance; and his family, flourishing under the beneficence of his year-
long support and devotion, and the ideal weather, is at maximum
strength.

Days are long; children are indefatigable; wives acquire an alarming propensity for shopping and house-hunting and "just walking
together, like a *real* family, in the park." In the early days I did not
have an ally among them, and my secret fishing life suffered much at
the hands of my family.

There were the little things: two missing barred rock necks that
turned up under Anthony-the-thief's pillow; a notorious departure
from the Schoharie in the midst of a massive Hendrickson hatch,
after I had waited three hours for it to appear (my wife called them
"Morgans" and pleaded that we leave "this bug-infested place");
innumerable engagements that took precedence; irony; caustic wit to
the effect that "grown men" did not act in the ridiculous way I acted

about trout. I must be painfully truthful about it, for it all reached a crisis, a momentous crisis, in an incident still painful to recall.

My fishing friends say I am too generous with women and little children. Perhaps. For I suppose Mari, Paul, Charles, Jennifer, and Anthony owe their survival of that Father's Day trip to my extraordinary equanimity. I am not at all sure how I survived.

The spring, troutless and city-bound that year, had been long, but Father's Day weekend was longer.

We left in a flurry, all six of us, on Friday, but despite my best efforts, my speed and my scheming, it was still too late even to make the latest moments of the evening rise on the closest streams. So I settled into a family habit of mind, decided to bide my good time, and set about enjoying a harmless day of visiting friends and swimming on Saturday. After that we could easily fulfill the most prominent of our trip's simple purposes: as I had engineered my wife into saying, "A few solid hours of fly fishing for Dad—poor Dad, who never gets out on the streams anymore because he loves us so much."

Not that I believed her, or had much confidence that at this particular season of my married life I would actually get to drop a few flies—but her gesture seemed sincere and I took it at face value. "A turning point," I thought with quiet satisfaction. Thus, hopefully, I had stashed my little Thomas and my vest carefully in the corner of our rented station wagon. I had heard of such turning points.

The temperature was ninety-eight degrees when we left our friends at three o'clock that Saturday: too hot to fish, no doubt, so I allowed Mari to persuade me that Vermont would be cooler, that we would have time to fish that evening and all day Sunday. "A nice drive will keep us cool," she insisted.

It was little less than one hundred and fifty degrees in the car once we hit the crowded highway: I cannot remember being able to drive faster than thirty-five. But up Routes 5 and then 91 to Brattleboro we went, pausing to examine, while we sped, a half dozen or more promising waterways. It had been part of my plan (cunningly conceived, I must admit) to inject my oldest son, Paul, with the trout fever, and the serum had taken with a vengeance. Before I could see a stream, he'd spot one and call out, "Can we stop here, Dad? It looks like a terrific place for tremendous trout."

He did this several dozen times.

The serum nearly cracked me.

By the time we reached Vermont, all four children were howling wildly, stepping on each other's toes and pride and souls. Dinner took two hours, motel-hunting another hour, and precisely at dusk we were established in cool Vermont, exhausted. Had I been on the Schoharie, at Hendrickson time, I would not have been able to lift my arm to cast.

"Tomorrow we'll get some big ones," I said to Paul as we turned off the lights and settled, all six of us, into the quiet and cool of the air-conditioned room.

"Do you promise, Dad?"

"I promise," I said.

"Can I get some big ones, too?" asked Anthony, my four-year-old, in the dark room.

"Maybe."

"Me too?" asked Charles with his foghorn voice. "If Paul does, I want to get some big ones, too."

"Let's sleep now, children."

It was quiet for five full minutes and, motionless, pooped, I was nearly into a pleasant dream about the Green Drake hatch on the Beaverkill when Jennifer whispered loudly, "You'll let me catch some big ones too, won't you, Daddy?"

"Shussssh!" said my wife. And then, sardonically, "*Trout!*"

Well, Sunday it was raining long thick droplets of rain: a day-long pernicious rain if I'd ever seen one.

"Didn't you say fishing was best in the rain, Dad?" asked Paul.

"You *wouldn't* take the boy out in a rain like this, would you, Nick?" asked Mari.

"Not when it's heavy, Paul," I said quietly.

"And you *wouldn't* expect the rest of us to sit in a muggy car while you were out catching pneumonia, would you?"

"We will not fish in this weather," I assured my wife, sullenly.

"You promised, Dad!"

"It will not rain all day," I told Paul. "And maybe it's not raining in New York State."

So we drove and we sang a hundred songs and we munched some of our genuine Vermont maple sugar—which did not quite justify Saturday's trip to cool Vermont, and which made Jennifer dreadfully nauseous—and we made our way slowly through the blinding Father's Day rain that was sure to kill any decent fly fishing for a full three days, along the winding, twisting Molly Stark Trail, and the children stopped singing, and then fought and bellowed, and Mari became irritated and blamed me, and then Paul blamed me for not finding him a "dry trout stream."

We crossed into New York, where it was pouring nails, at about twelve-thirty, had a long lunch, and then started gloomily, for a Father's Day—or any day—down Route 22. The Hoosic River, I noted, was impossibly brown, and the rain still showed no signs of growing less frantic. The Green River, a sprightly spring-fed creek, was clearer, but the rain continued and Mari would have none of sitting in a muggy car while I got pneumonia.

"If you could find us a nice clean beach, where we could get some sun and have something to do for an hour or so. . . . But you really can't expect me . . ."

"Scarcely," I said.

"You promised," said Paul.

A disaster either way. Straight home: the only solution.

There is absolutely no question in my mind that I should indeed have gone home. Right then. Tragedy was imminent. Had I simply read the signs of the times, I could have avoided disaster.

Yes, blithely I was heading home, peace in my soul, capitulation painless, when, as we approached Brewster, the sun broke out suddenly—brightly, fetchingly. I could not resist a quick look at the Sodom section of the East Branch of the Croton River.

"We won't do any fishing," I promised. "I just want a fast look at an old friend. I used to fish this stream when I was a kid, every Opening Day. Came up the first time when I was . . ."

"Thirteen. I know. You mention it every time we pass this silly creek."

"Do I really?" Do I mention it *every* time we pass?"

"Yes, you do. 'I used to fish the Left Branch of the Croydon every Opening Day when I was a kid.' Every time."

"East Branch. Croton," I muttered. "A short look. Three minutes. Perhaps less."

"I sincerely hope less."

Miraculously, the water below and above the bridge was admirably clear, not crystal but a translucent auburn, perhaps because it traveled to this point over a long cobblestone sluice after shooting down from the top of the reservoir. Interesting, I thought; very interesting.

I scurried back to the car with the happy news.

"Well, if you think you can catch a few trout for supper," Mari said, "you can drop Anthony and me off at a coffee shop for half an hour and take the rest of your children fishing in the Left Branch of the Croydon, or whatever it is."

"*All* of them?"

"I want to go with Daddy," shouted Jennifer.

"If Paul goes, I have to go too, Dad," said Charles petulantly.

"At least make it forty-five minutes," I said.

"With Anthony? In a coffee shop?"

"All right, children: a half hour to catch two fat trout for supper."

"Nick, you haven't brought home a trout in two years. You talk about fishing day and night; read about it constantly; tie those confounded bugs by the evening; go on and on and on—and never bring home any fish."

Since the clock was running, I did not choose to explain that despite the tragedy of being married I still *caught* trout now and then, though I rarely kept them anymore. One such argument, with my mother-in-law, who to this day thinks I keep a mistress on the banks of the "Croydon," led me to stomp out of the room with the profound truism: "Do golfers eat golf balls?"

"Two fat trout for dinner, children—in one half hour."

I dropped my wife off at ten of five, spent seven minutes acquiring some night crawlers, another four setting up Paul's spinning rod, and was on the stream by one minute after five exactly.

"Lovely," I said. "The water's beautiful, Paul. We're going to get four or five."

"Really, Dad?"

"Can't miss. Look: that fellow right under the bridge has one— see him splashing?"

The children crowded together along the bank, watching the brisk battle of a thrashing and leaping eleven-inch brown. I took the time to sneak in six or seven casts, but did not even get a tap.

Then Paul wanted the rod and I gave it to him, telling him how to cast across and slightly upstream, how to hold the rod tip down in anticipation of the strike, how to keep delicate control of the moving bait. He managed his casts well, and I watched eagerly as the night crawler floated downstream and out of sight. Before his fourth cast, Charles wanted his turn too. No, I had promised Paul he'd catch a trout first, I told him gently.

"I want *my* turn, Daddy," said Jennifer.

"We only have one rod."

"No fair. It's not fair, Dad," said Charles gruffly.

"Can't you keep these infants quiet so I can fish?" demanded Paul.

"Don't get nasty," I advised.

"They're bothering me, Dad."

"After Paul gets a fish," I promised Jennifer and Charles wisely, "you two get a turn each."

"Only one," said Jennifer.

"Two trout," said Paul.

But he got no strikes in the next fourteen or fifteen casts, and I noticed that it was now five-eighteen. I was glad I'd left my Thomas in the car. Another ten minutes of this madness—no more.

To get the younger children out of Paul's way, I decided to go up on the bridge itself for the last few minutes, though I noted with alarm how fast the cars sped by. I flattened the children against the edge, warned them sharply not to climb up the low wall, and leaned far over to peer down into the fairly clear auburn water.

A few flies were coming off the water—small darkish flies—but I paid them no heed.

Then I saw it: a long dark shadow, nose upstream, slightly to the left of a large submerged boulder. Now and then it would rise slowly to the right or left and, almost imperceptibly, break the surface of the flat stream. The fish was well over a foot long.

I tried to point it out to Jennifer and Charles, lifting one in each arm so both could see at exactly the same time, but when they scrambled further onto the low wall I spooked and put them back on the pavement, whereupon they raced back and forth across the bridge several times while cars shot by menacingly.

I told Paul about the fish and he promptly climbed up the bank and onto the bridge. He plunked his worm loudly down into the water and it bobbed to the surface and waved there, without the slightest threat of ever being disturbed by a trout.

But the long trout kept rising, once or twice every minute—God, was it really five twenty-three already?—and when I tossed it several bits of a worm, it swirled and snapped at them, though it did not finally take any.

Then a few of the small darkish flies rose to my level and I leaned out incautiously and grabbed several of them.

Dark blue; tiny. Most curious.

What were they? Iron Blue Duns. Not more than three or four a minute, but a steady hatch. *Acentrella*—about No. 18. Weren't they a late-April mayfly, though? No matter. *Acentrella*—nothing else.

Not much of a dinner, but the long trout was unmistakably settling for them. Had I tied a few last winter? Yes, one each, a No. 18 and a No. 16.

The trout rose again—and then again, this time with a definite sucking-down of the water, a turning of its sleek yellow body that showed it to be of considerable size and weight.

Five twenty-eight.

I could stand it no longer. Grabbing Jennifer and Charles by the collars, I rushed back to the car, plucked out my aluminum rod case and vest, and then tugged the children—silent, frightened—down the

muddy bank, past a flourishing garden of shiny poison ivy, and toward the downstream section below the bridge.

Swiftly I unhoused and jointed my delicate Thomas, a simple, lovely idea in bamboo. I managed to mount the fly reel and slip the line through the first two guides, but then began to fumble. The line slipped back through to the reel. Then I worked the line through four guides and discovered that it was twisted around the rod after the second. Then it was through all of them, but the spidery 6X tippet would not shake loose and got tangled in itself, and I had to select another. Then I couldn't find my Iron Blue Dun in No. 18. Should I try the No. 16? Or an Adams in No. 18? Or a small Leadwing Coachman?

Finally I found the Blue in with the Adamses, its hackles a bit bent, and I poked the film of head lacquer out after only six or seven tries and then knotted the fly to the leader on my fourth attempt.

Five thirty-five. She would be furious already—even on Father's Day.

"Quiet. You children have got to be absolutely quiet. Not a sound"—they had said nothing—"good children. You're not going to spoil Daddy's sixteen-incher, are you?"

"How big is a sixteen-incher, Daddy?"

"Big, Jennifer. Very big. Quiet. Quiet. Quiet, now."

"PAUL! DADDY'S GOING TO CATCH A SIXTEEN-INCHER!" Jennifer howled in her high-pitched shrilly voice.

"Can I help you, Dad?" asked Charles.

Paul, on the bridge, had leaned far over to see the action. Clouds were forming rapidly in the sky.

"*Paul!* Get back!" I called, nearly flopping over on the muddy bank. "But WATCH OUT FOR THE CARS! Not too far back!"

Damn, no waders. No matter. The moment was here.

I stepped in boldly—in my Father's Day shoes, in my neatly creased trousers, in my Father's Day sport jacket—tumbled to one arm on a mossy rock, climbed over the riffles slowly, bent my hand to steady myself on another rock (soaking the new sport jacket up to the elbow and along the hemline), and meticulously surveyed the long flat pool.

A few soft small drops of rain began to fall.

"Paul! Paul! Look what Daddy's doing!"

"Dad, can I go wading, too?" shouted Charles.

"Can we, Daddy?"

"Will all my very good children kindly be ab-so-lute-ly quiet for ten minutes. I love you all. I really do. But *please, please* be quiet."

"Daddy, Daddy," called Jennifer. "Charles is in the water. Charles is in the water. Charles is . . ."

"*I am not! I am not!*"

"Charles! Get out and stay out! Now!"

Another foot. Not too close. Whoops! Almost slipped that time, Don't rain. Don't rain, yet! "Paul! Will you *please* get off that railing?"

"My line's tangled, Dad. And I can't see a thing."

"Then come down. But carefully! Watch out for the cars. And the poison ivy."

"Will you fix my line, Dad?"

"In a minute. In just one minute."

Five *thirty-eight!*

"Charles is in the water. Charles is . . ."

"I am not!"

"Charles, if you don't stay out of the water I'll break your little arm!"

I could not see the fish beside the boulder, but thought that amid the steady raindrops and bubbles on the surface I detected the characteristic dimple of a trout's rise. "Now," I murmured audibly. I looped out several yards of line, checked behind me for trees or shrubs or sons or daughter.

The old feeling. That glorious old feeling. After twelve full months, it was all still there.

One more false cast.

"Now."

The line sped out, long and straight; the leader unfolded; the fly turned the last fold and dropped, quietly, five inches below the base of the bridge. Perfect.

I retrieved line slowly, watching for drag, squinting into the steadily increasing rain, along the rim of the dark water, to see that tiny dark-blue fly. In another moment it would be over the spot.

There was a heavy splash below me. Then another and another.

"Charles is throwing stones, Daddy. Charles is . . ."

"CHARLES!"

Whammo!

The tiny Iron Blue Dun disappeared in a solid sucking down of the water. I raised the rod swiftly, felt the line tighten along its length and hold. Not too hard. Not too hard, Nick. I did not want to snap the 6X leader.

I had him. A good brown. A really good brown. I felt his weight against the quick arcing of my little Thomas. Sixteen inches for sure. Not an inch less. The trout turned, swirled at the surface, and bolted upstream.

"Daddy caught one!" shouted Jennifer.

There were momentous splashes downstream.

"CHARLES!"

Out of the corner of my wet eye I could see Paul, in his short pants, hopping through the great garden of poison ivy. "Got a fish, Dad?" he called.

"Got a big one, kids," I said proudly, holding the Thomas high, reeling in the line before the first guide to fight him from the reel. "Your ol' Dad's got a good one this time—*whoaaa!*"

Just then Paul slipped on the muddy slope and slid rawly— through more poison ivy—to the brink of the stream.

The rain was steady and thick now, and I felt it trickle down past my jacket collar and along my spine.

The trout had run far up under the bridge and I was playing him safely from the reel. Several times he leaped high into the air, shaking, splattering silver in all directions, twisting like a snake.

"I'll help you, Dad," shouted Charles, splashing vigorously toward me.

"Didn't I tell you—?"

But before I finished, the huge trout began to shoot downstream rapidly, directly toward me. I retrieved line frantically. He was no more than four yards from me and I could see the 6X leader trailing from the corner of his partly opened mouth; the jaw was already beginning to hook.

Charles was quite close to me now, behind me, and I half turned to shoo him back to shore. His hair was plastered flat on his head from the rain, and he had a long thin stick in his hands and was holding it out, in the direction of the trout.

"I'll get him, Dad, I'll get him," he said. His tone was sincere and helpful.

"*No!*" I shouted, and turned to wrest it away from him.

The gesture was too sudden. The leather-soled shoes were no match for the mossy rocks. With gusts of heavy rain pelting my face, I felt my left foot slipping, tried to catch myself and my tangled line, felt my right foot slipping too, and, holding my delicate, my beloved Thomas high overhead, went down, disastrously, flat on my rump, up to my chest, and kept going, the Thomas slamming wildly against a rock . . .

I consider it a holy miracle of the first water that I survived that day.

And I consider it a fine miracle of physics that my Thomas survived. With only minor scratches.

And I consider it sure evidence of my extraordinary equanimity and good cheer that my family survived. Yet there may well have been a touch of clairvoyance in my ensuing patience: for pragmatically, how could I have known then that Paul would become my favorite fishing partner, Charles a skilled and careful net-man, and that on a memorable June evening I would baptize Mari in the holy waters of the Beaverkill?

Yes, Paul had caught the fever. And the very next year, fishing the little Sawkill near Woodstock, in mid-April, he caught his first trout.

We had taken only one outfit, his spinning rod, and I proceeded to give him some instruction, casting six or seven times up under the bridge. They had not yet stocked the stream but I knew there were always a number of solid holdover browns that survived in the deep ledge-pools.

Since the water was fairly low, I decided it would be best if we went upstream and Paul cast down, so that there would be less chance of the lure snagging on the bottom. He went up on the rocks by himself and cast twice, across and downstream, with no results. The casts were well executed and he retrieved the little C. P. Swing with neat, short jerks.

On the third cast the rod suddenly arced sharply. I thought it was a rock but Paul insisted it was moving.

I didn't believe him until the trout leaped. It was a splendid brown, well over a foot, and all of us—Paul, Charles, Jennifer, and Anthony—began to shout at once.

The fish raced across the little pool wildly. But he was well hooked, the drag gave line when needed, and soon Paul had him up close.

Charles, who was now a properly equipped net-man, slipped the net under the large fish with genuine talent. And we had him.

I grasped the trout around the head and flexed back its neck abruptly. Jennifer flinched and Paul asked me why I had to be so cruel. I told him that this was the quickest way, caused the least pain, and that it kept the trout from secreting bile. "If you're going to keep them," I began, but then realized that it does not occur to a young boy to release what he has caught. Especially not a first trout! That could come later.

It was a splendid event. Charles carried the fish, hung by the jaw from a forked stick, up the hill. Even Mari was impressed.

We took the trout directly to Frank Mele's house, and he treated that first prize with all the ceremony it deserved. First he got out his

ruler and measured it out at fourteen and a half inches. Then, with his razor-sharp pocketknife, he showed Paul and Charles how to dress it carefully, showed them how to slit from the vent forward, remove the innards, thumb out the blood clot, and cut out the gills. They were fascinated.

"Now," said Frank, "we'll have to trace it. Just like they do in the fancy sporting clubs."

He got out a strip of butcher paper and Paul laid his fish upon it and traced its outlines with my pen. Below it, Frank advised, Paul should put the vital information.

Years later, the memento of that first trout still hangs proudly in Paul's room. The brown butcher paper is rolling up on the ends but a few silver scales are still stuck on the body area, and beneath the silhouette reads:

brown Troute, 14½ inches
caught by Paul B. Lyons

Sawkille, Woodstock
4/16/67

MECCA

Mecca (mĕk'à), n. l. . . . a holy city;
hence, any place sought, especially by
great numbers of persons, as a supremely
desirable goal.

One spring there was no spring. March lingered into mid-April; late April was a wintery February; and by the end of May you might have been convinced that, since not even the Quill Gordon had arrived, God was taking a special vengeance on fly fishers. On all except me.

Emergence dates would be postponed; few trout would be taken in the fly-only stretches I had begun to haunt; June (unless God became ungodly vengeful toward fly fishers) would be perfect. While small clusters of distressed anglers grumbled in the tackle shops, I gloated. June was the only time I would be free, and June would be ideal. Even Brannigan was morose. I was serenely gleeful.

All winter I had corresponded from the city with Mike, a fanatic like myself but one who had taken the plunge and now lived chiefly— and blissfully—for fishing. What other way is there? Brannigan constantly wrote me of his friend Hawkes, a knowledgeable old Catskill trouting genius whom I had never met. But Hawkes was more than knowledgeable, more than a rumor: he was a myth. In an increasing number of understated and sometimes unconscious ways, the old trout fisher—in off-seasons, a cellist—began to emerge from Mike's letters as a figure of outrageous proportions. He had, so far as I could tell, a special formula for dyeing leaders to within a chromophore of the color of eight different streams at a dozen different times of the year. He no longer kept emergence tables, but could tell (by extrasensory perception?) not only which fly would be hatching on a particular day, but at what time of the day, even to the hour, the fly would emerge. And in what numbers! Of course I believed none of it. Who would? It was all the fiction of that wild Irishman. Brannigan was obviously a madman, more afflicted even than I, who had lost two jobs because of his trout neurosis, and almost a wife: he was given to exaggeration, fantasy, mirage, and fly-tying. I had only almost lost my wife.

But I was curious. Who wouldn't be? And I had asked four or five times, covertly, whether or not Hawkes would fish with us when I got away for a week in June.

"Rarely fishes anymore," wrote Brannigan. "Most streams have become rather easy for him; most hatches too pedestrian. Says he only fishes the Green Drake hatches—says there's still something to be learned there."

The Green Drake, yes—the most exciting and mysterious of them all. *Ephemera guttulata Pictet,* yes, which brought the lunkers, the old soaks, out of the deep pools, which emerged in massive and manic hatches, sometimes for only a few days, perhaps a week. Sometimes the circus occurred on the Beaverkill as early as the first week in June, but sometimes, according to water temperatures no doubt, it was delayed for several weeks. Yes, to fish the Green Drake hatch on the Beaverkill this year with Hawkes, that was an ambition worth the four months of brooding and scheming. To return to the Beaverkill, which I had not fished in ten years, with the old myth himself, yes—it would be Mecca, a vision to hold me throughout another long dry city winter.

But there was no adequate imitation of *Ephemera guttulata*— that was common knowledge. White Wulffs took a few fish; dyed light-green hackle flies took some; the attempts at exact imitation took very few; and, in the spinner stage, there was the adequate waxy-white and funereal Coffin Fly.

So I experimented that spring, to wile away the wait, and finally, in mid-May, accomplished what to my mind was a major innovation, a contribution to the angling fraternity of staggering proportions. I called it the Pigeon Drake, for the pigeon-quill body I had used after a long quill had fluttered down to me, quite mystically, at the very moment I was thinking about this fly one dreary lunch hour. That quill was a portent, and I promptly sent my two older sons out to collect me several dozen in the park at a penny a quill. They brought in ninety-seven, but I used only thirty in my experiments, and ultimately made only four or five usable flies.

The result is hard to describe. It was not a small fly, nor a particularly neat fly. The tip of the quill, through which I had inserted exactly three stems of stripped badger hackle for the tail, had to be strapped firmly to the shank of the No. 12 hook. Peering up through specially purchased contact lenses from the bottom of a filled bathtub at numerous flies floating there (the door had to be locked to keep out my skeptical wife and distracting children), I observed that the white impala wings of the Wulff flies, sparsely tied, closely resembled the translucent wings of the Green Drake (and many other flies, which perhaps explains part of its extraordinary success). I dyed pure white hackle in green tea. The pigeon-quill body, however, is what made the fly: it was natural, translucent, and would cock slightly upward if properly strapped to the shank. Frankly, it was the work of genius, and I could not wait to fish it with Mike and Hawkes on the Beaverkill—Mecca.

But it rained the first three days of my week's vacation, and all I could do was take Brannigan's abuse to the effect that a man who had not been out on the streams *once* by June ninth was a fallen man, fallen indeed, a man given over to mercantilism and paternalism and other such crimes and moral diseases as were destroying the world, or at least a noble sport. "These are dangerous years for you, Nick," he advised me. "Worse will lead to worse."

The fourth day was Brannigan's one day of work, his one day of homage to mercantilism and paternalism, and since Hawkes was not to be heard from (apparently he had disappeared), I went out glumly to a small mountain stream nearby and surprised myself by having a delightful day catching seven- and eight-inch brookies and browns on tiny No. 18 and No. 20 Cahills and Adamses, dry. It was fun watching the spirited streaks of trout shoot out of their cover and gulp the little flies; it was real sport handling them on 6X tippets. But it was not Mecca.

That night I could bear it no longer. Indirections lead to indirections, and I, a mercantilist, had no business being subtle. "Mike," I said, "it's the tenth of June. There have been no reports that the Green Drake hatch has started and it's due momentarily. Don't you have *any* idea where Hawkes is? Can't you simply hunt him up and ask him if he'll go to the Beaverkill with us tomorrow?"

Brannigan roared. "Sure. I know where Hawkes is. But you just don't ask him like that. It takes some engineering, and some luck. He's got to ask you."

"Dammit. What is he, Mike, a saint?"

Mike smiled and sipped at his fourth beer.

"Did you make the damn guy up?"

"All right. All right. I suppose I can find him. But I can't promise a thing."

Two days later, the night before I had to leave, after two days of mediocre fishing in the Esopus, Brannigan said simply, "Hawkes is going tomorrow; said we could come if we want to."

I tried to answer calmly. Though I still didn't believe a word about Hawkes, not a word of it, a myth is a myth, and it comes with ineluctable power, a power elusive and haunting.

The next morning at eight o'clock Brannigan was at his garage arranging his tackle, selecting from his six fly rods the best for the day.

"Hawkes thinks there might be a Green Drake hatch this evening," the bright-white-haired Irishman said, "but that there might not."

Already a hedge; the tricks of the prophets, the ambiguities of the mediums. He didn't exist. Not the Hawkes I'd dreamed about.

Then, as I got out my gear and piled it beside Brannigan's, Hawkes arrived in his forty-six Dodge. His gaunt, lined face was that of a saint, or of a gunman. His eyes were deep set, limned with shadowy black globes; his fingers were long and thin and obviously arthritic. He walked stiffly toward us.

"Brannigan, old Branny, so this is our young friend," he said, extending his bony hand. "Has he made all the adequate preparations? If he is to be admitted into our little club, he must agree to will his ashes to us, that we may sprinkle them upon the waters of the Beaverkill."

Brannigan tried to suppress a smile. I tried, gently, to remove my hand from Hawkes's firm but friendly grasp.

"The Beaverkill," he continued, looking warmly at me, smiling, "home of Gordon and Darbee and Dette: Mecca. Tell me, Nick, do you face the Beaverkill every morning and every evening at sunset? Do you pray to the gods?"

"Of course he does, Hawkes," said Mike. "Now let's get started. This will be his only real day of trout fishing for the year."

"Very curious," said Hawkes, shaking his head. "One day of trout fishing. I'm sure our young friend has the burdens of the world upon him, then. Nevertheless, one day of real fishing can be enough. Especially at Mecca. It can be made to serve the whole of the year."

I smiled, an embarrassed, naive smile that spread and spread all day, until my cheeks hurt, on that long unforgettable drive to Mecca.

The drive to the Beaverkill should have taken no more than an hour. It was nine o'clock, and I had all hopes of catching the late-morning rise. But it took about an hour for us merely to pack Hawkes's old Dodge, an immaculate, impeccably ordered vehicle, with each object in its proper place: rods, waders, vest, extra fly boxes, net, and Jack Daniel's whisky. There was a holder for his pipe above the dashboard, disposal bags, and four cans of beer neatly packed into the ample glove compartment. Hawkes placed each of our items of equipment carefully into the car, with such measured movements that he might have been giving them permanent homes. As he picked up each piece of tackle he would contemplate it for a moment and then comment on its appropriateness to the sport. "Branny, you know that felt is best for the Beaverkill—and yet you bring hobnails. Curious. Is there a special reason for that, Branny? Do you know something you're not telling? Have reports reached you of great mountains of silt and mud being washed into it? You surely would not be using them simply to impress the pedestrian likes of Nick and me, to taunt us with the fruit of some large sale of flies to a posh New York City tackle shop?"

And then, when the felt waders were brought out from Brannigan's garage, after another five minutes of slow, meticulous scrutiny, "I suppose you know that the glue you've used won't last the day. But the Irish are knowledgeable men, and if you've failed to use the preparation I gave you last winter, I'm sure you have your reasons."

At eleven we set out. Too late for the morning rise, but still early enough for a long day on the river. We wouldn't even have to stop for lunch, I thought, hopefully: pick up a sandwich or two for the vest, and hit the stream as soon as possible. I had a raging fever to be on the stream.

The old Dodge scrunched slowly out of Brannigan's pebbled driveway, made the semicircle onto the tarred road, and started, with incredible slowness, west—to Mecca.

Hawkes opened and closed his long arthritic fingers slowly around the wheel. "This is a day not to be rushed," he said. "It is going to be an experience, an event. It must be savored."

"Come off it, Hawkes," said Brannigan.

Hawkes stopped the car abruptly. Smack in the middle of the highway. Without taking his eyes away from the windshield in front of him, he said, with dead seriousness: "If this is to be a day of cynicism, of doubt, of feverish behavior by an unruly Irishman, I would be glad to turn around, return said Irishman to his own car, and make my peace elsewhere. I have my doubts that the Green Drakes will appear anyway; the temperature dropped to fifty-two degrees night before last—which, I take it, the less sensitive scholars of the streams *did not notice*—the barometer is falling, if slowly, and the moon was not to be seen last night. My fingers are tight, I have a telltale itch along my right thigh, and this *could* become a highly dubious proposition all the way around."

"Okay, okay, Hawkes. I apologize. Please—let's go."

"You're tense, man. Sink into the day. Don't force it. The electricity of such feverish thinking is transmuted imperceptibly but ineluctably to Mr. Brown Trout. The result you can well guess."

My smile spread, my cheeks ached. Three miles down the road Hawkes stopped at a gas station, got out, and asked the attendant about the composition of the gasoline. Hawkes got a drop on his fingers, smelled it, touched it gently to his lips, smiled, and wiped his fingers carefully on some paper toweling. "It is quite possible after all, gentlemen, that the Green Drake *will* make his appearance this afternoon. Very curious."

We started out again, and this time Hawkes was silent, thoughtful, meditative for five minutes. Several times he stopped the car at small mountain creeks, got out of the car, scrutinized the water, threw boysenberries into the eddies, and began to hum quietly. "Boys," he said, nodding, "it's really going to be a day. This is going to be an event."

Three more miles down the road, feeling immeasurably dry, he had to get a small bracer at a roadside tavern. We each ended having three tall beers apiece. Another mile, feeling too wet, he had to relieve himself, and did so in a conspicuously high arc. Half a mile farther and he stopped abruptly, whistled a long clear whistle, and watched a blond farmgirl carrying a child walk slowly across a field of knee-high corn shoots. "It is a day of poetry, of cosmic stillness," he informed us. "She is the Madonna agrarianistically developed."

When I noted, unobtrusively, that it was now two-thirty, he advised: "There are lessons to be learned on a day like this. Let it not be rushed; let it be savored. It is a day composed on the celestial lyre. An event. We need only stop at the Blue Goose tavern, my dear Nick, and we will get to Mecca in good time. Branny, where is that oasis?"

Mike did not remember, but several inquiries proved that it was seven miles out of our way, up an unpaved road. No matter. It was impossible to fish the Beaverkill during the Green Drake hatch without first stopping at the Blue Goose. It was a ritual. Part of the sacraments. The Blue Goose was a holy place, a temple pilgrimages were made to.

It looked like a cruddy overaged bar to me. We stayed an hour, but only two miracles occurred: the floor rose three inches on my fourth beer, and I was able to walk out. We took a six-pack with us and were on our way, due west, over the last little mountains, pilgrims, pioneers, seekers of the holy Mecca.

We arrived in Roscoe at five-thirty, still in time for a long evening's fishing, but Hawkes thought we should look up Bishop Harry Darbee before heading for the stream, to seek his blessings as well as his advice. This could not be done directly. It was first necessary to head for the Antrim Lodge, to the cool dark cellar for a few stronger snorts than we'd had. Hawkes invoked us each to empty two double shots of Jack Daniel's, which done, he launched into a series of incisive questions of the good bartender. But when that dispenser of firewater said that the water had been high and that a few men had been in that very afternoon with limits they'd taken on spinning rods, Hawkes became violent and Brannigan had to grab his arm, even hold his mouth, as he shouted, "Coffee grinders! Hoodlums! Saracens!"

Darbee was not to be found, but Walt Dette was home, and Hawkes conned him out of a dozen hackles from a natural blue, after an hour of talk about breeding of this rare bird.

At seven o'clock we hit the stream. Not ten miles downriver, where Dette had told us to go, but a spot directly below Junction Pool. One look at the water, after that interminable drive, and I had insisted. Hawkes shrugged. It did not make much difference, he said.

Once parked, Mike and I suited and set up hurriedly. Hawkes sat back and puffed at his pipe. "Long as you two have the Saint Vitus' dance, you might as well indulge it. Go on. Git, you two. Takes an old man like me a while to get into the proper frame of mind for his holy stream. It is not to be rushed."

We wasted no time. Brannigan headed downstream, I up—and we were flailing away wildly at the waters for a full twenty minutes before Hawkes, on stiff legs, puffing contentedly on his pipe, ambled to the spot on the stream nearest the car. Fish were beginning to rise steadily just at that moment, and the large pale-green duns began to rise in swarms from the water. I switched from a Cahill to a No. 12 Pale Watery Dun, and then to a White Miller, a White Wulff, and then to an imitation Drake. All in rapid succession. Nothing. Something was missing. My mind was beer-fogged, my casting was sloppy, I was wobbly, and something important was trying to press itself out of my unconscious. Below me, Brannigan, fishing nymphs dead drift, took nothing.

Hawkes waded out a few feet, stood stark still like a crane, fixed his glasses, took the temperature of the water, tested it with his hand, peered long into the swirling duns, the many dimples of rising fish, and selected a fly from his single aluminum case. It took him a full minute to affix it, but when he had he looked at the water again, clipped off the fly, and started the process again. He pulled the leader tight, clipped off the end bit, ran the leader through his mouth six or seven times, and peeled off line.

I was staggered when his first cast brought a strike only moments after the fly had alighted. Deftly he played an eleven-inch brown, drew it close until it turned belly up, and then neatly netted it.

The scene was unbelievable. The sun was several feet above the tree line now, and seemed to hang, luminous and diffused, ready to drop at any moment. The hatch was fantastic, the large pale-green drakes thick as locusts, heavy-winged and fat. Leisurely two- and even three-pound trout stalked them, inches beneath the surface. It was like a slow-motion film. They would cruise, like sharks, their dorsals extended above the water line, and heavily suck down the fallen drakes. Everything took place on the surface—methodically, devastatingly. There must have been fifty trout cruising in that long flat pool—no doubt, many were denizens of the large lakelike pool several hundred yards downstream. They were in no hurry. For them it was an event, an annual feast some of them had probably partaken of for four or five years. My hands and limbs were shaking.

Hawkes's next cast brought another strike, but it was short and he retrieved the line quietly, without a ruffle of the surface.

I made a full twelve casts before he cast again, and this time the rise to his fly—which I could not see—was not short. While playing what was obviously a two-pound trout or better, he called softly for me to come to his position. I scampered through the water like a water buffalo, convinced that he had both the right spot and the right fly, and scurried to his side just as he netted a fine eighteen-inch brown, broke its neck, and creeled it.

I was frantic. There could not be more than another thirty-five minutes of visibility. Wildly I tried four or five different flies, my back cast slapping the water behind me noisily. Hawkes did not frown. He did not take his eyes from the water. I had never seen such intense concentration.

Then I remembered—*how could I have forgotten?*—and my entire body shook with excitement as I did: the Pigeon Drake.

I was so unhinged that it took five cries before I got the leader through the eye of this miraculous fly, and when I jerked the knot tight the line broke. I tried again and this time managed. The Pigeon Drake hung convincingly from my line.

Carefully I false-cast out fifteen, then twenty feet of line. I felt calm and confident now, as icy and knowledgeable and canny as Hawkes. Then I released the last few feet of line, shot them through the guides, and happily, expectantly, watched the fly drop to the water.

It landed like a shot pigeon. But immediately one of those slow-motion monsters glided portentously toward it. I watched, heart beating wildly, while the dorsal neared. The spotted back of the fine brown and each and every aspect of his awesome body were clear to me as he moved, inches below the surface. Then he stopped, the fly not four inches from his nose. The trout was motionless, but not tense. "Take it. Take it, you old soak," I whispered. I twitted the fly. "Take it," I murmured again. Once more I twitched the fly, and this time the movement did it. When the reverberations in the water ceased, the fly began to sink, like the City in the Sea, majestically down. Unmistakably, the trout turned its nose up. It did. I'll swear to it. And then, with noble calm it glided toward a nearby natural, and took it. It had been a sneer—the sophisticated sneer of a wiseacre trout if I'd ever seen one. And it finished me. Dejectedly I retrieved my line, clipped off the fly, dropped it into the water (where it promptly sank like a stone), reeled in my line, and dismantled my rod.

In the remaining half hour of visibility Hawkes calmly took three more fish, the largest a full twenty inches, minutes before darkness set in.

The drive home, after Hawkes had finished three almost raw hamburgers and two cups of black coffee, took exactly sixty-two minutes. Hawkes did not particularly race along the road.

All the way back I had visions of those swarms of greenish duns rising from the flat pool, fluttering clumsily, falling back, drifting downstream, and being leisurely sharked down by slow-motion monsters. Brannigan had caught nothing; I had caught nothing; three anglers we met had taken one small trout among them; innumerable trout fishers throughout the East take nothing during the massive Green Drake hatches; but Hawkes had taken six in about an hour, using no more than several dozen casts. Alas, I can only further the myth about Hawkes: I certainly cannot disprove it.

He evaded all our questions for the first forty-five minutes of that quick drive home with a skill to dwarf Falstaff's.

"Yes, it did seem like the Green Drake, *Ephemera guttulata Pictet,* was the major hatch."

"You're not saying they weren't taking those duns, are you?" asked Mike pointedly. "I saw them take a dozen myself."

"Exactly what were you using?" I asked.

"How, how, how! An extraordinary question. Not at all an easy question to answer, my dear Nick. There are a dozen subtle factors involved that—"

"Come off it, Hawkes," said Brannigan.

"—that the unenlightened Irishmen who slash the streams—and whom it has been my misfortune to fall in with during my decline—would scarcely understand. Brannigan, Branny old boy, did you see the innocence, the absolute simplicity of that farmgirl holding her child this afternoon? The Madonna—no less."

"Will you simply tell us what fly you were using?" Mike persisted.

"A question impossible to answer, beyond my power to answer. Ah, but did you see the colors of the sun settling below the tree line, the ochers, the magentas, the great song of the heavens? You must scatter my ashes there, Branny. It is so written."

We were silent while he dropped us off at Brannigan's house, carefully unloading all our tackle—this time without comment. He asked if we'd like a fish apiece (though not the two trophies).

We both said no.

Then he got back into his car stiffly, turned over the motor, looked at us both with those ancient and shadowy eyes, smiled, and said: "It was an event, gentlemen—was it not? We have been to Mecca. And it will last longer than these six trout, which I shall dispatch shortly—the least part of our trip."

"You won't tell us what you took them on?" I asked.

"You've missed the point. Nick," he said, taking my hand in his bony fingers, "until next year . . ."

With that he drove off around Brannigan's graveled circle and up the road. We could see the old Dodge pause on the highway. Hawkes leaned far out of the car, looked up at the moon, and said something loudly that we could not hear.

"Perhaps it *will* last longer," said Mike, putting his arm around my shoulder and smiling broadly there in the moonlight. I started preparing for the long trip back to the city, for the long year.

"Perhaps," I said.

And it has.

from

Fishing Widows
(*1974*)

A FEW PREMISES

My life for many years has been bound by a city. A gray, dry, sunless place—swarming like an anthill with people. It is a world of "getting and spending," of busy offices and crises and gossip, of financial pressure and itching fear—of living, to a great extent, outside of oneself.

Fishing—in the brain and on the rivers—has been my antidote to all this. It is green and generous. If it is not always idyllic, it always gives me back part of myself that has been lost somewhere among the endless papers. I never go to rivers to kill hecatombs of trout or, actually, any trout: I go to unkill parts of myself that otherwise might die.

Fishing is an irrelevant passion. Wars, financial responsibilities, high art, politics, domestic relations—oh, one could name just about anything in the busy city world, or anywhere, and it will have more relevance than fishing.

Fishing is *complexly* irrelevant. Fishing—unintelligible and irrelevant to the uninitiate—is, as the wise judge Robert Traver wisely notes, *worse* than adultery. The very intensity of the passion—often private, occasionally even religious—is of course what creates fishing widows, and I doubt if the strange predicament of the women, the frequent chauvinism of the men, can be understood or appreciated without some disclosure of how deeply the fisherman's passion runs.

Mine's unfathomable.

I understand Kafka better.

THE LEGACY

I had never known Ed Halliday, of course—neither personally nor by reputation. For a while after that night I tried to find someone who had: someone who had fished with the man, someone who could tell me how he approached a pool, what rivers he loved, how softly he could lay down a dry fly, what size stripers he took from which lonely beaches, whether he preferred flat water or the riffles, whether he fished often, in the early mornings, weekdays, autumns, or when and where and how.

But I was not very successful, and to tell the truth I didn't try very hard. After that evening I had my own image of the man, and whatever he actually was has by now been transformed in my imagination. I have never even seen a photograph of him. Once I was tempted to ask Tom for one, but I never did. Not even after he finally saw his father. After all, his legacy was not mine.

My former student Tom Halliday had called late one night to ask my advice. His father had died a few months earlier and there was, he said, a certain amount of fishing equipment in the estate. Would I come over and give him an educated opinion?

"Doesn't anyone in the family fish?" I asked. I was rather too busy that wet December to go tramping the bleak cold city looking at some poor dead bloke's cod rods. I hadn't mentioned fishing for three months and my marriage was flourishing. I knew Tom had never cast a line, for

I now and then make allusions to trouting in my classes: there are metaphors in it for most of what goes on in the world. He had never risen, except once, to ask a sharp and probing question about the "morality" of trout fishing. I had rather worked my way out of the trout-killing business, and he said it was worse to play with them and then throw them back; he could understand a man fishing for food.

Tom had never mentioned his father to me, though the number of times he came to me for certain advice might have suggested that he had no father to ask—or that, as for so many young people today, the bridge had been blown up. I knew he was searching for values, for a guide; he was not by nature a rebel and his solitary nature kept him from joining the fashionable student mobs. We shared certain solitary habits of mind.

No. None of the family fished: neither of his two sisters, certainly not his mother, none of his uncles. And they didn't want to bring in a dealer until they had some idea how much the lot was worth. The man had fished a great deal, Tom told me, and his sisters thought the equipment might have substantial value.

"Are any of the rods in metal cases?" I asked. "Tubes?"

Tom did not remember. He only knew there was now a mass of it in several closets where his sisters lived and that he had been given a quick look a few weeks after the funeral.

"Didn't you see it in the house?" I asked. "When your father was alive?"

"I didn't live with my father. My parents were divorced. I was only allowed to see him three, maybe four times."

I agreed to take a quick look and, to the best of my limited ability with such matters, let him know if I thought the tackle had much value. The next evening I met him in the lobby of a dowdy apartment building on the Upper West Side.

The apartment was a shambles. Beer cans were littered everywhere; clothes and newspapers were carelessly heaped in the corners; I thought I detected the odor of marijuana. The television was blasting from the other end of the living room and the lights were dimmed. A seductive but sleazy girl in her mid-twenties was scrunched down into the shoulder of the couch and, as we came in, a bearded young man moved over to the opposite arm lazily, frowned, and then stared back at the set.

Tom said the girl was Clarise, his older sister; he'd never seen this particular friend of hers. He brought me directly into a large cluttered room and told me to wait a moment while he fetched his younger sister, Julie. I pivoted slowly in the dim room, trying to find some logic to this bewildering mess.

I could not.

A few moments later a whole spate of fishing rods, clustered and extended like lances, came thrusting into the room. There were eight or nine of them together, with one long stick projecting ahead of the others. Even before I saw who was carrying them, I saw the long rod catch against a cardboard crate and bend suddenly in a sharp arc. I leaped for it, shouted wildly, and managed to shove the crate back. I was too late.

"Damn," I muttered. "Clean split."

The girl—quite short, scraggly, and obviously very hip—was unruffled. "Did something drop?" she asked.

"No," I said after a short pause.

"What was that sound? Like, didn't you hear something, Tommy?"

"You broke one of the rods," I said. I still couldn't see, among the mess of sticks, which one had snapped. Most of them were thick saltwater affairs.

"I couldn't have!" she announced.

I turned the light on, went over to the pile of rods she'd summarily dropped on the daybed, and showed her the split tip section. I shut my eyes. It was a fine light-ocher bamboo.

The girl looked at it closely, running her fingers across the severed strands. Then she proclaimed, in the miraculous tone of admitting something she rarely admitted: "Like, you're right!"

Tom had come over, and he, too, wanted to see the rod.

I disengaged it carefully from the others and held it out, the splintered tip hanging limply where it had broken. It was a fly rod—about eight feet, I judged—and a fine one. I grasped the cork handle instinctively, thumb ahead. Fine fly rods come alive in your hand: this one leaped, then died. I could feel it in my stomach.

Then my eyes darted to the butt.

The signature read:

Dickerson   7604
            Ed Halliday

"No. No. No."

"Is it a good one?" asked Tom.

"One of the best," I muttered. "Custom-made, too. Is there another tip for this?"

The girl said she'd look and skipped out of the room.

Tom could see that I was upset and asked if the rod could be fixed. I told him it couldn't, not anymore, but that a company on the coast could probably match the broken section from their stock, or build another. It would be expensive, and the rod would probably never be quite the same.

" I don't like to see fine things destroyed," Tom said soberly. "I don't know a Dickerson from a Weyerhaeuser, but if you say it's one of the best . . ."

"It should have been in a metal case. I can't imagine why it was set up like that," I said, bending the splintered tip gently so that the pieces came together—imperfectly.

"Julie!" called Tom. "Have you found a case for this rod? Or another . . . another . . . ?"

"Tip," I said quietly. "Tip section."

"Another tip?"

She came into the room with a heaping armful of tackle, cases, and boxes, dumped them onto the daybed, and went back for more. "No cases yet. But I think I saw some near the radiator."

I shuddered visibly and Tom asked me if I wanted a drink.

"Two."

"Let's go into the kitchen."

Several quick shots of Jack Daniel's didn't help. And I was anxious and troubled about returning to the room. When we got back the pile had grown substantially. Julie was bringing in, she said, the last of it. She did. She dropped a couple of fly boxes, a handful of empty reel cases, and a net upon the rest, sighed, and said: "I never realized Ed had so much junk. Clarise brought some over the day

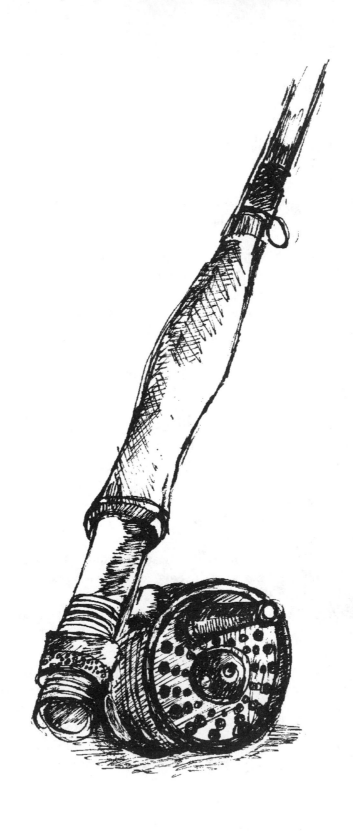

we closed up his place, and I took some over in a duffel bag on Harvey's bike, and the uncles carried some. I never saw it all together like this before. There's a regular mountain of it, this junk, isn't there, Tommy?"

Though the equipment was in wild disarray, and most of it buried, it was simple enough to see that it had substantial value. There were seven or eight Wheatley fly boxes, six or seven aluminum rod tubes in canvas or leather carrying cases, a fisherman's carryall, a fine pair of Hodgman waders, a lovely English wicker creel, seven or eight expensive saltwater reels to go with the heavy rods I'd seen. And more.

Much more.

It was also simple enough to see that though the equipment was heaped and disordered now, the man himself had been meticulous. One quick look into the opened top of a Wheatley fly box disclosed that. Here and there were corners of his fishing life untouched by his pelican daughters.

I held out my arms, smiled, and said, with as little irony as possible: "How can I help?"

Tom explained that the provisions of their father's will had simply said that all his worldly possessions were to become, jointly, the property of Julie, Clarise, and himself. His mother, Rena, had gotten some cash and, when it was secured, had gone off on one of her frequent trips—this time, one of the girls thought, to South America. But they weren't sure.

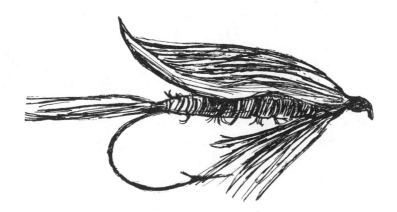

They had decided to sell all this "fishing junk" and divide the proceeds equally—if indeed it had any value; but Tom could have his choice of several items if he had any use for them; the girls certainly didn't. They had heard hostile talk about fishing from their mother for as long as they could remember. "I suppose what we'd like is some evaluation of it all," said Tom, "and perhaps some help for me in choosing one outfit. I didn't want any of it at first, but there's something fascinating about it, isn't there? I doubt that I'll ever use any of it, but I guess that since these things obviously meant something to him, I should keep some of it."

"All right," I said, "let's unravel the debris."

I began by extracting the saltwater equipment. The big rods were good fiberglass; I suggested their commonness and minimal resale value. Some of the big-game reels looked expensive and I mentioned several places that dealt in such used equipment; I told the confused legatees to try them all, and to take the best offer.

In a half hour we had gone through all of the heavy gear—surfcasting rods and spinning reels, boat rods and reels, carryalls full of hooks and lures and wire leaders. It all probably had cost in excess of a thousand dollars, but I told them to be satisfied with several hundred. Through private sales they might get more; but they would have to advertise, and without someone knowledgeable on hand, it would be a cumbersome business.

The freshwater tackle was another matter.

Nothing here was cheap; nothing was less than choice. The gear was all for trout, and it was the best. I could not quite reconcile it with the heavy saltwater tackle, but that was my fault: the world of trout has seemed mysterious enough to me since I found it, perhaps for a lifetime.

I said nothing for a long time while I carefully laid out the fly rods, cases, boxes, and miscellaneous gear, each separately and in a safe section of the room. Several times I thought I detected Tom's eyes searching mine while I fingered a particularly fine item.

None of the rods were in their cases. One other besides the Dickerson was fully joined, and I began with these first, trying to match up odd tips with mid- and butt sections, some of them warped from heat, nicked badly, and otherwise damaged.

"Why weren't these in their cases?" I asked without looking up, as I laid out the three sections of a handsome eight-and-a-half-foot Wes Jordan Orvis.

"We—ll," said Julie. "Like Harvey was over and he wanted to see it all . . ."

"Does Harvey fish?"

"Only from the piers at Sheepshead Bay now and then. He drives this motorcycle, see, and he likes to go down there and sit on the piers and drink a few beers on a hot summer evening."

"Why didn't he put them back?"

"Well, a couple of weeks ago we had it all out, every stitch of it, you see, and well, we were having a little fun with the rods and then it seemed like one helluva lot of trouble to . . ."

"Fun?"

"Some of us were . . . a little high, and we were like fencing with the really thin jobbies."

"Like this one?" I asked her, holding up the extra tip to the Dickerson. It had several bad nicks in its finish and one guide had been ripped off, but it looked straight and solid still.

"Guess that's one of them."

"And what's this piece of heavy wool doing on the end of this one?" My God, the fully joined rod was a Payne, seven-and-a-half feet.

"The cat."

Tom had grown strawberry red. "What about the cat?"

"We were fishing for it."

I closed my eyes and rubbed my forehead. Then I disjointed the rod, running my fingers along its smooth red-brown surface. With old Jim Payne gone, his fine rods had recently tripled in value; in ten years they would be priceless.

There were no reels to be found for any of the fly rods: no one knew what had happened to them. And there was one case for which we could find no rod. It had been an Orvis midge. Julie finally admitted she had given it to Harvey.

"The motorcyclist? The guy who fishes off piers?" My voice was high and shrill.

"Look, mister, don't talk that way about him. I can do what I want with Ed's possessions. What did he ever do for me? Clarise knows and she couldn't care less. Who are you to come in here making snide remarks? This is my apartment and my junk and I can do exactly what I want with it."

"Shut up, will you!" said Tom abruptly. "I invited him here to help us. The rod you gave away may have been worth a few hundred dollars. And it was Dad's."

"Well, it's not Ed's anymore. I don't care if it was worth ten thousand bucks. Like, it was Harvey's birthday and I told him to pick out a couple of things. He liked that skinny little stick and I'm glad he's got it."

"Look, Tom. Maybe I'd better go. This is family business. This equipment was obviously the man's life. It's the very best, and since I take it he wasn't very rich he probably bought it with every spare nickel he had, out of the deepest kind of passion and love. It has financial value. A lot. The demand for a number of these rods—the Dickerson, the Payne, that Garrison—will continue to increase, like blue chips. Make the lot of it neat, get a dealer in, or a couple of them, and get bona fide appraisals. I'll leave you some names. Maybe it will end up in someone's hands who will appreciate what's here."

I straightened my jacket and asked where my coat was.

"Stay a little longer," said Tom. "Julie, shut your mouth for ten minutes, will you?"

The girl balled up her fist and, shaking her head, walked slowly out of the room.

When she was gone I took two or three quick, deep breaths.

"It's a disaster, isn't it?" said Tom.

"It's criminal," I said quietly. "Look at these fly boxes: they've been left on a radiator—they're all rusted and most of the flies are ruined. See this fly-tying equipment? The man probably tied each one of those several thousand flies himself. It's meticulous work. Look closely at this Hendrickson. See how carefully it's made? See how straight the tail comes off the shank of the hook? The neat uprightness of the mandarin wings? The delicate pink in the body? The neatly tapered head knot?"

I held the fly out and Tom took it. He held it lightly at the barb and brought it close and then back a few inches from his face. He nodded his head and handed it back to me.

"And look at these feathers scattered across the floor," I said. "Ripped out of the necks. Look. Blue-dun hackle—excellent grade; you can't buy blue dun necks like this today. Mashed. Ruined. The net's broken, but you could bind up the wood carefully with bait-casting line and varnish it; you can't buy another old miniature net like this anymore: it's a beautiful little thing and probably helped the man with hundreds of memorable trout. Broken rods, missing reels, fishing for cats with a Payne! My God, Tom, whether you fish or not, it's absolutely criminal to treat fine equipment like this; it's like trampling on someone's white linen with muddy feet."

Clarise came in then, let her shoulders slump a full five inches, put a strand of hair in her mouth, and mumbled, "Oh, goddamn: this will take months to clean." Then she said: "Look, Tommy, there are a couple of dozen legal matters I've got to talk over with you and Julie since Rena's skipped, and she wants to get out and meet Harvey. So if you can spare ten minutes from all this heady junk, maybe we can get them done. Already it's time to be finished with this lousy cheap stuff—or are you falling in love with it, like Ed did?"

Tom agreed to go in and asked if I'd mind staying alone for fifteen minutes.

"Not at all," I said. "I'd like to look at all this . . . tackle carefully."

"Be back soon," he said and walked out the doorway. Clarise went after him, took his arm, and whispered loudly: "Can we trust him?"

"No," said Tom in full voice.

I picked up a couple of the rods and waved them back and forth, perpendicular to my waist. I popped open a few more fly boxes. *Perhaps,* I thought, *I should make a low offer for it all and try to steal the whole lot. In a week they'll mash it all anyway. It will be worthless. Cats!*

I picked up the vest, carried it over to an armchair, sat down wearily, and began going through the pockets. My wife would be wondering where I was; I had enough trouble breaking away for a few hours' fishing: I didn't much want this disaster to keep me out half the night, in December, when my most family instincts usually emerged.

But the vest was fascinating.

Leader material. Spare leaders, dyed blue-brown. Penknife, small and sharp. Fly dope. Leader sink. Rubber leader-straightening pad. Matted pack of matches.

I put my hand into an inside pocket. *What's this?* I fished out a little black notebook.

I thumbed through it slowly and saw that it was a record of trips, in a neat fine hand. There was a date, the abbreviation of several streams I had fished, a few scattered comments about the condition of the water, an emergence record, and finally, for each day, a list of trout caught and the fly that had taken them.

He had done well.

It was a pleasant, valuable little book—with a wealth of stream information of the kind that would fascinate any hard-core addict like myself. I would have liked to study it carefully, and half thought of taking it. Who would miss it? Who, among his children, would understand it?

Toward the end of the book he had written something else; it took the last six or seven pages. I cannot remember it all, but some words riveted themselves to my brain.

Raining. Sheets and sweeps of it. River growing browner by the minute. River pocked with bubbles and the lines slanting in. So I sit under this ledge, with pipe and pen, with my good Dickerson taken down and lying across my knees. Gulleys of brown water washing down around me. But it's dry here, and there are two nice trout in my basket and I released four more this morning, which started so quietly before sunup, alone, with the mists hovering over the river. Rena would never understand. Never did. Not Clarise. Not Julie. Not ever. Not even the shrill crisp of the morning or the quick disappearance of a dry fly. Not the swallows sweeping down the stream's alley, the stream birds beginning to work when a good hatch gets under way. Not the deep satisfaction of laying down a good cast, several in a row, sixty or seventy feet of line poised in the air and then reaching toward the eddy behind the midstream rock. Not the squirrel who shared my snack a half hour ago. Not the colors of the water or the sharp, sudden tug of a fat native trout. They never did. They never will. I was never able to tell them the slightest small bit of it, not any of them.

And Tom I do not know.

One calls it butchery while she butchers everything private and holy in her and everyone near her; another finds it merely boring. Fine. Each to his own.

Rena tells me I want to be a little boy again.

And Tom, they have never let me know.

Good ladies, I find myself here. The confusions disappear. The sweet mystery of it envelops me. It is full of sweet noises, the air. Perhaps I have failed with you all. You certainly have failed me and perhaps yourselves.

And Tom? I wish to God you could have been here this morning, my son. Whispering while we suited up in the dark before dawn, talking about flies and stream conditions, and a certain, particular trout one or the other of us raised six weeks earlier. He is the one person I would truly have loved to fish with, to communicate the loveliness of being alone with the streams and the trees and the mysteries under the surface. He is the one person I should have liked to tell this morning to, rain and all. Mud and all. Tom, you are my only son and I can give you nothing. You will not call now, now that you are a man. You *cannot* call, you cannot speak to me. I cannot even hope that someday, somehow, you will find me, or this piece of bamboo, or this corner of the world where a man can still husband that sure and gentle legacy that is every man's . . .

I closed the little black book and waved it back and forth vigorously. Then I rose, still holding it, and began to walk swiftly to the door.

I heard voices coming toward me. I picked up the vest, slipped the book into its hiding place, and dropped it casually on the heap.

"Well, I've seen it all, Tom, and there's nothing much more I can say. This trout equipment is valuable. The Payne, even though it's been used for cat fishing, is probably worth four hundred dollars or more; the Dickerson somewhat less; the flies can't be sold; the net and boots, this and that, have no resale value."

"What would you suggest?"

I hesitated. "I know you don't fish . . ."

"I think I'd like to try, perhaps this spring."

"It could be arranged."

"I might have to reimburse my sisters if I took it all. Should I?"

"That's your affair, Tom. But there's something of a man you never knew, who you've wanted to know, I think, in all this."

"Perhaps," he said, looking away from me.

Neither of us spoke for a moment.

"Well, take the Dickerson," I said, "and, if you can get it, the Payne. But if you fish, don't use them for a full couple of years. Learn on a good glass rod and use it until . . . well, until it seems to be part of your arm. I can show you a little about it this spring if you're really interested. Buy an inexpensive reel for the glass rod, and then, when you're ready, the best reel you can afford—a Hardy or an Orvis. The flies might still be good. Some of them. Go through them carefully some night when you have a few hours. But put away one of each pattern, in cork, for a reminder. The waders are ruined. Keep the net."

"Anything else?"

"No," I said. "I guess that's all."

"I'm grateful to you," he said, extending his hand.

I reached out to him, but drew my hand back. "Oh, yes," I said. "Take the vest." I picked it up and handed it to him. "It has no value," I said quietly. "No value whatsoever. But there are a few items in it that will show you what a proper vest should contain. Your father wore it often, I think, and perhaps you'll find something in it that will help you understand who he was. Otherwise, it has no value."

TROUT IN FUN CITY

My old friend Clyde Fish had gotten himself into a bag over mini-rods several months ago, and for the life of me I couldn't see it. He was a meater, a lunker-monger, a man who had always fished for everything from grayling to hackleheads—any fish at any time, whatever was available. He was not one of those refined chaps who has so much fame and money and distinction that he wants the ultimate distinction of being the only man who, say, caught a mako shark on a toothpick.

I reminded him of this when we met for our twice-a-week lunch-bag browse on the ninth floor of Abercrombie's. I told him that everything was getting smaller—the world, skirts, the trout, flies, fly rods—and that I simply could not buy it. Except I didn't mind the skirts.

"I need one," he said evasively, hefting a classic eight-foot Orvis he'd just removed from the rack, "for a very special purpose."

"But you don't believe that nonsense about the whole point of fishing being 'relativity'—fish to tackle size. It's the rivers and the flies, and the sight of a trout rising. You can return as many fish caught on a long rod, can't you? It's as sporting. A person ought to have the best possible rod for the conditions he's fishing—"

"Yes!" said Clyde emphatically. "For the conditions."

"Then why waste your money on one of those toothpicks?"

He simply smiled—a benign, condescending smile, I thought.

"Well, whatever the reason," I said, growing furious, "you're contributing to an increasing madness. Why, his fishing is getting so canny and persnickety and sporty that they're trying to get rods down to nothing flat. The time will come when you're not a sportsman unless you use a six-inch, tenth-of-an ounce stick. And after that, it'll be merely a long arm. And then trout fishing at the *highest* levels will be restricted to midgets with especially stubby arms—or infants. You'll want to found national associations of 'small fly-fishermen' and 'micro-rodders,' make sassy browns of, say, five inches seem like Atlantic salmon. You're the kind," I told him sternly, "who is ruining the classic art of Skues and Gordon and LaBranche. It's immoral."

He could see that I'd come unhinged and put his arm around my shoulder. "Nicholas, my classic friend," he said, "nothing of the sort is in the offing. Classic I'll never be. I'll still fish for whiting in the dead of winter, at night, on Sheepshead Bay piers; I'll still bounce lead for porgies and flounders in March; I'll still fish for *any* fish any-where at any time. But I agree in principle with absolutely everything you say about mini-equipment—for regular stream fishing."

"Then why this hang up?"

"At this very moment, Mr. G. W. Woodville, that master rod-maker, is making me a mini-rod of exactly one foot, two and three-tenths inches. Exactly. I *must* have it."

"Clyde, I'm all ears. I've known you for twenty years and not one of your schemes has worked. I remember your plan to stock the East Branch with bluefish. I remember when you showed me that fancy booklet about Mohangolookus Pool on the Rykol River, where 'on a night in June of 1937, the King of Laconia and his two companions killed seventy-three salmon, averaging over twenty pounds.' It was *only* eight thousand dollars per week per beat, including guide, and you didn't make that a year after taxes—and had three children. I remember how you went berserk, sold every last bit of equipment you owned, raised *worms* for sale, conned an agent into a special interim deal, flew to Norway fourth class, hitched to the Rykol River, walked four miles over a small mountain, and finally got to the pool—of which you'd purchased seventy-three minutes' worth for two ninety-eight seventy-five. Clyde, you didn't even have a rod left to fish with!"

"But I saw it," he said quietly, flexing the Orvis with obvious affection. "I actually saw Mohangolookus Pool."

"And now mini-rods?"

"Can't keep it from you, can I?" he said. "Well, you see this perfectly splendid and logical idea came to me last spring when my wife and three kids and I were ruining a perfectly splendid June afternoon drinking coffee and Cokes in the new vest-pocket Paley Park on Fifty-third Street. The one with the pool and the magnificent falls.

"'Isn't it lovely?' my wife asked.

"'Tremendous,' I said. 'Ideal for dries.'

"Well, she shuddered and frowned and insisted that I'd promised the family could have this one day, this one day all that spring together, without me traipsing off with my fishing nuts—no offense—without me even thinking fishing. So I apologized. But then it came to me that perhaps right there in the park wasting such a splendid fly-fishing afternoon other good men like myself were suffering—trapped by insensitive wives and indifferent children who could serenely enjoy themselves in stony Fun City while, two hours away, trout were rising steadily on the Willowemoc. I can feel them, you know. Up to one hundred miles away. Why not stock"—he glanced around and lowered his voice—"why not stock trout in the innumerable little fountains and ponds scattered throughout this asphalt jungle? The aerated water would be cool enough, the water in many of them had sufficient depth—"

"*You didn't!*" I said loudly.

He put his finger to his lips. "I envisioned," he went on, serenely, "dapper businessmen stopping by during lunch hours, blithely opening trim little Abercrombie & Fitch traveling cases fitted with trim traveling rods, rigging up, and deftly catching several lunch-hour trout. After an hour of fly fishing, think of how much more responsible they'd be at their desks!"

"That's true," I had to admit.

"Think of how the millions of trout fishermen who are moving out of this city would return . . ."

"There aren't millions of trout fishermen, thank God."

". . . how the economy of the city would improve and . . ."

"New York has survived, after its fashion, since the Indians without trout," I advised him calmly.

"I'd be the Madison Avenue Walton, the Great Emancipator, beloved by generations of stone-bound anglers the world over, immortalized in song and over martinis. Never again need there ever be a frustrated angler in New York—nor in any city! A trout in every fountain. Two trout in every fountain. A dozen!" He was beginning to lose control. I thought I saw his eyes roll. "There was the Revlon Fountain at Lincoln Center, the Grand Army Plaza fountains, a perfectly exquisite pond with bubbling waters at the Steuben Glass Building on Fifth Avenue and Fifty-sixth Street, and—"

"You're mad, Clyde," I said sadly. "This time you've absolutely lost your marbles. All of them." I took the Orvis from his hands gently. He had begun to shake uncontrollably. Then I gave him a half wave and a shake of my head and started to leave. It might be contagious.

But he grabbed my wrist.

"I decided," he said rapidly, "to start with Paley Park—for sentimental reasons. First I checked with the architect on the size of the falls and the depth of the water. Then I tested the water with my stream thermometer: fifty-eight degrees—perfect. I even got the parks commissioner and the mayor to approve, telling them about the important trout lobby."

"You actually did it?" I asked, incredulous. "They're there now? While we're talking?"

"Nope. No, actually they're not there now. Went too far. 'Why not salmon?' I asked myself. And then I had these four perfectly lovely little Atlantic salmon—grilse, actually—flown down from Nova Scotia and stocked them gingerly. Bad mistake. A lapse."

"I'm all ears."

"On the third day the salmon suddenly began leaping the falls to Doubleday's; Ed Zern, passing, saw them, went into shock, and nearly caused a nine-car accident. The traffic commissioner came down on me hard."

"A tragedy, Clyde."

"They hushed it up, of course. Fearing the trout lobby, no doubt. But I was not to be squelched. Two weeks later, without the approval of the mayor or the parks commissioner or the traffic commissioner,

I stocked eleven fat brown trout in the Steuben Glass pool on Fifth Avenue. They took to it beautifully and before work that Tuesday I tried them with my eight-foot Granger."

"But you couldn't match the city life that was hatching?"

"Nope. Took three on Lady Beaverkills. Dry. But then—"

"Don't tell me!"

"Then I caught the Fifth Avenue bus on a back cast."

I breathed deeply. "They can be damned sporty on light tackle."

"Nearly got the city struck by the union, that's what! Not one of the 'assumed hazards,' they said. Needed an increase to cover it. But that's why I'm having this one-foot, two-and-three-tenths-inches rod made."

"So you can fish the Steuben Glass fountain again?"

"Nope."

"All right, I'll bite. The Revlon Fountain? The fountains at the Metropolitan Museum? Downtown or uptown?"

"I see you've been looking, too."

I frowned.

"Couple of weeks ago," he said confidentially, "I poached a box of good stream life out of the Beaverkill and dropped it into the Seal Pool in Central Park along with a half dozen mixed browns and brookies."

"*Nooooo,* Clyde. You didn't!"

"I've been watching it, Nick," he said. "There are ab-so-lute-ly superb hatches in the evening and I plan to sneak in a dozen or so casts tomorrow at lunch hour. I'm getting the mini-rod so I won't catch any stray kiddies. Hooking one of those would be worse than catching a union bus."

I'd had enough. "Good luck," I muttered. And under my breath: "May your leaders rot and save you imprisonment, old Clyde."

And then I left rapidly. It was catching.

I met him several weeks later on Madison Avenue. He had a large bag under his arm and was headed for Abercrombie's. He was ecstatic. "What're they taking, Clyde?" I asked, taking his shoulder affectionately.

"Cow Dung," he whispered. "Twelves and fourteens—barbless."

"Where?" I whispered back.

"Won't tell anyone?" He paused. "Seal Pool."

"You're kidding!"

"Took two last night," he said matter-of-factly.

"*Trout?* In Central Park? You *really* took two?" I was suffering from a bit of trout deprivation myself, and the thought unhinged me.

"No, the seals got the trout before I could, of course—should have figured. But I took two small seals on a number fourteen Cow Dung right at dusk. God, what a fight they give on a mini-rod! My only worry was that truck that came around just as I released the second. Had on it, ASPCA. Are seals fish?"

"Mammals, Clyde," I said, recovering quickly. "And they're out of season. You're lucky the truck didn't say Bellevue. Perhaps we could just sit down, Clyde, old man, and talk this out. I'm starting a local chapter of Anglers Anonymous—when you feel this coming on again, just phone me, any time of the day or night, Clyde, and—"

"Oh, come on, friend," he snapped nervously. "If I don't get over to Abercrombie's, this bag of ice cubes is going to melt all over Madison Avenue. I don't much appreciate being humored. Certainly not by *you*."

Somewhere in his last words was a straight line, but I couldn't grasp it.

"Look," he said hoarsely, "we just have time to get this ice up to the A & F roof and get down to the ninth floor. We'll hide in the sail loft until they close. Then . . ."

Even when seized by the vapors, anglers seem to have a subliminal sense of communication—or, as they say, it takes one to know one. "Clyde, you don't mean . . ."

"Exactly!" he shouted, grasping my arm. "The casting pool on the roof."

He reached in his pocket and shakily withdrew a bill of lading marked Alaska Airways. He held it close to my face.

"Since lunchtime today, pal," he announced triumphantly. "Stocked with Arctic grayling."

THE FINE ART OF HUDSON RIVER
FENCE FISHING

Fly casting on the new-mown grass in Riverside Park, I was pleased to see a fellow brother of the angle walk briskly through the crowd of skeptical onlookers. He had an army carryall slung on his shoulder and a long and heavy saltwater rod in his hand; his nose was bright red and there was a pint bottle stashed neatly in the back pocket of his baggy gabardines. *Stenonema fuscum* had appeared on the Schoharie, my scouts had reported, but I had only caught a half dozen good clumps of fresh-cut grass in an hour of serious casting. They were about five or six inches apiece, I suppose, and I had slipped them off the unbarbed and, in fact, untipped yellow fly easily. They gave no appreciable fight.

"You never ketch 'em here," the angler advised, with a loud laugh.

"Where're *you* going?"

"The river." He came over and shook his head at my bamboo fly rod.

"What do you get?" I asked.

"Fish," he said. "What you get with toot-pick?"

"Grass," I replied.

He waved his hand down, laughed loudly again, and then, somewhat surreptitiously I thought, marched quickly off. I had seen that particular step before. It was somewhat too determined and hurried. A telltale phenomenon. The man had information that he was keeping from his brothers. Was there a striper run on? Could shad be in the river and available to the initiate? Herring?

My four children were with me and we had an intolerably long June afternoon, hot and landlocked in the city, stretched in front of us. Even Clyde was in the Catskills.

Why not, I thought: I'll try the river.

I sent Paul back for his spinning rod and Charles to the fish market on Broadway for twenty-five cents' worth of squid. Pier fishing, if that's what it was to be, was not new to me. When I was a kid I'd bike down to Sheepshead or Steeplechase piers and fish for porgies, ling, whiting, blowfish, hackleheads, and whatever else could be scared up from the bottom. Most of them had scared me—with their horns and prickles, their ignoble inflating and deflating. It was a weird business, practiced in snow and boiling sun, and I had not regretted relinquishing it when I fell in love with trout—which at least had no horns and only grew fat in one's imagination. I had never tried the Hudson, though we lived only a block away, in the center of Manhattan. A slide presentation by Bob Boyle at the Theodore Gordon Flyfishers' dinner in March had intrigued me with the fecundity of the river, and I had, years before, caught stripers and even herring on flies as far north as Barrytown.

Without disjointing my fly rod, I took my two young ones by the hands and headed for the river. Twenty minutes later the spinning rod and squid arrived, and I was ready for action.

It was an exquisite day.

The sun was bright, the sky was pleasantly flecked with soft white-gray clumps of clouds. The New Jersey palisades were firm, angular, and green. A couple of posh cabin cruisers headed upriver; a long brown barge headed down. Several women were sunbathing against the slope of the hill; they had hardly any clothes on; one of them was more angular and firm than the palisades. A helicopter fluttered up the mighty Hudson like a bloated swallow—but found no mayflies rising.

I saw at once that this was not pier but *fence* fishing. There were some eighteen or twenty anglers spread along a hundred yards of fence. Their heavy saltwater rods were leaned at precisely the same angle against the railing, and all of them were standing back ten to twenty feet, alone or in little groups. There was one spirited group of eight to ten Puerto Ricans whose lively chatter rose above their loud radio music.

I found an unoccupied few yards, laid my fly rod carefully against the fence, set up the spinning rod, cut and threaded on a slab of squid, and cast out. I have never been the sort to leave a rod unattended—neither on the forked sticks common to reservoir fishing nor on piers—so I held it lightly couched in my arm, with my right index finger pressing against the monofilament. I even gave the line a few sporadic tugs, to impart some action.

After an hour, my older boys grew bored and went off to play baseball; Jennifer and Anthony ran to investigate the boat basin a couple of hundred yards downriver. I had experienced my share of family disasters while trying to fish for trout, and was enormously grateful that they could thus occupy themselves. I had perhaps discovered an anglers' paradise in the midst of gray New York. There were escape facilities for the children, music (if that's what you wanted), company, a beautiful landscape across the river, shapely sunbathers; there was no wasted time getting to the fishing grounds; there would be no anxiety lest the day's hatch be missed, or go unmatched. If it wasn't the Schoharie when the Hendricksons were on, and you were alone with fish feeding in every run and pocket, it was still—I rationalized—a line in the water.

But I soon discovered that Hudson River fence fishing is an art not to be taken lightly—an art with its own traditions and lore, its own ethics and mores; it is also essentially a traditionalist's art, for I'll wager there have been few changes over the past seventy years—nor any tolerance or encouragement paid the rebel. Innovation, as for the fabled lotus-eaters on the Beaverkill, is met with distrust bordering on disgust.

At precisely three twenty-seven one of the Puerto Rican anglers let out a momentous howl, not unlike that of the hound of the Baskervilles. He raced down the slope, grasped his rod, and struck it back five feet. "*Grande, grande!*" he shouted, and was soon surrounded by seven or eight onlookers. He reeled his line in without hesitation, with a sweep of his arm heaved his fish directly out, and a moment later there was a long green eel flapping and squiggling on the grass.

An interesting tool was then produced, which I had never seen used before. It looked to me like a piece of twisted wire hanger. It was carefully placed just ahead of the hook, with eel hanging down. Then, with an abrupt movement, the eel was flipped in a circle around the tool. Whatever was supposed to happen did not. The maneuver was nevertheless tried again, and this time the eel came quickly and miraculously off the hook and flopped to the ground. There it was ceremoniously kicked at and stabbed with a long knife until it lay motionless. A mutt was brought near, but it showed singular disinterest in the long corpse.

Then a general query was raised whether anyone wanted the remains. There was no response and the eel was thereafter handled meanly by several children—until it disappeared.

I asked one of the men the name of the instrument used to disgorge the hook so handily. "Wire," he replied.

Soon another cry went up and another young man raced to his rod. Within the next twenty minutes another and then another rod were struck back fiercely, and four more eels were swiftly brought to fence. The rise was going full blast and, frankly, I felt somewhat left out. I reeled in my strip of squid and discovered it to be singularly unmolested. Anthony had returned and I asked him to seek out a good angler willing to part with a few worms—for that, I had now substantiated, was what they were rising (or sinking) to; I gave him a quarter and made him swear not to spend it for ice cream. He acquired four night crawlers (though bloodworms are considered slightly superior), and I promptly threaded a whole one onto my No. 10 Eagle Claw hook.

I continued to hold my rod and in a few minutes was rewarded with a few faint but telltale taps.

I must have been overanxious, this being my first eel, for I struck quickly and came up with a shredded worm.

My second strike came at four twenty-seven. I gave this one more time, but again came up with only a mutilated worm and a long strip of tissue paper.

Several other eels had meanwhile been caught, and also one striped bass. My field notes concerning the striper read as follows:

> Striper caught at 4:20. Bait: worm. Size: about seven inches. Fight: negligible. Miscellaneous comments: Angler claimed: "Got one about the same size, same time, day before yesterday." May be significant. Fish stashed quickly in bottom of metal box.

Soon after I missed my second strike, I realized that much more careful thought was necessary if I were to master this art. Careful observation is indispensable to the serious angler, and I soon noted the following: no other angler was holding his rod. In fact, there seemed a deliberate attempt not even to notice it. The fishermen would stand in a crowd, and then, either by instinct born of long experience, by sight, or from the tinkling sound of one of the small bells attached to the tip of many a rod, they would leap to the fence for action. The Hudson River fence strike is sudden and abrupt, delivered with killing force; I presume this is to compensate for the bend the river must put in the line, though it may simply be the natural hostility of urbanites.

There seems to be the widest latitude concerning the proper clothing for this kind of fishing. Short pants, Havana shirts (not tucked in), or no shirts, and leather moccasins appeared to prevail; though I observed four or five anglers in traditional street clothes. I could come to no conclusion concerning the logic for dress, and must assume my subsequent failures were in no way related to what I wore—khaki trousers, an Orvis vest, and my slouch stream hat.

I queried several fishermen who had displayed conspicuous success. Their characteristic mode of expression was laconic, authoritative, unequivocal. The following conversation transpired:

"Ever use plugs?" I asked.

"Nope."

"Spoons?"

"Nope."

"Any kind of artificial lure?"

"Nope."

"Why not?"

"No good."

"Have you tried them?"

"Waste of time."

I had noticed that one fisherman spit on the bit of worm he affixed to his hook, and asked him: "Why do you do that?"

"It helps."

"Ever catch anything on top?"

"Nope."

The angler I'd met in the park made me his confidant. He was extremely knowledgeable and perhaps felt some sympathy for me because I seemed to try so hard, I had two small children who were by now embarrassed at my ineptness, because anyone who used toot-picks was in need of counsel, and perhaps because he had been the instrument of my conversion. Taking me under his wing, he promptly advised that I would never catch a thing if I persisted in holding the rod.

"You ketch 'em in the country like that, maybe; not here. See these places?" He pointed to some old notches in the railing; I had not seen them before. "You put rod there."

I was tempted to ask him precisely why, in order to learn whether these long green ropes were so tender-lipped that they could sense the presence of a fisherman, but he was intent upon imparting a great deal of information to me quickly, in order to get back to his bottle of Old Grand-Dad, so I let him go on. I was not at all sure such an opportunity would present itself again. If he were indeed a deputy of the Castle, a secretary of the curia, I would not be caught napping.

"Your weight no good; you need three, maybe four ounces." I was using about a half ounce of split shot, pinched on and strung along a foot of line. It seemed to hold the bottom, and the spinning rod could not manage anything heavier. I told him so.

"You never ketch 'em," he told me flatly.

Spiritually, I could not quite work my way around to the four ounces.

"Your bait wrong," he said. "You need him little piece of worm, like this." He squashed off about a half inch of worm and was about to put it on my hook. Before I could tell him that I had always, in my salad days when I fished worms, done better with a whole bait, he added: "No. No. Hook wrong, too. You need long hook. I get you one."

This was downright decent of him, but I thought I could get them just as well on a short-shank hook and told him so. He shook his head and was about to give me up when I asked him: "Tell me the truth. Why don't any of you guys hold the rod?"

"No good."

"Don't you *like* to feel the fish biting?"

He roared with laughter and took my rod. "You hold this," he said, giving it to me.

I took the rod back.

"Now put finger on line." He gave the line at the end a few small twitches and then broke up laughing. I had to agree that this element of the sport had little enough to recommend it.

Since I had seen my friend keep several eels, I asked him if he ate them.

"Sure," he said.

"Even from the Hudson?"

I might as well have cursed his mother. He said nothing.

"Well, how do you cook them?"

He came over close to me and whispered: "You put nail in his head, then strip skin off, cut him in chunks and fry or stew him."

"Easy as that?"

"You stew him like beef stew." He made several facial expressions indicating gastronomical happiness.

When he left me, I condescended to put a bit of worm on my wrong hook and cast it out. Then I went back to the grass and lay down on the slope, closing my eyes against the warm redness of the sun, listening to the pleasantly rhythmic chatter, and thinking back a month to a May afternoon when the Hendricksons were popping up out of a still pool in the Catskills and riding slowly downriver like little sailboats until they were sucked under, dramatically, by the trout. A sparsely tied Red Quill, with genuine blue dun hackle, had done some happy business for me.

I was on my third trout when I heard Jennifer shout: "Our ball's in the water, Dad." They had been playing nearby. I got up slowly and went over to the fence. A tennis ball was bobbing slowly along the rim of the rocks. It belonged to the son of one of the regulars.

There was some immediate interest in this, and four or five of the more agile anglers hopped the fence and vied for the honor of fishing the ball out. One of them got way out on a rock and with a long stick proceeded to prod at the ball. It only bobbed under and farther out.

"What are those?" Jennifer asked, leaning far over the railing and pointing.

I looked. "Balloons."

"Oh."

The young man with the stick was now holding on to his companion's arm with one hand and leaning still farther out.

"Look," said Jennifer. "More balloons."

There were two more. "There must be a party upriver," I told her.

"Can we go?" asked Anthony.

"Look, he's got the ball," I said.

The young man had indeed dropped his stick and grasped the ball, but as he did so his foot slipped against the slippery rocks and he careened over into the river. Rather than alarm, this caused numerous shouts and cheers and considerable excitement. The man went under once, losing his baseball cap, splashed and shouted with animation—as one might, say, if he had fallen into a sewer—and then got a hand on the rocks, forced himself up by sheer will, and was finally lifted out.

There was mucho celebration.

But then it was noticed that his hat was gone.

Several men reeled in their lines and tried to probe for it with the rods, but only managed to push it farther out. Finally it got some twenty feet out into the river, with only a bit of the peak showing.

One good turn deserved another, so I reeled in my line, took off the half inch of worm, pushed the split shot down flush with the hook, and made several short underhand casts. I could not hook the cap.

Then I saw the fly rod.

While the hat was ever so slowly moving farther away, I clipped off my yellow practice fly and tied on a No. 8 Eagle Claw hook. Then, stripping line off my reel, and to the utter amazement of all the onlookers, I began to false-cast. They watched in silence as the white line sailed back and then forward.

On the third cast, I was able to lay my line over the hat, and then, drawing it slowly in by hand was lucky enough to catch the hook onto some part of it. Alternately filling with water and losing water through the air holes in the top, and hooked but lightly, the cap rode in majestically across the majestic waters of the Hudson. It took some care and strategy to bring it to the rocks and then up and over the fence. At its best weight, the cap went a full two pounds, I guess, and gave a good account of itself.

The landing was watched with muted silence, and then, when the hat was safely landed, the event was greeted with what I took to be somewhat extravagant praise. I was toasted, congratulated, invited to share in the community bottle, and offered a long, thin, green rope, which had once been an eel.

It was late now, and I took my toot-pick and headed hand in hand with my young ones up the hill. A cool breeze had come on, and the near-naked ladies had long since left; the globed sun was cherry red and serrated with soft Payne's gray clouds. I could smell the new-mown grass and listened to the sweet methodical hum of cars on the West Side Highway.

At home a patient fishing widow waited, one who, like me, had never reckoned with the special delights of Hudson River fence fishing. Fortunately, I doubt if I can ever master this art. But it is well to remember that there's more than one way to skin a cat—or an eel.

HOW TO GET THERE: All major airlines to Kennedy, Newark, and LaGuardia airports. All regular train and bus lines come directly to New York City. The No. 5 Riverside Drive bus stops on the corner of West Eighty-third Street. Crosstown buses at Eighty-sixth and Seventy-ninth. Seventh Avenue subway. Do not come by car—parking not available.

BEST TIME: Same catches reported all year long. Come when you can.

ACCOMMODATIONS: Great latitude—from Waldorf-Astoria to nearby furnished rooms. Rat traps a necessity if you choose the latter.

COSTS: Will vary greatly; generally astronomical.

CONTACTS: Ask for Joe at the Eighty-fourth Street fence.

WHAT TO TAKE: Bring cheapest and heaviest saltwater tackle; four- and five-ounce sinkers; No. 8 long-shank hooks; a couple of night crawlers or bloodworms will last a day; all clothing acceptable. Transistor radios useful.

ADDITIONAL INFORMATION: Literature on Hudson River fence fishing is currently unavailable. No books on subject now in print, though it is probable dozens will be written in the coming years.

ON THE DIVIDE

For three days we fished the lake without a strike. We rose each morning at four, dressed quickly by the bald light of the bulb in the kitchen of the cabin, and then carried our rods and tackle bags silently through the darkness, down the hill, and to the aluminum boat.

The motor started only once on the first pull of the cord. Neither of us was adept at motors, and we wore our hands raw with frantic tugging. Once, far out on the lake, when the winds came rushing along the Continental Divide, in which the lake was set like a glittering blue jewel, we pulled anchor, could not start the motor, and drifted half across the lake before another fisherman came after us. I tried to row, busted an oar, and ripped more skin off the palms of my hands.

On the fourth morning the alarm was only a dull ringing far back in my head. The ringing stopped and then the memory of it woke me. I went into his room to wake him, but he only turned and arched up his body like a cat stretching. "I can't . . ." he said. "I can't make it today."

I dressed and gathered up my fly rod and the little teardrop net I always wore fastened to my vest, and the burlap creel in which I carried my reels and flies. I went down to the lake alone, which is how I usually fished anyway. It was better alone, I thought. Then you didn't have to worry if the other person was enjoying himself, whether he would catch the fish you had dreamed of all winter, whether he would see your poor casts. Sometimes with the experts, I'd seen fishing turn to fierce competition.

The boy had stopped casting that last afternoon. I had asked him why, and he had answered curtly, "What's the use?"

"They're here," I told him. "Big ones. Up to four, five, even ten pounds."

"Sure," he said.

"They are. Dave told me he hooked a tremendous trout here last September. He had it on for nearly an hour. He said it was actually—"

"Towing his boat. You've told me that. In Cincinnati, Sioux City, Cody, and—"

"Guess I did," I said. "But they're here. I'll swear to it."

"Then why haven't we caught any?" he asked.

"Maybe they haven't come into the channel yet; maybe we haven't found the right fly or lure; maybe—"

"Maybe they're not here," he said. "Maybe they were here sixteen years ago, when you say you caught all those monsters."

"Yes, they were here," I said quietly. "I killed a great number of trout when I came to the lake sixteen years ago."

"You said your arms were tired from catching so many."

"They were."

"You said *my* arms would be tired."

I had looked out across the lake, at the surrounding sagebrush flat with its pastures and fences and scattered trees, and at the mountains of the Continental Divide that rimmed the lake, some still snowcapped though it was midsummer. We had fished seven hours without a strike, and the sun was now high and hot.

"Can't we go back," he said, "or run the boat around the lake a couple of times? I like to run the kicker."

The word sounded strange on his tongue. It was a new word and fit him like a ready-made suit. We had not been in a boat together before, and I was pleased that he enjoyed running the kicker.

"I'd like to fish," I said.

"For how long?" he asked, turning from me and fingering the rubber covering on the handle of the kicker, turning it slightly several times without pulling the cord.

"We came a long way to fish this lake," I said. "More than two thousand miles. I think we'll get some trout if we'll . . . only . . . be patient enough."

"Well, I'm tired."

And then he put the rod in the bottom of the aluminum boat carelessly and tucked his head down into his mackinaw jacket though the sun was high and hot. I fished for another half hour and didn't catch a thing.

On the fourth morning the air was wet and cold. There was a thin drizzle and I rolled down the rim of the expensive khaki hat I'd bought in the city a week before the trip and lifted the collar of my old hunting coat. This time I pressed the rubber bulb near the gasoline can four or five times sharply before I pulled the cord, pumping it until it grew hard. The motor started on the first pull, and I backed out of the dock and out into the springs.

There were a few lights, and the moon still gave enough light to see by. I eased the boat under the wire that stretched across the springs into which the fish came when the weather warmed, and headed out into the channel. When I was parallel to the great clump of willows on shore, I turned left and cut my speed, running the boat slowly out until I thought I was in the deepest part of the channel; "Glory Hole" the spot was called—and I had only learned of it the day before, from the manager of the cabins. I had fished in the springs the first time I'd come to the lake; there had been thousands of trout in the springs and no need to fish from a boat. I had caught and killed a great number of them one night sixteen years earlier. It was better that the springs were closed, but I had hoped the boy could fish in them and catch some of the huge trout I had caught. One fish would be enough, if it was the right fish.

I let down the large tin can filled with cement. The anchor chain felt cold and harsh against my torn hands. The barest light was breaking behind the mountains to the east; it came first from the V of the mountains, where two pyramids crossed, and then the whole sky to the east grew lighter.

I tied on a long brown Leech, with a brown marabou tail, wet it in my mouth, and then began to strip line from my new Princess reel. Soon I had a good length of line working back and forward, and then

I laid it out as far as I could and dropped the rod tip to the surface of the water, as I'd seen several men do the day before. In a minute or so, I began the methodical short-strips' retrieve, slowly bringing the fly back through the black waters. It was a rhythmic process and not at all like the dry-fly fishing I had always done in the East. Everything was feel. I had fished the lake with spinning lures that summer after my release from the army; I had come alone and stayed for four days that had stayed pristine these past sixteen years. But now, with flies, I had not been able to induce a strike. Five, six times I cast, and each time waited and then brought the fly back slowly—strip, strip, strip, pause; strip, strip, strip.

It was good, I thought, that the boy had not come out with me. The air grew colder as the mists formed on the lake and the drizzle grew into a light rain. My hands were already numb, and no one else had yet come out onto the lake. I heard unseen sheep bleating in one of the meadows.

I enjoyed being on the lake alone, and I enjoyed casting the long line and then bringing back the fly with that slow, methodical retrieve. The years had been long and crowded and hard, and I had watched some of my dreams die and I had not been home enough—not nearly enough—and I had thought all winter and all spring, for several years, of coming back to this lake, where I had once made such a large catch. I wanted to catch some of the big trout very much, on flies. You progressed from worms to lures to flies, and then flies made all the difference. I had wanted the boy to catch some of the big trout, it didn't matter how.

The tip of my rod jerked down sharply. I raised it and felt the heavy throbbing as the line arched out and away. It was a good fish.

The fish moved off to the left and I reeled in the loose line so I could fight him from the reel. Twice he broke water but did not jump. Cutthroat, I thought. I knew that the cutthroat broke water but that the brooks in this lake usually did not. There were hybrids in the lake, too, crosses between the rainbow and the cutthroat, but they would not often jump either.

The fish was not as large as I'd pictured him, and I soon had him alongside and into my little stream net. It was about two pounds, and since we wouldn't be eating them, I took the hook out and then turned out the net. In the net the fish was bright red; and I watched as he wavered slowly, his back spotted and the red no longer visible, and then darted down and out of sight.

I cast out immediately, and after waiting for the fly to sink, began the slow retrieve again. Again the rod tip shot down, and I took another cutthroat, about the same size. When I had turned this one out of the net, I sat down on the green boat cushion and took out a cigar. I breathed deeply several times, lit my cigar, and looked over toward the east. It was still raining lightly, and the sun had not yet broken. Christ, it was good to be out on this lake alone, after all the years, after all the changes.

Several other boats were anchored in the channel now, and a man in one of them was fast to a good fish.

"On the Leech?" the other man called out.

"Yep. Brown and long, with marabou."

I waited another ten minutes, while the fish was brought in. As the man finally lifted it high with his huge boat net, I could see it was a gorgeous male brookie.

The other man had a fish on now, too. The trout had come into the hole. There might be hundreds of them, staging into the channel that led to the springs.

I cast again, and again took a fine trout. I was in the right spot, in the right hole, and there were many fish and I had the right fly.

I took two more, about three pounds each, and then, after three fruitless casts, hooked a fish I could not stop. I felt when he took that he was heavy. He did not rush like the others, angling to one side while the line angled up and up. This fish moved straight away from the boat—slowly and steadily. *Thump—thump—thump.* Soon he had all my stripping line out, and then began to take line off the reel with the same slow, confident power.

And then he stopped.

I lifted the rod tip to be sure it was still there. There was a heavy weight, but I felt no movement. Perhaps he was sulking, I thought. I lifted the rod again and felt the same dead weight. For several minutes I stood, putting constant pressure on the line but not enough to break it. My chest was beating heavily; my right hand shook.

"In the weeds?" one of the men asked.

"Don't know. Something's still down there. I can feel something."

"Better pull the line with your hand," the man said. "If he's still on, you'll feel him."

I did so and only felt the dead weight.

I gave the line a few more steady pulls, and then drew it tight and gave it a sharp tug. When I got the line in, I saw some weeds still attached to it. The fish had wound himself around and around until he was able to break off; I'd never felt the break.

"Tough luck," one of the men called. "Must have been a big brookie—or a hybrid."

"I couldn't turn him," I said.

"One of the big hybrids, probably. Eight, maybe ten pounds. Larger even."

I took a deep breath and sat down. My hands were still shaking so I pressed them against my knees. Then I went into my fly box and fumbled for another of the Leeches I'd been given by a neighbor the day before. I breathed deeply again, thought of the boy, and decided to head back to the cabin.

"You really took five and lost a big one?" the boy said as we sat at the linoleum table. His eyes were wide and his bushy black hair, dried by the sun, stood up wildly. He was rested and I could tell he was excited as he wolfed down a doughnut we'd bought in town the night before. "Five? And they were about three pounds? Why didn't you keep them? I'd have kept them. Every one of them."

"All the men were getting good fish," I said.

"Why didn't you wake me?"

"I tried to, old man, but you wouldn't be woke."

"Want to go back out? Do you think I can get a couple? *Everyone was getting them?* How many fish did you actually see caught?"

"Whenever you're ready we'll go out," I said, smiling.

"You're sure I can get some? They're in the channel, like the manager said they'd be this week?"

"Let's find out," I said.

The lake was crowded now. As I moved the boat out of the springs and into the channel, I could see at once that the Glory Hole now had eight or ten boats anchored in or near it. The sun had burned off the mist and the rain had stopped; it was late morning, and I could see down into the water, right to the bottom in the areas that didn't have weeds. It was a shallow lake, and not particularly clear, and in the summer the weeds grew thick and high. I saw several large fish swimming slowly along the bottom and cut the motor. The boy looked over the side as we circled back, and he saw them too. They were large brook trout—four or five pounds apiece.

"Did you see them, Dad?" he asked. "Did you see the *size* of them?"

"I saw."

"Shall we fish here?"

"Let's head farther out," I said. "Near where I got them this morning."

We headed out toward the hole, but several boats were anchored where I had been. I did not want to fish too close to them. I wished there were no other boats on the lake.

Finally, we cut the motor at the edge of the weeds, where the hole abruptly ended. I told the boy to cast in toward the other boats. His rod was rigged, and he began to cast before I'd fully lowered the anchor chain. He drew the lure back quickly, with the rod tip held high and steady. He made four casts this way; I watched him while I tied on another Leech and checked my leader for frays.

"Put the rod tip down and bring the lure back in short jerks," I said. "You're bringing it back too fast."

"Like this?" he asked, and lowered the rod and brought the lure back even faster, still without the short jerks that had worked so well for me sixteen years earlier.

"No, no," I said. "Slower. Slower."

One of the men in my morning spot had hooked another fish on a fly rod, and he fought it noisily, with Texas howls. The boy looked over and then began to reel his lure in fast again.

In a few minutes another man had a fish on his fly rod, and then another rod bent in that high curving arc, too. I began to cast now, from the bow of our boat, and on the third cast hooked a solid cutthroat.

"This spinning rod is no good," the boy said.

"It will catch more and bigger fish than a fly," I told him.

"That's what you said while we were driving here. All the way across the country you told me I'd have no trouble catching fish with a spinning rod. I haven't gotten a thing. Not a strike."

I put my rod down and took his spinning rod. It was a strange weapon in my hands. I had not used one in many years. I had stopped using a spinning rod after I'd fished this lake the last time, and I had gone through a long apprenticeship learning the magic of a fly rod. I had caught nothing for a long time, and then suddenly the line no longer whipped down on the water behind me, and the fly no longer slapped down on the water, and my distance grew from twenty to forty and then maybe sixty-five feet.

I flicked the metal lure far out into the hole and let it sink, and then brought it back in short, sharp jerks. I cast three or four more times, drew the lure back with those slow, sharp jerks, and then handed the rod to the boy. He cast again, and then again. He imparted a better motion to the lure now, but he still caught no fish. The other men took three more fish on their fly rods.

I cast again, and then again. On the fourth cast I hooked another cutthroat; he splashed at the surface several times, and then came in without difficulty.

"I can't get a thing," the boy said. "I'm just no good at it. I'll never catch anything."

"You will. I'm sure you will."

"You've been saying that."

"Try a few more casts," I coached.

"Why?"

"You can't catch anything if you don't cast."

The sun was bright and hot now, and many of the boats were beginning to head back to the dock. I pulled the anchor and headed closer to the center of the hole.

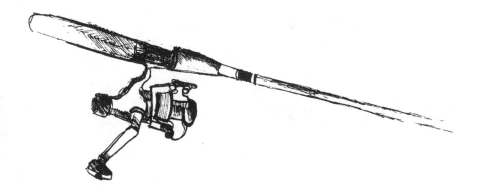

But when we'd anchored in the new spot and he'd cast four or five more times, he gave it up and sat down.

"How long are we going to stay here?" he asked.

"We can go back now," I said. "I only wanted you to get a couple of fish."

"I haven't caught any," he said.

"I know," I said.

"Look, Dad," he said. "I like fishing, I really do. And I like being out here with you. But I can't catch anything on this spinning rod. Maybe if I knew how to use a fly rod it would be different. But I don't. And I don't have the same kind of patience you have. I like fishing, but I don't like not catching anything. You don't care. You really don't. But I do. And I'm not going to get any. Not today. Not tomorrow. Not any day this week. I know I won't."

"Well," I said, scratching my head, "why don't you try twenty more casts, and if you don't get one we'll head back to the cabin and maybe visit Virginia City or the Park this afternoon." Perhaps we should head back at once, I thought. I had enjoyed being on the lake alone at daybreak—catching some fish, losing the big fish. Perhaps it had been a mistake to come back to this lake with the boy. He would have enjoyed the beach more, and I wouldn't have wanted to fish so much. I never seemed to fish enough but it mattered much less when there were no trout nearby.

The boy began casting and counting, bringing in the lure much too fast. Thirteen, fourteen, fifteen. Nothing. Sixteen. Nothing.

On the seventeenth cast, the little glass rod jerked down in a sharp arc. A good fish. A very good fish.

"Good grief!" he shouted. "Can't hold him!"

"Let him have line," I shouted back. "Don't force him. Keep your rod tip high. It's a good fish, a *very* good fish."

The fish moved steadily from the boat. I could tell by the way the line throbbed slowly that it was a substantial fish, a brookie I thought.

The boy lowered the rod tip and I leaned over to lift it up. The boat swayed and I never reached the rod, but the boy smiled broadly and raised the rod so that the full force of the bend could work against the fish.

Don't lose it. For godsake don't lose it, I thought.

"He's still taking line, Dad. I can't stop him."

"He'll turn," I said. "He's got to turn in a minute or two. Don't force him. Don't let him get into the weeds, but don't force him. *Don't drop that rod tip!*"

The line went slack.

"No. No!" I said.

"Have I lost him? No. I *can't* have lost him."

"Reel quickly," I said. "Maybe he's turned. Maybe he's still there."

"He's there," the boy shouted. "I can feel him. Good grief, he's big. Can you see him yet? I won't lose him now."

I looked over where the line entered the water. I strained to see the fish, but could not. It had to be a big brookie.

Now the fish was angling off to the left. He might go completely around the boat. As the line came toward me, I lifted it and let it pass over my head: for a second I could feel the big fish throbbing at the other end of the line. The fish came around the front of the boat and the boy fought him on the other side.

We both saw it at the same time. A huge male brookie. We saw it twisting and shaking ten feet below the surface, the silver lure snug in the corner of its mouth.

"It's huge. It's the biggest brookie I've ever seen."

"I'm not going to lose him," the boy said. "I can't lose it now."

"You won't lose it. He's well hooked. He's too high and too tired to get into the weeds. You've got him beat, son. I'll get the net." I looked down under the seat and came up with the little teardrop stream net.

"He'll never fit," the boy said. "He'll *never* fit in that—*whooooa.* He's taking line again. He's going around the other side of the boat now."

The fish was close to the boat but not yet beaten. He went deep and around the corner of the boat. I watched for the line to angle out, on the other side of the boat. It never did.

"The anchor chain!" I shouted. "Don't let him get in the anchor chain."

"I can't feel him," said the boy. "The line's on something but I can't feel the fish fighting anymore."

I scurried the length of the boat, bent under the rod, and then lowered myself where the anchor chain entered the water. At first I could see nothing. But then I saw it. The huge brook trout was still on the line; I could see it five feet down, the silver lure still in the corner of its mouth. He was circling slowly around the anchor chain, and I could see that the line was already wound six or seven times around the links. It would not come free. Not ever.

"Is it there?" the boy called. "Is it still there?"

"You're going to lose him, son. He's in the anchor chain. There's no way I can get it free."

"Oh, no, no," he said.

I put my nose down to the surface of the water. The fish had gone around the chain twice more, and his distance from the chain was growing smaller and smaller. It kept circling, slowly, every now and then jerking its head back against the tug of the line.

"I can't lose him! I can't," the boy said.

"There's nothing to be done. If I lift the chain, he'll break off; if I leave him, he'll pull out in another couple of turns. "

"What about the net."

"Don't think I can reach him."

"Try, Dad. Please try. I can't lose this fish. Not this one."

I took the little stream net and dipped it far down. The cold water stung my raw hands, and the net came short by more than a foot. The fish made a lunge and I was sure it would break free.

"Got him?"

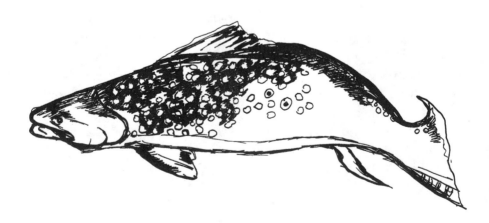

"Nope. Too far down. Can't reach him."

"Maybe someone with one of the boat nets . . ." But he stopped. The other boats were gone from the lake; we had the Glory Hole to ourselves.

The fish went around the rope again. There was only a foot and a half between him and the chain now. The big brookie was tired. It was half on its side.

I took the boy's arm and pulled him down to where I knelt. It didn't matter if he let the line go slack now. Together we pushed our faces close to the surface of the water and peered down. In the liquid world below us, we looked through the reflections of our faces, side by side, overlapping and rippled, and saw the huge fish.

I reached again, pressing the net down through the water as carefully as I could, trying hard not to frighten it again. My arm was in up to my shoulder and I felt the cold lake water slosh onto my chest. The fish came a little higher this time. I could almost touch it with the end of the net—and I saw clearly now that even if I could get near enough to it, the fish was far too big for the little net, and the lure was almost torn out. There was no chance.

"You'll never get him, Dad," the boy said.

He was holding on to my shoulder now with his left arm, and looking constantly through our reflections at the shadow that was his fish.

"It's lost," I whispered.

And then the fish floated up five or six inches, I pressed the net toward its head, felt cold water on my face, saw the head of the huge fish go into the net, saw the line break behind the lure, and lifted madly.

A year has passed, and the etching remains, as if fixed by acid in steelplate: our faces in the water, merged; the tremendous circling trout; the fish half in and half out of that tiny teardrop net, and then the two of us, side by side in the bottom of that aluminum boat, our raw hands clutching a thing bright silver-gray and mottled, and laughing as if we were four days drunk.

A TALE OF TWO FISHES

I had rather gotten out of the habit of vacationing. For seven years, bucking the New York current, I'd held two full-time jobs and more, and with four young children and no car we traveled little and never for more than a day or two at a time. I had to borrow time from each job to meet special commitments at the other, and if I managed to take two weeks a year it was always in dribs and drabs.

But in early August, abruptly, without warning, there opened before us a full week—with two weekends—and it seemed just this side of heaven. The children were in summer camp, and Mari and I looked at each other with newlywed wonder. A whole week!

Naturally I decided we should go to the Battenkill. There was a huge dusk hatch of mayflies in early August, and the trout rose freely from eight-thirty until midnight. "We'll stay at a motel right on the river," I told her as we sat at the dining room table, scheming, "and I'll fish every evening."

"*Every* evening?" she asked quietly.

"Unless it rains."

"Sounds like fun."

"I'm mad to catch that dusk hatch. They're big cream mayflies, size ten or twelve, and when they come off the water the fish—"

"I'm sure it will be wonderful for you." She lowered her head. "Couldn't we perhaps spend a few days, just two or three days of the vacation, on Martha's Vineyard? I'd love to swim and sunbathe and paint; I hear it's absolutely breathtaking."

Martha's Vineyard was not one of our household words. I waited for the pitch—obviously planned and timed—to continue.

"Edna St. Vincent Millay raved about it," she said. "And it's romantic and windswept. Oh, Nick, wouldn't it be wonderful to swim in the ocean before breakfast and lie out in the sun all day and walk along the beach at night? You really need a rest, you know, and there's no place like the shore for a real rest. You can sleep all day in the sun, with the surf pounding in your ears, and swim—"

"They have a pool at the motel," I said quietly. "And I don't even know where Martha's Vineyard is."

"We'll get a map."

"It might take three days to get there; there could be all sorts of complications. You mean you don't even know where it is?"

"It's in New England, isn't it? An island, I think. And the Beaverhead or Bottomkill or what's-its-name is in New England, isn't it?"

Yes, the Battenkill was indeed in New England, I admitted, and thought that, alas, if *I* hadn't had a vacation in seven years, neither had Mari. "All right," I said, with magnanimous condescension and the wisdom of Solomon, "we'll split it in two: five days on the Battenkill, three on Martha's Vineyard."

"Four," she said.

"Three. Not a day more."

We rented a car on Saturday morning and, without reservations, found a good motel with a pool not far from Manchester. It was directly on the highway and cars rushed past constantly. But the rooms were comfortable, when you were in the pool you could almost forget there were a dozen people sitting on chairs around the perimeter and cars rushing by a couple a minute, and it wasn't far from the Battenkill, and they took Magi-Card.

I had the river much to myself and fished a stretch above Shushan, New York, that in May was more crowded than a rush-hour subway. At dusk, when the stream grew still, the large cream mayflies began to come off the water—two, three, and then the water was pocketed with rising trout and the air full of fluttering duns. Swallows began to dip and dart, to hover in the air and catch the rising mayflies. Even when I couldn't see the flies anymore, I could hear and see the birds working, all up and down the river.

I stood in the hushed alley of the Battenkill, gaining back some of myself, some of that which the city had sorely threatened, and caught four or five modest brown trout on Cream Variants, just at and after dusk, and then released them. It would have been enough without the fish—only to be standing alone in the river at that hour, feeling the bamboo of my delicate Dickerson fly rod come alive and work out the line with measured rhythms. But there was more: I missed a fish that first night which was extremely large. I'd failed to change to a heavier leader after dark, and the fish took in a splashy rise and snapped off almost at once.

Mari had not wanted to remain alone at the motel, and when I came off the river, about ten-thirty, she was curled miserably into the corner of the car, half-asleep, half-starved, bitten to shreds by no-see-ums and mosquitoes. She was such a mess that, as I rushed her back to the motel, in a rash moment, I promised her *four* days on Martha's Vineyard.

Several days later I realized quite how rash I'd been. The fish I'd lost was indeed huge. I hooked him again the next night, and that time he jumped twice—high and thunderously—and then summarily headed downstream and broke me off in the dark. He was a full twenty inches, a superb old Battenkill brown, and a fever to land him raced through me. The next night, fishing the same run, I caught two good fish, but could not raise the big one. Battenkill browns strike hard after dark; the alley of the river is all hushed and misty and you can barely see the fly as it comes downstream toward and past you. The fish took like bass, crashing up, exploding the water, and often jumping immediately after feeling the hook. Each time I thought I had the big one again.

On my last night I saw the huge brown rising steadily far beneath a wide batch of overhanging willow branches on the far bank. He began to come up for the mayflies just at dusk, and then stayed fixed in that position under the willows, his body a long shadow and his fin and tail partially above the surface. I knew I'd have trouble casting to him; the fly would have to be presented upstream of the branches, and then floated down under them. The angle was difficult and I knew the fly would drag uninvitingly. I tried a dozen casts and each time knew the fly was dragging badly by the time it reached the huge fish. The only way to take him, I finally reasoned, was to cross the stream to a spot directly above him, and then fish directly

downstream with a lot of slack line. It is extremely difficult to wade any river after dark, and sections of the Battenkill, with its deceptive current and smooth stones, are especially hazardous. I inched my way upstream, with a kind of shuffling movement. The air was now quite cool and it had begun to drizzle. Thirty feet above the willow, I began to work my way slowly across stream. I took three small steps, tripped, held on tight to my precious Dickerson, and then went down on one knee in the river. The cold water shot into my waders, I regained my balance, and I knew I was done for the night.

No matter, I thought, as I headed back to the motel: I'll raise him tomorrow.

Mari smiled broadly when I came in, drenched and shivering. She had already packed our few valises, and wondered whether we couldn't leave right then, after I changed, for Martha's Vineyard. I knew I could take that huge brown the next evening; I knew he'd be there, and I knew how to raise him. I'd use a sturdy 3X leader, take up my position *above* him while it was still light, and then . . .

"Why *don't* we leave now?" asked Mari. "It's probably not more than a few hours."

I was about to ask her, plead to her, if we couldn't stay over one more evening; I desperately wanted one more try at that fish. But I saw it was no use. "All right," I said. "But not tonight. We've never even located the place on the map."

"We always do it that way, don't we? We live with our heads in concrete all year long, and it's sort of like pioneering to head out and not know precisely where you're going."

"The great adventurers," I said.

The next day it took us about seven hours of dull driving to reach Woods Hole, which a good guidebook proclaimed was the gateway to the Vineyard. It was an excruciatingly hot day, and the traffic on Route 7 was heavy; we fell behind some slow-moving trucks and crawled out of Vermont and down through Massachusetts. We breezed along the Massachusetts Turnpike and my only worry, after several hours, was that I'd spent half my vacation on the road.

We got to Woods Hole about 3:45 and were directed onto a long line of cars. A few discreet inquiries made me realize we should have made reservations in advance—years in advance—but I trotted over to the ticket office and thought myself lucky to get signed on (one-way only, since the Steamship Authority was booked solid for all return trips through Labor Day). I took the opportunity to note that I had only about $35 left in cash; Magi-Card had proved its worth—would it hold up for three days on an unknown island? We managed to become the last car wedged—brilliantly, I thought—onto the ferry, and as the boat and dock diverged it occurred to me, fleetingly, that if all return trips were booked through Labor Day, we might not get back to New York for a month. Which my publishing house might not appreciate.

I mentioned this to Mari, but she considered it too sober an issue to consider at such an exciting time. We had three days to worry about that, didn't we? Anyway, she was too busy watching some of the initiates feed popcorn to the trailing gulls, letting the kernels sweep back until one of the poised birds caught it in midair.

We got to the island about six. Vineyard Haven was crowded, and we'd seen its likes before, so we drove to Oak Bluffs, which was about the same. We saw a few motels here and there, and a number of inns, but none of them displayed the prominent golden-orange Magi-Card sign.

"Why don't we explore the island before we eat and find a place to stay?" said Mari. "Maybe there are sections that aren't so crowded." This was a fatal suggestion.

The New England guidebook's map of Martha's Vineyard showed us where we were and suggested that up-island, near Menemsha, Chilmark, and Gay Head, we'd find the quiet we were seeking. It was nearly seven now, and we both rather could have eaten dinner; but we decided that the island was small enough for a quick tour, and maybe we'd find something pleasant and isolated at the other end.

We drove for more than a half hour, looking at the small farms and weatherworn saltbox houses, the ponds and salt marshes. Finally, driving slowly through a nest of unmarked roads, I saw a small sign that read LOBSTERVILLE BEACH. We hadn't seen the ocean yet, so I took the road.

It was a lovely beach, strewn with small pebbles and curving in a wide arc. The sun was half-down now, and the clouds were richly maroon. I took Mari's hand and we walked up over a bluff together and stood quietly, looking out over the lakelike cove. It was rather a holy moment. There wasn't an evening hatch to worry about, not even a twenty-inch brown trout, and I sort of began to think that friendship with one's wife was almost as pleasant as trout fishing.

We held hands for a full five minutes and spoke softly, as married people sometimes do, about bringing some canvas down the next day, for Mari to paint, and collecting some of the brightly colored rocks, and of how much the children would love a beach like this. It had been, by now, a long, hot, tiring day—a full twelve hours since we'd left Manchester. I flexed my aching shoulders back, snapped a small crick out of my neck, and asked Mari if she was hungry.

"Hmm, yes," she said, "but it's so-oo beautiful here, isn't it? So absolutely quiet and still. The skies are unbelievable. You couldn't paint them. No one would believe those colors. The ocher bluffs up there on the left, the little town way off there; the way the sky is divided into shifting planes of maroon and crimson and gray; the way those birds are cutting the stillness of the background. See how excited they are."

"Birds?" I asked.

"Over there." She pointed to the left and I saw a great flock of terns dipping and swooping. Something was agitating the surface, too, and as the birds came closer I could hear their shrill, excited calls.

"What is it?" asked Mari. "Is it a raise?"

"Rise," I said absently. "Yes, rise. No. But they're after something. Minnows. Killies. I don't know what you call them. Small fish of some kind. Not much." I looked more carefully. The water beneath the screaming birds, only a few hundred yards from us now, was tremendously choppy. I saw several sharp splashes, and then the silver-blue back of fish—two, four, a dozen very large fish. But the area was a hundred yards long—and it was all choppy and agitated. Bluefish. A huge school of blues had trapped baitfish and were on a massive feed; the birds were picking up the pieces. I'd read about blues and I'd caught a few, on a party boat out of Sheepshead Bay, deep and on heavy lines, when I was young. They're a ferocious fish—powerful and savage. I'd never seen them working like this—and the action was coming directly toward us, and now not more than fifteen or even ten feet from shore in some places.

I could feel my heart beginning to pound heavily. Mari said something but I didn't hear her. Several wild men came racehorsing up the beach with huge spinning rods and cast long plugs far out and then jerked them back quickly, quicker than I'd ever seen a plug worked, across the surface. In less than a minute, both rods were bent in sharp arcs and the reels were whirring as line raced out; they were hooked up to heavy fish. The birds were directly over our heads now, and the chopping water directly in front of me. I took my cigar out of my mouth and flipped it like an immie, as far as I could. It disappeared in a massive swirl.

"Where are you going?" shouted Mari.

I didn't answer. I chewed up the beach toward the car, unlocked the luggage compartment, and began to take my bamboo rod out of its aluminum case. My whole body was shaking uncontrollably now. I soon had my Dickerson jointed, and was about to fit on the Hardy reel when the men came rushing up the bluff, leaped into Jeeps, and roared off around the cove. I trotted to the top of the bluff, rod and reel in my hands, and looked for birds. There were none.

"Mari," I shouted. "Let's go."

When she came up, somewhat slowly, I rather roughly hustled her into the car. "Good thing," I said excitedly, "I didn't get the Dickerson set up in time. Damned good thing. Did you see those monsters? Eight, ten pounders. No less. They'd eat twenty-inch trout, wouldn't they? Good thing I restrained myself: I'd still be picking slivers of my Dickerson out of the sand."

"Beginning to like Martha's Vineyard?" Mari asked.

"There are the birds again," I said. "Over there." And I began racing along the narrow macadam road. A mile down the road and the birds seemed to be hanging in the air directly to my left. So I ran the car high up into a sand dune where it would be safely off the road, leaped out, and raced to the top of a nearby dune.

The birds were too high; they were only circling; the fish had either gone down deep or moved out. I breathed heavily and walked back to the car, where Mari was sadly shaking her head and smiling.

"Gone," I said.

"Good," she said.

"Let's go eat," I said.

"And find a place to sleep," she said.

We were both starved and tired; the sun was low and the air had begun to grow cool. I started the motor, switched into reverse, and stepped on the gas. The car wiggled back, the tires spun, and I thought we sank a bit lower.

"Ha!" I said.

"Stuck?" she said.

"Have to do this slowly," I said, and began to push down lightly on the gas pedal. The car wiggled, the tires spun, and again I thought we sank a bit lower.

"Slowly?" she said.

"Maybe it's fast," I said, and gunned the motor hard. This time there was no doubt at all about the issue: we sank so deep into the soft sand I could hardly open the door to get out and begin my shoveling, with a weathered board, riveted with nails, I found nearby.

I dug for twenty minutes, furiously, but the car only seemed to sink lower. "Hopeless," I said. "We'll be here for a month." We were at the end of the island, with no houses nearby, with only the faint outline of a town off to the right. I decided to head for the town.

It was nearly dark now, so I trotted away at a brisk clip and found that on this magical island, beloved by Edna St. Vincent Millay and my wife, the towns receded. This one did, or seemed to. It even did more. I chugged up a little hill and, looking down, discovered that it had disengaged itself from the land I was standing on: it was actually on the other side of a moat—or maybe an inlet. So I walked back slowly, barely able to face my good wife, who had suffered once again such humiliation and privation at the hands of a fanatic fisherman.

But Mari was almost cheery when I returned—and the car was out of the sand.

"Pushed it," she said.

"Like hell!"

I got in and started the motor. "At least I didn't use my Dickerson on those monsters," I said. I put the car in forward gear and almost leaped into the sand trap again.

"Fish!" muttered Mari. "At least the fishermen who pulled me out know enough to come in Jeeps."

I didn't say a word until we got to Edgartown and Mari wanted to stop at the first lodging place we passed. Then I reminded her that we had to live on Magi-Card alone, and we drove slowly and intently in and out of the narrow one-way streets until finally, like palm trees in the desert, a golden orange sign sprang up in the window of the Harborside Inn.

It was cheap at any price, and soon we were changed and washed and eating huge platters of roast beef. We even drank cool wine and danced a middle-aged fox-trot—something we hadn't done for years—in the Navigator Room. It cost only a signature.

The next day I rented myself a saltwater spinning rod and caught bluefish until I couldn't move my arms—also my first striped bass, about twelve pounds, on a surface plug, and fell in love with that grand fish for life.

Mari found herself some sun and some rocks, some beautiful views and some quiet sandy beaches. We swam and we walked hand in hand for miles, barefoot, along the north shore, filling a fish creel with brightly colored stones and shells. We walked along the road, too, barefoot and content at dusk, beside the bouncing Bet and the blue-petaled chicory, listening to the long sweet songs of the cicadas. And at night we walked through the narrow streets of Edgartown and looked in galleries and shopwindows and ate more roast beef and lobster, and danced close. I fished only that first day, intently, in the brightest sun, without a hat or shirt.

We had to return on Sunday, and so did a couple thousand other people. Obviously they all couldn't get into that ferry—and at this time we learned about the standby system. We stood by and stood by from eight that morning until ten-thirty that night, when they put on an extra boat. About three that afternoon, when we were nearly roast beef from the heat, I saw John Updike blithely drive up, get on line, push his sunglasses up on his forehead, and move on board within fifteen minutes.

"Place is loaded with famous writers," I told Mari.

"Who plan ahead," she said.

We got back to New York at five-thirty in the morning, with seventy-three cents between us, too tired to take more than essential luggage from the car. The next morning, before racing to the subway, I noticed that the car had been broken into and all our shells stolen. No matter. I still had my brutal sunburn, an epic rash of poison ivy on both legs, and a wallet full of Magi-Card receipts.

But it wasn't so bad, I thought, as I pleasantly elbowed an old lady who'd elbowed me on the sunburn in the jammed subway: maybe I won't be able to vacation again for another seven years.

MY SECRET LIFE

I had not wanted to remain in the stream late. I had wanted to meet the ecstatic rise I was confident would appear again in the July dusk, and then be back at the inn shortly after nine, making the best of two worlds. We were away for a long weekend without the children. An infrequent business. It was not to be a second honeymoon—but we had our plans.

We had spent a long day shopping and playing tourist in Manchester, and in the late afternoon my wife had insisted we could not pass through our brief vacation without at least one leisurely meal together at the inn: meals came with the price of the room and were reputed excellent. We had missed them all. Why did fishing always take place at odd hours? Afterward, she suggested, there might be other treats that middle-aged folk are still heir to.

We were seated at six, and it may be that the waitress, who arrived late and flushed, had other affairs in the kitchen. I thought she'd never come. When she did, my wife said: "Let's have a drink first. I want to relax." My wife takes apricot liqueur. She takes it slowly.

The meal was a model of leisurely eating: a fifteen-minute wait for the fruit cup; a seven-minute wait for the empty cup to be taken away; salad served separately; twenty-three minutes for my wife's chicken to be cooked to order; a thoughtful few minutes selecting from the spice and cheese plate; warm comments on the charm of the spice and cheese plate; a long small dessert. And then, about ten to eight, my wife had done more than linger leisurely over her cup of coffee: she had lingered leisurely over three cups of coffee, the clock on the wall spinning madly, my heart heavy, my whole chest choked up with a lump the size of an avocado.

For I had fallen feathers and bamboo for the Battenkill and her sweeping glides and rose-moled trout. I had fished her enough during our three days in Vermont to know that I could not resist her. She had coaxed my deepest passions, won my heart. She had played the coquette with me, teased me with her ample hatches and selective trout. But I had felt, all day, in this curio shop and that basket barn, that I now knew enough of her mysteries to do some business with her that evening. The day had been warm and overcast; if it did not rain the evening would be sensuous and full.

"Well," I said, rising vigorously and patting my stomach. "I'm delighted you suggested this. An absolutely delicious meal. Delicious."

"I'm not done with my coffee, Nick."

"Third cup," I said. "Bad for your liver."

"A few more minutes. Please, Nick? It's been so pleasant. I really didn't believe you'd actually do it—have dinner with me."

I sat down on the corner of my chair, smiled, and drummed my fingers a few times. I *had* promised a leisurely meal.

"Do you have to?"

"What?"

"Drum your fingers and tap your foot? It makes me nervous."

"It's ten after eight."

"And you want to catch the match, or whatever you do."

"Yes. Yes, actually I do. It's been a wonderful day. Wonderful. Great meal. Great." I smiled with infinite sweetness, rose, told her to sign the check, told her to have another coffee, two more coffees, told her I'd meet her in an hour and a half, that I loved her, that I'd always love her, more than anything—and then I bolted.

No doubt I drove recklessly down the gray highway with its drab gas stations and gaudy motels, but I hit no one and only ran the wheels off onto the gravel siding twice. I was suited up and heading on down the steep bank at precisely eight twenty-three.

Through the spruce and birch and alders, down past the rocky ledges, I could see her and hear her: the river. Clouds of flies were coming off the surface, rising against the dun blue of the evening sky. The sun had already dropped below the rim of the western mountains and a breathless calm hung over the valley of the Battenkill.

I scurried down the slope to what I had named Marietta's Pool, after the name of the man who owned a house on its high bank. I have since infancy watched rivers from the corner of my eye, from speeding cars, and I had first spotted this run in this way. I had named it for myself, as I had named a hundred others—their names secret and hallowed and full of memories.

It was a breathtaking run of several hundred yards: a series of quick twists and angular turns along a sharp gradient, an undulating series of deepening riffles opening into a magnificent pool farther across than could be cast, deeper than could ever be known fully. There were overhanging willow branches on the opposite side, and, as the stream widened, almost no possibility of wading—since the water flowed deep and flush to the banks. On the side I fished, the only side that was wadable, the water coursed against the bank with true velocity: the drop-off was sheer and probably lethal. For a hundred broad yards, there were numerous portions that simply could not be reached, areas that had to offer fine and permanent cover. I had seen a mounted nine-pound trout that came from the Battenkill on a spinner; it might well have come from such a pool.

Its tail was long and flat and wide—the water no more than three feet deep at any spot. In the mornings, when the mist swirled from the surface, I had seen large fish cruising in these flats; but I had not been wise enough to raise one. Working upstream I had been surprised, at midmorning, to see, in the very deepest water, the steadily pocked water of generously feeding fish. And I had seen the ecstatic evening rise the night before, fished over it for two hours without pricking a fish. It was a pool of many and subtle moods.

I waded in along the boulder bank where the water was deep and slow and full, feeling the cold thrust of the heavy current against my waders. I took a bit of water along my left leg, felt its sharp chill, and noted that it came in below the knee.

Then I began to inch downstream, where the fish were working steadily in midcurrent. It was treacherous work. I had to manipulate my feet along the tops of high and mossy rocks, in fast current, at dusk, where a wrong step could mean far more than a bad spill; to the sides of the boulders I stepped on, the water might easily be ten feet deep. But the fish were working twenty yards downstream and there was no other way to approach them. The river's most evocative parts were the hardest to penetrate. I wanted to be even with them, perhaps downstream of the great feast.

The dusk was now sensuous and ripe. The stream birds glided in quick parabolas through the clouds of dancing mayflies, pausing and fluttering when their bills found a soft ephemera. The fish, all native browns, were not rising so much as lolling several inches below the surface, waiting for the nymphs to rise to them or for the duns to fall back and ride the little waves. The surface of that deep center water, with its sinewy currents, boiled without pause. I could see the tails and fins of the fish shift a foot, two feet, to take a hatching or floating dun. From every safe covert and cover, every fish in the run must have been lured mindlessly to the top for this sweet and leisurely feed.

I had been told there was no Cahill hatch on the Battenkill, but, catching one of the whirling duns in my hand, I thought the species seemed close enough for me: perhaps a bit creamier, but I would have to prefer the mandarin wings to the unmarked hackle of a Cream Variant here. I had tied a dozen Cahills with cream hackle and cream bodies; they work well on the Amawalk. My clumsy flies seemed a reasonable imitation of this too easily crushed little insect in my hand, a fair bait.

There is a rhythm to the Battenkill, a haunting music in its ways. As I worked downstream, grasping this alder branch and that for support, probing tentatively with my feet before I made any step, I could feel it: an undulating pattern of sound and sight. Perhaps it is the clear meted flow, the deep glides, the incessant slurping of the trout; perhaps the birds and fish feel it, live in it, create it; but it is there. I could feel it and tried to enter it.

By the time I had reached a position slightly downstream of the main feeding area, the dusk had nearly set in; there was only a grayish glow in the sky. The feeding had reached an excited yet curiously unhurried pitch; the scene had the frenzy and stillness of Poussin's *Rape of the Sabine Women*.

I cast several times, without haste, and soon took and released a firm ten-inch trout. Beneath a low-slung willow a heavier fish was rising in a fixed area and I lengthened my casts to reach it. I could not quite do so, so I probed with my feet and found several boulders beneath the deep water that would keep me emerged only slightly above my waist. My felts held, and though I could not now readily reach back and grasp a branch should I slip, I felt safe enough to manage a few long casts from this perch. I was intent now upon doing so. The large fish, or several fish, made huge slurping patterns beneath the willow.

The extra feet toward them and the added room for a back cast were enough. I made one short cast, let it ride out the float, and then shot the line within a foot of the rise area. The trout took instantly and leapt three times in rapid succession: high, twisting, breaking the rhythm of the stream electrically. By the time I brought him to net, after he had drawn line from the reel four times in heavy runs, darkness had settled into the borders and alley of the stream—and also a chill breeze.

I killed the brown, creeled it, and then tucked the rod under my arm. I had taken a slight shiver, from the water in my boots, the absence of enough warm clothing near my chest, the slightly spent feeling after an intense closing with a good fish. My mouth was sticky and dry; I cupped my hands and drew several small quick drinks from the river: they were sweet and cold.

The moon was not full. I could not see it, but remembered the honeydew arc I had seen the night before. Through the latticework of the branches, now radically changed to weighty shadows and abstractions, masses and patches of some deftly crafted tapestry, streams of light lit the surface of the river enough for me to see that flies were still coming off and that fish were still taking them. The adult mayflies were playing out the last hours of their brief lives—rising up out of the cold depths in swarms, dancing in crazy flight over the stream, fluttering into nearby branches. Now and again the gauzelike wings would catch a fraction of the light; in the dark they were mating and dancing their life's sole song, dipping to deposit eggs, fluttering and falling back to the water whence they had only recently emerged, fulfilled and spent.

At the inn, my wife was expecting me. But I could not yet leave. Too far out into the cool and heavy water, I packed a pipe, lit it, and stood for a moment listening to the river and the fish and the birds. I stood alone in the cave that was the stream's alley, a long winding covert cut from black woods, its form elusive and not entirely safe from the encroaching darkness. My pipe's pocket was a bright orange glow; several bits of tobacco sputtered out, stung my hand lightly and disappeared in the river.

When I cast again, I could not see the fly but only the streak of the white line on the surface. Several times I saw the line twitch, and struck—coming up fast with a bent and throbbing rod. I do not remember how many trout I brought to net, perhaps five or six, but I killed one more and remember that the action was intense and exhilarating. I stopped when I lost my second fly and leader tippet on a back cast. I could not, even holding a big Wulff fly against the sky, fit the heavy leader point in the eye; and, my hands shaking now, I could not tie on a new tippet.

Working my way back, with every deceptive shadow a possibly final trap, I realized with stark clarity quite how dangerous a position I had put myself in. The thirty yards back upstream to where I had entered took a half hour or more. I slipped twice, caught a branch, scratched my face and tugged a rip in my waders, and finally reached the familiar birch clump exhausted and severely shaking. I lit another pipe at the car and sat stone still for ten minutes—weary and spent.

My wife was reading in bed and did not look up when I entered. *Done it again,* I thought. *Insulted her, neglected her, let the fever lure me away.* She looked lovely: thoughtful, beautiful, warm.

I put my gear carefully in the bathroom—vest and hat and creel. I flexed the kinks in my shoulders and felt the deep tiredness throughout my body. I flushed my face with cold water, combed out my matted hair, and changed my shirt for a pajama top. In the corner, against the wall, I leaned my uncased and disjointed rod.

"Mari?"

She did not answer but lay, face from me, deep in her book. I plucked a fly out of the lamb's wool patch on my vest, clipped the excess leader, and placed it with others of its kind. "Mari?"

"In a minute. In a minute."

I finished a few more chores and then opened the creel for another look at the two browns I had kept. Their spots were still bright red. The cool evening air had kept them fresh. They were considerably larger than I had first thought.

"Whew," my wife said loudly. "Tolstoy is incredible. You wouldn't believe the way he can make a scene come alive." She twisted on the bed, smiled, and then jumped off and toward me. "Catch anything?"

I held open the creel toward her.

"They're exquisite. I've never seen such bright coloration. It must have been an exciting evening for you. What time is it?"

Later, when the lights were out and we were close in the bed, she said: "Of course I don't mind if you fish. Wouldn't do any good if I did. I've learned that much. And I'm happy when you are. It was a delicious dinner, and reading Tolstoy in a warm bed is a lot better than being bitten to shreds by bugs along one of your streams."

We lay touching in the dark room, listening to a car pass now and then, a muffled voice in another room, applause and laughter from a television set in another world.

"Nick." I heard the word but did not answer. "Nick?"

"Yes."

"I'm going to get a secret lover, too," she whispered flatly. "The Empire State Building or something. You'll see. I'll meet it at night, and dream about it." She sighed and pulled me closer. I could smell her fresh perfume; I felt her hair against my cheek. "Meanwhile, I guess you'll do. Even if you are a madman. And an adulterer."

I felt my mouth widen in a smile. I changed position and put my lips to the soft nape of her neck. Eyes closed, I could not help but see the river at dusk, and after dusk, and I could still feel her undulating rhythms on my mind and thighs. I wondered if the hours between twelve and six were as generous.

from

Bright Rivers
(1977)

GRAY STREETS, BRIGHT RIVERS

Every object rightly seen unlocks a quality of the soul.
—Ralph Waldo Emerson

In the evening on upper Broadway, two blocks from my apartment, lynx-eyed women stand near the bus stop as the buses go by, waiting. They wait patiently. Their impassive rouged faces show only the slightest touch of expectation; their gold high-heeled shoes glitter. Their dresses are exceedingly short. One of them hums, and the sound is like a low cacophonous motor, in perpetual motion.

A man asks, with startling politeness, "Would you be kind enough to spare me fifty cents, sir, for a cup of coffee?" Later I see him caterwauling, along with a young tough, eyes wild, waving a pint bottle of Seagram's. Nothing here is quite as it seems.

Four blocks away, only last month, an ex-cop "looking for action" found himself dismembered by a pimp and then deposited, piecemeal, in several ash cans in front of a Chinese laundry I once used.

On a given evening you can see:

The diminutive Arab who every night paces rapidly back and forth in front of the old church, talking incessantly to no one in particular; men rigged up to look like women, with bandanas and false breasts, arm in arm, leering; more lynx-eyed women, one of whom, quite tall and extraordinarily thin, reminds me of a Doberman pinscher; a few tired old men closing up their fruit stalls after working sixteen hours; some fashionable people in front of Zabar's or one of the new restaurants, who look like they've been imported, to dress up the place, from Central Casting; the bald, immie-eyed Baptist—his eyes like those little marbles we used to call steelies—his face bass-belly white, with placards and leaflets, proclaiming to all who will listen that the end of all things is surely at hand. Perhaps. Or perhaps not.

Everyone is an apparition, connected to me by eye only. Why am I always looking over my shoulder, around corners, then, to see who's tracking me or what will be? Hunted by ghosts. I want to become part of them, any one of them, to feel their pulse and know their heart, but I fail; some part of me is locked. Bill Humphrey says these people are only ahead of their time: we'll all be there soon.

And sometimes I see, in the early evening, a glimpse of sunset through the rows of stone, catch the faintest smell of salt, and even see the Hudson itself, sullied but flowing water.

I know no more than ten people among the thousands who live within two blocks of my apartment. Next door, for five years, I used to see a grizzled old fart by the name of Mr. Maggid look out of his second-story window now and then. Sometimes he would call to my sons in a high-pitched voice and throw them pieces of candy; at first I half suspected the sweets were poisoned. A year ago, another neighbor from that building came to me one night, his wife with him, and said, "Mr. Maggid is dying."

"I'm sorry to hear that," I said. I didn't know Mr. Maggid. I didn't know what to feel.

My neighbor paused, then added, "He won't leave his room. You can hear him coughing and groaning in there—it's awful—but he won't answer. The door's locked. About a week ago he told me he wanted to die in his own apartment, no matter what happened. He didn't want to die in some sterile hospital. What should I do?"

A moral decision.

Suddenly, in death, Mr. Maggid's life is linked to mine. No more casual encounters by eye; no more candy dropped thirty-five feet down, suspect, never eaten. He is no longer a stranger like that woman who collapsed on the pavement last winter; when I stooped to help her, a passing lawyer told me I'd better keep my distance—I could be held liable for her death.

What to do?

"I really don't know the man," I explain.

"You can't just let him die like that," says my neighbor's wife.

"He wants to die in his own room."

"Maybe he didn't mean it," says my neighbor.

"He meant it," I say. I have known lonely men.

"Maybe not."

"Does he have any relatives? Any real friends?"

"None." The word is absolute.

"The poor man," says the woman. "You can't let him die all alone up there. You've got to call a hospital, or the police. Maybe they can save him."

"That's the point," says my neighbor. "Maybe he's not really dying."

Finally the neighbor calls the police. On my phone. Does that make me liable? And for what? They come, three of them in blue: solid men who will know what to do. They pound on Mr. Maggid's locked door. They shout. There are a few moans, as if some inhuman creature had been walled up in a Poe story and wanted to stay there. Ten minutes later a bright white-and-red ambulance, its top lights turning and flashing, arrives; someone produces a crowbar and brings it upstairs; then I see Mr. Maggid come down the stairs he rarely used, feet first, on a stretcher, an oxygen mask held to his mouth, his eyes wide, then small, staring, then still. An hour later we learn he has died in the hospital. The next day, our neighbor describes to us Mr. Maggid's room. It has not been cleaned in more than fifteen years. Garbage was never taken out. Hundreds of pornographic magazines piled with soiled clothes in the corners and closets. Dust. Dust over everything. The landlord, who had taken legal measures to get Mr. Maggid evicted so he could jack up the rent, can't face the place and takes a year to clean it. A dour bearded guy who edits movies lives there now. We never speak.

Downtown, where the game for the big green is played, I go to a meeting that lasts eight hours. After the first ten minutes, I feel the tightening in my chest. I begin to doodle; I scribble out a meaningless note and pass it to someone I know across the table, because I've seen executives in the movies do that. I look for the windows, but they're hidden behind heavy, brocaded draperies so that the air-

conditioning will take—anyway, we're in the back of the hotel so even
if the windows were open, I'd only see the backs of other buildings.
Everyone is talking with pomp and edge; I jot down Evelyn Waugh's
observation, "that neurosis people mistake for energy." I drink two
glasses of ice water. I speak like a good boy, when spoken to.

Suddenly I begin to sweat. I've been in this windowless room
for fifteen years. I have been a juggler, flinging my several lives high
and carelessly into the air, never catching them, barely feeling one as
it touches my hand. Nine to five I am here; then a salt stick on the
subway and five hours in the classroom; then I am the fastest ghost-
writer in the East, becoming a lawyer one week, an expert on Greece
the next, then an adopted girl searching for the blood link. When there
is time, after midnight, I write high-toned scholarship—on Chrétien
de Troyes and Thomas Nashe and William Ellery Channing and Saint
Augustine—and shaggy-fish stories; or I prepare a lecture on "The
Generosity of Whitman." A smörgasbord, my life. Five hours of sleep
and back at 'em again, the ghost who is not what he seems, back at
meetings like this one, dreaming.

I say my piece in front of all these important men as enthusiastically as I can. These are the rules of the game. Part of what I say—
a few words—has to do with rivers. From my words I catch their
briefest warbling sound, like the faint rush of wind among the leaves,
or a rushing faucet, and when I sit down, there in the back of the
hotel, with the windows covered by heavy drapes and the smoke from
cigars (mine among them) thick around our heads, as strategies un-
fold and campaigns thicken, I see a glimpse of them, inside. Deep
within me they uncoil.

Rivers.

Bright green live rivers.

The coil and swoop of them, their bright dancing riffles and their
flat dimpled pools at dusk. Their changes and undulations, each
different flowing inch of them. Their physics and morphology and
entomology and soul. The willows and alders along their banks. A particular rock the size of an igloo. Layers of serrated slate from which
rhododendron plumes like an Inca headdress, against which the current rushes, eddies. The quick turn of a yellow-bellied trout in the lip

of the current. Five trout, in loose formation, in a pellucid backwater where I cannot get at them. A world. Many worlds.

> *. . . oft, in lonely rooms, and 'mid the din*
> *Of towns and cities . . .*

as Wordsworth said in "Tintern Abbey," about a nature he felt but never really saw,

> *. . . I have owed to them,*
> *In hours of weariness, sensations sweet,*
> *Felt in the blood, and felt along the heart . . .*

Yes, I owe rivers that. And more. They are something wild, untamed—like that Montana eagle riding a thermal on extended wings, high above the Absaroka mountain pasture flecked with purple lupine. And like the creatures in them: quick trout with laws we can learn, sometimes, somewhat.

I do not want the qualities of my soul unlocked only by this tense, cold, gray, noisy, gaudy, grabby place—full of energy and neurosis and art and antiart and getting and spending—in which that business part of my life, at this time in my life, must of necessity be lived. I have other needs as well. I have other parts of my soul.

Nothing in this world so enlivens my spirit and emotions as the rivers I know. They are necessities. In their clear, swift or slow, generous or coy waters, I regain my powers; I find again those parts of myself that have been lost in cities. Stillness. Patience. Green thoughts. Open eyes. Attachment. High drama. Earthiness. Wit. The Huck Finn I once was. Gentleness. "The life of things." They are my perne within the whirling gyre.

Just knowing they are there and that their hatches will come again and again according to the great natural laws, is some consolation to carry with me on the subways and into the gray offices and out onto upper Broadway at night.

Rivers have been brought to me by my somewhat unintelligible love of fishing. From the little Catskill creek in which I gigged my first trout to the majestic rivers of the West—the Madison, the Yellowstone, the Big Hole, the Snake—fishing has been the hook. And in the pursuit of trout I have found much larger fish.

"Must you actually *fish* to enjoy rivers?" my friend the Scholar asks.

It is difficult to explain but, yes, the fish make every bit of difference. They anchor and focus my eye, rivet my ear.

And could this not be done by a trained patient lover of nature who did not carry a rod?

Perhaps it could. But fishing is *my* hinge, the "oiléd ward" that opens a few of the mysteries for me. It is so for all kinds of fishermen, I suspect, but especially so for fly fishermen, who live closest to the seamless web of life in rivers. That shadow I am pursuing beneath the amber water is a hieroglyphic: I read its position, watch its relationship to a thousand other shadows, observe its steadiness and purpose. That shadow is a great glyph, connected to the darting swallow overhead; to that dancing cream caddisfly near the patch of alders; to the little cased caddis larva on the streambed; to the shell of the hatched stonefly on the rock; to the contours of the river, the velocity of the flow, the chemical composition and temperature of the water; to certain vegetable life called plankton that I cannot see; to the mill nine miles upstream and the reservoir into which the river flows—and, oh, a thousand other factors, fleeting and solid and telling as that shadow. Fishing makes me a student of all this—and a hunter.

Which couldn't be appreciated unless you fish?

Which mean more to me because I do. Fishing makes rivers my corrective lens; I see differently. Not only does the bird taking the

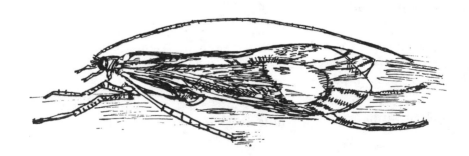

mayfly signify a hatch, not only does the flash of color at the break of the riffle signify a fish feeding, but my powers uncoil inside me and I must determine which insect is hatching and what feeding pattern the trout has established. Then I must properly equip myself and properly approach the fish and properly present my imitation. I am engaged in a hunt that is more than a hunt, for the objects of the hunt are mostly to be found within myself, in the nature of my response and action. I am on a Parsifalian quest. I must be scientist, technician, athlete, perhaps even a queer sort of poet.

The Scholar smiles wanly and says, "It all sounds like rank hedonism. And some cultism. With some mumbo jumbo thrown in."

Yes, I am out to pleasure myself, though sometimes after I've been chewed by no-see-ums until I'm pocked like a leper you wouldn't think that. There is a physical testing: the long hours at early morning, in bright sun, or at dusk; casting until your arm is like lead and your legs, from wading against the stiff current, are numb. That is part of the quest: to cleanse through exertion.

And the cultism and mumbo jumbo?

Some of trout fishing has become that, perhaps always was that. It is a separate little world, cunningly contrived, with certain codes and rules and icons. It is not a religion, though some believers make it such, and it is less than an art. But it has qualities of each. It touches heart and head; it demands and builds flexibility and imagination; it is not easy. I come to rivers like an initiate to holy springs. If I cannot draw from them an enduring catechism or from their impulses even very much about "moral evil and of good," they still confer upon me the beneficence of the only deity I have been able to find. And when the little world becomes *too* cunningly contrived? Wit helps.

My friend the Scholar says he is not a puritan or a moralist but that it seems to him it would be more satisfying to make something that would last—a book, a poem, a cabinet, a wooden bowl—than merely to fish well. He quotes Cézanne, from a letter, after a day of fishing: "All this is easier than painting but it does not lead far."

Not hardly. Not very far at all. Except that this may be precisely where I want it to lead. Let the world lead far—as one should frame it to do; let art last long and lead far and to form. Let a few other human activities lead far, though most of them lead us up a tree or up the asshole of the world. Let fly-fishing be temporary and fleeting and inconsequential. I do not mind.

Enough. Enough.

Too much theory and this pleasant respite from the north Broadway renaissance and gray offices will become an extravagant end that leads too far. Fishing is nothing if not a pastime; it would be hell if I did it all the time.

Beyond the dreams and the theories, there are the days when a close friend will pick me up at dawn on my deserted city block and we will make the long drive together, talking, connected, uncoiling, until we reach our river for the day. It is a simple adventure we are undertaking; it is a break from the beetle-dull routine, a new start, an awakening of the senses, a pilgrimage.

Flooded with memories and expectations, we take out our rods, suit up in waders and vest, special fish hats and nets, arrange flies and leaders, and take to the woods. Each article of equipment, each bit of gear in our ritualistic uniform, is part of the act. The skunk cabbage is thrusting up, lush and green-purple out of the moist brown mulch of last year's leaves; we flush a white-tailed deer that bounds off boldly; we see the pale-green buds pressing out of the birch branches. "Spring has come again," says Rilke. "The earth is like a little child who knows poems by heart—many, so many." We wonder whether the Hendricksons will or will not hatch at midday. We have our hopes.

With rivers as with good friends, you always feel better for a few hours in their presence; you always want to review your dialogue, years later, with a particular pool or riffle or bend, and to live back through layers of experience. We have been to this river before and together. We have much to relive.

Then we are on the river. It is still there. So much is perishable, impermanent, dispensable today, so much is gobbled up by industry and housing and the wanton surge of people, we half thought it might be gone, like that river we used to fish in Dutchess County, now bludgeoned by tract homes and industrial plants and trailers, now littered and warm and dead. Trout are yardsticks; they are an early-warning system like the canary in the mine—when they go, what will happen to the rest of the planet, to the quality of life?

Yes, this river is still there, still alive, still pregnant with possibility.

"There's a swirl," I say, pointing.

"I saw one upstream, too."

"A few flies are coming off, see?"

"Yes, we're going to make a day of it."

My pulse quickens, the long gray city winter vanishes. In a moment we separate and belong to the river and to its mysteries, to its smooth glides and pinched bends, to the myriad sweet problems that call forth total concentration, that obviate philosophy.

Yes, these are Hendricksons, *Ephemerella subvaria,* and the hatch, on schedule, is just beginning. I am by profession neither an angler nor a scientist but there's always more pleasure in knowing than in not knowing. I take the lower pool and spot four good trout, poised high in the clear, flat water, waiting for the duns to hatch in the riffles and float down. By tilting my head close to the surface, I can see them, like little sailboats, drifting down. Two, three, there's another. Not many yet. A couple of birds are working, dipping and darting; against the light sky above the tree line I pick out one mayfly, watch it flutter, watch a swallow swoop, hesitate, and take it. What looks so pastoral is violent; it is, only on a smaller, more civilized scale, a horde of bluefish slashing a bunker school to bits, leaving blood and fin and head everywhere, to be picked up by the ravenous seabirds. The bites are cleaner here: the birds and trout take a whole creature in one mouthful.

Then back to the river. There are circles below me; the fish are feeding steadily. Shall I fish above or below them? They are so still, so firmly established in an irregular row across the channel in that clear flat water, that I elect the road less traveled and decide to fish down to them on a slack line—this way I won't have to cast over their backs.

It is delicate work, but I know that this year I have an excellent imitation of the natural fly, that my 5X leader is light enough, and that I've done just enough slack-line downstream casting to manage. Fishing is cumulative, though you don't learn all of it, ever.

I position myself carefully on the bank—it would be fatal to wade above such fish—strip about forty feet of line from my reel, and false-cast twice.

My rod jerks backward. I've hung my fly in that low brush.

The interruption of the music, like the needle hitting a scratch on a recording of the Brandenburg Concerto, irritates madly but is not final.

When I return, the fish are still feeding, more steadily now, even rhythmically.

My cast lands well above the fish, and my fly floats without drag a few feet short of their feeding station before the line tightens; a little V forms upstream of the fly and it goes under.

I retrieve the fly slowly, unwilling to ruffle the surface until there are no more than ten feet of line still in the water, then cast again. The fly floats freely and I hold my breath. This time it will go far enough. It's two feet upstream of the first fish; I'm still holding my breath; the snake in the line unwinds and begins to straighten, slowly, then faster; I lean forward to give it another foot, another few inches; I watch the fish move slightly, turn toward the fly, inspect it, nose up to it, and then the fly drags and the fish turns away.

A deep breath.

Two more casts: one that quarters the river too amply and causes the fly to drag within two feet; another that floats properly but gets there a second after the trout has taken a natural. Then a good cast, a good float, and the fish pivots and takes, feels the hook, jumps twice, and burrows across and upstream. It's thirteen inches and not strong enough to cause much mischief; anyway, after the strike, after I have successfully gulled this creature from another element, linked my brain to its brain, I am less interested. After a few minutes I have the fish near my bank, lean down and twitch the hook free, and it is gone, virgorously—sleek and spotted and still quick.

When I've taken the slime off the fly and air-dried it, I notice that most of the fish have left their stations; only one fish is working in the pool now, across the main current, in a little backwater. It will require a different approach, a different strategy. I take fully five minutes to work my way downstream along the bank, into the water, and across to the other side, moving slowly so as not to disturb the life of the river. I am only its guest. The fish is still working when I get there.

I am directly below the trout now and can see only the periodic circles about forty feet above me. I don't want to put the fly line over it, and I know its actual feeding position in the water will be at least several feet above the mark of the rise form, which is floating downstream and is the final mark of his deliberate inspection ritual. I elect to cast into the edge of the main current above the fish and hope the fly will catch an eddying current and come down into the trout's position. The cast is good. Squinting, I watch the fly float down, then free of, the fast center current and my fly line hug the nearly dead water. There is an electric moment when the circle forms. My arm shoots up. The fish has taken the fly solidly and feels like a good one. It does not jump but bores into its little pool, then into the current; then it gets below me. I slip, recover, and begin to edge downstream, the fish stripping line from the reel now, boiling at the surface twice, then coming upstream quickly while I raise the rod high and haul in line to keep the fish from slipping the hook.

A little later I release the fish from the net, turning it out—a beautiful seventeen-inch brown.

I take two more fish, smaller ones, in the riffle below the pool, then head upstream again to where the first fish were feeding, approaching the spot from below. The hatch has peaked and is tapering now; the late-afternoon chill of late April has set in and I feel it for the first time. One fish is still feeding but I cannot, in six or seven casts, raise it, and finally it stops.

I breathe deeply and take out a pipe. There may be a spinner fall in another hour but I am exhausted. The river is placid, calm now. No fish are rising. The drama is over; the actors have retired to the wings. I have been caught for two hours in an intensely sensual music, and I want to stop, perhaps for the day—to smoke the pipe now, watch that squirrel in the oak, look for deer tracks and chipmunk holes. The city has become a bad dream, a B movie I once saw that violates my imagination by returning at odd moments. Most of the world would be bored by these past two hours. Most of the world? Most of the world is polluting the rivers, making the worse appear the better cause, peacocking, grating on each other's ears, gouging, putting their fingers on others' souls or their hands in the wrong pockets, scheming, honking, pretending, politicking, small-talking, criticizing.

"Is that *all* you find?" I hear the Scholar ask me.

"Nope. But there's a damned lot of it."

"You're a misanthrope, a hater of cities," he says. "You claim to love gentleness but . . ."

I don't especially want to answer his questions now so I look back at the river. We invented the non sequitur for just such moments.

Yes, we have made a day of it. Two, three hours sandwiched in. Little enough. But deep. And durable. And more than a day's worth. We've earned memories—full and textured—that live now in our very marrowbones, that make us more alive. Our thoughts will be greener, our judgments perhaps sharper, our eyes a bit brighter. We live day by day with little change in our perceptions, but I never go to a river that I do not see newly and freshly, that I do not learn, that I do not find a story.

On the way home I still feel the tug of the river against my thighs, and in my mind's eye I can see the largest rising trout, the neat circle when it took a natural, the quick dramatic spurt—electric through my whole body—when it took my fly and I felt its force. And I wondered why I had not raised that last fish.

It was not the ultimate river, the ultimate afternoon; it was not so exquisite as a Keatsian moment frozen and anguished because it would not last. There will be others—never equal, always discretely, sharply different. A thousand such moments. Days when, against all expectation, the river is dead; days when it is generous beyond dreams.

A luxury? A mere vacation?

No, those rivers are more. They are my Pilgrim Creek and Walden Pond, however briefly. Those rivers and their bounty—bright and wild—touch me and through me touch every person whom I meet. They are a metaphor for life. In their movement, in their varied glides, runs, and pools, in their inevitable progress toward the sea, they contain many of the secrets we seek to understand about ourselves, our purposes. The late Roderick Haig-Brown said, "Were it not for the strong, quick life of rivers, for their sparkle in the sunshine, for the cold grayness of them under rain and the feel of them about my legs as I set my feet hard down on rocks or sand or gravel, I should fish less often." Amen. When such rivers die, as so many have, so too dies an irretrievable part of the soul of each of the thousands of anglers who in their waters find deep, enduring life.

Visit a few of them with me. We won't linger long. I know how fearfully busy and hurried you are. But perhaps a few moments will be of some profit. Perhaps you will meet some old friends, smile (without seeking to gull someone thereby), and make a new friend or two as we travel: first near, then far.

PILGRIMAGES

And smale fowles maken melodye,
That slepen al the night with open yë,
(So priketh hem nature in hir corages):
Than longen folk to goon on pilgrimages.
                        —*Geoffrey Chaucer*

I was not born near rivers and I have not lived my life near them. From the beginning, my fishing has been a matter of excursions. Usually I went for a day, perhaps two days at a fling. For this I would prepare weeks, sometimes months in advance, buying new bits of tackle to meet new knowledge I'd acquired, tying leaders, rewinding guides, selecting the proper flies, lures, or, much earlier, bait.

In my teens these were massive, exhausting treks, beginning in dark basements in Brooklyn at three in the morning, ending when I returned at midnight. Everything was carried in great packs on my back—waders, gear, extra clothing, food, all. Had not some friends got the use of the family car when we were seventeen, I would to this day be humpbacked.

That first day out in April was holy to me. It meant the first break of the year with the gray, indoor winter. I needed it to freshen my eye, to remind me that I can still explore, adventure. It was a beginning and augurs a wealth of days from then until autumn, when the bright rivers will be available, waiting. My feet pick up a quicker pace those first few days in April; my wife says my eyes light up. In my green years I did not miss an Opening Day—but now the season begins somewhat later, under less frenzied, less crowded conditions. I have learned to wait. Another week, another few days will not matter that much. Not now. I could still bear that cold, with the ice freezing at the guides, and no doubt some fish can be taken on a fly. Some fly fishermen I know even make a ritual of the day, complete with a traditional lunch or breakfast at home or at a favorite restaurant; some seek chiefly the celebration—more natural than a Lincoln's or Washington's birthday—of the new year. Who can blame them?

Chaucer begins his *Canterbury Tales* with such a magnificent celebration of the power of spring. When April with its sweet showers pierces to the root "the droghte of Marche," and small birds, too filled, apparently, with the excitement of spring to close their eyes, sing all night, then "longen folk to goon on pilgrimages . . ."

It is a pilgrimage indeed. Chaucer's "palmers" come from various parts of England and travel to Canterbury, to seek the "holy blisful martir," who has helped them "whan that they were seke. . . ." Fly fishermen, with little less zeal, seek moving water again. They want to touch that which is awake, alive. All is awake. All begins again. Sometimes, deep in the city, the first touch of spring, a wraithlike dream—green and bright and flowing—seeps through the gray and starts the awakening. Or perhaps, on dark forsythia branches still flecked with snow, bright green buds appear.

All is growing. *Anthony* has grown. I measure him with my eye and see that he is older, calmer, less a child, more a bud about to bloom. Perhaps he is old enough this year. Perhaps. Certainly he's willing. All that winter he had been after me: "Dad. Dad. You promised. Can I go with you and Mike? Can I?"

His older brothers always got the largest piece of cake; he always wore their hand-me-downs; he always got interrupted at the table. But he is older now, pushing thirteen, holding his own, full of his own mischief and play and purpose. I have tried, with mixed success, to convert people I love to this fly fishing I love; I do so no more. It is, after all, a private affair and must come or not come as it will. But since I talk fishing *ad nauseam* and find few listeners anymore in my own home, I leap upon Anthony's interest. The addict needs allies.

What is this hook?

Sparse Grey Hackle says that "you will search far to find a fisherman to admit that a taste for fishing, like a taste for liquor, must be governed lest it come to possess its possessor." I cringe when I think of those times when my taste for it has come to possess me: the long hours snatched from employment that would lead further, when I've tinkered with tackle, tied flies, eyed choice bamboo rods at Abercrombie's (which I could scarcely afford), gabbed incessantly with other addicts, thought fish, read fish, dreamed fish. For while the worries vanished, so did my commitments. I'd return three hours late, my ears filled with the rush of the river, frazzled, freaked out on fly hatches, my wife livid, her gold wedding band gleaming brightly on the top of my Tackle Satchel.

I cannot give up a rising trout any more than I can the search for the irresistible fly, the ultimate fly rod. I am forever searching for a better leader formula, a more efficient vest, an answer to this or that trout mystery. Why wasn't there a rise at two o'clock on the Green House Pool? There was one last year at that time. Why did the Lady Blitz work well at dusk last night, not tonight? Why, when trout were rising all afternoon, couldn't I even raise a chub?

Why?

That, I suspect, is the ultimate hook. Men by nature desire to know; trout by nature are capricious, mysterious, unpredictable—at least to me. Your disposition, their disposition, maybe even the phase of the moon affects the outcome. Nothing is certain in trout fishing, says Arnold Gingrich, "except its glorious uncertainty."

Of course there are days when, miraculously, all goes well—when you are far from the quiet desperations, closer to nature than you've ever been, calm and contemplative, when the flies hatch on schedule and you have the right fly and the fish become particularly human in their predictability. I've had a few such days when nearly every cast brought a trout.

"And you weren't bored?" the Scholar asks.

No.

"And that didn't satisfy your longing to strike through the 'pasteboard mask' veiling the elusive mystery?"

No. No more than catching nothing bores the addicted angler. Catching fish and not catching fish are both drugs. Each hungers where most it satisfies.

"But you can't always fish," says the father of Roland Pertwee's boy-addict in *The River God*.

"I told him I could, and I was right and have proved it for thirty years and more."

"Well, well," the father, like any good condescending nonangler, says, "please yourself, but isn't it dull not catching anything?"

And the boy answers, as he does a thousand times thereafter (even as I have done a thousand times), "As if it could be."

Would Anthony be bored? Did he know how cold it would be in April? "That doesn't bother me, Dad. You know." Did he realize, his mother advised, that old Dad *talked* good fly fishing but—so it seemed—rarely caught anything? "I'll catch some for him." Did he *really* know, one of his brothers asked, how downright boring it could be? "Dad doesn't get bored." Nope. Not ever. Not for one minute of it.

Well, we would try.

We picked Mike Migel up at eight on a cold gray mid-April morning. Anthony knew and liked him. What twelve-year-old wouldn't like that tall thin white-haired gentleman, with a handshake that gobbles up your fingers with a firm warmth. And he tells stories, too! Wide-eyed and unusually silent, the boy listened as Mike began to tell about growing up in Arizona a half century ago. We began, at the George Washington Bridge, with the Apache massacre in which one of Mike's uncles died, before Mike went to live on the ranch, and progressed quickly to the sheepdog that used to lie beneath the porch on a hot day and nip a bit of the tail off the pet monkey whenever he could; he'd gotten all but a couple of inches of it, during the course of a summer, when we shifted abruptly to the lion hunt. The lion hunt! No sooner were the words out than the boy's eyes widened like a camera lens, catching everything. Mike was only fourteen and went with some men down into Mexico where a lion had been lunching on some unfortunate townspeople. They took guns and mules and tracking dogs. I glanced from the road to the boy's face. The story continued ever so slowly with substories about Mike's first use of a gun, about tracking other wild and dangerous beasts, and we had just picked up the sure scent of this particular cat when we discovered we were two hours upstate already and that it was time for coffee before hitting the river. We hoped the Hendricksons would be hatching. But we were early—they wouldn't be off for another few hours.

In the diner Anthony kept looking at Mike and finally asked, "Well, what happened? Did you get the lion?"

"There's a remarkable story concerning that."

The boy waited.

Mike finished his bite of a doughnut.

"It'll take some time," Mike said. "Perhaps we should save it for the trip back, Anthony."

"Well . . . I'd just as soon hear it now. If that's okay."

I said, "We've got to plan out the fishing now."

"Oh. Does it have to be planned?"

Perhaps not. But that adds to the pleasure. So we talked leaders and flies and particularly choice days in the bright past and, after some debate, chose our section of the river for the day, and after a half hour I could tell that Anthony rightly considered all this trout talk somewhat less important than lions.

Or maybe he didn't.

An hour or so later, Mike and I were a hundred yards apart in a cold, deep riffle below the Big Bend. It was far colder than we'd thought, the water in the high thirties, the air not much warmer. There was still no sun. It had begun to drizzle steadily. At the bend, a long flat glide turned with deceptive speed into a treacherous, sweeping rapids. I was fishing a Red Quill upstream, a bit too quickly, without great expectations; Mike, from a fixed position below the bend, where the pinched flow began to widen, was fishing a wet fly in the currents, casting slightly upstream, mending, letting the fly work as slowly and deeply as possible. We'd been at it for an hour and the signs were not good. The water was too heavy and too cold; no flies had shown— and wouldn't; we were too early for this run to produce. We shouldn't have chosen a river so far north.

But it was the first day out and I could feel a deep stillness inside me. I enjoyed casting; I enjoyed watching Mike cast. But we were too early, much too early; the green was still sleeping in the alders and the trout were slow.

While I worked rapidly upstream toward Mike, I could see Anthony fishing along the bank above us. His white face glistened out of the dark low alder branches and surrounding grasses.

"Anything at all?" I asked Mike.

"A tap. Maybe two."

"Any size?"

"Couldn't tell."

"I don't think any flies will show."

"I saw two. Exactly two. Quill Gordons, I suppose."

"It's a start. We're a week early. By Thursday, if it warms, they should . . . Anthony!"

The boy had waded out into the glide in his brother's baggy chest waders. He was coming toward us. "Anthony! Go around! The water's too deep there. Too fast. Don't try to wade! Go through!"

Had he heard me?

The sound of the bend rapids was a steady rush in my ears. Mike started to move brusquely upstream. I followed, rushing now against the heavy press of the current. I knew that stretch. The boy was not going to make it. I waved him back frantically. I shouted. Didn't he hear me? Mike kept moving quickly around the curved edge of the bend.

Then, while we were still fifty yards from him, hopelessly too far, I froze, then lunged forward again, up to Mike, past him. Anthony started to lose his balance as the current quickened. We could tell his feet had slipped; we could see his small body twist and struggle against the greater force of the water. He slid forward now, almost racing at us, weirdly, as the water leaped toward the turn. Then he was off his feet and under, all the way under, over his head, splashing, flailing out, his feet out from under him now, then up, fear in his eyes for the first time, his movements jerky, wild, as the water deepened and sped out toward the fastest white-capped broken water where we'd never be able to reach him.

"Anthony! No! No!"

But then he was up somehow, with a toehold and we breathed deeply as he lunged toward the bank, *willing* himself there—slipping back, forcing himself on, safe.

In a small covert among high dead grasses, in the cold wet air, we stripped off his jacket, slacks, shirt, undershirt, underpants, socks, everything. He stood stark still and wide-eyed, unashamed, shaking only slightly, as we wrung out each bit of clothing: silent, white, like something sprung suddenly from winter earth on a spring afternoon.

An hour later I was still shaking.

It had been as close as it can get.

In the warm car, heading home, with my old fishing coat snug around him, Anthony sat like a prince. Mike and I talked about the two flies he had seen, the one I saw later and positively identified as a Quill Gordon, and then Anthony heard all about the lion, in effusive detail, and he said, "You guys don't catch anything but you sure have fun out here."

He and I fished together on brisk, misty mornings in May; and then in June, standing by my side in the Esopus River, he caught his first trout on a fly. And last week, as the time for another pilgrimage approached, he came over to my desk one night, hung on my shoulder, and said, "About this book you're writing, Dad. I mean, you'd better get it done in time, by April, so we guys don't lose any of our fly fishing time."

A month after Anthony's first trip, I took another pilgrimage with Mike, to the big Delaware. I'd never fished it before.

Mike was an hour late, which was all right because he's often late and the fishing didn't start, he'd told me, until "very late in the day." Then he was two hours late, and it was ten o'clock, and by the time he finally showed—his dark-blue Pontiac rounding the corner of my city block—I would have given up on the trip and gone back to bed had my expectations not been so high.

We were going to fish for rainbows with Ed Van Put, and I had been looking forward to the trip for weeks.

The lateness was simply explained. Mike had left his car in front of his apartment building for a few minutes while he went back for a second fly rod he'd leaned against the elevator. When he returned, the car was being lifted behind a police tow truck. He shouted, they were deaf; he pleaded, they drove off. He had to follow the truck by cab to the city lot and pay a $75 fine to retrieve it. One never extricates oneself from the city easily. It must love us too well.

Well, there was a long, rich day ahead of us, and those "muscular rainbows" Mike had described danced in my imagination. I speculated as we drove that for the overworked inner-city angler, fishing often became less *what* than *who* you knew. I was going to be admitted to Kafka's Castle without delay that afternoon. No more for me the long disastrous escapes from the city—driving hundreds of miles to barren streams, meeting crowds or high water, fishing an hour too late or leaving an hour too early, arriving a day after construction started upriver and the water was in cocoa-colored spate; no more the exhaustion and frustration and discovery, three hours from the city, that what I'd labored so hard to get to was not there.

Now, instead of trips randomly stolen from the maelstrom of the city, I more and more made the long up-country pilgrimage when I had good information. "Hi, Nick, my boy," would come Art Flick's hearty voice on the phone. "They started coming off today. You ought to get up within the next few days while they're still strong. The 'Kill, eight miles below the bridge, above Old Oak Pool. I'll be there tomorrow at noon if you want to meet me." An offer too good to refuse. With that kind of advice one forgoes the sage advice that the best time to fish is when you can. The best time to fish is when Art Flick tells you to fish. As I proved next day. The Hendricksons began to hatch and the fish to rise, right on schedule, and I was actually there, at the right place and right time, with the guy who wrote the book and who had given me some of his Red Quills, which imitate the male of the species, as all initiates know. Who couldn't have caught fish? Even *I* got a few.

This remarkable principle worked for me in Provincetown, thanks to the "swami of the surf," Frank Woolner, and on the Yellowstone River, thanks to Charlie Brooks. Clearly I had the system beat, the inscrutable mysteries of trout fishing solved. Or thought I did—forgetting that time and chance and the fickleness of fish and my own brand of city-bred ineptitude happeneth to me quite often.

A well-planned and advised trip to Henrys Lake, that extraordinary fishery in Idaho, ended in near disaster when I managed, with much effort, to get my fly line caught in the Johnson fifteen-horsepower motor. That's not easy to do. I tipped the motor up to get in at the blades and began to pick away the weed and untangle the line. When the motor kept slipping down, I leaned farther out, to get beneath it. I'd taken out six or seven healthy clumps of weed and unwrapped the line a couple of turns when the motor slipped again and I with it. I lost control, dunked my head in upside down up to my nose, rammed my leg against the gunwale so hard I could barely walk for a week, jerked myself back up and into the boat, kicked the plug out so water began rushing into the bottom like a reservoir sluice, rubbed my head, wiped the water out of my eyes, cursed my leg, shoved the plug back in, and tipped the boat so violently I almost fell into the lake again.

Even expert advice cannot keep you from a trick like that. It takes practice.

For years I'd heard rumors about the increasingly good fishing for large rainbows in the Delaware River, and the name Ed Van Put came up repeatedly. As a Catskill-region fish-and-wildlife technician, he was both a knowledgeable biologist and a man with regular access to and understanding of the river. Mike had met him, and we were going to be taken by Ed to one of the best pools on the Delaware. I couldn't miss.

There were a few chores first: to visit a house Mike might want to rent, then over to Len Wright's cabin on the Neversink, to pick him up. By the time we finally met Ed at four o'clock at the Roscoe Diner, I was exhausted; it had been eight hours since I'd officially started on this fishing trip, and though the company was good I was anxious to be on the water—this was beginning to look too much like all those bumbling trips I'd made before I got authoritative advice.

Besides, it had started to rain—first steadily, then fiercely, then not at all, then steadily again. There was a time when I didn't much mind fishing in the rain in early summer, in fact thought it brought better fishing, but I was older now and didn't have a rain jacket with me; about six years earlier when I'd gone outside my apartment to wait for Mike, it had been sunny.

We packed into two cars, and Mike followed Ed upstate, along Route 17, to the Delaware. It would have been downright unsociable and cowardly of me to ask, but I rather wondered what the bar of the Antrim Lodge looked like at this time of day. An hour later, about five o'clock, we headed down a dead-end muddy road, stopped, stretched, suited up, and headed for the river.

It was still raining—not as hard but steadily. I tried to light my cigar but it kept fizzling out.

What a river! Its huge sweeping turns were more than a half mile long; where we came out of the woods, there was nothing to indicate the hand of man but an old railroad track. Clusters of aspen, willow, birch, and alder graced the far side of the river. Some rhododendron was in bloom. This was a gloriously wild stretch, equal to anything I'd seen out west, and only—at least that day—nine hours from the city. As my eye swept down the length of the river, I saw fish breaking water only a few hundred yards away. They were obviously big fish, in the shallows, and there were a lot of them. Good grief, I'd fish in a hailstorm for creatures like that! They were monsters. I'd hit a bonanza again and I was all for trotting down the tracks in my waders to get at them.

"Shad," said Ed. "Probably spent, and almost impossible to catch. They'll be heading downstream in another week or so."

We marched slowly down the tracks in the rain, watching the water constantly. This was as lovely a stretch of river as I could remember ever having seen. Ed said it would be lovelier if the reservoir people let a steady flow of cold water out from the bottoms of Cannonsville and the Pepacton. He said that in another few weeks the water would become so warm that fishing would stop and the fish might die. It sounded criminal.

"What's the drill?" Len asked when we got to the bend. Ed wanted to fish. We'd walked about a mile in the rain.

An Adams or Gray Fox Variant, about size 16, would be best; we might pick up a fish or two during the next hour or so, but the real fishing would start at dusk. Ed did better than catch a fish or two. In ten minutes he was into a really large rainbow that took him into his backing. Then he had another on, then another. He'd earlier told me he'd caught more than two hundred rainbows each of the past two years, most of them over fifteen inches and at least forty or fifty over eighteen. Today, no one else caught even a chub. For me that was not surprising, but I'd expected more of Len and Mike.

I fished from the tail of the sweeping pool up into the run where the current struggled to keep its definition, then into the fast, choppy water, then into the head of the riffle—thinking that the rainbows might go into the fastest water during the day. The trouble was, besides not seeing a fish—except the ones on Ed's line—I couldn't keep a cigar lit; either I'd get one started only to have the rain snuff it out a moment later or I'd spend ten minutes trying fruitlessly to light a soggy cigar with damp matches. I fish better with a lit cigar; some people fish better with talent. But I fished downstream diligently with a large Whitlock Bronze Nymph, which had raised some good fish for me in the West, and watched Ed catch still another muscular rainbow. He casts an immaculately slow and graceful line, and I had the distinct impression that he was also doing something I didn't see, like humming or whistling to these old finny friends to perform for the crowd. He could tell by his taggings that he'd caught several of these fish before; no doubt they were aware that he released every fish he caught and thus had no reluctance to renew acquaintance.

As for me, I sloshed around despondently, bone tired now, whipping the water to a froth, getting wetter by the minute, wondering precisely why I wasn't home reading *The Turn of the Screw* instead of making such a fool of myself. This was strictly a regression.

But finally, about eight-forty, just after the light grew dim, two splendid events took place: the rain stopped and the fish began to rise ferociously, dozens of them. I promptly lit a new cigar, clipped off my large nymph, and rummaged in one of my fly boxes for a No. 16 Adams. Well, I was going to make a day of it at last—or at least a fifteen minutes of it. I could *taste* the rise and run of one of those sleek rainbows.

My hands began to tremble All the old fever and expectation returned, all fatigue vanished. I fumbled with the fly, couldn't get the leader point through the eye of the hook, raised the fly against the dun sky, manipulated the thin monofilament with the deftness of a surgeon, and at last got the pesky thing done.

Eight forty-five, and nearly dark.

The circles—rhythmic and gentle—continued to spread in the flat water where the current widened. Ed was at my left shoulder now, willing to forgo these fine last moments of the day so he could advise me. A saint.

"Cast to specific rises, Nick, as delicately as possible. Some of these are really big fish. Over twenty inches. Strike them lightly."

With not a second to lose, I took my dry-fly spray from my vest, held the Adams near my face, pressed the plunger—and went stingingly blind. The little hole had been pointed in the wrong direction. I'd given myself a triple shot of fly dope in the eyes, and even after I doused them with a bit of the Delaware I could barely see.

But I squinted bravely, puffed with vigor on my cigar—whose tip now glowed like a hot little coal in the dark—and began to cast in the general direction Ed was pointing.

"That looked about right," he said as I laid out a surprisingly accurate cast to one of the inviting circles. I couldn't see the fly but that didn't matter.

"Can't imagine why he didn't take it," Ed said.

When I miraculously repeated the feat, a good cast, he said, "They're awfully picky sometimes. What have you got on?"

"A sixteen Adams."

"That *ought* to do it."

Another cast, my third good one in a row, a record. It was a magical, witching moment, the far bank receding in the swirling mists, the river sounds filling my ears, my squinting eyes seeing only that faint multitude of spreading circles. I could not see my fly but knew exactly where it was by estimating the distance from the end of my bright yellow fly line.

Nothing.

"Strange," said Ed.

"Maybe this time."

Still nothing—and nothing for the next fifteen minutes, when a moonless sky finally pulled the curtain on us and we began to head back up the long stretch of railroad tracks to the cars.

In the headlights I saw a strange sight, which I took the liberty of not reporting to my fellow anglers. There was no fly on my leader! There was only a blackened, melted end, as if, just possibly, it might have been burned through by a cigar.

Mike and I made the long trip back in silence. Had I really fished through the entire rise, the twenty minutes I'd waited for all day, with no fly? No doubt. I was capable of it. My face still smarted in the darkened car with embarrassment, my eyes still stung. I tried to keep my eyelids from drooping, and I tried to talk—because good talk with a good friend after a long day on a river is one of the best parts of any trip. But I was bushed.

I closed my eyes and dreamed of muscular rainbows dimpling to a No. 16 Adams, then skyrocketing out and taking me into the backing. That huge bend of the river was alive with rising fish and each cast was true. I heard Ed say, "They're awfully picky sometimes. What have you got on?"

And I answered, moaning, knowing I had developed a pattern even the experts had never thought of, "The emperor's new fly!"

EXPERTS AND FRIENDS

Whatsoever thy hand findeth to do, do it with
thy might; for there is no work, nor device, nor
knowledge, nor wisdom, in the grave, whither
thou goest.
—*Ecclesiastes*

There are advantages to being known as a fly-fishing expert. People
send you free flies and ask for your opinion of the thorax tie; you
get to try out (and keep) marvelous new equipment and to take paid
trips to famous rivers where brown trout grow as long as one of Wilt's
stilts; other fly fishermen make a happy fuss over your mere presence;
you can become a well-paid consultant, a lecturer on the trout-talk
beat, an author, a panelist, a clinic instructor. Being an expert mas-
sages the wallet and the ego. Some people even make a living at it.

I always wanted to be an expert. It seemed a good kind of creature to be. I especially dreamed of being asked to fish the bright rivers of Argentina, New Zealand, Iceland, Wales. Being an expert would
without fail put me in dramatic connection with rivers. But though it
grieves me to do so, I am forced to confess that I am not—and never
will be—an expert. Not only am I an amateur but I am about to become
an apologist for amateurs. Amateur fly fishers, that is. For if a man is
going to write or act or sing or paint or fix plumbing or carburetors
for his supper—or his soul—he should try to be the best he can be at
it, the best there is. "Whatsoever thy hand findeth to do, do it with
thy might," sayeth the preacher, and he is no doubt right.

But *not* about fly fishing?

Well, we do it chiefly for recreation, don't we? It is, in the best
sense of the word, a pastime, isn't it? Most of us fly-fish for the sheer
pleasure of it, to heal the sores of work—to refresh, pursue, make

whole again. At least that's what I thought until I started trying too hard to become an expert. *That* nearly killed my love of rivers.

Frankly, the problem became this: near and far, as far as two thousand miles from home, friends and perfect strangers—out of a variety of false assumptions (mistaking passion for expertise, labeling me by association with my betters)—actually considered me to be an expert. Alas. There is a time in every man's life when he must see himself for what he is. It is not so. It will never be so. My grasp of Latin entomological names is rotten and improves not at all; I spend too little time on the rivers I love; I am mostly inept, careless; I mismatch the hatch and slap the back cast; despite my most patient patching, even my waders leak.

Witness this bogus expert during a splendid caddis hatch on a popular section of the Yellowstone River in the park. The little gray whirlers are coming off in clouds. Cutthroats—fifteen, sixteen, seventeen inches—are lying high in the water, tipping their pretty snouts up to take the duns. Everywhere you look trout are rising in the clear, riffled flow. Charlie Brooks has brought me. He has seen this before; I have not. My blood, which should be cool, turns to a swift boil. Did I actually froth at the mouth? Maybe. It would have been consonant with my mood. I rummage around in my vest and pluck out the only reel I've brought, forgetting until that moment that I'd lent the reel to one of my sons, who'd gotten such a brilliantly complex series of wind knots in the leader that I'd cut it through a foot below the nail knot.

My hands tremble. I look out at the Yellowstone and those cutthroats have gone berserk. There must be a thousand of them. Charlie, who has indeed seen this before, says, "Problem with your leader? Let me tie a new one to that stub." He has (may his leaders never rot!) a special knot for tying thinner diameter monofilament to twenty-five-pound-test butts. Who'd have thought the problem would ever come up? Who'd have thought that an expert like me would be ignorant enough to come to the river without an adequate leader? Actually, I had been on the verge of trying to push that fat stub through the eye of one of George Bodmer's deadly Colorado Kings, size 16.

I have come as Charlie's editor, and though I have made no boasts I fear he now thinks me the perfect fool.

Well, he gets the thing done, patiently instructing me as he does, though I hear none of it since I'm looking mostly at the river, and I string up the rod, turn and head for the river, turn again to thank him, trip and nearly bust my rod, and arrive at what must be the closest thing to heaven—a river alive with rising trout.

Two casts from the bank and I've got something: a seventy-foot pine tree. Unlike most of the large things I hook, it does not shake free, nor can I disengage it before Charlie comes over and politely plucks it out for me. The third cast stays cunningly out of the trees— and hooks me neatly in the earlobe. I have fished for more than thirty-five years and have only heard of this embarrassing phenomenon. Play it nonchalant, Nick, I think, and say, "Got a clipper, Charlie? I just want to snip this barb . . ."

The man still hasn't rigged his rod—is he human?—so he comes over, looks at the sweet little thing in my ear, and says, "Out here we just pull them straight back out. Only stings for a moment."

"That's the way they do it out here, is it? Straight back . . ."

And the thing is out.

Though these huge cutthroats are rising no more than a foot from shore, in the little eddies beside our bank, in the first riffles, I decide to wade out. Perhaps it's safer out there. But the current is stronger than it looks, and naturally I have not replaced my worn felts this year; soon I am safely stuck between two rocks, there for the afternoon or longer, and flailing away. When I manage to snag a few of these generous fish and see that Charlie has caught a few and put down his rod, I feel much more relaxed. He's a friend, after all, not a judge. But turning toward the bank after releasing a fish, I notice that Charlie is now talking to several fishermen. They begin to watch me intently—and promptly everything goes wrong again. My line

tangles in my net; I try to take a step and nearly keel over in the current. Then I try an especially long cast and the line does not come forward after the back cast. I have hooked another cutthroat—on the slap as it were—and try desperately to pretend I had fished it that way. Do they know? Do they see the blood on my ear? Does one of them have a camera?

I am an expert at hindsight. Ten minutes after I've left a luncheon at which I babbled and mumbled, failed miserably at comebacks and bons mots, I become extraordinarily brilliant. Walking home, I become like one of the other maniacs on upper Broadway, laughing and giggling out loud to the tune of some hidden inner dialogue; my wit and courage astound me. Some people's minds work like that: ten minutes too late at a minimum. Mine does. Always.

I'm also not bad at second-guessing my fishing mistakes. In the late fall or in the dead of winter, when I've put all my rods and tackle in order and safely away, I can think of a dozen things I should have done had I been even part expert.

Many of these things fall into the category of tackle care, a subject I flunk regularly. The slightest piece of equipment reminds me: leaky waders, a broken leader clipper, sunglasses that should have been Polaroid. A quick look in my fish closet and I know why my casts hooked and fell awkwardly on that last trip: my fly line has a bad crack above the nail knot. Had I been *that* unconscious on the stream? Why hadn't I noticed it? And even if I had, would I have had the skill and patience to clip the raw end and tie on a new leader with a good nail knot? Not hardly.

And why hadn't I rewound the frayed winding on a middle guide of my fly rod instead of having to pull a Band-Aid off my scratched finger to keep the guide in place? It would have taken me no more than ten minutes to do at home, and I knew it had to be done.

While I am asking myself such embarrassing questions, I notice the fly box still in my vest, which reminds me that—with twenty good grasshopper imitations in my storage case—I took only mayfly patterns with me in early September. The fields had been full of plump, leaping grasshoppers, and I got skunked on mayfly imitations. Was I saving those Whitlock Hoppers for Opening Day?

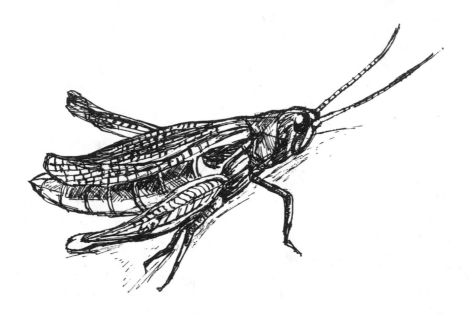

Hindsight? I'm flush with it.

So much for would-be experts who had once the longing but never the hand. What about the real thing?

There's Flick, of course, who's more than an expert: he's a fisherman. He's so skillful that I had to fish with him a handful of times before I realized he was not a magician. He'd caught a half dozen good trout in the middle of a hot July afternoon on the Battenkill—when *no one* catches trout—and another half dozen one evening on the Schoharie when I didn't see a fish move; before a Hendrickson hatch one early May afternoon, he'd taken a fat eighteen-inch brown from high roiled water when I'd had trouble casting, knowing where to fish, or what fly to use.

But I finally realized that he wasn't a magician, a trout hypnotist, a possessor of occult wisdom. He's merely an enormously skillful and practical fly fisherman who has reduced the great mysteries of the sport to a minimal number of working and effective maxims—and, while others fret and puzzle over complexities, debate esoteric theories, and fiddle with their fine bamboo and nine thousand flies, he has fun—and he catches fish.

Of course Art has one great advantage over most of us. Though he isn't a professional fish expert—one of that peripatetic breed who roam the world over—he can fish virtually every day of the open season, and this is exactly what he has done for the past forty or fifty years, fishing every inch of the fifteen or sixteen miles of his beloved Schoharie. For years he fished no other river, but he missed little. The Schoharie is blessed with every important kind of water: turbulent runs, bright riffles, pocket water, pools.

The Flick magic is simplicity. He once spotted a man on the Schoharie, taking literally dozens of fly boxes out of his pockets and putting them on a rock. He thought the man must have fallen in, was drying out his flies, and rushed to his aid.

"Can I help?" he called.

The man looked up, scowled, and said, "You can if you've got a computer. I've got so many darn fly patterns I can't keep track of them."

Art has insisted for years that "less is more" is a better maxim for the trout fisherman to live—and fish—by than "more is better." His *Streamside Guide* stresses just this, and he himself uses remarkably few patterns. He uses his own simple, spare dressings for the principal Catskill hatches: the Quill Gordon, the Hendrickson, the March Brown, the Cahill, the Gray Fox, and several others, but when there are no flies hatching he invariably fishes his favorite Gray Fox Variant (the best all-purpose fly I've ever used) or, recently, his Dun Variant in the later season. His basic equipment is as simple as the fly patterns he carries. He uses a twelve-foot leader early in the season and increases this to thirteen or fourteen feet as the water drops and grows clearer. His vest is sparsely furnished with a few flies appropriate for the day, a privately made clip-on container for fly dope, a good knife, and an ancient teardrop net. His approach is always simple, functional. He's even modest enough to say of his methods, "For someone who has fished as long and as hard as I have, I am probably the worst fly fisherman in the world. I pay little attention to technique, use only the two or three basic casts. All those fancy, complicated casts! They're taking the fun out of fishing." His casts are merely straight, quick, and true. They merely send the fly where the trout is. They merely get the fly onto the water more than it's in the air.

So. Part of the mystery of Flick is this: He fishes one river and knows it better than any man alive (and can translate his knowledge of the Schoharie's pools and runs to his infrequent forays to Montana, where he caught a five-and-a-half-pound brown in the Yellowstone several years ago, to Labrador, and to several other Catskill rivers); he knows fly fishing from its roots, the water he's worked at preserving, the trout-stream insects he's collected, charted, and written about; he has been a guide and fished day after day through more than fifty seasons; and he has unflinching confidence in a few of his own proven fly patterns. He goes out at the right times, keeps his fly on the water, and catches fish. He's a fisherman first, an expert merely by virtue of his excellence at it.

"For the average person," Art says, "every time you add complications, new gadgets, more flies, the chances of taking fish go down. There's simply less time left for the fishing itself."

Art moves faster and has his fly on the water far more than any other man I've seen or heard of; frankly, I'd say he fishes five times as fast as the average fisherman, even at seventy-two. "If your fly isn't on the water," he says with a light laugh, "you can't catch any fish." He also knows his river so well that he's always thinking of the spot "just a little upstream" where he raised a good trout the year before, and he will know more quickly than most that there are no fish in a particular spot that he can catch. For pocket-water fishing, which he insists is too often overlooked by fly fishermen but which he likes best, you *have* to fish fast. "Anyway, I'd go crazy," he says, "to go to one pool and stay there, like so many fishermen do, for a long period of time. That's one reason I don't like pool fishing, except the last thing in the day. It's not in my nature."

Fitting his nature to his fishing, Art has become incredibly adept at pocket-water and riffle fishing. Those half dozen trout he took from the Battenkill at midday were from the riffles, where the trout have more cover during the day, more oxygen—and are cooler. "Fishing the riffles," he says, "you must be alert every second. More often than not you won't even see the fly taken, just the hit. You have to concentrate every minute and forget everything else."

From his knowledge of water, weather, and entomology, Art has a sure sense of when fish will be available for the taking. You do not appear on a stream at four in the morning to fish a Hendrickson hatch that will appear in the early afternoon; at best, you come a few hours early to fish the nymphs that will be active then. He is also, today, less interested in the less selective, smaller fish—a natural evolution—and fishes when there is a decent chance of taking a tough, larger trout. There is another reason Art spends less time on the water today. It's not his age; I'm nearly thirty years his junior and he'll wear me out any day.

"Lots of times now," he told me confidentially, "when March Browns or Gray Foxes are on the water, I'll be on the stream in the late morning or afternoon, when they should be coming. But if they don't I think of my long-suffering wife"—so he has one, too!—"who has never said one word about my fishing, or when I should or shouldn't fish, in fifty years." Mine has. "I just haven't got the heart to stay out on the stream anymore, and lots of times now the flies will come after I've gone home to dinner. Back in the old days, I'd want to be there. I wouldn't miss one minute of it. But I've gotten over that feeling." He pauses reflectively, then adds, "If I don't catch them today, I'll catch them another day."

Art Flick, fisherman, usually does.

There's also another breed of expert. A friend of mine once spotted one of these bona fide famous people far downriver on some choice club water in the East. From coast to coast the bards sang of this man's exploits in the white wine–tinted glides. So my friend relinquished a perfectly good night of fishing and, like a sleuth or secret agent, crept into the bushes and took up his surveillance. It might prove more valuable than any book he'd ever read to watch this expert in action, to see his method of approach, the way he cast a fly and where, to chart his success.

Anyway, he was curious as all hell.

He'd heard a great deal about this expert. We all have. He was the Fisher King himself, ready to lead us all to the Holy Grail.

So my friend parked himself uncomfortably, and cravenly watched as the expert came around the bend, surveyed the long stretch of water before him, dipped thoughtfully intro a large box of flies, chose his pattern, and began to fish. His casts were wondrously smooth; he laid the line out long and like a feather, probing the pockets and riffles deftly.

At first he caught no fish. My friend could not see if they were rising but he knew this stretch, knew it contained good fish, knew that on a June evening the browns should be rising to sulfurs. Nothing. The man pricked not one fish.

Then the expert changed his fly. Now, thought my friend, we'll see some action.

Again the line went out like a dream, and the skilled practitioner plied his art for a hundred more slow yards of gorgeous water. Nothing. Nothing even unto dark.

It had been a memorable performance, though, and my friend was glad he'd watched. Did it matter that the man had caught no fish? Not at all. Isn't one of the finest books of angling memoirs, by that grand legendary sparsely hackled angler, called *Fishless Days*? In it the author catches two barely legal fish. The expert had caught no fish, which did little more than affirm what we all know: sometimes they won't be caught.

Back at the lodge, where the men gathered to swap flies and lies, someone asked the expert how many fish he'd caught that evening. Suddenly the chatter stopped. Not a glass clinked. Everyone, including my friend, turned to the famous man. Without a second's hesitation, the expert said, "Thirty-two."

Why?

Why did he feel compelled to tell such an outrageous stretcher? Would it have been so dreadful to say "Nothing" or "Not one" or "Skunked, most magnificently skunked"? I don't think so. In fact I can imagine that he would have given the others, who'd all taken a few that night, much pleasure to think they were a little more gifted than they'd thought. And would the expert's reputation have been diminished? Not the diameter of a 7X leader point.

And why did another expert feel compelled to have a local fish hawk catch and ice up some huge western browns whole—so that when he got out there he could hold the fish up and have his picture taken with them for the magazines?

I happen to know and like these men, though I've fished with neither of them. I expect, sadly, that they were locked in by their expertise. No one was less free. They were condemned, like G. E. M. Skues's ill-fated Mr. Theodore Castwell, *always* to catch fish. What hell. And they had to do it; they weren't entitled to any more fishless days. What a pity. For aren't those days precisely what hook us most? Don't we remember most the big fish that we've lost, the days when the sweet mysterics of the river and its inhabitants eluded even our most sophisticated angling? Or perhaps it was not the cunning of the trout that made us fishless, but that we failed: our timing was off, we were impatient, we missed our chances. When then? Twenty years in the classroom have taught me this much—we often learn most from failure, though few people have the heart to see it. Why should we hide our failures or fear them? They are the emblems of our humanity, beacons to what we yet may be.

Ah, dear. Preaching again. Isn't it all an attempt to justify my own admitted failings, to worm out of the embarrassment of putting flies in my ear and nearly falling on my assumptions? Probably. But at least if I am condemned *not* to catch fish, I am *free* not to catch them, either.

Still, there are times when the season is hot upon us, when I would like to get just a little more of the hundreds of miles of drag-free float the experts promise us; when I would like to know for sure whether the thorax tie will work best for a Hendrickson imitation; when I am more than a little curious about what the trout really sees; when I long for a bit of professional coaching and wish I could tie flies along the banks of a stream in my fingers. Like all of us, there are times when I would like to know just a little bit more.

As long as it doesn't interfere with my pleasure along the rivers.

This urge for privacy and pleasure and freedom from the connections that lead us to compete makes me a dismal friend along rivers. No sooner do I see moving water—its currents tangled and alive, its surface creased with the rings of rising trout—than I am lost, quite lost. The urge for expertness vanishes and I feel few of the juices of genial angling brotherhood well up inside me. I don't want to speak. I don't want to share my thoughts or my pool. I don't want to prove. I want no fishing friends, expert or not, near me.

I watch the water, then the world above and around it, make my calculations, and want to be quickly about the business of fishing. That's what I've come for, that and the solitude. If I take someone, I'm compelled to give him the best position in the pool—and to regret it all day—or not to give him the best position in the pool— and to regret it all day. Will he judge my casting? Shout when he raises a fish? Put down my fish? Breathe too hard? All manner of nasty speculations flood my mind.

This is my own problem, one happily that few fishermen share. Mike Migel, for instance, is a perfect saint along rivers. No sooner do we arrive at a new stretch of water than he directs me to the private haunt where the biggest, most generous old hookjaw is bound to be lunching that afternoon, and then he promptly retires to a rock, looks away, and begins a miraculously long and involved charade of putting new line on his reel, fussing with leaders, piddling with fly boxes (all of which, I swear, he arranged in perfect order in March, for he is a meticulous man). Worse, I've seen him make new friends along rivers—inviting perfect strangers to share whatever information he possesses.

This is all quite unintelligible to me, though I am forced to admit that I've been the glad recipient of such treatment.

But once off the rivers, once out of the maelstrom of quiet passion, I'm all ears. I can't get enough fish talk. And since I'm off considerably more than I'm on, I've discovered that a large portion of my delight in angling comes not on the stream at all or even in print, or even in tinkering with my tackle, but in talking or corresponding with friends who also love rivers. Some of them—among them my best friends—I've never even met.

But what is the source of that bond which makes us, in the best sense of that weary old phrase, "brothers of the angle"? An expert I will never be, nor am I linked to a man by virtue of his expertise. There are other links. A golfer does not feel the connection with nearly the same intense familiarity as a fisherman does; after the handicap and the courses played and one's best game or shot are discussed, what's left? One grips his hands as if around a club, smacks an imaginary ball an old country mile, perhaps mentions that the Japanese write haiku about the sport—and then changes the subject. Nor do two sports fans want to do much more than acknowledge that they both saw the Oakland game last Sunday, or O.J.'s run, or Namath trying to run. Nor is the bond as sure and firm and intimate between businessmen, stamp collectors, skiers, Scrabble players, or even, necessarily, members of the same religion. Two Catholics, two Jews, or two Protestants who met and recognized each other as such would not quickly lapse into a discussion about the difference between Augustinian dualism and Thomistic reconciliation, Maimonides' *The Guide for the Perplexed*, or Channing's brilliant apology for Unitarian Christianity, now would they?

But two fly fishermen, on short notice and with impassioned wit, may well discuss such sacred matters of practical piscatorial philosophy as the virtue of the thorax tie or the relative merits of Garrison and Payne rods; both may well have read the same Traver or Haig-Brown or Skues story, fished or wanted to fish a particular river. They would be interested in the esoterica of entomology—I have never fished in South America and probably never will, but the pancora crab and its imitation, and its effects on the growth rate of trout (they're ten-pounders in four years!) can capture my imagination for hours— and how to increase productivity in rivers. They will have favorite memories, cut from the gray fabric of humdrum days, that leap, fresh and green, from the mind of one to the common experience of them both.

Green thoughts, technology, triumphs, hilarious mishaps. Common and fascinating tackle (of great variety), a common language and a common and well-read literature, an inherent love of the vastly differing worlds of wild nature, an ethical base (increasingly concerned with matters of conservation), mysteries that are quite wonderfully unsolvable, or differently solvable, and so much more—these things surely bind us. Age and status don't count a whit. Among my closest fishing friends I number a twelve-year-old redheaded girl with freckles and pigtails and an intuitive love of rivers; a maverick twenty-eight-year-old moviemaker; people in England, Maine, Montana, California, Bermuda, and Arkansas; mechanics; doctors; farmers; some guides; an expert or two; several octogenarians; professors in Chicago and Pennsylvania and Vermont and North Carolina. All but the fact that each of us is sweetly hooked on rivers vanishes.

Some of these friends I've never met, and one I now never will. Father Paul Bruckner, S.J., first wrote to me three years ago, after I'd sent him several books at the suggestion of a common friend and former student of his. I was told he'd been a magnificent English teacher at Marquette University for many years and had recently become quite ill.

Words flew from the doubting sinner in New York to that grand warm priest in Minnesota and back again, sixteen times. He passed shrewd and accurate judgment on some books I'd published, tested their theories with a steely Jesuitical logic against a knowledge of rivers he no longer fished.

He is gone now and I miss those letters—and the friendship. I don't know what he looked like, I never heard the sound of his voice, I did not listen to him teach Wordsworth or Newman or Waugh, but I shared a part of his life—rivers—an important part for us both, among the many parts we might have shared; and this meant much to us both. When I heard not long ago that—probably to keep from being a burden and expense to his brothers as he grew sicker and more dependent—he had shot himself (willing the worst for himself, for them), I wept. We had shared dreams and bright rivers and lore; we had been brothers under the skin.

Who will say we did not fish together?

Who will say we were not the closest of river-born friends?

A CATSKILL DIARY

Go fish and hunt far and wide day by day—
farther and wider—and rest thee by many
brooks and hearth-sides without misgiving.
. . . There are no larger fields than these.
—*Henry David Thoreau*

We are finally settled in "Eastover," a weathered board house at Byrdcliffe, high on the hill outside Woodstock. It is an ample, dark- and pink-wooded house, built for the artist Herman Dudley Murphy in 1903 by Ralph Radcliffe Whitehead, that follower of William Morris who chose Woodstock for his colony out of innumerable possible sites because of its elevation and beauty. He had a theory that important art could not be made at sea level.

Eastover is an artist's house, dominated by a massive studio on the first floor with a thirty-foot ceiling, high windows, a huge bluestone fireplace, a space oil-heater with rusted curving pipes; there is one small ash-stained chair, made by the original craftsmen, and a shredding couch that we've placed directly in front of the fireplace. Mari has set up her easel, laid out her paints; I have stretched a half dozen canvases for her, my one craft.

I have a small room for myself on the second floor and have arranged my few books and papers and equipment. A whole summer! The first in more than fifteen years. From early June to September, with little to worry about other than the vastly complicated business of learning a bit more, as Yeats says, "to articulate sweet sounds together"—and finding some generous trout.

It is a vacation, I remind myself: respite, not removal. It is a chance to look more deeply, for a while, into rivers—and myself. It suits my growing misanthropy to be here, to be alone with my family. I have some private business to transact.

The town itself has grown chichi and is far more crowded than when we were here ten years ago. But it is isolated and quiet here on the hill, beneath the two huge maples. The house has wood sparrows in the eaves—there are fledglings in one nest—squirrels in the woodwork, two raccoons under the shed, two small rabbits that nibble on the large lawn, and a porch on which I have set up summer quarters for my tackle. I have hung my new waders on one nail, my old vest on another; I have laid out my leader spools and fly boxes and set up two fly rods. I have resolved to read the newspaper only once a week, the critics never, and to spend this one summer with my fly rods set up for the entire three months.

I fished only once this spring before we settled into Eastover—that day on the Beaverkill in early May. I got to the No-kill section about noon, in good time for the Hendrickson hatch that I knew had started several days earlier, took three very small fish on a nymph above Cairns's Pool, and kept waiting for the hatch to begin. About one-thirty a few Hendricksons began to show but there was curiously no feeding to them. I stayed with the nymph, then tried, in succession, one of Art Flick's Red Quills (which have always been so successful for me), then Del Bedinotti's excellent tie of the Marinaro Hendrickson. Nothing. About three o'clock, when no fish had risen and none had been taken by the dozen or so other fishermen within sight, I switched impulsively to a huge Yellow Stone tied and sent to me by Charlie Brooks. I've had stoneflies on my brain all spring. Sam Melner tells me that Walt Dette has a bottle of stomach contents of trout, and that 70 percent of the nymphs were stoneflies; and I know they are in the stream all year long and represent the largest insect food available to trout. In the West they're taken for granted; here they're virtually ignored.

On my second cast, across and upstream. I had a sharp take as the fly swung below me. Really sharp. But I'd ignorantly not changed the light dry-fly tippet, and I broke the fish off. So I still have stoneflies on the brain.

Then, about four o'clock, when I was about to give it up, I spotted the form of a large dark fish over a broad flat light-gray rock; it was high in the water, feeding. Then I saw another, and then another: long dark shapes, holding their positions. There were fifteen or so feeding freely now within my sight; they'd risen to just below the surface and were taking in that leisurely way I had seen trout rise on the Battenkill at dusk.

But rising to what?

At first I thought they had finally gotten a sweet tooth for Hendricksons, for there were still a few in the air, so I tried the Red Quill again on one of the nearest fish, a fourteen- or fifteen-incher. The fish rose an inch or two to inspect the fly, then drifted back; the second time I floated the fly past it, the fish didn't budge. I looked again. In the water and in the air I could see the telltale transparent wings of spinners; on the flat surface of the river they were like specks of mica.

Now the fish were lolling just under the surface, merely tipping up, snouts out of water, and allowing the flies to drift into their open mouths. I had never seen this before, but if you spend enough time on rivers I suppose it's logical that you'll see more of what occurs, after its own laws, in moving water.

A No-Hackle with russet body and hen-hackle wings took five good browns for me, and I felt very satisfied with myself.

But on the way back I realized that I had been fishing in a bell jar, or fishbowl. However interesting the hatch itself, I was sharing that run with more than a dozen other fishermen, with the trucks to Binghamton that roared along Route 17, and with the thousands of other fishermen who had fished this popular run earlier in the season. I wondered whether the fish were really worth the loss of that part of fishing I value most—solitude. If you concentrate on a small patch of water and a few working fish, you forget all else—but isn't that an illusion? If the Catskills become very much more crowded, one will merely be going from "the desperate city," as Thoreau says, "into the desperate country."

The Esopus is the closest major river to Woodstock, and though it's never been a favorite of mine, I have reread Paul O'Neil's brilliant article, "In Praise of Trout—and Also Me," one of the finest profiles I know of any river. Perhaps I can renegotiate my uneasy détente with this river. It has always seemed inhospitable to me—a bit raw and rough and crowded—though before I fly-fished I used to catch hecatombs of trout in it.

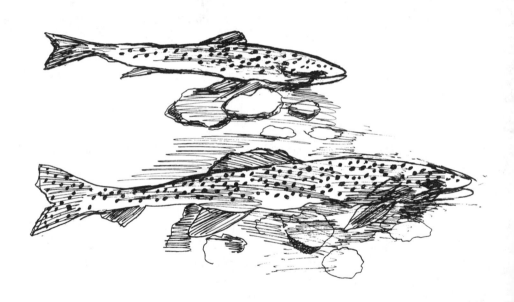

I went upriver from Mount Tremper with Anthony tonight, to an old run I remembered from my teenage years. A lot of caddisflies were dancing on the surface, and a number of small fish were splashing for them. I tried a wet fly first but didn't get a tap. Then I switched to a small Gray Fox Variant—since the caddis were grayish—and raised several nine-inch rainbows. They were bright silver, bred in the river.

Anthony sloshed out to me without waders—since the spring, when he fell in, he finds it simpler to start wet—and I gave him my fly rod. The run is deep and fast, and I stood behind him and to his left, holding on to the bottom of his vest tightly, feeling him shiver in the cool June evening air. At first he slapped the fly down on the water brusquely, like a whip, but soon improved enough to take his first trout on a fly. It was a small fish, but he struck it well and smiled more brightly than the full moon as he reeled it in, almost to the tip-top guide.

On the way home, he was wet and shivering beside me. We sang "Summertime" and "The Battle Hymn of the Republic"—"Mine eyes have seen the glory . . ."—and saw, frozen in the headlights by the side of the road, a gorgeous amber deer.

Heavy, steady rains for two days. The Esopus is high and roiled. Worse, it is positively crammed with salmon-egg, corn-kernel, and minnow fishing fiends; this afternoon I counted fourteen of them in a stretch of river I had wanted to use to exorcise the stoneflies from my brain. They were another breed. Is it snobbishness that I resent them? My fishing troubles them—and the river—not at all; theirs destroys mine and depletes the river. Anyway, I don't like the looks of them.

I have been learning the names of trees, weeds, birds, and flowers: sumac, locust, black walnut, ash, poplar, hickory, mountain laurel, whortleberry, rhododendron, anemone, finch, starling, bloodroot, marsh marigold, bluet. With names the eye sees more, in the fields and along the bright rivers.

One of my sons, studying for a college-entrance examination, is also learning words: plethora, derogatory, experiential, phenomenon, magniloquent, malevolent, conciliatory, concomitant, bemuse, garrulous, misogynist.

* * *

More rain. Art Flick—who lives over the mountain and has been inviting me over, when the weather is right—says he has never seen a worse season, either for gully washers or heavy heat and drought. He thinks the water will keep the rivers alive in the late summer, though. The portal at Allaben has been delivering surges of silt to the Esopus, which has been unfishable for a week.

You notice the weather more in the country. It has more of a direct link to your life. Everything is connected here. In the city, rain merely irritates.

Drove to Phoenicia, the same sleepy town it was twenty years ago; Woodstock has, by virtue of its name and the presence of large corporations near Kingston, expanded in a half dozen bad directions at once, and Hunter, because of its ski slopes, is radically changed from the tiny three-store town I knew as a child, when my grandfather owned the Laurel House in Haines Falls.

Reread Keats's poem "To One Who Has Been Long in City Pent" and found it true, not soft; and read Gauguin's *Noa Noa* and found this remarkable passage: "Civilization is falling from me little by little. I am beginning to think simply. . . . I have escaped everything that is artificial, conventional, customary. I am entering into the truth, into Nature." But Woodstock is not Tahiti, I remind myself; and much, much of the Catskills is merely the desperate city transplanted, on vacation, its roads raw gray veins connecting major urban and industrial towns.

I have reread *Walden,* too, and found this passage. As Thoreau leaves John Field's house at Baker Farm and hurries off to catch pickerel, "wading in retired meadows, in sloughs and bog-holes, in forlorn and savage places" appears for an instant "Trivial" to one "who had been sent to school and college." But then his Good Genius seems to say, "Go fish and hunt far and wide day by day—farther and wider—and rest thee by many brooks and hearth-sides without misgiving. . . . There are no larger fields than these, no worthier games than may here be played. . . . Through want of enterprise and faith men are where they are, buying and selling, and spending their lives like serfs."

And so I have gone off for a little while to play worthy games. I am not blind to the fact that I did not build the house I live in, that I use gas to cook on and gas to heat the house, that I have a telephone which connects me in an instant to Art Flick in West Kill or business associates in the city, that I travel to the rivers in a car and even use fly lines and leaders that are the product of modern technology, that the electric light permits me to read and write at night, that the plumbing carries away my wastes with a quick flush, that the food I eat is processed and packaged thousands of miles away, that the river I fish is not wild but merely a sluice between two reservoirs that supply the city with water, that this summer will cost me one hundred times what a whole year cost Thoreau, and that the trappings of modern society are not only part of my life here but conveniences I would not do without.

I find the notion of a permanent escape from the modern world just that—an escape. A removal. It is not, I now see, what I want. In *Walden,* all radiates out from the pond, which could still be central. Today, ponds and rivers radiate from—and exist at the pleasure of—the cities. If the cities need their water, they will take it.

Even in *Huckleberry Finn,* which I have also reread, the rivershore dichotomy is misleading. Beyond the truism that there cannot be a river without a shore, the simple pleasures of the river take their meaning from what happens on shore. And, ironically, there is more vigor and wit and interest in the shore; the river is idyllic, removed, illusory, and, in permanent doses, dull.

Have begun to fish the Ashokan Reservoir for smallmouths nearly every evening at dusk. Still water is not flowing water, but it too has its appeal. Frankly, I don't know if smallmouths can be caught on a bug from the shore; I have asked no one, and no one else appears to fish this way. But I strongly suspect that fly fishing for bass in reservoirs like the Pepacton and the Ashokan may be one of the great unexplored joys left in the beleaguered Catskills.

Anthony and several of his friends have been coming with me and are able to score well on wet flies for sunfish and rock bass. Last night Anthony took a gigantic crappie, a Moby Dick of all crappies— but he did not like its name.

The view from the Hurley Embankment where I fish is extraordinary, stretching back over the miles of the reservoir into the many layers of mountains. The sun breaks through the clouds at dusk far to the west and streaks down and infects the entire sky, like a medieval painting. The vast sky reminds me of Montana, where I have been lucky enough to fish several times, briefly.

But the Catskills are far, far from Montana. Why do I perpetually dream of other places? I am in the Catskills now; Montana will come later.

Drove with Mari along the pleasant, winding Route 212, then took Routes 28 to 42, and over the mountains to West Kill and an evening of fishing with Art Flick. His hearty hello and unflagging vigor!

We immediately raced off in his car to the Schoharie, and he deposited Mari on top of a high rock embankment backed by the highway and overlooking the river and a spectacular patchwork quilt of meadows, farms, and hills. From far below, where I began to fish, she was small and practically camouflaged among the rocks as she began to work patiently on a watercolor.

I saw eight or ten fish come up, raised four or five on the small Gray Fox Variant Art advised me to use, and caught two.

About eight-fifteen, a wind came up and Mari called down to me that she was cold. I had vowed to avoid the tragicomedies of my "fishing widow" days and decided simply that I'd had a good evening of it and would walk the three hundred yards upstream, then climb the rocks and give her my jacket. Art would be along before too long; he'd said he was only going a short distance downstream. But just then, a really huge hatch of *Potamanthus* began to emerge and the fish began to whoop it up royally. Up and down river, wherever I looked, the water was pocked by feeding fish.

The marriage or the trout. What to do?

I hesitated and Mari called again, plaintively but not unfairly under the circumstances: she was perched on rocks in the near dark and was freezing.

I still had not made my decision and was watching an especially bold riser when Art drove up. "Stay where you are!" he shouted. "Stay as long as you want, Nick!" He'd left his favorite river in the midst of a major mayfly hatch, perhaps the first really good one he'd caught all this fluky year. A spectacular display of old-time chivalry. "Thought Mari might be cold," he called. "Don't hurry!"

So I didn't.

Fished the Esopus this evening a good distance above the Five Arches Bridge. Found a huge hole, the size and glory of a salmon pool, and raised two very acrobatic rainbows of perhaps fifteen inches each on a Dun Variant, just at dusk. There was twenty minutes of frantic feeding and the river was electrically alive with fish porpoising out of the whirling water, chasing the duns, but I could only raise those two and lost them both, one on a broken hook, the other on a pullout.

If the Esopus could produce many evenings like this, maybe I'd stop dreaming about Montana.

What a pleasure it is to find such an isolated pool. I suppose, if one looks hard and long enough, there are still such places left, tucked into corners and away from roads. They are worth the exploring.

This afternoon was bright but cool, and after a shopping chore I explored several mountain brooks and finally stopped at the Little

Beaverkill, an Esopus feeder and an old friend. The Esopus is unfishable *again* with the portal wide open.

A ten-inch brown was feeding regularly in the center of a small pool below a bend, and I naturally had my fly rod in the car, rigged with a Colorado King. I crept down the high bank onto a slate rock, made one long cast above the fish, and raised it—a bright jewel flashing, turning in the sun. I pricked it but no more, then made a half dozen fruitless casts and returned to the car.

Such brief, electric encounters are a simple, lasting joy this summer. They grace a day. They brush it with a touch of the wild. That fish will be there tomorrow, and next month, for me. And I now know four or five others—not large but native, I think—in the now-unfished Sawkill and Mink Hollow Brook.

But I won't tell you where.

I drove to Manhattan and back today for some business and could feel the tension mount the moment I left the West Side Highway. Traffic jams. Arrogance and hatred in the streets. Corrosive politicking at the office. In the newspapers, clever men crying the catch-cries of the clown. The same crew on upper Broadway in the early evening. This place on the hill is not Walden Pond or Tahiti, but it permits certain values to be maintained, husbanded—electric lights notwithstanding. Here I can choose as much of the modern world as I want to partake in my life and exclude the rest. There is no fallacy in taking some, in riding the railroad rather than allowing it to ride you. The electric light does me no harm; it enables. So does the stillness of the night and the grass, woods, and view from my window here.

The hot, heavy days of mid-July have started, but there's still a lot of water I want to explore. Len Wright has given me "poaching privileges" on his upper Neversink water, above what's left of Hewitt's old section of the river, and I'll probably go over later in the summer. And I will want to try the Beaverkill and Willowemoc, very early in the morning or perhaps at night, and perhaps the East Branch (if those bastards who control the water flow will let in cold water), the upper reaches of the Rondout, and more of those small, cool, clear mountain brooks.

Sparse has invited me for a day on his DeBruce Club water, and that's always a joy. I have my dreams. Somewhere, mingled among them, is a wish to return to the Laurel House, which more and more takes the shape of a spring from which so many of my waters flow.

The Sawkill heads in Echo Lake, near Overlook Mountain, flows through a backwoods valley lush with birch and poplar, crosses Route 212 at Shady, turns with the road at Bearsville, and then winds down past Woodstock, through the golf course, toward Zena. Much of the upper water is small and posted, but I have fished the five or six miles between Shady and the eastern edge of the golf course, every pool and run of it, many times in the past. The Sawkill is always a genial, clear, underfished creek, rather small and growing smaller each successive day of the summer; some years the water simply vanishes—slipping between the rocks to some underground shelf and leaving small, unmoving, stagnant pools.

At its best, ten years ago, it provided a pleasant evening's spotfishing for ten-inch browns, with always the chance of moving a holdover of some size on a delicate cast to some deeply undercut bank. I once found an eighteen-incher locked in a small bend pool—and raised it three times, its rise explosive in such small quarters.

Not a little of my interest in spending a summer in Woodstock was the thought of the Sawkill just down the hill. So when we arrived in early June I picked out a calm evening and went to a back-section I knew. The cream-colored dorotheas were on, and I took seven fish up to twelve inches in little more than an hour. I released the fish and returned to Eastover elated: I would have fish all summer, and the river to myself, since I remembered seeing few fishermen on it after May.

Wrong. When I tried the creek on a drizzly day several weeks later, a half dozen teenagers were fishing the section on which I had caught the dorothea hatch; they were using live minnows, about an inch long, and three of them had a dozen trout, hung by strings from their belts. They had cleaned it out.

And as I fished that day, and others, up past other sections I remembered with affection, I saw the extensive bulldozing had flattened the streambed and that there were now many more houses near the banks. The little creek could not bear such pressure.

So I did not fish it again until this afternoon, a hot, bright, mid-July day. The family decided to go swimming about two o'clock. Fine. But I bathe in other waters. I was off to explore a section of the Sawkill I had not fished yet this season, that I remembered holding up well in the summer. Ten years ago you could take some nice browns, even on such a bright July afternoon as this, on a No. 18 Hairwing Royal Coachman. I remembered the way the bright little fly danced down the clear rapids, the take of a foot-long trout, a barracuda in these waters. I remembered the surprises in this section that year: that eighteen-incher, and specific thirteen- and fourteen-inchers hidden back in the root-tangled pools and undercut banks that the town kids had been unable to fish out in May.

My rod was in the car, set up; I had only to add a length of fine tippet and the small ocher Colorado King that has been working so well for me. No boots today—just my vest and old fish hat, and then a bit of quick mountain-goating down the rocks to the streambed.

But the stream was far different from the brisk water I had fished when the dorotheas were on, or ten years ago. The flattened bulldozed pools were long shallow runs with only several inches of water in them now. There was no visible holding water and I was convinced, even before I cast, that there were no fish. Still, the little rock-strewn creek with its dancing spring water—cool, sparkling, clear—was better than the public swimming pool with the name of Swim-o-Links. There might still be a lesson or two to be caught here—a sound, shadow, image I might creel forever.

I fished downstream first, using ten- to fifteen-foot spot casts into the head of the diminutive riffles, watching the fly dance down into the slicks. The spring water seeped into my old sneakers and was cold. My face perspired heavily, and I had to take off my sunglasses and wipe them clean. The creek was a major river in microcosm—but without fish.

There was nothing downstream but a few pecking dace, so I headed up, moving quickly, hopping along the rocks, most often keeping a short length of line moving in the air even when I was not fishing. I found a larger pool and put one cast into its tail. Nothing. Another at the base of the riffle. Nothing. One into the head of the riffle. Yes—only no. A dace.

At the bridge I spotted my first trout of the day, a quick darting shadow. It had been resting beneath the rock in the tail of the pool and, after darting back and forth, settled beneath the little boil of falls and foam. A sensible choice for a hot afternoon. I knew I couldn't take it then but decided to come back that evening or early the next morning. I knew I could take that trout easily after a careful approach at the right time of day.

Better yet: I won't fish for you at all, old last Mohican.

I have found pockets and patches of the serenity I expected in the Catskills—a pool on the Esopus, the headwaters of a few feeder creeks, a run on the Schoharie—but year by year they too are encroached upon. Where I remember a pleasant meadow, there's a garish shopping center; where I fished an isolated stretch of river, a superhighway now skirts its path, and the river can never fully come back now for the cars will always, in increasing numbers, rowel your ears. I fished such a run at three o'clock one morning—and the cars still came by every minute or so.

Kurt Vonnegut recently told some graduating seniors that things are rotten and are going to get worse. "Some men, like bats, have eyes for darkness only," says Dickens in his marvelous *Pickwick Papers*, disclaiming such eyes, at least there. One surely does not want to be so, but even on this pleasant hill, this pocket of quiet patrolled by oak, maple, and pine, within twenty minutes of five rivers, it is hard to avoid that ocular disease.

A number of unpleasant episodes that I hope are not auguries of innocence permanently lost. Last night on the Ashokan, just when I got my first strike, some overgrown no-neck monsters began to set off firecrackers and toss cherry bombs at the car in which Mari was reading. There were a dozen of them, drinking beer, shouting threats, and they scared her half to death.

Then tonight, with the Esopus high, I went up near Shandaken and found a pleasant run with eight- to ten small rainbows rising playfully in it. I had taken one when a green apple the size of a golf ball hit the water in front of me. I thought it might have fallen from a tree but there was none nearby. Then three or four others, in rapid succession, pelted into the water or against the rocks. Some kids had to be throwing them, but they must have been behind the bushes up near the road for I couldn't see anyone. I thought they might not know I was there, so I simply waded downstream, but the pelting followed me. I breathed deeply, then shouted; the apples kept coming. Finally I crossed the river, climbed the bank, and saw half a dozen of them standing up the road beneath an apple tree, cackling like daws, leering. One of them had been serving as point man, directing their fire. When he saw me he raced across the road, and all of them scurried behind a barn. Like chickens.

Both incidents recalled the eerie story Mike told me, of his being caught midstream in the heavy Saranac River and having rocks thrown at him by four leather-jacketed motorcyclists. One of them had shouted, "Let's give Pops a lesson"—Mike is over sixty—and they headed into the river after him. He was several miles back in the woods, waist deep in strong current, standing on slippery rocks. He had feared for his life.

Sooner or later, probably sooner, the mad world will fully find every corner of our gentle rivers where we pursue—to no one's harm and our quiet joy—this simple passion. It is hard at times like now not to have eyes like bats.

In the Pepacton, at night, the men fish with lanterns hung from the ends of their boats, lowering huge sawbellies to depths of thirty and forty feet. This is an exotic sight on a trip back from the Beaverkill, but I cannot imagine I would enjoy fishing that way—even for the ten-pound browns that are regularly extracted.

Is there no way to fish for them with flies?

In Henrys Lake, small shrimp and damselfly imitations take trout up to seventeen pounds. I should like, one whole season, to explore the Pepacton with streamers, large nymphs, bass bugs, and Thom Green's Leech. I'm sure big bass and some of the larger browns can be taken on a fly.

But then, I'd like to spend a whole season doing other types of fishing much more, and in other places. In the night, despite all my vows not to think of other rivers, I often dream of the Yellowstone and the Firehole and Henrys Fork of the Snake and other rivers of the West—and sometimes of one truly gigantic trout I once hooked, and lost, in Henrys Lake.

They are a long way from here.

I have been studying, for several hours each day a rich, complex, and difficult book called *The Ecology of Running Waters* by H. B. N. Hynes. This is my first exposure to scientific works on rivers—or science of any substantive nature, except for piscatorial entomology—and it is deeply revealing. Watching rivers now, I see more of the many physical laws that are their fiber and bone and blood. "A river channel," says Hynes, "is thus an almost infinitely adjustable complex of interrelationships between discharge, width, depth, rate of flow, bed resistance, and sediment transport. Any change in one tends to be countered by adjustment in the others, and the whole system tends towards conservative dynamic equilibrium." I like that last phrase. It explains much.

Nor does science in any way spoil my pleasure, as at times I feared it would. It scarcely troubles me that ichthyologists consider my lovely trout a "low form" of fish. The job was done right that first time, and the *fact* of it supports my general and increasing skepticism toward the new and the novel.

I always knew that all rivers were different; it is good to learn from science that they overlap.

We drove to Haines Falls last week, to the Laurel House, where I caught my first fish in the weedy lake and gigged the first trout I ever saw, beneath the bridge over the unnamed mountain creek.

The main road is three-lane—it had barely been two, and rough macadam then—and new motels and restaurants have sprung up everywhere. Ski madness has hit the remote valley and fashionable condominiums and chalets festoon the hillsides, built of dark wood, each with its own terrace and fireplace—a bit of mock Switzerland grafted onto this backwater Catskill valley that once supported only small, modest, family resorts.

"Is there anything to do there?" my son asked as we turned off the highway at the little old church, exactly as I had remembered it: tawny wood-slab sides, white shutters, the pretty garden in front, behind the picket fence.

I remembered that I had always had too much to do at the Laurel House. The days were too short. Every minute was crammed with some game or discovery. I would be up at five, with the first touches of light, and down at the creek or on the lake. I began to see my white-bearded grandfather, whom I loved, sitting in front of the little cottage off to the left of the hotel in the cool evenings, reading the *Daily Forward;* the orchard across the creek and up to the left; the creek I tramped daily, catching untold numbers of crawfish and frogs and tiny bright trout that skittered and flopped in your hand like long spotted jumping beans; the long walk to the lake in the early mornings, when slants of sun broke through the heavy pines and hemlocks and my heart was light and open and pounding like mad.

You think at such moments of the bends your life has taken, the course of the river from there to here, then to now, from its simple source to who knew what. How because you were very young and your stepfather was a cold fish and a martinet, you studied business at college, "so you'll always have it," then switched abruptly after the army years to English; how you wanted to write—that most of all—but taught and edited and then wrote other people's books for them; the editor had said you were the fastest and best ghost in the East, which he meant to be a compliment. Small apartments, many children, debts that covered your heart like weeds, barbed wire through your veins, senseless bickering. Now you did not edit anymore and did not ghost and would not be teaching for much longer either, though you loved your students. This was a year for a new beginning and this was a long summer, and we were going back to the Laurel House. It would be good to see the old hotel, where the river took its source.

"Are you sure this is the right way?" Mari asked.

The sides of the road were pocked by cheap shacks and trailers—little tinny worlds inhabited by sloppy people. There were thirty or forty on little half-acre plots where there had been only two houses on the road thirty years ago: a neat clapboard cabin, rarely occupied, and that Old Victorian spook house I had once climbed into with my cousin. We were where the cabin had been and I had not seen it as we went by; the foundation of the old mansion was up on the left, a trailer on either side of it now. "This is positively ugly and slummish," Mari said. "It looks like they've moved half of upper Broadway up here. You said it was isolated, covered with blueberries that you picked on the way to town."

"It was."

"Is this where you used to ride on the running board of someone's old truck?" my son asked.

"Joe's. The handyman."

"God, that must have been fun."

"It was."

After we passed the ruins of the old Victorian house, its chimney stack halfway broken off, its shrubs run wild, I recognized nothing. Maybe Mari was right. Maybe, somehow, I had taken a wrong turn. It could happen. I had taken wrong turns before. Those ruins might not even have been the building I remembered; they might have shifted the course of the road. I slowed to twenty, then fifteen miles per hour. There had been a view, I remembered, of the surrounding mountain peaks; I would often pause, with my cousin, and look at it on the walk to town. The trees now so overhung the road that I felt I was driving in a tunnel.

"Can I get a strawberry cone when we get there, Dad?"

"Sure," I said, abstractedly. There was a canteen in the basement of the hotel. We could buy the ice cream there.

I scrutinized each dirt road on the right now, looking for that familiar turnoff with the swinging sign mounted on the cedar-log frame. There had been no other roads off to the right. That entire side of the road, all the way to within a quarter of a mile of Haines Falls, except for the cabin, had been wild, filled with low blueberry bushes that I had plucked in August, tangled raspberry and blackberry vines clustered thick among the low birches and alders and towering oaks, dark mountain laurel shrubs with bright pink flowers in June—and always the view, stretching across the deep valleys to the far mountain ranges, cobalt and mauve on a lazy late-August afternoon like this.

"Laurel House Road."

Even at fifteen miles per hour I almost missed the foot-long sign, and the dirt road, which looked exactly like so many of the others. I felt a flutter in my chest. I could not wait to see the old place, walk several of my old trails, across the nine-hole golf course where the blackberries would already be ripe; down the hill to the swimming pool, with that silver-green creek, always icy cold and clear, behind it. I didn't even know its name but I was ready to bet anything I could remember every rock of the place where I had gigged my first trout. Perhaps I'd take my son on the path to the lake or down to the famous falls behind the hotel, where I had carved my name among so many others on the big flat rock. I always remembered the place scene by scene: a particular morning on the lake; the night of my grandparents' fiftieth wedding anniversary, with those glorious swans of ice I had watched being carved in the afternoon and the platters of cold cuts and bowls of fruit, and my grandfather, still stern but with happy glossy eyes, a patriarch there on the dais, surrounded by hundreds of his friends and relatives. He was dead now. I saw few of my relatives. I had slept until eleven-thirty the next day, after the midnight supper, and my cousin and I had talked about it for weeks.

Memories had mingled with affections, becoming so much a part of the fabric of my bone and blood that they often had to be pried loose, one by one. I could see the large white-pillared hotel itself, as clearly as if it were yesterday, with the circular drive and the ring of lilac bushes that were always in full bloom when we came up each June; the back porch where my uncles, with great hairy chests, played pinochle in the sun; the tire swing and compost pile behind the kitchen, where I dug worms for bait; and the old bridge across the creek and the barn with its cows and huge silver milk cans, and my grandfather in the shed, whacking the heads off chickens he seized mercilessly from a jammed wooden cage, feathers flying furiously— blood on him, on me, on the sawdust floor.

Mostly I remembered the lake and the creek. I remembered everything starkly but piecemeal; I couldn't quite put the parts or the years together—when what happened, where it all stood in relation to everything else. But I remembered, in careful sequence and unchanging image, the lake and the creek and all the times I had become a part of them.

Was that why I wanted to come back?

Did I really think I could recapture something I had at this place, at that time when all the world was young, now gone perhaps forever?

I raced the car as I made the sharp turn down Laurel House Road and felt the wheels skid on the dirt and the car swivel.

"Nick!"

"I've got it. Don't worry. I remember the place now. This is the right road. I've got everything under control. The golf course is just around the second bend."

"Can we play, Dad? Can we? I hit golf balls last summer, on that range in Connecticut, and you said I was terrific. Can we, Dad?"

But there was no golf course around the second bend. When we came past the turn I saw only a lightly wooded field. The grasses were over two feet high, I could see no mounds that might have been greens, and the entire area was so sprinkled with trees—some of them four and five feet high—that it was impossible to conceive where a golf course might ever have been.

"Where's the golf course?" Mari asked.

"I don't see a golf course, Dad."

"It was . . ."

"You promised we could play, Dad. You promised."

"I did *not* promise."

"Are you sure you got the right road, Nick?"

"I am quite sure," I said, my voice taking on an edge, "that I took the right road."

Poplars and birch, four or five feet tall, rose out of the high grasses. If there had been greens, neatly trimmed, they were long gone. There had been a small clubhouse where, after the season, I had often found golf balls, tees, a broken club or two, some small change. In the lower corner of the field, near the road, there was now no structure.

Huge logs blocked the main road, so I stopped the car, got out, and walked to where the clubhouse had stood. I bent over. Nothing. Only thick shrubs, sproutlings, high grasses.

"You'll love the view from the falls," I told Mari, my voice beginning to rise slightly. "It's right in back of the hotel. I once carved my name in the rocks—my real name, before my mother remarried. It's just a short walk around the bend and down the hill. Behind the hotel."

We walked, the three of us, slowly down the hill. I told my son how the old barn had stood over to the right, near a huge patch of blueberry bushes. There had been four milch cows and hundreds of chickens whose stock was replenished weekly by a truck that came with dozens of wooden cages on it, crammed with squawking white birds fated for the hotel dining tables. I held my son's hand, put my arm lightly around my wife's shoulder. From the condition of the road, the neglect of the golf course, and the logs across the path, I knew the hotel—already a hundred-year-old relic when my grandfather owned it—would be unused, neglected, fallen into disrepair, but it would be good to see those large white pillars, the great circular drive, the old porch in back, that world that had been my childhood, every long summer from before memory until I was thirteen.

Suddenly I wanted to share it all with my son. I wanted this place not only for myself but for him, with whom I quarreled too much, knew too slenderly, loved.

The boy was quiet. He held on to my hand tightly.

We turned the bend in the road—and it was not there.

I looked down into the hollow where the hotel once stood and saw only a tangle of high grasses and brush, small poplars, birch, and pines. There were half a dozen mountain laurel bushes; there was no hotel.

"Where is it, darling?" asked Mari.

"It was right there."

"Where?" asked the boy.

"There, there," I said, pointing. "Don't you see?"

"Nope."

"I'm afraid I don't see anything either, Nick."

"They tore it down. That's all. But the foundation will be there. I'll show you."

We walked more quickly now, down into the hollow which, on a Fourth of July or Labor Day, once teemed with people I knew, many of them family: uncles, aunts, cousins, second and third cousins, friends of my uncles and aunts whom I also called "uncle" or "aunt," my grandparents. There would be old Dodges and Buicks parked in the road that led to the falls; children playing in the sandbox behind the back porch; that interminable pinochle game; dozens of people in the circular driveway, talking, laughing, heading up the hill to play golf or to the old concrete swimming pool; people arriving and hugging old friends; people chatting with animation, laughing at some old story, of which there were hundreds. I knew all the people; the same ones came back every year and I was related, somehow, to every one of them. They were all "family."

I ran the last forty yards down the hill alone and was walking now on the ground on which the hundred-room hotel had stood.

Nothing. Boulders. Wild grasses. Several clumps of tiger lilies. Saplings. Clumps of high weed. Brambles, tangled and untended. I thought I remembered where the neat grove of lilac bushes once stood, off to the right. In a cluster of thirty or forty trees, I saw three, past their bloom. I walked slowly over the humps in the ground, pushing away the high timothy and weeds with my feet, looking down at the roots of all this dense growth for some specific sign, any sign, that this was exactly where the hotel had stood. I found none. The land was wild. There was not one indication, anywhere, that the Laurel House or any other human structure had stood in this place.

Only the falls were still there—the flow less than I remembered it, but the same crystalline creek, flowing out of the heavy pine and hemlock forest, down over slate-bottomed pools, over the great cleft and down into the awesome clove. The space stretched out, and then farther out and down, and I felt the hollow twinge in my loins which I had always felt when I was a boy and played too close to the brink of this ledge, and the three of us looked silently out across the illimitable space, across the clove, toward the intersecting mountains in the far distance, cobalt and mauve and gray, layered, textured, growing dimmer as they stretched back farther and farther into the distance until the eye could see them no more.

Later we searched the rocks for my name but could not find it among the hundreds of others; perhaps the water, in spring torrents, had washed it away. I had been ten years old when I scratched it into the stone and perhaps had not dug deeply enough. We walked up the creek toward where I had caught my first trout. We could not reach it. The forest had claimed its own. The entire hollow had returned to some primitive state. It was as if nothing from my past existed at all, as if, were I to build here, ever, I would have to start, not from family or hotel but from the rocky earth, the maze of brush tangles beneath my feet, the same bright creek flowing out of the wild forest.

Auguries of autumn: The day is bright and warm in the later morning and afternoon, but about five o'clock a coolness enters the air that has not been present since May. Is it different in itself or only in contrast to the recent summer heat? It *feels* of autumn; it has the tang and hue of the fall, though there is still a week left of August. Last night darkness came by eight-fifteen. This morning I turned on the space heater. The trout will begin to move soon; the smallmouths will surely be up out of the depths more regularly now.

The blast of cold these past few days of early September brought with it the sure shiver of recognition: summer is nearly over. The time to return is nearing. I cannot resist counting—and trying to hold back—the few days left. Brief patches of red and red-gold on some oaks and maples; pale orange splotching the birch.

We returned to Eastover to retrieve the last of our clothes and supplies. Despite the heavy rains, the ash, maple, and oak have kept most of their leaves, some of which are now orange and red.

I had hoped to fish the Esopus one last time, but the river was unfishable again. I had had a number of really good days there and had been fishing below the Five Arches Bridge.

So in the evening I headed back to the reservoir, which has been such a salvation all summer. While I was stepping into my waders, a funny little man, no taller than four feet, eight inches, came up with his spinning rod and a scowl. "Last week I caught an eighteen-inch pickerel," he said.

"That's a good fish."

"Best I've taken."

I slipped the suspenders over my shoulders, straightened them, and put on my vest.

"Hooked one even bigger this afternoon. Much bigger. Maybe a foot longer he was, like so. Brought him in and knowed right away he was a bigger one'n I'd ever caught. Well, I get him and puts him on the stringer and ties the stringer to a log and keeps fishing a little ways off and when I comes back he's gone and so's the stringer."

I looked up. "You sure no one stole it?"

"Couldn't of. Didn't see no one come near it. He done pulled it out. Biggest pickerel I ever caught. Damned shame. Never get another like him," he mumbled, "not if I fish ten more years." And then he went off to his car.

Mari looked up from the Evelyn Waugh novel she was reading and wished me luck, and I headed down to the water, promising without fail to be no longer than an hour and a half. "Sure," she said, with a mock scowl.

On my first two casts I took large bluegills—fat, orange fish that raced in circles. Then I took two smallmouths, little ones that I threw back. And then a rock bass. Well, there was some action, and the light was still good. Another fifteen minutes and the big bass would start to move; I could feel it. But then the sky clouded over suddenly and a sharp wind came up—much too hard in which to cast a bug—so I breathed deeply, looked out across the long reservoir to the mauve and pale cobalt mountain ranges, and decided to fold up the season. It had been a long, interesting summer, not nearly as fertile as I would have liked, but I had brought a great portion of the lakes and bright rivers into me.

For the first time since June I unjoined my fly rod, wound in the line, and then took off the reel and slipped it into the inside pocket of my vest. "You're forty minutes early!" Mari said when I got back to the car. "Are you sick?"

"Too much wind," I said, putting my gear into the back of the battered station wagon.

"Wind? You're fished out!"

"Never!"

"Fished fully out!"

She looked at me carefully. "If you're not sick, you're fished up to the gills. You've had all you can take for one year."

"The wind . . ."

"Bull!"

So we talked about it, laughing, on the short drive back to Eastover and made a large bright fire in the fireplace, and in front of the fire, while she finished her Waugh, I clipped the flies out of the lamb's-wool patch on my vest, slipped my reels into their chamois bags, took down two other fly rods and slipped them into their cases, and packed everything into a carryall. I thought of Thoreau's "I love best to have each thing in its season only, and enjoy doing without it at all other times."

Then, for some unaccountable reason, I began to think of Montana.

WESTWARD

I love the wild not less than the good. The wildness and adventure that are in fishing still recommend it to me.
—*Henry David Thoreau*

On the day before I last flew west, for a long-awaited week of fishing in September, I witnessed this event on my upper Broadway.

First, according to what I saw, a cab driver leaned out of his window and hollered at a double-parked sky-blue Cadillac that was blocking his way. Then a long-haired kid—lean, with pinched cheeks, about twenty—put a bony hand out of the Cadillac's left window, with the middle finger extended and jiggling up and down.

"Get the hell out of the way," the cabbie yelled, "you lousy bastard!"

This time the lean young man decided that no mother could talk to him like that, leaped out of his car, and strode boldly toward the cab. In his right hand he held a baseball bat. As I watched, quite disembodied, with no urge or reflex to move, the boy reached the cab, lifted the bat, and began an incessant battering of the top of the trunk. Again and again he lifted the bat and smashed it down with all his power.

A group of onlookers quickly assembled. Several took out cameras. No one said a word. They, like the great movie heroes of the West, let a man play his own hand out. So, apparently, did I.

A moment later I heard the cab driver shout, "Is he hitting my cab? Is that what the bastard's doing? Is that *my* cab he's hitting?"

There seemed no question of this to me; it could not have been otherwise.

In a moment the man was out of his cab, and at the same time—freed by a latch on his dashboard—the trunk door swung up. He raced toward it. The young man loped back to his Cadillac, laughing wildly, and locked himself in. The cameras clicked, the onlookers kept gathering.

In the trunk of the cab I saw one object: a gigantic hammer, the largest hammer I'd ever seen. Its handle was the length of a tennis racket. It was not a mallet or an axe but a hammer. Why would anyone buy such a tool? What was its use? Why would one leave it, alone, neatly placed in the center of a trunk that flipped open with the flick of a switch? The cabbie grabbed the hammer on the run and headed toward the Cadillac. He was yelling, over and over, "Hit my cab, will you? Hit my cab, will you?"

What now? I wondered. Surely the man won't hit the car with *that!*

"Hit my cab, will you? Hit my cab, will you?" He was brandishing the hammer, waving it back and forth like a weapon of early war.

He'll merely threaten, I thought. No one would wield a thing like that with serious intent.

The crowd had increased considerably by now; people lined both sides of the street. They were back just far enough to enable the hand to be played out. Some were cheering. They were having a perfectly marvelous time.

The cabbie got to the front left window—behind which I could see the lean boy laughing wildly—and abruptly swung the hammer at it with full force, fracturing the glass. One second it was whole; the next, a mosaic of tiny irregular rectangles radiated from a center hole. "Hit my cab, will you?" he shouted and fractured the front window just as the boy leaped out the door on the passenger's side and high-stepped across the street, his face sober now, yelling, "What are you doing? What the fuck are you doing, man?"

"Hit my cab, will you? Hit my cab, will you?" The cabbie began to batter the hood of the Cadillac, denting it sharply. He would swing and there would be a strange loud sound and then I would see the dent. The crowed cheered. The boy was across the street, waving his arms, shouting; I could not hear what he said. Without turning to the crowd, the cabbie methodically smashed both headlights.

I turned then and headed home. I wanted all my affairs in order before I went west.

I was on a plane, high over the Midwest, suspended in time, traveling in a modern machine to Montana by myself, and I wanted to think of what would be and of the other times I had been to the West. At first the images were scattered, fragmentary, blurred, but I took out a pad and began to write them out, slowly at first, then with my hand racing across the page until I had to slow it down, make each letter more deliberate.

I thought of that first time, when I had been an eastern innocent out West. "The lake for big ones," Sandy Bing had written to me from Croix Chapeau, France, twenty years ago. I had been discharged from the army several months earlier, and when I wrote him that I was bent on driving across country, he had sent me a concise letter listing a dozen or so good waters. I had driven out alone, exploring here and there, picking cherries in Colorado, washing dishes in Wyoming, and when I circled back, not yet having fished, I sought out his lake "for big ones." The lake was on the Continental Divide, surrounded by dreary sagebrush flats, and I had caught huge trout on a Wob-l-rite from the shore, in the springs. I had taken an enormous number of big trout on my spinning rod—trout to make the eyes of an easterner weened on hatchery fish bulge.

When I drove out again, five years ago, I planned to stay at that lake again. I thought that my son Paul might take his first really big fish there. Hadn't Dave Whitlock told me of a whalish trout he'd hooked on a fly in that lake, that had actually *towed* his canoe for twenty minutes?

By then I had long since lost my heart to the fly rod. I had grown to love rivers—and my plans featured the Madison, the Firehole, Henrys Fork of the Snake, perhaps the Big Hole, hopefully Armstrong Spring Creek, probably the Yellowstone. Nelson Spring Creek? Rock Creek? The Beaverhead? I had lived with those names all that winter, for a half dozen city winters. I had lived with the huge trout I had seen in Dan Bailey's and Bud Lilly's catalogs. I felt, as I drove west that time, like a little boy heading into a candy shop, where he'd be surrounded by innumerable bins of sweets, where he'd be unable to dispose calmly of his well-earned nine cents.

I dreamed of the rivers, but it did not work out that way.

On our third day, fishing a long brown Leech on a Hi-D line, I hooked something that went steadily, merrily on its way, that stripped line to the backing without so much as a nervous wiggle or rush, that then wound my four-pound-test leader summarily around some weeds and swam off, no doubt chuckling mightily at this eastern dude. And I was hooked. Except for three short forays onto the rivers, I never left the lake that trip.

"You'll get the unbelievable cutthroats and brooks," Bud Lilly told me at his Trout Shop in West Yellowstone, "once you learn the house rules." I had gone out that first night, an hour after we arrived from the grueling four-day car trip, not knowing one of the house rules, and I had fished three hours without a tap. I had never fly-fished a lake for trout before, and as I looked out over the huge expanse of this slate-gray lake I did not know where to cast, how deep to fish my fly, what time of the day to fish, what fly to use, how to retrieve. I thought of what I'd learned on the Beaverkill and the Battenkill and the Willowemoc and shrugged my shoulders.

Others caught fish that night. But they were casting a full forty feet farther than I could. What flies were they using? Was everything I learned in the East—from casting to fly imitation—useless?

I had an eight-and-a-half-foot glass rod, a sinking No. 8 line, and a four-pound-test leader. The leader had seemed adequate at first, but when I caught nothing I thought of going finer. Was that why others caught fish? I knew nothing about the proper flies for the lake and bought a dozen weird woolly-worm patterns, from bright chartreuse to black, from the tackle shop at the lodge. I would not have used them for sunfish back East, but I had seen local patterns work too often to think of trying my delicate Eastern flies.

My luck changed when I met Thom Green. He hailed me from the porch of his cabin, which was next to ours, and soon gave me three flies. They were long brown woolly-worm patterns with brown marabou tails. The Leech. That's what the fish were on. How would I have known? I used nothing else in the lake for ten days. One of the flies took eleven fish and is now a ragged memento, its leaded body bare, of the trip. I lost the other two in fish and Thom replaced them with three others, fresh from the vise he had set up on his dining room table.

I watched Thom carefully that night. He was tall, solid, nearly bald and consistently amazed me by throwing out well over a hundred feet of line. I did not realize until later that he and most of the other fly fishers were using a shooting head, which I had never seen before. He would cast and then he would wait, and *wait,* and then he would finally retrieve with studied slowness. I had not waited, and I had been retrieving far too fast. I changed to a Hi-D line and fished deep and slow and with slow twitches, pointing my rod toward the water as Thom did. He also told me that an important part of this fishing was *position.* There was a channel in this lake, headed by a major spring—the one that I had fished from shore many years earlier, now properly closed to fishing. There were deep holes here and there, if you knew where to find them. When the weeds came up in early July and the water warmed, the fish schooled in the channel and headed toward the springs. You had to position your boat just right to fish the channel properly; there was a pole and a chimney which, if properly aligned, told you you were in the right spot. And in the early morning, before the sun broke over the mountains, there was one man, an old "regular," who could find his way in the dark; other boats waited for him in the cold darkness, then used him as a point man and found the hole and channel after he had anchored.

I began to catch fish sporadically. I fished for two or three hours, slowly, steadily, without a strike—and then took three fish one after the other. These were big fish by Eastern standards: two- and three-pound cutthroats and brooks. I would be plying the dull art of the slow retrieve and suddenly the rod would thump down. My four-pound-test leader held, and I did not think to change it. Paul caught two fine brookies, and Mari caught a couple of landscapes.

By the end of our stay I had learned most of the "house rules" and was ready to cast off all further worldly responsibilities and resign myself to living at the lake forever, lulled by the long casts and slow retrieves and shocked into unforgetfulness by the big fish. Someday

I would come back and fish the rivers. But I had gotten hooked on this lake, this still and slate-gray water, and my winter dreams—despite all my plans—would be of it and of the slow, thumping power of its huge fish.

I remembered, too, high over the Dakotas, the next year, and a particular trip floating the Madison. Paul caught his first trout on a fly that time. Thinking of that, I began to think also of how fly fishing differs from all other forms of fishing and how desperate fathers become, sometimes, to share their deepest pleasures with sons. I had already heard of innumerable cases of children who had been given vigorous, tenacious, and even expensive training in a sport only to despise it for the rest of their lives. I suppose we like what we like not out of obligation, ever, or because we would *like* to like it, but because something in us responds as naturally as a trout to a mayfly to something in the action. It cannot be forced. Particularly not fly fishing, which is a rather demanding affair.

Still, we dream. Paul *seemed* to have a genuine liking for fishing, especially when he caught some fish, which he often did. He had natural coordination and a good eye and became an excellent spin-fisherman by the age of nine or ten.

"Why didn't you start him with a fly rod?" asked several fly fishing friends.

A good question. I was already deeply hooked on the fly rod by then, and I wanted to share with Paul fly names, hatches, rises, leaders, and all the other arcane details that so absorb and delight the lover of fly fishing. I told them that I had not started with a fly rod and that I wanted him to catch fish.

"Did you always have to catch fish?"

"No."

"Anyway," one said, "he'll catch plenty, soon enough, because the fly rod, properly used, will catch as many trout as bait or spinners." I had to agree.

I had rather slowly worked my way toward the fly rod over a good many years, I told them. No one I knew fly-fished, and it seemed an impossibly complicated way to catch trout—if indeed you could catch them that way. I wasn't convinced, not until the day I watched a man take four, on a dry fly; each time a fish rose, I felt a sharp twinge, like an electric shock, in my chest.

Robert Frost, when asked why he still wrote with a defined meter and often in rhyme, replied that it was no fun to play tennis without a net. Part of the pleasure we take in any sport depends upon the reasonable limits we set to our freedom: the slalom skier must move between certain carefully positioned upright poles, the baseball player within foul lines. The basketball hoop is neither too small nor too large, but as basketball players grew taller, rules were added to maintain a fair chance—the three-second rule, goal tending. This denied to the merely big man an unwarranted advantage by prohibiting him from camping under the basket or stopping the offensive shot when it was on its downward course. Rules enhance the quality and pleasure of a game, rarely diminish them. It is not sporting or even reasonable to play basketball with a ball so large it will scarcely fit through a hoop, or with one hand tied behind one's back. This becomes affectation, fiddling around.

The object of all fishing is to gull a fish. Some anglers find pleasure in doing this by any legal means; I like a prescribed court, a code of reasonable limits. My object, by choice, is to gull the fish with a single fly. I would use a ten-pound leader if that would fool it; it usually won't. Smaller rods do not increase my pleasure, nor are they necessarily sportier—since you may tire a fish and even kill it in the longer fight required, and most casting situations demand a longer rod. Dry flies are more pleasurable than wet flies, at least for me, because you can see the fish rise to them. But often only sinking flies will move the bigger fish, or any fish, or even reach any of them. Some attempt at imitation of the natural insect on which trout are feeding brings me more satisfaction than merely luring them to an attractor pattern, because you have had to live more deeply in the trout's domain, solve the riddle of its selective feeding. Ultimately, I do not fish for the trout's pleasure or convenience but for mine. I do not think the fish has a sense of fairness—or a sense of very much at all.

On that trip Paul had caught a fat cutthroat in the Shoshone, as we approached Yellowstone Park, and several good fish in Henrys Lake—on his spinning rod. He had confidence in it. He was unwilling to give it up. He had traveled two thousand miles and he wanted to catch trout—which meant, for him, the spinning rod.

I had traveled two thousand miles, too, and I wanted to enjoy myself, not worry whether or not my son became a fly fisherman. So we both fished the lake and I enjoyed myself royally—as I always do when I fish—and Paul got good and properly bored and began to go mountain climbing.

On our last day I arranged to take my first float trip down the Madison with Mike Lilly, Bud's son. He asked if I would be going alone, and I said I wasn't sure. Then at the last minute Paul decided to forgo mountain climbing and come along, though he only brought his spinning rod. I took two fly rods.

In the morning I raised a few fish but each time struck late; we were floating too fast for a second cast. Then I took a few small fish and Paul took a small rainbow on a spinner. I could see that he did not want to use a fly rod in the boat.

We had a pleasant lunch in the grass above a fast run and then walked to where a channel entered the main river. The smaller water immediately appealed to me; with its bends and pools and gentler speed it reminded me of Eastern rivers I loved. We came to one run where a narrow, brisk current widened into a pool about fifteen feet across. I asked Paul to try it first, perhaps with a fly, but he preferred to use his trusty spinner. He cast upstream and retrieved the lure with short deft twitches. A trout struck and then was off. On the next cast he pricked another. The run was filled with good fish.

"Try a fly," I suggested.

"I didn't bring a fly rod."

"I brought an extra," I reminded him.

"Well . . ." He looked at Mike. "That's all right. I'll try the spinner again, if you don't mind."

Mike told me of a pool around the bend, where the conservation department had shocked up several four-pounders, and said he'd stay with Paul and show him another spot or two among the channels.

I did not catch one of the big ones, but I did take a good seventeen-inch brown and several smaller ones on a Whitlock Hopper. It was fine, careful fishing, and I enjoyed being able to wade—and being off by myself. My code did not have to be Paul's code. One came to rivers to pleasure oneself, not please one's father's whims.

When I came back around the bend an hour later, I saw Paul, knee-deep in the first run and fast to a good trout. He was smiling broadly and Mike was coaching him in a quiet voice.

Paul was using a fly rod.

I came up close to Mike and asked if this was Paul's first trout. Yes, it was his first trout on a fly—and he was radiant.

"He came right up, Dad," the boy said, scarcely willing to turn his head away from the splashing fish. "Mike said they'd be up next to that rock, where the current slaps against it, and they were. And one came right up and sucked it down. And I struck just right—"

"He struck it perfectly," said Mike.

"And he was on."

"And there he is!" I said as the fish jumped, a brightly colored fourteen-inch brown. Paul netted the fish himself, on the third swing, and then raised it high, that huge smile still plastered all over his face.

And in the darkened car, riding at dusk back to our cabin after Mike had left us, Paul chattered on in luxuriant detail about the other two fish he later caught that afternoon on a dry fly. He also told me about a good one Mike had caught under an alder, while he looked on from the bank not ten feet from where the trout rose.

"I saw it all," he said with animation. "He cast perfectly. Just five feet above the tree. And he snaked the line a little—you know, to give it a good drift . . ."

"I know."

"And the fly floated perfectly. He's a terrific fisherman, and a terrific guy; he told me to crouch right there above the tree, so I could see it all. He said there *had* to be a fish there. He'd changed his leader tippet and put on a little gray caddis imitation—because he'd seen some caddis, of course . . ."

"Of course."

"And he only false-cast once and then laid the fly down perfectly. The water was just like a piece of liquid crystal. I could see everything. I think my heart stopped as that fly floated down toward the tree, then under it, and then the trout came from nowhere—from under the bank, I think. It was the fastest thing I've ever seen. The water was so clear I could see everything that happened—and, wow, that was the most beautiful thing I've ever seen. I felt this strange shot of electricity go through me when I saw it come up suddenly, from nowhere, and turn, and take the fly. The most beautiful thing . . . "

"I know," I said quietly.

We watched the last purple and pink of a Montana sunset fade below some shadowy mountains far off to the right.

"Like electricity. *Wham!*" He slammed a fist into his palm. "*Wham! Just like that.*"

"I know."

In the plane I dreamed of other voyages I knew: those of Odysseus and Pound's seafarer, Hölderlin to Patmos and Yeats to his Byzantium, Ahab in his mad pursuit and Whitman's passage to "more than India," and Keats—"on the viewless wings of poesy"—with his nightingale, voyages near and far and inward to places holy and dangerous and rare . . . and then the plane angled, swooped like a great bird, and touched down at the airstrip in a place called Butte.

RIVER TOURING

Eventually, all things merge into one, and a river runs through it. . . . I am haunted by waters.
—*Norman Maclean*

Suddenly you're gliding. The rubber raft comes clear of the shore, gravel, swivels, picks up the main current, and the guide's oars grow rhythmic, then faint in your ears. Sitting in the front seat, with only inches between you and the water, you look out over the winding expanse of river before you, up at the yellowed cottonwoods and pink and yellow aspens, at the slope of the hills and at the stark gray buttes, up toward higher peaks—with jagged patches of snow at their crests. The air is crisp. The vast sky is pale blue, almost cloudless.

You strip line from your reel, test the knot on your fly.

You look backward and a ruddy face nods, so you turn front again and begin to watch the ever-varying line where the moving river meets the shore. Sky and hills disappear. You feel the raft slip into faster current. The willows, where they border and droop into the river, are moving upstream. Motion. All is changing now. You pass a pinched bend and watch the lace of the current dance and widen; you watch the eddies behind a dozen rocks, the slower water beneath overhanging willows, slight changes in the conformation of the shoreline that create a constant series of small, moving targets, each different, each racing upstream as you float, never stopping.

Targets, one after the other now; pinched pockets, patches of backwater spotted with foam, swirls. Targets. Every one of them slipping noiselessly upstream, back, past you and out of range.

You begin to cast. There is time for one shot, maybe two if you're lightning fast, a third before the target is gone. Inches are critical. Too far out and by now you know there will be nothing. You must watch the current: with fast water between you and the shore you must curve-cast properly, put the fly downstream of the line. Every muscle and nerve of your body is awake. Your eyes cannot turn for a second. You do not want to miss one likely spot. There! And there! That run behind the boulder. Under the tree. In the slack water right up against the shore. Again. Then into the pocket where the mudbank goes concave. Pick that pocket. Into the foam line. Into the two-foot eddy behind the boulder. It is like jump shooting, but faster—extraordinarily fast. The targets never stop.

Then down a quick sluice, a moment's rest, quick glances to both riverbanks now. Left or right?

"There!" Phil says, his voice a sharp invitation, and I cast backhand to the right bank, into that pocket. "Again," and the fly is up and, without a false cast, upstream and into the same pocket. "And again!" I strain, accelerate, and force the fly upstream farther this time. It lands within inches of the bank, pauses, then begins to shoot downstream as I strip line frantically. A good brown rolls, lunges, misses. I feel it in my chest. I breathe out sharply and turn to Phil. He nods; yes, he saw. I start to reel in. "Left side. Left. Quick!" he says, and I look and see the pocket and put line in the air again. My wrist already aches, my casting hand is callused. A deep, dull, but satisfying pain is beginning to work into my shoulders.

We are floating the Big Hole below Divide, Montana. We have floated the river three times this week, and slowly I have been learning the mechanics of this new thing for me—float-fishing—feeling the full challenge of it grow, and earning some of its special rewards. Later this week we may try the Beaverhead, then perhaps the Jefferson or Madison, whichever is fishing better.

On the far side of the heavy main current, in a flat backwater pool, I saw the fish rise. A good trout? Perhaps. You could not tell for sure, not at this distance: the pool was more than a hundred feet away. The autumn afternoon was bright and the pool was flat, so you could see the widening circle clearly enough, but you could not fish for the trout from where I stood. The main current was heavy and deep, with rolling whitecaps a foot high, impossible to wade; the cast was far too long.

I fished slowly upstream until I was opposite the backwater pool and could see it better. A small channel came in out of the woods, or perhaps it was a feeder creek from the sloping sagebrush hills; it hit up against a huge slate-gray boulder—twelve feet high, the size of a trapper's cabin—pinched into a riffle, met a channel from the main current, swirled, flattened out, became glassy, and washed slowly over some small rocks into the main river. Fish could come into the pool either from the feeder or from the main current. There would be ample food and cover—the depth beneath the rock would have to be eight to ten feet. I ached to fish the spot but there was no way I could reach it. The main current, for as far as I could see down and upstream, was too heavy, the depth too great; I could not do it, and it was impossible to cast across the broad current, then the small spit of rocks, into that pool. It was much too far. And even if I could reach it with a cast, the main current was so surging and powerful that it would tear the fly away in an instant when the line hit the water.

So I kept working my way carefully up my side of the river, which was quite safe and easy, first fishing a caddisfly into the slack eddies directly upstream, then casting a large Marabou Muddler directly across and into the heaviest flow and, as it swung below me, working it back with short, sharp strips.

Nothing. Not even a follow.

I had not seen a fish in two hours of hard fishing. Surely this was the side everyone fished; it was not far from the road—in fact, it was a run named after a famous writer. *Everyone* fishing this river would have made a pilgrimage to this spot, to fish where that man had fished; I had done exactly that. If there were trout on this side, they would be wary, jaded, used; there probably were not many of them. And I did not particularly want to fish where everyone else had fished. I had not come all this distance to do so. I had come from that crowded place, where I always felt myself pinched and torn and manipulated. I had tried to save a few fresh places in myself, somewhere. I tried often to smile there—until my cheeks ached—but I laughed less there lately. I often felt there as if puppet strings were attached to my limbs—and soul. You could not see them but they were there. Here, the mornings at the old cabin, one of the oldest in the valley, had been so cold they sparked your face, and at the main house there had been good food, long hours of pleasant talk, and enough Scotch. But I had not come for that. I had come to be on the river. To be away. Alone. It was only for a short time. I knew that. I knew I would have to go back. But I did not have to think about that, not yet.

I had left the small party of men that morning and gone off by myself. I had liked being with them all. They were easy to be with, each of them; I liked to talk to them and I had learned from them. I had looked closely at each of them: they were younger and older men, and you knew who they were and that they knew where they were going. I was in the middle of things, not sure which way, of many, I should turn.

I was upstream of the backwater pool now. Oh, it was a perfectly marvelous pool; you might have painted it, although it was almost too pretty—wild, untouched, picturesque. There were three or four yellowed cottonwoods on the far bank, a bright yellow and pink aspen, a jam of gray weathered logs and deadfalls above the big rock. The feeder creek was bright auburn in the sun, and it sliced through a tunnel of overhanging willows, which were also spotted with yellow. I could see several of the dusty pink flowers of Indian paintbrush, and beige rabbitbrush along the far shore.

The fish rose again, at the tail of the little foam line, where the riffle widened, bubbled, and flattened out. Had anyone fished that pool? Ever? It was late September and the river was low, probably as low as it ever got, and you could not cross it; in the spring and early summer the main current must have been a torrent. The high sagebrush hills were backed up close to the far bank, and there were no bridges for ten miles in either direction. Floaters might have paused there, on the long spit of land; yes, a good guide would have brought a boat up below the pool, on the far side. It was probably not virgin. You could not expect that anymore, hardly anywhere. Not even in Montana. But certainly it was less fished.

That circle formed again in the middle of the pool. It spread, then vanished.

I waded steadily upstream now, my fly stuck around the brace of the lowest guide. Above me the river was turning in a broad, sweeping bend before it drew itself tighter, dropped, and swept heavily for at least a mile downstream. In the middle of the bend I saw a patch of lighter, shallower water. The river was a hundred and twenty feet across here; the water was heavy, perhaps deeper than my waist at all times. Should I try it? Upstream I could see a series of long, deep pools, separated by short, heavy runs. If I were to cross, it would have to be here.

I studied the water. Was it possible? If it simply could not be done, I did not want to try. I could not see the entire riverbed. A pothole, a slip, a fall in such water—I did not want to think of what would happen. Footloose, there was little way a wader could regain footing; he would be swept, tumbling, into heavy water, several hundred yards of white water without a break. That would do the damage, all right. And for what? That pool was a pretty little place, and it held at least one feeding trout. Was that enough? There were other days, other portions of this river to fish.

I had already caught some good fish on this trip and knew I would catch more. I was not hungry. That first day I had been frantic to catch some fish; it was cleansing to do so. But today I could pass up that pool. Perhaps the water would drop a few more inches and I could fish it later in the week. And if I did not? Perhaps the next time I came out here I could get across. I would surely come here again and the pool would always be there.

But I felt drawn to it. I did not know what it contained and would never know until I had laid a fly on its surface. It was there.

Yes, I'd try.

I checked that my fly was secure and then shuffled slowly into the heavier current. I felt it tug and bend my legs. My cleated felt soles would hold the bottom, but I wished I had cut a thick willow branch for a staff. I leaned upstream into the flow and nudged forward. Each time I lifted my foot away from the firm riverbed, the water caught and forced it downstream. I shuffled. I saw an old aspen on the opposite bank, ten yards upstream, and headed for that. The water came up to my waist, then an inch higher. The flow was growing heavier with each step I took closer to the center. I shuffled another foot, two feet farther, then stopped. I wanted to turn around, to see how far I had come, how far I would have to return if this venture proved impossible. But I could not turn my body, only my head, and that not far. I realized, suddenly, with a spur of fear, that the current was now too heavy for me to risk turning. I was balanced sideways against the current; I was quite sure, if I faced my body flush upstream or down even for a moment, even with the good grip my cleated soles had in the riverbed, even if I summoned all my strength, that the force of the current would spill me. I knew it would happen. I could feel the river's power when I turned even slightly. It was like holding a plank of pine in the water: if you faced the thin edge to the current, it held: if you turned the wide part upstream, the current kicked it high and you could not possibly hold the bottom no matter how hard you tried. If I wanted to head back toward the safe side of the river, I would have to back out inch by inch, with the chance of bumping some unseen rock and losing control. I had been able to get out from the safe side, but unless I found the exact same way back I might not be able to return.

I held my position for a moment. The water was crystalline but deceptive. It seemed to hold at its present depth but I could not be sure. I bent carefully at the waist to check more carefully—and almost lost my balance.

"Careful. Very steady, old boy. Steady now," I said audibly. They were the first words I had spoken in several hours. They sounded hoarse, alien.

"I'd be dead without the cleats and felt."

I shuffled a bit father. The water was at the tip of my vest now; I felt its surging, forceful rhythms against my whole body. My foot bumped a rock, felt left, then right. I raised my foot ever so gently, trying to get above the rock—teetered wildly for a moment—then scratched it across.

"I'm not going to make it. It's too strong."

I had fully half the river to cross, perhaps a trifle less. I could not turn back and was terrified of pushing even one foot ahead. "It's not possible." My palm, where I held my rod, was slippery. My face was drenched. A couple of caddisflies danced on the bright surface. The sun was strong on my neck and wrists and on the water. The aspen on the far bank did not seem much closer. I did not look toward the sky.

I tried to conjure a picture of the pool but could not. I had words for it now—I could have described it—but I could not see it clearly. I knew only that I wanted to fish it. Fishing that pool was all that mattered to me; it was a thing I was determined to do. I might catch nothing, I might never tell anyone of this fling, I might catch merely a whitefish or a chub, but I was going to fish that pool.

Methodically, ever so slowly, I inched closer to the aspen. Half a foot at a time. The soles of my waders merely pushing along the riverbed. A pause. The grating scratch of my cleats against a mossy rock the size of a grapefruit. Water high above my waist now. Two inches from the top of my waders. A slight depression. Tiptoes! The cold spurt of icy water slipping past my stomach into my trousers. Slowly. Very slowly. A minute, two minutes for each couple of inches. Scratch and nudge and tiny shuffle.

And then I felt the slight waning of the current pressure against my body, watched the water line drop two inches, four, felt my step grow surer, and bolted—splashing, high-stepping—the last five yards to the shore.

I breathed heavily and felt my entire body soften. I felt the rowel of pain in my arches and the biting sting in my right shoulder, merely from holding my rod high. I kept breathing heavily, panting, smiling broadly to myself, and then, without waiting to calm down, I half ran, half tumbled through the stand of cottonwood and aspen to the pool.

When I got down to the end of the woods, I stood for a moment looking at my pool. There was no hurry now. I had spent more than an
hour getting to this place, and I did not want to spoil it.

What I had thought was a feeder was really a back channel of
the main river. The hole was far deeper than I had guessed. Where it
hit against the rock, it was so deep you could not see the bottom;

angles and fractured planes of light descended toward the point of a cone and disappeared. One had to imagine what lay in the depths. The water might have cut under the rock a full ten feet. Big trout, really big trout, could live under there for a lifetime, having all their food washed down to them, being perfectly safe from all manner of predators. You could not work a fly under that rock; it went back too far, the current was too rough. You would even have trouble working bait back down into the recesses of that hole. Whatever lay down there was safe. There was no honorable way to take a fish that lived there.

Perhaps, though, one of them would come into the pool at times, take a position where the foam line of the current grew lazy, and pluck some hatching fly from the surface. It would not have to, any more than I had to cross over to this far side of the river—for there was surely enough food at the bottom of the hole—but it might, someday, for some reason.

There were tangled currents at the head of the pool where the two channels met; one might find trout there, too, not five feet from where I stood. But the glare of the sun was strong; they had no protection but the broken water. Any really large fish would surely be on the far side, near or under that boulder, in deeper water.

I was still breathing heavily as I watched the pool. I leaned my rod into some low willows, took off my hat, and scooped some water from the main current onto my face. Nothing could have felt finer. There was plenty of time. I had gotten to this pool. I saw some deer tracks in the mud, rabbit droppings along the rocks. I saw how the water broke ever so slightly, down where the foam line widened, not in a rise but perhaps a bulge. I measured with my eye the kind of cast I would have to make to reach it. Forty feet downstream, perhaps, but with slack enough so that it would not drag too soon. And I would have to cast over the tangled currents. I could do that. The alley of the channel would support my back cast, and I could probably stop the rod short enough to lay down five feet of slack line.

But the better cast, surely, would be from *below* the rock—a short upstream cast, over flat water. That would take another fifteen minutes.

I had come this far, I thought, why not do it right?

I walked a short way up the shallow channel, crossed to the base of the hill, and walked down toward the rock. Those deadfalls and weathered logs were jammed high, from some spring freshet, and I had to climb through and over them, then under a huge fallen pine whose stubby branches caught my vest. The trek took a good while, and I was sweating again when I stood on the rock bed below the pool, in exactly the right position. I was precisely where I wanted to be.

I watched the water closely for five minutes. I had been careful, but perhaps the noise or my shadow had spooked the fish. There was no hurry, no hurry at all. A few small tan caddis danced on the surface. A magpie fluttered noisily out of the cottonwoods. The sky was bright cobalt, flecked with white. Then, suddenly, a fish rose at the end of the foam line.

The water was so clear and open that I feared I would get only one or two casts here. I wanted to cast at once but I stepped back a few feet, sat on a rock, and slipped off the No. 12 caddis I had been using. I took out my pipe, packed it slowly with tobacco, and puffed deeply. Then I tied on a length of 5X tippet, tested it, and fetched out a No. 18 tan caddis. I pulled the tippet through a patch of rubber I carried to straighten it, then ran it through my mouth to help it sink quickly.

"Now," I said. "Now."

I drew eight or ten lengths of line from my reel slowly, so the click was muffled. I false-cast across the stream three or four times, then swiveled slightly and cast two feet upstream and somewhat to the side of where the fish had risen.

The fly floated several inches, swirled languidly in a pinch of the current, came out of the little eddy, floated another inch, then another . . . slowly, now—and the fish took.

If I fish another forty years I will never forget the quick little splash, the spurt of water, the circle forming on that glassy, silent pool; nor the speed with which my rod hand raised firmly and hooked the fish; nor the sight of its three hard jumps, smashing the stillness.

It was a bright male brown, about fourteen inches—wild, brilliantly spotted, quite plump. It had never seen a fly. In a few minutes I slipped the hook out of its jaw and turned it free.

Later, my friends asked me what luck I'd had. "No luck," I said, laughing. "But I managed to take one fish, on the far side of the river."

"How big?" one of them asked.

"Not very," I said. "But sweet. Very sweet."

Three men about my age, from Iowa, came into the shop, looked at the register, and said, "Good heavens! Nick Lyons has been here."

I wasn't sure whether that was good or bad—since I am too well known for bringing monstrous luck wherever I go (hurricanes to Martha's Vineyard, torrential rains to the Beaverkill). It certainly was not the same as George Washington, Ernest Schwiebert, or Kilroy's having been there. But they seemed like kindly folk, not superstitious, and had already mentioned that they had had good luck, so I took a chance and said, "Yes, and he's still here."

"*You're* Nick Lyons?" they said, almost in unison. And then, in unison, went silent and scrutinized me. Then one of them said—did I detect a touch of reverence?—"You are the master of frustration!"

"Sure, you speak for all of us," said another. "For the poor guy who sits in his office all year dreaming, gets out for only two weeks a year, and then bungles everything."

Was it true?

Perhaps.

Next to Sparse, who lets us know in *Fishless Days, Angling Nights,* quite modestly, about only two small trout he caught—but whom everyone knows to be a man who simply does not bother with smaller than fifty-pound Scotch-guzzling browns—I have probably written more about *not* catching fish—about getting hooks in my ear, falling in, nearly losing my prized equipment and lovely wife—than anyone else, ever. It is not a distinction I particularly sought. I would much rather be known as the first man to cast three hundred feet backhanded or to take a ten-pound brown from the Blue Kill on a No. 24 Blue Spinner. But in what I have seen of my future, those things are not in it.

I cringed to think that about the only three people in Iowa who knew me, knew me for my blunders. I half expected them to ask not how many trophy fish I had caught but which guides I had hooked in the nose with a Marabou Muddler. In fact, I thought I saw one of them looking closely at Phil's left ear.

The truth, though, was that I was not in the least frustrated and had had a minimum number of disasters that week. None worth talking about. Actually I felt positively gleeful about a couple of dazzling casts I had made that very afternoon—they would have knocked your eye out. But then I worried. If I got really good—I mean, like the experts—would I have anything to write about? What could I say then? I caught ninety-three trout in two hours? Rumor has it that George LaBranche gave up trout fishing because he no longer found it a challenge. Would I ever come to the same sad end? Well, I wasn't going to get *that* good, not ever.

I found myself mumbling, trying to avoid bragging about several good fish I had moved. I really wanted to tell them about that, but they kept quoting my disasters to me. Had I really exposed my secret fumbling life so well? Didn't I know it all already, to my great shame? Still, the disasters *were* rather amusing and fun to tell, and true—how true!—and it would have been downright boastful of me to mention that I had taken, oh, seven or eight decent fish that very day. There didn't seem much point to such a story.

After they left, I was on the verge of asking Phil if he knew some brushy irrigation ditch where I might catch some funny disasters, when I thought, boldly, No. I am going to play this straight. I am getting unbelievably good and there is no truth in downplaying it any longer, letting misconceptions gather in Iowa. I will have to start admitting to my success even if it spoils my reputation forever.

So I promptly asked Phil whether, if I gave up the city and all its exotic pleasures, he could make a steely-eyed Montana guide out of me. To my shock he said he could and later even sent me a guide's application.

The Beaverhead is a strange, deep, bushy-banked trouty river. Norm Peterson, a local fisheries biologist who has stocked and studied the river carefully for years, told me it has one of the highest populations of trout in Montana, more than four hundred pounds per acre; he also suggested that the infamous Girdlebug—a positively ugly fly of black chenille body with rubber legs, which is used quite frequently on the river—imitates the "green worm," crane-fly larvae that run up to two full inches in length. So curious a fly is the Girdlebug that Glenn West and I contemplated a series of them. If the standard fly worked so well, why not a *Spent* Girdlebug? An Emerging Girdlebug? Even a Stillborn Girdlebug? When I used a dropper and the two Girdlebugs came back locked together, we even contemplated Mating Girdlebugs.

The Beaverhead is a difficult river to fish, and I know many dry-fly fishermen in the East who would rather eat worms than fish it. The river is narrow and deep, lined with overhanging willows, deadfalls, tangled mazes that cover sharply undercut banks. It winds and twists so severely that at one moment you're traveling south, another north. Some sections, in the fall, are filled with heavy green weed, the edges of which invariably produce good fish.

The afternoon we checked into a motel in Dillon, the bright warm weather suddenly turned sour; there was a steady drizzle and a sharp chill that crept beneath four layers of sweaters and shirts and a parka, deep into my bones. But we were all anxious to be on the water and fishing, so we managed a four-hour float.

We used the abrupt, hard cast, as close to the shore as possible, and found fish in the crook of each big bend, and in the little pockets along the bank, under the fly-snagging deadfalls, deep in the eddies, just beyond the steady foam lines. You can't wade. You must expect to lose half a dozen flies. Little is delicate. Floating, you forget everything but that endless series of small targets against the shore. You begin to concentrate on what you cannot see, what you imagine is underwater. You fish the Girdlebug on a stubby six-foot leader tapered to sixteen-pound test, almost exclusively—casting it hard into the pockets, splatting it down, flirting it in the current, teasing it through one enticing lie after the other. You know, always, that a big one, a hog, a brown that has been safely hidden in those tangles for four or five years, fat on green worms and wild and brilliantly colored, might on any cast, any time you put one of those outrageous rubber-legged monstrosities in the water, blast up, jaws open, and scare you out of your long johns.

Bill had one on that bore deep and never showed and finally pulled free; Betty Meier, who, with her husband, Jack, fished down with us in another of Phil's boats, had one on in the current that "felt like a log." They were bright, firm, wild fish, all of them—and after I stopped pulling the fly away as a fish burst toward it, I got a batch that went about fifteen or sixteen inches those two days we floated the Beaverhead.

Then it rained hard we returned to Phil's house and checked the Big Hole. It was high and discolored but I could not bear, being in that country for only a few more days, to miss an afternoon of fishing, despite all the good days I had had. Glenn suggested the upper Wise River, where the Wrights also lease water. It was a splendid choice. Glenn had been guiding hard all summer and fishing practically not at all; he needed an afternoon to himself, and the intimate Wise proved just the place. The water was fresh and quick, light auburn, like a cold white wine, and he and I fished it for two hours, he downstream, I up. It was a pleasant, relaxing river after the hard float-fishing we had just finished. Glenn got a fine thirteen-inch rainbow—a trophy in that water—and I took a slew of small fish that popped up in the silvery riffles to nab my Hairwing Royal Coachman.

We had one last leisurely float on the upper Big Hole. It was a quiet day on exquisite water. We chatted and laughed and loafed and spent an hour fishing over a batch of incredibly picky seven-inch rainbows: they were taking spent *Tricorythodes,* we finally discovered, and Phil had to go down to a 7X twelve-foot leader before he hooked one. Bill, who had once rowed crew for Harvard, took the oars for a while. Phil got a chance to do something his guiding had left too little time for all summer—fishing—and Bill got a chance to do something he and I had wanted to do all week: tease and coach the steely-eyed Montana guide.

It was a sweet day, without any of the pressure hard floating demands; we caught a few fish but that was the least of it; we laughed a lot at Bill's marvelously dry New England wit, chided the guide when his cast was four inches to the left of a pocket, and ate the last of Joan's magnificent streamside lunches—after Bill said he was so hungry his stomach was beginning to wonder whether his throat had been cut.

And then it was over.

After I left the Wrights the next morning I began the forty-mile drive to Butte. I was early for my plane, so I stopped on a rocky hillside overlooking a broad bend in the river. I looked down at a huge boulder, with eddies behind that *had* to hold good fish, and at the rocky pilings of an old bridge. Yellowed cottonwood and willow leaves drifted lazily in the current, and the week in all its richness flooded my thoughts: the long good talks with Bill at night, the crisp sound of frost on the ground each morning, the warm hospitality of the Wrights, the new skills I had learned and the fine water I had seen, the fish that had—in their own good time—been so generous.

I knew I would make such forays to such bright rivers again, and that I had taken so much of them inside me now that I need never worry again that I would be without them. The river that had started as an unnamed freshet, far back in the Catskills, was broader, richer, more complex now, and I had tools to fish in it and a lifetime still to fish. The circus of upper Broadway, the cold gray isolation of cities, could trouble me no more. Perhaps, like Walton, I would someday leave my London, "judging it dangerous for honest men to be there." Not yet. I took my life from another source. I had fashioned my craft to float any waters. I welcomed the work of cities. I welcomed the tangle of deadfalls in which one probed for the largest truths.

I looked at the bright river below me and thought of what Cézanne had once said: "My eyes are stuck to the point I look upon. I feel they would bleed if I tore them away."

I looked once more, deeply.

I tried to turn but could not.

Then I tore my eyes away, and found that they did not bleed, and headed home.

Confessions of
a Fly Fishing Addict
(1989)

FISH TALES

It's winter again and I have been fussing with all my flies and rods and reels, wondering (as I periodically do) why and how I have been gut-hooked by fly fishing. Surely the sheer wondrous technology is part of it, I think, looking at the immense variety of flies in my boxes, mumbling their names as if I were saying a mantra, running my fingers across the subtle tapers of rods, listening to the particular sound of a reel on which I wind a new fly line. When I squint, all the flies I've dumped into a shoe box look like so many jewels.

But my eyes look through the brilliance of the "things" of fly fishing to the stories—those odd, compelling, hilarious tales, in and out of print, that are so irresistible, and to the images and mind-pictures we record. "Had all Pens that go salmon fishing," wrote William McFarland in 1925, "devoted themselves to jotting down notes about why the big fish did not gobble a grasshopper, we should have lost many a page of sunshine, fresh air, and good fellowship, and reaped a crop of fireside Disko troops who thought like the fish."

In the best stories about fly fishing—by Norman Maclean, Roderick Haig-Brown, Robert Traver, Sparse Grey Hackle, William Humphrey, Howard Walden, and ten thousand others who tell them in camps and at lunch tables but do not write—we find the best clues to why some of us fish. Odd, funny things happen; there is mystery and suspense, challenge and discovery; the words have the warm colors of earth and water, not the jargon of the specialist; we meet real people, with warts and wit and maverick gestures; big fish are caught or lost; people say wild and spontaneous words; event becomes memory and sometimes, in the hands of a master, bleeds into art.

Such is surely the case with Sparse's story "Murder," about a man who catches a gigantic trout while trying to escape the doldrums of the Depression—and discovers that even fishing won't let him escape the harried world of affairs (though I've found it a good start), and Howard Walden's "When All the World Was Young," about a boy becoming a man, and William Humphrey's hilarious dissection of days (and nights) in a Scottish salmon-fishing hotel, *The Spawning Run*.

Many of the best fish tales only begin with the fish. There is a scene in Maclean's *A River Runs Through It* in which the narrator and his brother go looking for a pal who has taken a local lady of low repute along on the fishing trip, and downriver. The pal has taken her way downriver. The lady's name is Old Rawhide. The men turn a bend and come upon an odd sight in the middle of the Big Blackfoot River. "Maybe it's a bear," says the narrator. "That's no bear," Paul says. They study the sandbar. Maybe it's two bears. "Bear, hell," Paul says when they get closer. "It's a bare ass." "Two bare asses," says the narrator, and reports: "You have never really seen an ass until you have seen two sunburned asses on a sandbar in the middle of a river. Nearly all the rest of the body seems to have evaporated. The body is a large red ass about to blister, with hair on one end of it for a head and feet attached to the other end for legs. By tonight it will run a fever." And a page later he adds: "I never again threw a line in this hole, which I came to regard as a kind of wild game sanctuary."

Sometimes a fish tale is a brief image, a moment, a few words: an angler I'd met for the first time, telling me about a gigantic rainbow trout he'd been pursuing all morning on Bonefish Flats of the Henrys Fork with No. 22 midge pupae. The man's eyes, half-crazy, were nearly out of his skull. Or my marvelously fanatic French friend, Pierre, breaking his rod, then his line, losing a record one-hundred-eighty pound tarpon at the boat, and leaping onto it, straddling the thing like the cowboy pilot straddling the bomb in *Dr. Strangelove*. Or me, sinking slowly into the mud (on which I guess I thought I could walk), right up to my tweed jacket, on a gentle British chalkstream, in front of some perfectly bewildered British friends who'd never dreamed they'd see such a sight on their genteel waters.

Fish tales can occur anywhere, even in the bowels of cities, where some of us spend a few too many of our days. I once sent a young, rather shy English friend, on his first trip to America, to see Jim Deren, the late proprietor of the Angler's Roost in New York City, about buying a dozen flies for a weekend in the Catskills. Jimmy was scrunched behind his counter in that tiny, crowded, inimitable shop, and when Neil introduced himself, with quiet British courtesy, he growled: "I can tell from that accent that you're from across the pond—from over there. Well, mister, we use small flies here, too." And he reached under the counter and brought up a cupped hand. "Have you ever used flies *this* small?"

Neil looked into the hand. There was only pure pink palm. He thought this might be some sort of American joke he didn't understand and said, "Well, they're pretty small—but no smaller, old sport, than the ones I use." And Neil put *his* hand into his pocket and brought it out empty, too. Later he told me in perfect wonderment: "Nick, we talked about those empty hands for a full twenty minutes, and then I asked for some Hendricksons, like you told me, and he tried to sell me some air, and I walked out of the place in shock and never bought a thing."

The first plumes of skunk cabbage out of the brown earth; the spectral light and delicate green of the willows in April; Hendricksons popping out and then floating downriver like little sailboats on the Willowemoc; a trout tipping up ever so slowly for a drift of spinners; collecting scraps of sable and fox with Justin from the side streets off Seventh Avenue in June, which (converted into trout flies) we reckoned had a street value of $28 million; bleak days when not a fish showed; a day on the Beaverkill when every trout in the river went bananas; Lee Wulff talking quietly about his pioneering days of flying and salmon fishing in Newfoundland, buzzing the river valleys to spook schools of salmon and thus locate them; a Connecticut lake at daybreak, when largemouth bass crashed up out of the mists for hair bugs as big as bats, which Larry and I threw at them—their rises less like a trout poking its snout up than like a garbage can being chucked into the lake; the Delaware at dusk, when the sun slanted silver and red down the alley of the river, distances blurred, a certain sweet chill entered the air, the surface was suddenly pocked with a dozen rising trout, and Ed took a gigantic brown that for twenty minutes he thought must be a shad hooked in the tail; the flow of the lower Neversink in my ears and against my body; the deep, happy ache in my shoulders after a long day of casting; my first sight of a landlocked salmon, skyrocketing into the air, a gash of silver; a letter from a friend out West, describing the pursuit and capture of a twenty-four-inch brown—with the postscript that the one he was *really* after could have eaten the one he'd quickly traced for me on newsprint; a brown with shoulders angling up from beneath the willow on the Beaverhead, its mouth fearsome, like a dog's, to take a tiny Elk-Hair Caddis—these and a thousand other moments and images, remembered as I fuss with tackle in the dead of winter, are the stuff of fly fishing for me, and perhaps some of the mysterious "why" of it.

There is some lunacy in it all—and some playing Huck Finn, to regain our childhood. But that lunacy and those images are specks of sand that, like the sand in an oyster, become a fisherman's pearls. Some are funny jewels, some sad, and some touch our hearts. All are part of the great storehouse of memories and tales that make up a fisherman's quirky and crammed brain, keeping us gut-hooked from one season through the long gray winters until another season starts. In the end, the fisherman avoids the glitz of the new, the quagmire of too many innovations and new techniques, and this competitive monster the Fishing Contest, and returns to the simple, lovely pleasures of the sport itself: days filled with "sunshine, fresh air, and good fellowship," and sometimes a bit of raw hide, and a pursuit that never quite ends, and images and words that brighten our often darkened spirits.

It is late winter now and I have grown restless, grumpy, sour. I am beginning to count days until the season opens again. I fiddle with my rods and reels and flies, put away the books, check my waders for leaks, and then take out all the jewels that are my memories, and, silently, gloat over them.

CONFESSIONS OF AN EARLY WORMER

When I was fifteen and we lived in Brooklyn and all the other guys were off hunting girls, I would often sneak out of my house on a muggy late-March evening, wearing sneakers and carrying a flashlight and coffee can. On the corner of Bedford Avenue and Avenue J, I would meet my friend Mort, and the two of us, with great bounding strides, would head without a word for the huge abandoned house several blocks away, its windows dark, a FOR SALE sign stuck prominently into the front lawn. And among the high clumps of untended grass, only barely green, our hearts would quicken and we would begin to hunt worms.

More snake than worm, these night crawlers were long, floppy, gooey things, often stretched out to six or seven inches on their spawning crawl. We would shine the light so that only its edge illuminated the shiny back of a worm, then plunge quickly to catch one where it left the earth, pinning it lightly, firmly, then easing it up out of its hole. Later we learned to put red paper over the faces of our flashlights, and we could shine the dimmer light directly on these night crawlers without their moving. We often caught the old hermaphrodites at it, quite passionately joined together at the necks, and now and again Mort or I would say, in a loud whisper, "Double," and we'd display two with as much pride as a wing-shooter after his feat.

We were always quick and intent about our business. We had to be. More than twenty minutes on any lawn usually meant the cops.

We had "safe" lawns, where we could linger, and some well-tended lawns whose owners thought we were madmen, burglars, or worse. Carefully trimmed and watered lawns were usually the most fecund, and one old lady, whose immaculate lawn was irresistible, often sat shotgun so we "beastly boys" wouldn't pinch *her* worms.

It was a strange, mystical rite—this catching of night crawlers on moist spring nights—and we somehow took almost as much pleasure in it as we did in fishing. Rarely did we return with fewer than several dozen good worms. We even experimented with scores of different materials in which to store the bait—from cut newspaper to grass—and finally settled on sphagnum moss, which we bought in vast quantities from a dealer in Arkansas. We packed the moss and worms in shoe boxes, and I, who had an understanding mother, kept them in the vegetable section of my refrigerator.

They were our foremost baits for trout, these snakelike night crawlers, and for several years we caught all our early-season trout on them. Though by May, when the water was low and clear and we switched to small garden worms—a firmer, more compact creature— all our April fishing was done with these preposterous monsters. And we caught fish. Big two- and even three-pound holdover brown trout, from hard-fished public waters, fell to our ungainly rigs.

We gave them up not for flies but for spinning lures, and spent the last few years of our teens becoming lethal with this new tool that enabled you to flip a 1/16-ounce spinner forty feet, to the base of a fallen tree, and retrieve it with subtle fluttering.

Spinning taught me much that I've put to good use when streamer-fishing—but probably condemned me to a floppy casting wrist for life; only years of careful fly-casting have burned away the haste, the impatience, the nervous movement spinning taught me so well. None of my previous fishing prepared me for the challenge of the dry fly, and only recently have I begun to appreciate how much I learned about wet-fly and nymph fishing from my early worming.

At first we fished worms on long, unwieldy telescopic fly rods. We did not so much cast as heave or lob the rig out—a big night crawler hooked lightly in its orange band with a No. 8 Eagle Claw hook, then ten inches of leader, then as much split shot as we needed to get the thing where we wanted it. We used four of the biggest shot in the Big Bend Pool, merely one in the deep Swamp Pool, none in several slow glides where we'd fish it straight upstream and follow its progress down with the tip of the rod. On Opening Day, we used the most primitive methods and fished the deepest, slowest pools, smack in the middle, dead still, right on the bottom. On warmer days, we'd fish the head of a pool, drifting a worm from the riffle down into the center or sides—still as deep as possible. And even with "bugs" hatching all around us and trout rising with bacchanalian slurps, we fished—and caught fish—with worms. We'd use the smallest worms then, the lightest leaders; we'd fish shallow runs or riffles, or wherever we saw fish rising. We fished upstream and watched the worm come back toward us, a few inches beneath the surface—and often enough we'd see one of the better trout cease all that peanut grabbing and head for a good, decent munch of worm.

How did all this early worming affect a closet fly fisherman?

I suppose at first it merely humiliated me to have done it. I mentioned it not at all, could find no connection between it and the dry-fly fishing I now did—except that I had always caught a lot of fish on worms.

But then I realized that there was a certain "pool" of streamlore I had developed before I caught any fish, even on worms—a knowledge of where, at a particular time of the year and day, fish would be; a sense of what will frighten them; an inkling of what they would eat and under what circumstances they would take it. I had begun to learn this kind of lore while worming. Before long, I learned that trout were rarely taken in open, exposed water; they wanted protection from the heavy flow, and from predators, and they wanted a spot where vulnerable food would come to them. Pockets behind rocks, with their broken water and eddies, were ideal: here the trout had protection and had ready access to food caught and stunned and perhaps eddying in the broken water.

After the holocaust of Opening Day, our most regular success came from fishing these spots, what Al Troth calls the supermarkets of the river, with immense care. We learned that we could not drop a worm smack in the middle of such a pocket because the turbulence would scoot it right out and into the main flow; we had to get the worm slightly upstream first, then give enough slack so the bait would sink to the proper depth, then manipulate the rod in such cunning ways that the bait would remain in the pockets. Bends in the rivers created undercut banks and greater water depth, and we also took fish by working a worm slowly, naturally, into their depths.

Naturally.

That, I think, is the key word. Mort used to say, when a dumb hatchery fish took a quickly retrieved worm: "Mistook that one for a worm swimming upstream." And we'd continue the conceit with references to "hatches" of upstream-swimming worms and other unnatural absurdities. No. The tough fish, the good-sized fish, were only caught when you fished the worm naturally. And since a worm does not usually swim upstream, or hang suspended from a leader on the bottom of a river, *natural* meant dead drift: with the worm cast upstream, gaining a bit of depth as it moved down, without encumbrance, tumbling as close to the bottom as possible.

We learned to hold the rod forward and then bring it downstream as the worm came toward and past us. We learned to see the telltale twitch of line or leader, the wink of white underwater when a trout's mouth opened. We learned to manipulate the bait to the depth at which the fish were; we learned to judge currents and eddies in the process. We learned holding water and feeding lanes and how to use our eyes and hands, and we learned the absolute need for quick, light strikes.

Though we didn't know it, we were beginning to learn how to fish the nymph.

Now and again, when I hear someone tell me how they learned to fly-fish when they were five or ten or twelve, I get a touch of envy, a sense of regret, a feeling that all of my green years, when my feelings and passions were freshest, might have been better spent. As I look back, I was from the beginning fated to be a fly fisherman: everything I love about fishing pointed me in that direction. Now and again, when I think back on my early years, I regret I did not find fly fishing sooner.

But lately, especially in late March, when Mort and I first went forth with flashlight and coffee can, I remember the lowly worm: the moist nights on which we hunted them, the engaging *peck-peck-peck* when a fish took one, the whole ritual of worm fishing. But beyond all that, beyond that world to which I cannot return, I am grateful to the worm. It was a damned good teacher.

HOMAGE À BLUEGILLS—
AND PUMPKINSEEDS, TOO

Durocher once said of Eddie Stanky: "He can't run, he can't field, and he can't hit, but he's the best player on the Dodgers." It could be said of bluegills and pumpkinseeds that they run to no size, can be caught in dreary field ponds, and will hit even cigarette butts—but I won't say it.

They are the harlequins of kids' hearts, a grand and generous fish, a whiff of youth for many a middle-aged trout snob.

Me, for instance.

Lepomis machrochirus—it belies the lovely simplicity of the bluegill to drape it in Latin; pumpkinseed, *Lepomis gibbosus,* of the bright orange belly, with shimmering green-blue sides and that prickly dorsal you must smooth and lock back with a thrust of your palm: low on the pecking order, high in hearts.

They were the first fish I caught on a fly, the first I caught by *any* method, and in my dotage, when the fly comes no longer lightly to the rise, I hope some good soul will wheel me to the bank of a weedy field pond with lots of pancake-sized spawning nests in view, so I can slap my Bumble Bee down while shuffling slowly through senility and off this mortal coil. Often enough, the fly comes not light even now—and a good substitute for throwing myself upon a sword when I've botched the trout game is surely to let the *Lepomis* massage my ego a bit with their ready antics.

If only they weren't so small, I used to moan when I first caught them in South Lake and in the lake runoff (where they were positively stunted). The cork bobber, threaded through, would begin a spritely jig, then dart down at an angle; I'd yank, and there it was, flopping in the boat a second later—four inches of flopping blue, green, and orange, maybe five. One didn't particularly have to be a big-fish fisherman to desire more for one's cranelike wait: they were midgets; they were—no doubt about it—a one-yank fish.

When I was sent, rather against my will, to a gloomy boarding school in Peekskill, bluegills and pumpkinseeds were my salvation. I credit them with no less. I was five, then six, then seven, then eight there—and they yanked me through. For all the gray of grayness, for all the chest-wracking loneliness I felt in that old Victorian spookhouse of a school, the little Ice Pond—a couple of acres of it—was green and live and generous. Though quite alone, I was never once lonely there. I can look intently at one photograph taken of me, knee-deep in that muddy pond, in short pants and a sailor's blouse, holding a crooked bark-stripped poplar pole, and there is no touch of loneliness on the face. The eyes are intent, awake, as if through the pole and cheap green line I am plugged into some life current.

It was only a muddy pond with no current, a big basin of tepid water near a highway, this Ice Pond, but it was the home of harlequins. I learned to wait and watch, to stalk with some caution, to *think* underwater. Mostly I caught bluegills, fewer and bigger than those at South Lake, and a few bright, mature pumpkinseeds that circled with tough tugs and had to be eased, not yanked, from their element. On a Saturday afternoon in May, when others went with their guests, I could stand there hour after hour, my toes curled into the mud, my corn-kernel can of dug worms on a nearby rock, my eyes unflinchingly locked to the cork bobber.

And so, on bluegills and pumpkinseeds, the hook was set deep, into the marrow and into the affections—and when the hook grew feathers, the fish were still there, still as happily accommodating. (I only wish my own children had come to fishing on them, for their trout days have been long and often fishless and frustrating.)

I was seventeen or eighteen when I bought my first fly rod for fly fishing; I'd had a telescopic steel rod first—after the cut or cane

poles—then a twelve-buck Heddon bamboo that broke on a foul-hooked ten-pound carp, then an array of spinning rods with which I learned to perform prodigious feats. But I never used flies with those first fly rods, only bait. That summer in my late teens, while waiting on tables at a summer camp, I earned enough to buy an eight-foot glass fly rod, a dozen cheap, snelled flies, and a level-C fly line and spool of level leader. I had been watching, with increasing awe, the fly fishermen who plied their elusive art on afternoons when I was about to leave the East or West Branch of the Croton. They seemed no less than an advanced stage of evolution; there was grace and delicacy in what they did. Better, they never snagged bottom—and they *did* catch fish when even I, the master of worm and spinner, could not.

So I bought the ill-matched mishmash of gear that summer, and since Ellis Pond was handy and I had my evenings free, I'd head off beyond the docks to a weedy flat near the bend of the shore and flail away. No one taught me—which showed. (And still does.) I put back casts into rocks and shrubs, slapped the water to a thick foam, tangled myself in my level-C fly line—and caught bluegills.

Did I catch bluegills!

That ragged No. 8 Bumble Bee could take thirty in an evening. Whipping and waving, I'd get the fly a few feet beyond my nose, down on the water like a tossed rock, and they'd riot for it. Against the soft bend of the rod, they couldn't be yanked, and I learned finger positions for drawing in line, getting it back on the reel, keeping it from tangling at my feet. We educated each other, those bluegills and I: by late August, they were warier, I was defter.

Not deft enough for trout, not nearly so—but better. Good enough to cast, say, twenty-five feet. Good enough to jiggle the fly, twitch it just right, so it brought that pinched swirl that let me know a fish had taken the slightly sunken, battered Bee.

Now and then the chance comes to taste a food you loved as a child— fresh wild strawberries, perhaps, or tart blackberries from a thorny bush. Berries with memories. Bill Humphrey and I had found his local creeks dead as trapped mice one hot June afternoon, and he whisked me up to a little weedy pond on a neighbor's land. It was rarely fished. It was quite choked already with lily pads and long, high weeds. It was perhaps fifty yards all the way around. But what fat bluegills it had, and how readily they came to tiny popping bugs that evening! And what simple good fun we had, mingled with memories, as we stalked through the high grasses along the shore. We'd cast one of those six-for-a-buck poppers out, twitch it, let it sit, twitch it again. A midget would tap the thing, *splat-splat,* then a big gulprise and a plump bluegill was on, circling at right angles against the tug of the line, tugging with its jerky tugs, twice its weight in pluck.

They were fat, but if only they were still a *little* larger, I thought.

And then, last week, Thom Green called me from Tulsa. He is a big-fish fisherman of the first water. He takes big lake rainbows on his big brown Leech; record white bass; cutthroats the size of your arm.

He casts his shooting head a hundred feet and prowls big waters for big fish. There was this pond in Utah, he said.

Did it hold rainbows, big browns?

Nope.

Fat smallmouths, maybe?

Bluegills.

Bluegills?

"Well," he said, "I'd heard about it, and the reports told of bluegills up to a pound, pound and a half."

"Those're big bluegills."

"But then I was working in that area last fall and got to speak to the local conservation officer. When I asked him about the pond, he said, 'Would you believe two to *three* pounds?'"

"The conservation officer said that?"

"Can you go this summer, Nick?"

"To Utah? For bluegills?" I'd rather been working my mind into a salmon mood, or perhaps the Madison during stonefly time. I had the Henrys Fork on my brain—and the East Branch, the Firehole, and dusk hatches in long Montana evenings.

"The man said, 'Would you believe two to *three* pounds?'"

"But that's two thousand miles . . ."

"On popping bugs. *Three-pound bluegills.*"

Lepomis machrochirus monstruosus! Wouldn't dreams of *those* enliven my dotage!

"Will you go?"

"I'm already there," I said.

THE CASTING PERPLEX

That March, while I was in college, I often trotted over to the Palestra with fly rod in hand. The basketball season was over, mounds of sooty snow still spotted the street corners of Philadelphia, and I was mad for the trout season to begin.

I had not really started to fly fish yet, but the tool—a white Shakespeare fiberglass rod—intrigued me. I had used it for bait-fishing the previous spring and with flies, for bluegill. When the season opened that year, I was determined to try fly fishing for trout.

My prospects were discouraging. The mismatched level line was too light for the stiff rod and would not work it. I snapped the thing back and forth like a bullwhip. The line came back too slow, my loops were ludicrously wide or else got tangled in their absurdities, and I jerked my rod hand around so much I nearly ruined it for spinning.

I was crazy for distance. Standing at midcourt, I wanted to wing the thing far beneath the backboard and into the stands. The harder I tried the more I flopped. I could not do it.

On short casts—very short casts—I wasn't nearly so helpless. With no more than twenty feet out, I almost thought I could manage this madness. My barbless hook dropped with unerring accuracy on the foul line. But at thirty feet I ached for a spinning rod, at which I was a master.

I fumbled here and there, split time with other fishing tools, and then, some years later—without prompting, without a coach, and without more than a fool's sense of what I was doing—committed myself the whole hog to the long rod. And then, to do what I wanted to do, to reach that eddy near the far bank or get a drag-free float through the riffle, I began to take my casting with a terrible seriousness.

I began matching my line to my rod. This proved one of my wiser decisions. I used a tapered line: also not a bad idea. I considered the size and taper of my leader and, without too much tinkering, found that it was not inevitable that a leader should jerk and hook and then lie like a half-moon on the surface. I learned that less could indeed be more: by firming up my wrist, keeping my casting arm closer to the vertical, and allowing the line to work the rod, I cast farther and with far less energy. Gone, suddenly, was the feverish bullwhip mentality; gone, too, were the maddening tangles and loss of control. Phil Wright taught me to control the line with my line hand and then, to my astonishment, got me to do the double-haul in fifteen minutes one afternoon—well, my unique version of that valuable cast.

So I began to get the business done a bit better, to reach the line a bit to the left or right when needed, to cast sidearm or backhand when I had to, to send the fly out far enough to get a fish or two now and then when they were beyond what I'd thought was my limit, and to roll out a creditable cast or two under branches. Except to myself, in giddy moments, I had few pretensions. I had begun to see what magic others could wreak with the fly rod; I knew my limitations. And I had other fishing interests to fry: there were new kinds of streamcraft, a growing interest in still waters, entomology, tackle tinkering of a rudimentary stripe, tying, improving my eyesight and hindsight.

But you can't do a thing at all unless you can cast: it's that fundamental. And now and then, watching one of the masters in motion, I had an itch to become truly dazzling with the tool.

But they all did it so differently.

Art Flick, moving with astonishing speed and purpose, had his fly on the water five times more than anyone I'd seen. He flicked his fly here and there, followed it, lifted, cast again, had his fly working for him while I dawdled. But when I went fast, I fumbled again.

I watched in wonder when Ed Van Put laid out a long, lazy line and then watched in dismay as my line, at twice his speed, crashed to the surface behind me.

When I saw Lee Wulff put his index finger up on the cork handle and cast eighty feet without much more effort than I used to breathe, I immediately tried this and found I forced the line too hard and it did whacky things.

I only saw a movie of Lefty Kreh, but when I tried for his distance, I was the complete tangler again. What authority and ease he had. And just when I thought I'd learned something about casting, I knew I knew nothing.

I knew it would take me twenty years, fishing every day, to fish the way Doug Swisher did that day on the Big Hole, dancing his line, attacking the river with deft skill. And if it took the balanced, classic casts that Schwiebert made that day on the Grimsa to catch salmon, I'd have to go back to chub on the short line. He was quite marvelously fine.

Thom Green laid out a hundred and twenty feet of line on Henrys Lake, with a shooting head, and I watched as he drew his rod arm back, almost parallel to the water, then, with his whole body, winged it forward. The line went out and out, and then the leader turned over with a last little flip and I bought myself a shooting head for Christmas. With it, with a great deal of effort, I could cast almost as far as I could with a standard double taper.

Beyond my pleasure in watching all these men at work—and once, Joan Wulff made it all look ludicrously easy—I was perplexed. Was there a *proper* way to cast? I didn't have to be particularly perceptive to notice that each of these fly casters was different. Each had, what we call in stuffy English departments, a style of his or her own. *Style est l'homme.* Flick flicked and Van Put putted slowly: they both got the work done. Bob Buckmaster cast as if he were driving a nail, with sharp *thwack, thwacks,* and Pierre Affre (that afternoon at Riverside Park) cast like a tooled machine, all in a rush of frightening motion, his rod going back far farther than even Thom Green's, the line no more than four feet off the ground, and then the awesome shoot.

I was baffled.

I had a sincere desire to improve myself and thought I *had* been improving myself, but these birds were all so different. One proved his theories with the help of an orthopedic hand doctor; another used a classical exemplum, such as Steve Rajeff; others recommended wristbands, books under the elbow, and whatnot else. Worse, with my ear not particularly flush to the ground, I began to hear rumblings of backbiting and rivalry. "What does Swisher know about casting?" "Do you really call Schwiebert a caster?"

Yes, Virginia, I do. And Swisher knows awfully well whereof he speaks. So do the others. Some are professional coaches and greatly skillful at it. Had I the time or money I could invest it in worse efforts than a casting clinic with the Wulffs or with Swisher. They'd make anyone better.

Someone recently wrote to a magazine saying that his son could tell wines like Ernest Schwiebert and cast like Nick Lyons. This is no lie. You can ask the editors. He couldn't have mixed us up because I can't tell a Riesling from a Margaux. And I read his sentence as a compliment. But the man must be a lunatic. No one would *boast* that he or anyone he knew cast like me.

How does Nick Lyons cast?

I could answer, with false modesty: painfully, with limited success, rarely reaching the foul line. But though no showman, I'm better than that, though it's less fun to say so.

How do I cast?

Like Nick Lyons. I cast my own way. I use my wrist a bit too much, my back cast often goes too high, I have been known to slap the water (fore and aft), my puddle cast too often collapses like a mess of spaghetti. But most of the time I get the business done—each year a bit more handily.

Isn't that what it's all about?

JUST A CAST AWAY

"I'm a lousy caster," the guy shouted, smiling broadly, "but I sure have a lot of fun."

Since I'd heard the same sentiment from my own lips. I felt I'd earned the right to mumble: "I'm a better caster than I was, and I have more fun than I did."

The guy was flailing away on the Yellowstone in the Park, having as much fun as a clown; the fish were out there, rising by the hundreds, just a cast away, but he was catching nothing. How could he? He slapped the water only a bit less on his back cast than he did on his front cast. His high loops, buffeted merrily by the wind, dropped the line fifteen feet short or to the left of the rising fish to which he cast. His wrist, flopping back and forth, was a speeded-up metronome. Twice his fly actually floated over the fish, but at a gallop—for his cast those times had been *too* accurate, without slack to eat possible drag. Three times he had to cut a cast fly out of his vest or shirt, once by taking his vest off, losing a fly box in the process, and nearly losing his footing, which is easy enough in the Yellowstone. I feared for an eye or a cheek or an earlobe.

And through it all, thousands of those generous Yellowstone cutthroats kept tipping up and feeding safely on a perfectly splendid and generous hatch of tan caddis, perfectly safe from this poor bumbler.

Had he not been happy as a pig in mud, I'd have waded out and shook him by the shoulders for a full minute. Why so many of us fly fishermen have felt, for so long, comfortable with our incompetence, I don't know—unless it's because when we try to learn and can't, we feel like three-thumbed imbeciles, so we don't try and are insulated from possible failure. Or perhaps we think of fly fishing as merely a "poetic" leisure sport. and of practice as too much like work.

Anyway, I'd been where this guy was. A lot of times.

I'd stood in the same river during the same hatch—and caught nothing. Funny as that genial bumbler looked, on the river in front of me and in my memories, I turned my back on him in a few moments; I'd never enjoyed being there, though I had liked to write about it, and I soon found the scene too painful.

On the drive out of the Park I remembered the sudden change from frustration to pleasure after Phil Wright taught me the double-haul; I could not only cast farther but with more control; I gained line-hand control when I'd thought you only cast with your right hand. I remembered the day on a Madison River float when Glenn West taught me to cast lower and harder into the wind, and a particular moment on a small secluded pond when I saw something in Craig Mathews's casting that helped me from then on to lay down a dry fly more gently. I remembered the authority and power I'd seen in casting demonstrations by Steve Rajeff and Lefty Kreh and Mel Krieger and Joan Wulff, the fluid strength and control and purpose in their casts.

Fly fishing is composed of many interrelated skills: poor approach will spook your quarry before you can strip line off your reel for the first time; too thick a leader will give a fish acute anxiety, and using too heavy a line for particular water will put a fish on a fast just as fast; the wrong fly—because of size or pattern or design—will draw no rise, no matter how brilliant the cast. But all other things being proper, you *must* cast well or you will catch few fish. And casting well—whatever you have been promised—ain't easy: it is the development of skills that will meet a couple of thousand special fishing situations, and that takes more than an hour.

Perhaps a fish is rising seventy feet away and cannot be approached closer—and you can only cast an honest sixty; or the wind is from the right and you don't know how to use a backhand cast; or you must hook to the left, or to the right, or get decent S-curves into your line if you want to avoid drag on a particular stretch of river; or you want to throw an especially heavy bass bug or a No. 24 Trico on a twenty-foot leader.

You are finally *there*, in the right place at the right time; you even have the perfect imitation of a dorothea, the fish's lunch. The fish is only a cast away . . . and that's too far.

Those situations occur far more frequently than I'm willing to admit.

I was fishing not long ago on a very shallow, very clear river with very large and very skittery trout. The fellow I was fishing with knew the river well, and I'd heard he was a truly great caster—though no hard chances had come his way that day.

We came around a back bend and together looked up a hundred-foot stretch of this water—narrow here, with a glassy surface, little cover, none of the water more than a couple of feet deep. As we stood beside each other, scanning the water for a feeding fish, I saw at once how difficult this river was. The shallow water meant that the fish had a tiny cone of vision and a fly would have to float within inches of their lies if they were even to see it. There were no trees, nothing to cast shadows, so the full light of a bright blue sky was over the water—and these fish suffered most from airborne predators; so anything moving, such as a fly line, would scare them silly. I took a step and the ripples and little waves went out thirty-five feet ahead of me. I moved an arm and a fish from the far bank darted madly upstream.

Ah, the sweet mad toughness of it.

We stood for five or ten minutes, still as poles, scanning the surface for a dorsal, a wake, a delicate rise. There were none. Then, where the current hit off a point seventy-five feet upstream and made a slight but discernible ten-foot foam line, a fish came up with authority. There were a few No. 18 Pale Morning Duns on the water, and they must have been what had brought this fellow up. Up he'd come, every minute or so—not much more frequently than that. I imagined him a wise old dog of a trout, fat and territorial, not given to feeding binges anymore, having a sweet tooth for these little sulphur bonbons. The way it lolled just under the surface, its dorsal out, and the steady, heavy way it moved, suggested it might be one of the larger fish in a river not known for its pikers.

I could not even contemplate the cast necessary to take such a fish. I knew just enough to know I'd botch it. You could not cast directly over the fish or it would surely bolt for safety. If you cast to the right and hooked the line left, the bulk of the line would fall on the shore. If you cast too roughly, by millimeters, no matter where the fly landed the fish would vanish. False casts would be disastrous. The water dropped off toward the left, and some brush there would make all but some brand of steeple cast impossible from that side—and such a cast inevitably would come down too hard. And you'd get one cast, no more: the water was too thin, the fish were too wary—like a Japanese brush painter, you'd have to catch it just right on the first try or try again some other time.

Five years ago I wouldn't have thought twice about turning such a fish over to the better fisherman. Now I thought twice and then decided to turn it over. I was a better caster now but not nearly good enough for this situation.

My friend grunted and said all right he'd try it, and then he stripped off a great number of coils of line, hesitated, and (without a false cast) made the most astonishing cast I've ever seen. I've always valued trout rivers precisely because they're so far from the modern technological world—but I'd have welcomed an instant replay this time. As best I can reconstruct what happened—and I have replayed it a dozen times—he cast partially *underhand* (so that the line never rose more than a foot off the surface of the water, and thus could be laid down lightly), he cast far to the *left*, across the stream (so the line never came near the fish); and then he hooked the line back to the right, so that the fly flipped up near the spit of land, several feet above the fish, caught the little line of current exactly, and came down over the place where the rise-form had been just a minute before. I should add that there was a brisk downstream wind against us and that the cast was comfortably seventy-five to eighty feet.

It was a magical moment.

I let out an immense gasp of air.

And the fish came up as nice as you please and took the fly.

* * *

Until I can cast eighty or ninety feet (honest count) with one false cast, lay my fly down like down on a dime, with an S-curve or a triple air-mend or a left hook, or whatever else is needed, I guess I'll keep trying. Fishing may not be a spectator sport, but I sure had fun watching that cast. Being able to make it myself would have been even more fun.

THE OLD MAN

The old man was there when I came out of the wood line and into the clearing, when I turned the last corner. At first I smiled when I saw him casting from a chair perched on one of the wooden ramps. The Connetquot had dozens of these ramps and I do not like them. "That's the life," I thought, "but not for me."

Then I saw that the old man was sitting in a wheelchair and that he held the slack line for his casts in his mouth.

I had walked briskly that bright, hot autumn afternoon—the last day of the season—and sat down for a few moments to rest at one of the bench-tables near the hatchery. From where I sat I could see only the old man's right side and back. He was using a small bamboo rod and cast ably—his loops tight, his forward thrust authoritative—but not very far. I could not see his face, but I could tell by the way he leaned forward and studied the water that he was intent at his work. And he was surely outfitted for the kill, with a long-handled net propped against the chair, an old wicker creel beside that, a full vest, and a khaki hat with a lamb's-wool band crammed with bright flies.

I watched for ten minutes. He would cast across and slightly upstream, follow the fly down with head and rod, then pick up, false-cast once, and cast again. He was catching nothing.

I knew this stretch of what had once been the famous old Southside Club and now was run as a state park. The several hundred yards above the hatchery were reserved for the handicapped and aged. He'd earned it on both counts. A neat little sign at the tail end of the run announced these restrictions. Once, several years ago, I came to the stretch from another road, for the first time, failed to see the sign, saw a dozen fish rising, and got an ego as big as the Ritz when I took just about all of them—and had to smile when I learned from where. The few hundred yards of sap-green water contained hundreds of trout. You could see them holding over the lighter sand bottom between the lines of elodea, or they would bust out from the darker patches of waterweed—three, four at a time—to chase a fly. Too many fish. Far too many. They were too hungry, too unselective. They lacked that critical eye without which gulling a fish becomes child's play.

The old man was catching none of them. His casts were true and the pretty little stream is so small here that he could reach across it. Perhaps his fly picked up too much drag; perhaps he used too large a fly; perhaps the water held fewer trout than the day I fished it. It was the last day of the season: maybe the fish had seen enough artificials and would starve before they'd chase another. I don't know. I rather wanted him to catch a trout. I rather wanted to see him play and land one. Then I would get on with my own affairs, those I had come for, the last rites of not an especially productive season.

Lulled by the quiet of the place and the warm afternoon, tired from my rush to get here, I leaned on an arm, watched the old man, and amused myself imagining this feeble old sport as a young man. Had he been a member of this club? Had he once fished the four-mile length of it, each run and pool of it? Did he resent being condemned to this one rather privileged spot, on a ramp? Did the river's new public role disturb him? Did he resent newcomers and plebians such as me and wooden ramps and the death of an old order? He was old enough—in his late seventies at least—to have fished in the twenties and thirties. What fabulous fishing he might have known! He might have known and fished with Hewitt and LaBranche and Jennings. He might have fished . . . well, anywhere; he might have caught wild trout in rivers that are polluted or madly crowded now, that were ruined before I saw my first fly. Had he been vigorous and adventurous once? Had he pioneered new waters? Had he been truly exceptional at this game, one of those private, unheralded masters at it—a man quite as good as the experts, and I have known a few, but quite uninterested in the public or commercial aspects of the sport? He certainly cast with distinction, though not far and not consistently well. Even his right arm creaked, hitched, failed to follow through. He was a very old man. Twice his fly slapped on the water. Once it hit an overhanging branch and luckily came free. Had he been disappointed, discouraged to the point of despair, when his body betrayed him? Who brought him here? A son perhaps. Maybe an abler, younger friend. Someone he had once fished beside, as an equal. He was dependent now, tethered to those who could and would help, a burden, an inconvenience. Were they condescending? Did they *pity* him? And what *had* happened to his body? A stroke? An accident? How long ago? His left hand appeared to move not at all; I could see that his legs were pinched together, thin under bulky pants, lifeless. Had he thought when all this happened that it was at last over for him—wading swift streams, tying cunning flies, pursuing sport and mystery and independence and perhaps—like me—his soul in moving water? Perhaps. And perhaps not. He might have been paralyzed fifty years ago, or thirty years ago, or after he retired; he might even have started to fly fish after this mangling of his body took place. Fly fishing in this fashion, as he now practiced it, might be the only kind he knew, his salvation. But I did not think so. There was something too intent in his manner, his gestures, too skillful in his cast. The man had once been a superb fly fisherman. And when you have once done something well, quite as finely and purely as you are able, there must be a deep humiliation in being reduced to such a state. Once his eyes might have seen the quick, bright wink of a trout underwater, on the far side of the river. Once he could fish all day, on any man's river, from first light until the hushed gray of dusk. Once he could fit a 7X leader point through the eye of a No. 20 fly the first time he tried. Once he could tie midges, wrap rods, move lithely in a river, become one with it. Once. Had he slipped slowly over the years, so slowly he could not feel the fine edge vanish? Was this to be his last time out, a final trip, a last fling at it before a winter he might not survive? Had he stopped *liking* to go out—worn down by the cruelty of expectations, the blunders, the memories? How much did he hurt from being unable to do what he had once done with such delight, what he was now reduced to practicing crudely and in the tamest of places?

I could not see his face. I could not tell.

Now and again he leaned perilously forward to get an extra foot or two to his cast. He strained. Then he put his fly firmly into an overhanging branch. He pulled the line taut with his mouth, grasped the line with his rod hand, pointed the rod at the place where it was hooked, and pulled straight back. He could not do it. On his third try I found myself rising from my seat to help him. On his fourth try the leader broke.

Then he retrieved line, brought the leader to his mouth, leaned the rod against the chair, secured a fly box, and out of my sight, fumbled for ten minutes before he was ready to fish again. He appeared now to have some little use of his left hand. Once he raised it—clawed and crabbed—and held the fly to the light. Before he cast, he let the fly hang loose from the propped-up rod, cupped his right hand under his right leg, and raised the leg and repositioned it a few inches to one side.

I went off then, restless as always, brooding, making up fantastic stories, remembering the boy I once was, barefoot in a mountain creek as clear as truth, as cold as snow.

As always, I was glad to be on the water. I piddled here and there and found a few large brookies camped under a long willow branch and coaxed them out; I made some blunders you'd have thought impossible; and after the sun had vanished and the sky was merely bright gray, I returned to clean my few fish on the bench-table near the hatchery.

I had forgotten the old man.

He was there on the ramp. But now his rod was sharply bent. Twenty-five feet downstream a heavy brook trout rolled and pocked the surface. The old man held his rod high and the arc grew sharper. Then the fish turned. Then, in a few minutes, I could see the white of it on the surface, and the man was transferring the rod to his crabbed left hand, supporting it between his legs. For a moment he faltered. I found myself rising to help him. Then he grasped the long-handled net with his right hand, lowered it, and scooped up the fish.

It was a pretty brookie, all right—plump, bright, about seventeen inches.

"Bravo," I said softly. "Well done! old man."

And then he turned, still holding his trout in the net; he turned, looked around him, saw me, held his trout a bit higher, and smiled. I saw his eyes. I looked closely, beyond the crabbed body, at his eyes. His eyes, large and bright behind thick glasses, were smiling, too.

WILD STRAWBERRIES

There is a picture of me taken last summer, holding a trout in one hand, a graphite fly rod in the other. I am standing near a cluster of lodgepole pine, near the brief falls of a meadow creek. It is a color photograph and the river is tawny, speckled with silver. The spots on the fish, a brookie, are bright red. I am quite ridiculously plump.

Dave took the photograph. We had followed the creek from its confluence with a famous trout stream high up into a second and then a third meadow. We had leapfrogged—first one of us fishing a bend or pool while the other watched, then the other fished. We are good old friends and it was a truly bright summer afternoon and we were in no particular hurry. So we fished slowly, and we talked when we felt like it, and we tried to make our few casts count.

Had someone been watching us from the tree line he could have told easily that the silver-haired man was by far the more adept fly fisherman. He would have seen that man show his portly friend how to stand ten or fifteen feet back from the bank and how to cast so that only the leader and fly rolled over the little hedgerow of grass that bordered the creek and fell into the water. Twice he would have seen the silver-haired man kneel, bend low, cast to a pool, wait, cock his head, and then suddenly strike. He might not have heard the splash behind the high tufts of grass, but he would have seen the rod bend in that happy arc and the portly man walk up quickly to be near his friend while each fish was played and released. Both fish were rainbows. They were as silver as the man's hair.

Had someone been watching, he would have seen that the portly man (whose girth was of such a fine, full dimension that it threatened to split his waders if—as he was told to do—he knelt) wasn't catching any. If there was some little trick or mannerism that his friend was employing, he did not see it. He managed to cast quite honorably; from a distance he might even have looked adept. And he quickly picked up the technique of dropping his fly over the grasses. But he caught nothing.

I looked back into the woods, wondering how we looked, but no one was watching us. We had the river very much to ourselves. I liked it that way. We followed the meandering creek from one S-turn to another, one after the other, and fished the deeper bends and a few of the back reaches where the creek narrowed to no more than several feet wide and was perhaps five feet deep. It was leisurely, fascinating fishing. There were sometimes big browns in such water, Dave said—alligators; he had caught them. They came up from the main river to escape the late-summer heat, and you had to tempt them with a large fly into doing what they did not particularly want to do. As I cast, I imagined a ridiculously large splash behind the tuft of grass and the fight of an eight-pound brown in such small water. The fish were there for the coolness of the water, for the respite, not for the regular business of foraging. But they could be caught.

Dave had tied the flies we used. In fact, they were a new version of an old and famous fly he had invented, and they imitated grasshoppers. We were a little early for grasshoppers, though there were a few small ones in the meadow, and perhaps we were a little early for the run of truly large trout out of the main river. Perhaps not. There were a few fish to be caught and Dave was catching most of them. That's a habit of his. The air had a habit, I remembered, of being warm and fresh on days such as this in Montana, and it was. The sky was brilliant blue, with evanescent shreds of clouds. On another day I might have been troubled that I was not catching any fish whatsoever, a habit of mine. This day it was more a source of quiet amusement than displeasure. I enjoyed seeing my friend catch a few good fish and I enjoyed hearing him tell me the fish had come to the fly "like a beggar to a five-dollar bill."

We had fished steadily for about two hours, leapfrogging, before we came to the second meadow. Here there were hot-spring seepages and a tawny tint to the water. All was wilder. The fields were flecked with the white, yellow, crimson, purple of wildflowers. The mud near the seepages bore the tracks of many elk, and we saw several elk back in among the pines. Along some stretches, the creek was no more than a few inches deep and a half-dozen feet across; there was no cover, no protection for a truly large fish here. What they wanted was what I had come up this creek for: a respite.

What a wearing, forgettable, wearying year it had been. How often I had felt like Eliot's "pair of ragged claws scuttling across the floors of silent seas"—quite unbrained, disembodied, and my body blowing up like a blimp. To pay the piper, the bamboo was gone, books would follow: a year without color or taste, without rivers, without words.

I had snatched at a chance to come West, but that first week had been a tumult of conferences. There is a business and a politics to fly fishing, even as there is to everything else. Some of it must be done, and often good people do it and advance the sport and protect such rivers as the one I was fishing, without which there would be no sport. I admired the work and many of the people who did it—but I had an itch to be alone, not in crowds. Now there were a few days and I wanted to see if rivers and woods could work their dark magic again. I had a few good tools left and I wanted simply to fish again.

The little creek was there—splattered with foam and winding its tawny way through curve after curve, down to the main river. It was the smallest of waterways, but it held promise. The big browns might be there. They might bust up behind the grasses and shatter my heart. Now and then I cast into the creek and waited, and then cast again.

In the late afternoon, I sat on some roots covered with lichen and moss, took off my glasses, smoked a pipe slowly, and watched Dave fish. He took several small fish, then stooped and poked into the grasses a moment. I thought he was collecting insects.

"You won't believe how these taste," he said, standing up.

"I'm not sure I'm ready to try."

When he came over to where I sat, I saw he had a handful of small wild strawberries.

A dozen of them were soft and crimson in my hand. You could not press them or they'd squash. I held them gingerly for a moment, then popped them, one at a time, into my mouth.

Dave picked a batch more and I put them all up to my mouth at once, smearing my lips. They were the choicest of foods, astonishingly sweet and tart, an emblem of something.

In a few minutes I stood, walked to the creek, and cast into the bubbles and swirls where the brief falls met in the pool. A fish snapped at the large grasshopper, hooked itself, fluttered at the surface, and I hoisted it in.

As I raised the fish, Dave said, "We really ought to record this trophy," and snapped his camera twice.

In the photograph, which I took out and grinned at a bit too often all year, the man is smiling rather smugly. The brookie—its little crimson spots the color of wild strawberries—is barely four inches long. The man appears to be either a lunatic or a clown. Or perhaps he's merely giddy with the pleasure of having returned to a thing he was born to do, and to write about, for as long as there are rivers and for as long as he has words to write and there are a few people who want to read them.

THE DIRECTOR

There was fear and trembling among the outfitters and guides of West Yellowstone when news reached them that "Fast-Fly" Lyons was scheduled to direct a month's program last summer at a local fly fishing and conservation foundation. And with good cause.

When ten thousand fly fishermen signed up for Fast-Fly's clinic, seminar, whatever it was, would any of them ever again need an outfitter or guide? Fast-Fly would surely give away all the best spots within fifty miles, instruct so that instruction would never again be needed, and offer cheap (Fast-Fly is nothing if not cheap) what else-where has become so dear.

In fact, Fast-Fly's first week was somewhat undersubscribed. He waited for an hour that first morning but no one appeared. He was a director with no one to direct. How could anyone pass up this mag-nificent cheap chance? he wondered. Clearly he was the bargain of a lifetime.

Finally, one customer showed up. Well, he did not actually show up. He left a message that he would be the tall, thin guy in the gray sweater in one of the local fly shops, and if Fast-Fly so chose, he could look him up. Fast-Fly did not hesitate to so choose. He ran to the shop in search of a tall, thin, gray sweater.

The lucky fellow's name was Les Ackerman, and he had been fishing the West Yellowstone area every day since early June. It was now late July and a Monday.

A truly wise guide neglects no opportunity to learn, even when he is learning from his customer. (One honest outfitter so represented himself in an advertisement several years ago—as someone who was not too proud to learn from those he guided—and is now apparently out of business, if he ever got any.) But Ackerman sounded as if he knew what of he spoke, and Fast-Fly thought he would give the man the unique opportunity to learn the guide's trade. So several times that week he suffered Ackerman to drive him to interesting new spots on the Madison and the Gallatin, and Fast-Fly watched his mentor-customer catch numerous fine and noble trout. Fast-Fly was not in the least troubled to learn that Ackerman, who was skillful with the long rod and knowledgeable about the how and where of local fishing, had begun to fly fish seriously only a year or so earlier. He did not write any articles about fly fishing; and he had read less than a dozen books about the sport; and not least, he lived in Dallas. He merely fished well and caught trout and was of wise counsel to Fast-Fly Lyons, who needed quite as much wise counsel that week as he could catch.

Meanwhile, in every spare moment, Fast-Fly whizzed around the middle Madison and the Henrys Fork and a dozen other rivers—for the West Yellowstone area has a great plethora of fine trout water, more than a man could fish in a lifetime—and he looked for spots where he might take his clients the next week—a week that would surely boast many times more clients. Hundreds, perhaps.

In pizza joints and from behind bushes, Fast-Fly listened for those telltale hints of where the big fish were. There were rumors that Hebgen Lake was hot and that Henrys was cold. Someone spoke of the Yellowstone's being high and the Gallatin's being low. Listening, in the West, can be a dramatic experience, given a certain high diction now and then. He heard that someone had lost "Mr. Plump" on the Madison, and someone else had been "hog haulin'" in the Canyon. Fast-Fly listened with wide eyes as Fred Arbona whispered half-sentences and hints about certain "tortugas" to be found in remote ponds—huge brookies, the size of logs, you couldn't believe the size of them, and when they nosed up to a little streamer you'd cast in the path of one of them, you'd nearly die of the tension. So Fast-Fly slept, that night and for many nights thereafter, while visions of tortugas danced in his head.

To sharpen his thinking, he floated one mighty river with a true guide one day, sponging up information he might later use. But when the Mackenzie River boat docked, a local angler's wife looked at him and said: "You're from New York. I could tell." Fast-Fly had not said a word. Now that he was a director, almost a true guide himself, he had been anxious—like Lawrence of Arabia—to be accepted by the natives and to become a native himself. How had this sensitive lady found out? What had he done wrong? And then he remembered that, when he took off his waders, his pants had come off, too, and it was clear that the good local people merely assumed that everyone from the East exposed himself.

The second week provided a unique opportunity.

There were no clients.

Not even Les Ackerman—who was signed up for every week but figured he'd learned enough about guiding, which was the only opportunity Fast-Fly could give him.

So Fast-Fly explored further. He accepted Dwight Lee's invitation to fish one evening up a road called Mosquito Gulch. This might be an absolutely unique place to take his clients the next week, when surely all of them would appear. Dwight had some trouble finding the spot up Mosquito Gulch, but then he finally did and they got out and followed the river for a mile downstream, where they fished steadily for a few hours and Fast-Fly was bitten so often by mosquitoes that he felt he had become a single throbbing lump. Had they caught more than three fish, no more than four inches long apiece, he might have remembered the spot, but on the long drive back to town he did everything he could to forget about the place. He would have thanked Dwight for the interesting new experience, but his lips had been bitten so thoroughly and enthusiastically by the mosquitoes that he could only mumble something about the need to make such a place well known to people to whom you'd like some harm to come.

It was not until the third week that some customers finally appeared, anxious to learn from that dazzling international sport Fast-Fly Lyons.

And despite his worst fears, the week went marvelously well.

The group could not have been made up, he thought, of nicer fellows. There was Russ Willis from Seattle and George Burrows from Michigan; Bill Johnson had come up from Texas, and Donn Griffith, a veterinarian, had driven in from Ohio. And Les Ackerman reappeared. Griffith, who was still learning the fly fisherman's skills, had a marvelous evening and was converted fully to the fly. Russ Willis, who could cast a fly half across the Madison—by virtue of a couple of decades of double-hauling for steelhead—needed only a quiet word or two about fishing the *edges* of the current in the Madison to have several startling evenings. And Johnson and Burrows both took fish, including several on the Henrys Fork on a particularly blistering summer evening. And the group talked about the rivers of the area and the need to protect them, and the essential message of conserving and protecting became an integral part of pursuing and catching.

So by Friday, Fast-Fly was quite pleased with himself and thought himself considerably abler than he'd thought, and he decided to share with his new friends a spot on the Firehole that he had once—six years earlier—fished with great success. It was one of his favorite spots, and he had been reluctant ever to take even his best friends there.

So they set out, in six cars, and slowly wended their way into Yellowstone Park. He felt it incumbent upon himself to stop and point to an elk in the run above Grasshopper Bank and a series of deep holes about which they had spoken during a slide show the night before, and he felt really quite comfortable in this role of genial guide until he turned off the main highway onto a dead-end road and went about a mile and then realized, with a shock, that he didn't have the foggiest idea where he was.

This was a terrible predicament.

It was a miserably hot August afternoon and he was on a dead-end road and he really had no idea whether his secret spot was or was not within twenty miles of where he stopped.

There was no room for the six cars—patiently waiting one after the other—to turn around. He had no idea what was ahead, other than a dead end. And he was pouring sweat and wondering whether he should just throw up his hands, abandon the car, and run to the tree line and live thereafter with the bear and the moose.

But he got a good grip on himself, walked pleasantly past three cars without saying a word, and stopped next to Bill Johnson's station wagon. This was a stroke of genius. Johnson, a wise old Texan, told him exactly where they were and how to get to the section of the Firehole he wanted to fish, and Fast-Fly swore eternal loyalty to this good man who should have been guiding him.

But when they got to the secret section of the Firehole and tested the water, it was at once clear to Fast-Fly that he had made a small miscalculation. The Firehole did not fish best in August. It was better for bathing in August—or for boiling eggs.

Well, Fast-Fly is safely back in the East now, and the guides and outfitters of West Yellowstone are surely safe from his devastating raids and depredations, and he's fixed his trousers and vowed never to guide again—should someone go perfectly loony and ask him—and he deeply appreciates the nice Christmas card he got from one of his clients, quoting the immortal words of Ann Landers, otherwise not much of an authority on the subject: "If you want to catch a trout, don't fish in a herring barrel."

WHERE TO GO

I was in Vernal, off U.S. 40 in northeastern Utah, pursuing with my friend Thom Green rumors of gargantuan bluegill—which, from where I come, is a long way to go for bluegill—when Thom told me: "You realize, Nick, that you have an obligation to your readers to tell them exactly where you've been."

I was not so sure.

"Let them find their own bonanzas," I said.

"That's the wrong attitude. That's what they're buying the magazine to have you do for them. That's what you're paid to do."

"Not that I've found so very many hot spots," I said reflectively.

"Still, when you do—"

"But do you know what happens when someone announces such a place in a magazine with one hundred thousand or two million readers? Such publicity can wreck a river or a lake overnight. Someone goes there a year later and they think you've lied; but you've really *caused* the disaster. There are places, Thom, where you can get trampled to death during a Green Drake hatch because someone has been just a little too explicit about his where-to-go."

Thom knew that. He had seen it happen. But he insisted I had an obligation.

"The first thing," I said, "you get none of the solitude that brought you there. Everyone and his mother-in-law are suddenly flogging the river to its doom. Then the size of the fish goes down. One year the average size is five pounds, the next it's three, and then you're fishing for guppies. If someone's subscription is a month late, they're liable to find something that looks like a New York street after a blackout." I was becoming hysterical; nothing looks quite that bad.

"Still," Thom said, "that's what you've been paid to do; that's what readers want. They get two weeks' vacation and they want reliable information, not mystery lakes. You shouldn't take an assignment if you don't expect to produce hard facts."

"But does everyone want to vacation where everyone else is vacationing? If you tell everyone about a posh lodge in Canada that costs three thousand dollars a week, you won't get many takers, not with taxes what they are, but if you mention a public river, you'll spoil it. No. I'd rather go into the worm business than become a popularizer of secret spots. Some writers even make a profession of such discoveries, to the loss, Thom, of their immortal souls. I saw one writer photographed on *four* different rivers—all of which are now on the decline—with the same eight-pound brown trout!"

Thinking of photographs of big fish, we could not help noting, as we walked in and out of several Vernal tackle shops, that all had dozens of unique shots pasted on the walls near the cash register. They were Polaroids mostly, with one unusual feature in common: they were of positively gigantic trout. Eight-, nine-, and ten-pound fish. We had not come for trout, but these were irresistible. Were they from Flaming Gorge? Perhaps we could catch some on a fly designed to imitate the reservoir's principal trout food: Rapala lures. No. They were from Jones Hole Creek.

Anyway, we were in a regional storm and the lake we had intended to fish was unfishable. Perhaps we could amble over and snoop around this new discovery.

Jones Hole Creek. What a lovely mysterious name. And true. You can find the place on any local map. And those big trout, dozens of them, had all come from Jones Hole Creek within the past two weeks. No question about it. Here was an unexpected story: "Lyons Clobbers Trout in Unknown Bonanza." I had written some stories on which bored Madison Avenue editors, in a fine frenzy, had slapped such a title—but I had never found more than two cents' worth of a bonanza in my life.

Nor was there any mystery about the place. Not only would the tackle dealers readily tell of the creek, but the Vernal Chamber of Commerce had a printed map of how to get there, which looked simple enough. How to get there. Ah, dear. Not only "where" but "how." The ultimate sin. Well, this time I would see and catch and tell. The townspeople, photographed in flagrant numbers and in flagrant pride with their monster trout, did not seem shy or secretive. If they did not care, why should I? Let Jones Hole Creek be damned.

So we started out, Thom and I and also W. Earl West, Jr., and Dr. Ed Reasoner from Casper, Wyoming, in Ed's van—and I swore to them all that I would tell everything this time, the whole truth.

It was only a forty-mile drive, mostly over paved road (except, the brochure mentioned, from mileage 16 to 25.5). For my readers I want to be very explicit about how to get to Jones Hole Creek. At mileage 2.9 there is a junction, at which you take the left road. You take the left road again at 7.8 and then the right road, across Brush Creek, at 10.0. At 15.7 there is another junction and you must keep left; the right road is a dead end. The sagebrush begins to give way to cedar and piñon pine here, the brochure says, but frankly I did not notice: we were climbing slowly upward now, hitting the unpaved section (which I did notice), and executing a series of sharp horseshoe turns on a dirt road with no railings. Actually the road is not dirt after a rain. It had rained quite heavily that particular morning. We squooshed our way up the sloshy, muddy ruts, looking down into an eight-thousand-foot drop. My stomach felt approximately that deep.

"Put the car into low gear," said Earl.

"Mind your own business," said Ed.

I was not particularly in the mood for bad Casper, Wyoming, jokes and elected at 21.2 miles not to look out the window anymore, not even when Earl pointed to Diamond Mountain and told the story of how two 1870s hustlers named Arnold and Slack salted it with diamonds and got a San Francisco syndicate to raise $10 million; those investors must have been as light-headed as I now was. At least not many people could travel a road like this: Jones Hole Creek was surely loaded with lunkers. Those in the pictures were the size of baseball bats.

After having not spoken for fifteen minutes, nor done anything but pray quietly, I launched compulsively into a story I once heard about a man who came back to an eastern hotel with several outsized brook trout. When asked where he got them, he gave detailed instructions ending with the general caution: "One small problem, though. Rattlesnakes. Once you get past the fallen oak and the quicksand, if the mosquitoes—they're the size of hummingbirds—don't get you, the rattlesnakes will. They lie on the rocks, dozens of them. I've seen them hanging from the trees. But those brookies! You really ought to try Rattlesnake Creek."

I finished the story and Thom said, No. Jones Hole Creek could not possibly have rattlers. The Chamber of Commerce recommended the trip for little kiddies, along with Dinosaurland. It had to be safe.

At 22.3 we passed Diamond Gulch Junction on the plateau. At 25.5, hallelujah, we reached paved road again; but at 31.0 we began a severe descent into the narrow and rugged canyon that I was quite sure would be my final sight. It was not. At 40.0 we finally reached the Jones Hole National Fish Hatchery that stood at the head of the creek. The forty miles had taken nearly two hours. I was limp. Had I traveled all this distance to fish in a hatchery?

Now the sun suddenly made a bright appearance; the wind stopped. We saw dozens of birds working in the pit of the canyon. Not only had we found a bonanza, but we were surely there at precisely the right time—there was a gigantic hatch in progress—and not one car in sight!

Unfortunately, a few people had found Jones Hole Creek before us, which was where they fished, not in the hatchery. An old Fish and Game hand with a narrow, bumpy face and the scratchy voice of truth said: "Well, there was some big fish in the crik. Mighty big fish. They come up from the Green for a couple weeks in the early spring. But there ain't none anymore. No, sir. You bet."

"Have they gone back down?" I asked.

"Didn't have no chance to," he said. "We had three hundred people a day up here for two weeks. They got about every one of them trout, you bet. There ain't none anymore. All fished out. Not a one left. No, sir. All gone."

We spent an hour verifying his story. Jones Hole Creek proved to be a spritely little brook, spring fed, clear as fresh tap water, filled with watercress and rich in streamlife. Mayflies and caddis were hatching profusely. But the old guy was danged right. You bet.

A couple of days later we pursued a rumor that Ray Lake in Wyoming was yielding ten-pound brown trout. The lake had been closed by the Indians of the Wind River Reservation for four years and it sounded like a sure bonanza. But we discovered, five hundred miles later, that it was infested with carp. Thom got a couple on flies, big ones, three- or four-pounders, and they were rolling and jumping out there as if it was a hustlers convention.

I could tell you exactly how to get there from Jones Hole Creek. But that might be more than you want to know.

ON MY BRAVE WIFE

The other night, sitting with two fly fishing friends, addicts both, who had come over to see my new seven-and-a-half-foot Kushner rod—an extraordinary instrument—I mentioned a trip I'd taken with my wife and oldest son to a remarkable valley in Colorado. My voice beginning to rise, I recalled the long haul over dirt roads, the frequent false trails we'd followed, following the briefest hint, from a friend's letter, that at the end of our trek we'd find one of those rare untrammeled corners of the trouter's world.

I have followed slenderer trails—and usually found less than I'd sought. It is the fisherman's way, exploring, and I shall follow such slim promises until I follow no more trails at all.

I spoke of that first sight of it—bright and silver through the trees, the river—after three hot summer hours on dusty roads; and of how we found a pleasant ranch along the bank, paid a modest rod fee (I had only enough money with me for one rod, so Paul and I would share), and went down to the water.

Mari came in with coffee, smiled, and stopped to listen patiently. My voice was quite shrill now, my eyes huge. Having made conspicuously little headway in interesting her, ever, in any matter piscatorial, I rarely allow the fevers to take me when she is present anymore. Still, we had found a happy truce. I lived that part of my life a bit more inwardly and she began to take her watercolors to riverbanks, perhaps because the mosquitoes seemed to bite less when she was working.

I knew she loved this valley. We'd spoken often of it. We'd even asked whether there might not be a few acres for sale, along the river. It is an isolated place, desolate for some, far from any town, far from any of the modern world's entertainments. One defiles such a valley by bringing anything but oneself. If one brings enough, the valley provides all else. Its long sloping and overlapping hills, spotted with small pine and hemlock, give way to broad, lush meadows; snow-blotched peaks reign at a great distance; cows grace the fields with their slow, heavy grace; and a bright dancing river runs through the heart of the place.

Peace. I'd never been to a place so peaceful.

Deep, quiet, lasting peace. Like a rare elixir.

Mari felt that way, too: I knew it.

In the winter, we learned, the snow was ten feet deep and the elk herds raided the cow barns; in late spring, the river was high, unfishable, but already the meadows were spotted yellow and purple with wildflowers. Then, in August, when we came, the waters came down and the river was a mecca: quick glides, riffles, bend pools studded with boulders and fallen trees. The water was emerald. The river was just small enough for the fly fisherman to touch its hiddenmost secrets, large enough for demanding casts and large trout. We saw no other fishermen along twenty miles of it.

And it was gorgeous.

"The whole valley was gorgeous, wasn't it, Mari?"

"Absolutely," she said with genuine enthusiasm. "I'd move there tomorrow."

Emboldened by her interest, I let my voice touch a wild note or two and went on to tell how Paul and I had gone upstream to the first great bend pool while Mari got out her watercolors. It was late afternoon and the valley was hushed. I was going to ask her to verify what happened next—how we'd seen a good trout turn in the current, fished for it with a Rio Grande King, taken it, taken three others in rapid succession, first Paul, then I, all fat wild rainbows, fourteen to eighteen inches—but I remembered suddenly, three years later, that Mari had not showed. We'd met her back at the car, after dark.

I squeezed my memory and it came up with roses: she hadn't been bitten to shreds by no-see-ums, there had been no visible scowls on her face, she'd seemed positively beatific.

At the time, I'd asked her nothing. Paul and I had been in a state of acute neurotic joy: we'd finally taken fifteen or so fish, all over fourteen inches, all spectacular jumpers. We'd never budged from our position just to the left of a boulder where the current broke and swirled. We'd said little. Mostly we'd smile when another fish rose and was properly struck, each turning to the other with an electric jerk, knowing and feeling together. His line went out more deftly with each cast; his reflexes were better than mine.

On the way back we relived it a dozen times, saw a slew of deer in the headlights, and were still in a trance when we returned to our cottage.

"Did they really get that many? That size?" one of my friends asked Mari. They were no worse than me: off the river, I rise regularly to such tales, demand proof and detail.

"Ask Paul," I said.

"He's just another fisherman. I asked Mari."

"They said so," she said.

"You didn't actually *see* it all?" the other asked. "There are rumors that Nick *never* catches any fish."

"They may be true," I muttered, taking back the Kushner and simulating a little side cast toward the pocket between the couch and the bookcase.

"No. I was busy," Mari said placidly.

"Painting?" I asked.

"No."

"You didn't spend the whole time in the car, did you? The sunset was incredible."

"No. I saw it. I got a good long look."

"Maybe *she* caught more trout herself, downstream," one of those jokers said, "and didn't want to embarrass you."

"Not hardly," she said, laughing.

"Well, what did you do?"

"If you must know," she said, "I got out my watercolors as I'd planned, went through the barbed-wire fence to the bank of the river, and sat down to work."

"I never saw that watercolor," I said. "I'd like a watercolor of that spot."

"I'd made a good start—a rather greenish landscape, of the river and some willows on the far bank, with a few cows off in the meadow, when I saw a black bull on my side of the water rear up, lower its head, and start toward me at a trot. I dropped half the paints, smeared the painting badly, and got behind the fence just in time. It was after me, all right. I ripped my dress and put a bad gash in my left ankle—"

"I don't remember a cut on your left ankle," I said.

"On fishing trips you don't often look at my left ankle. Anyway"—she was speaking in a perfectly normal, mild-mannered tone, and there was even a Madonna-like smile on her face—"I put the watercolors in the car and sat at the base of that huge rock hill a little downstream. You remember. The one about eighty feet high, of crushed boulders. The valley was exceptionally beautiful, so peaceful, and I was watching the way the hills changed color as the sun dropped, thinking of Turner, hoping you and Paul were having a good time—you'd dashed off so quickly I didn't have a chance to wish you good luck—when I saw something move out from one of the rock crevices just below me."

"Good grief."

"It was a snake. About six feet long." She held out her hands, but they didn't go far enough. "Black. Making a rustling sound. Flicking its tongue. Slithering toward me."

"No!"

"Oh, yes. So I fumed and scrambled right up that huge hill of rocks."

"You can't climb rocks!"

"You never saw anyone climb them faster. I shot up, bruising both knees, one elbow, my jaw, scratching my—"

"I never noticed," I said quite sheepishly.

"You never noticed!" said my friends, the Andrews sisters.

"It was dark when we got back," I explained.

"Anyway," Mari continued, her voice like honey, "I finally got to the top, looked back, almost fell down, and then turned at some noise and saw the hugest, shabbiest, fiercest wolf of a dog I've ever seen. It was growling in a low, steady growl and gnashing its huge teeth, and I almost fell down . . . where the snake was."

I couldn't say a word.

"That dog kept gnashing and growling for a full five minutes while I stood shivering with absolute terror on the tip of the rocks. Oh, yes. I could see clearly. All the time. The sunset was exceptional."

I looked at my friends. They were on the edges of their chairs.

"But then," Mari said, "a young boy came along."

I breathed deeply.

"He was quite young, but he was whittling on a stick with a ten-inch knife and looked like he'd come from the nearest reformatory—and he had the short butt of a cigar in the corner of his mouth, and his eyes . . ."

And the story went on, another ten minutes of it, interrupted by the chorus chanting, "Peaceful valley!" "Brave woman!" "Brute."

When she was done, she smiled pleasantly and excused herself; she was rereading Henri Focilon on "The Life of Forms in Art."

My friends shook their heads in unison; they positively refused to look at my new fly rod, though I'd especially wanted them to feel how much more power the second, heavier, tip gave the rod. Finally, one of them said: "And she didn't say a thing until now? Three years later?"

"First I've heard of it," I said glumly, beginning to put the rod into its cloth bag.

"Remarkable."

"A brave, wise woman."

"All that ammunition and she's never used it. Jean would have . . ."

A few minutes later, they got up to leave. But first they went into the dining room where Mari, demurely, was reading.

Reverently, as if she was the sainted herald of a world that might be, they placed kisses upon the forehead of my brave wife.

I noticed, for the first time, she had a thin, white scar on the tip of her chin.

LEFTY AND ME

There is a photograph of the great Lefty Kreh holding up a gargantuan tarpon. Lefty is straining and smiling while with both hands he grips the rope of a flying gaff whose point protrudes from the huge fish's lower jaw. The tarpon—so vast a fish that only its head and a quarter of its body show in the picture—must be six or seven feet long, perhaps one hundred and twenty pounds. Lefty's huge barrel chest is prominent.

"So that's what saltwater fishing is all about," I thought when I first saw the picture. "And on a fly! What an event."

Preston Jennings found saltwater fly fishing "too athletic," but Sparse tells me that George LaBranche, in his last years, forwent the pleasures of a dry fly in fast water for the lure of fast bonefish on the flats. Frank Woolner, that sweet, crusty surf-fishing master, whetted my interest in the salt, and then so did Art Flick, with tales of snook and trout and tarpon fishing down south. And the late Charles Ritz, at a luncheon in New York City, positively rose from the table and shouted to me when I asked him about saltwater fly fishing: "Ahhh. It is only for the strong man with a hard stomach. It is like sex after lunch!"

He was past eighty at the time.

So I began to dream of gigantic tarpon, leaping snook, savage bluefish, of tussles that made my arms ache and my stomach collapse.

Lyons against anything that roamed the sea! Against stripers, barracuda, dogfish, redfish, permit, anything. Against white sharks, sperm whales, even!

Yes. I'd try it. I'd grown a soft belly but I'd been athletic enough in my salad days; I could stand it. I could stand a dose of such monsters very comfortably, indeed.

So I began to take a heavy fly rod for a No. 9 line with me whenever I knew I'd be within ten miles of a beach. I even bought a batch of huge saltwater poppers to go with the Lefty's Deceivers the master himself had given me.

But for several years I never uncased the rod. The wind was bad, the boat's motor conked out, the fish were too far offshore.

Then, last summer, I managed to engineer a three-week vacation on the island of Martha's Vineyard, off lower Cape Cod, and vowed: I will not leave this place until I take a blue on the fly rod.

Strong words. Determined words. The words of a man who will do what he says.

I had a very clear image of an evening, four years earlier, when the blues were careening back and forth along Lobsterville Beach near Gay Head, so close I could flick a cigar butt out and they'd slash at it. I'd take them. A dozen. Two dozen perhaps. And right from the shore.

I fitted my largest fly reel with more than one hundred yards of twenty-pound-test Dacron, triple-tested the knot joining fly line to backing—making sure it was not only firm but would slip through the guides smoothly—and bought a coil of single-strand wire to make into three-inch shock tippets.

When the blues did not show the first evening, I was scarcely troubled. I still had nearly three weeks: they'd be in, and I'd be ready. To prepare myself, I decided I'd better practice casting. So one night, while everyone else was merrily flinging three-ounce plugs and catching nothing, I decided I'd just as well catch nothing with my fly rod.

I rigged up carefully, clipped off my leader to about seven feet, attached the wire and then the fly, and got a tremendous shock: I couldn't cast the thing ten feet. Now, I've seen movies of Lefty casting a saltwater fly, and it's obviously as easy as tossing a ball. The long line goes back effortlessly, there's a double tug, and then the line shoots out and out . . . and out. I had resigned myself to half, maybe a quarter that distance, but not this. I'd juggled the pacing of my cast with a bass bug, but I'd never had this problem. The huge popper jerked back like an apple on a string, dropped, hooked upward, turned in a gigantic, flopping motion when I brought it forward, and collapsed on the surface. It was not a graceful affair.

I tried harder.

The results were worse.

I tried to let the line lengthen more slowly behind me, to let the popper straighten before pushing it forward. A bit better but not much. I clipped my leader back to *three* feet: it was thick enough to spook a Battenkill brown a mile upstream. Now the big popper straightened more easily behind me, rolled out with fewer somersaults.

Still not far enough. Without the double-haul, without an even heavier rod, I was quite doomed not to be able to reach any fish that did not seriously want to feed close enough for me to spit on its dorsal fin. And the wind? It made bird's nests of even my best efforts. And the whole affair was positively dangerous: that 2/0 hook came winging past my ears and jugular, slammed into my sunglasses once, whacked me on the back so hard I thought I'd been shot.

So I put my long rod away and waited and watched. Each day I went to the beach with my children and looked for birds working, for some disturbance on the water that would indicate feeding fish close to shore. I listened for reports. I checked the tackle shops every day. Nothing. The fish weren't in. No one knew where they were.

Then, several days before we had to leave, I spotted some kids on a dock catching an occasional snapper blue—baby bluefish perhaps six inches long—on spinning rods. I'd caught snappers at Sheepshead Bay when I was their age, dozens of them on a cane pole and frozen spearing. Perhaps. It was better than nothing, and I could surely use my fly rod.

I bought some small freshwater streamers with Mylar or tinsel bodies, rebuilt my leader to eight feet, with a 3X tippet, and began to explore.

In Menemsha, where the Pond fed into a channel and washed into the bight, there was a strong current on either the incoming or outgoing tide; the wind was minimal. If you squinted, the moving water looked exactly like a river; and if you looked closely, you could find little eddies, backwaters, and breaks in the steady flow where snappers might hold, where bait fish—buffeted by the tidal surge—

might cluster. I slipped on my waders and sloshed to within forty feet of one such hole.

For years I have followed the Numbers Game with morbid fascination: this expert caught forty-three trout in two hours, that one got twenty-seven at dusk. Were I ever by wild chance to catch more than five at one time, I'm sure I'd lose count. I fish for fun, not to improve my mathematical skills. But I caught a hundred, maybe two hundred snappers in the next few days.

There was action on every cast. Four, five of the silver-blue darters would lunge at the fly, hit it once, twice, three times before they hooked themselves. They tore the half dozen streamers to shreds, to the bare hook, with only a few strands of impala or squirrel tail holding desperately to the shank; they chewed up three bluegill poppers—leaping over each other to get up at them. What savage beasts! They rose and charged and swirled and ganged up on every fly I cast to them—and they were just where trout might have been, in the eddies and breaks. Pound for pound—though they were admittedly only six or seven to the pound—they were the scrappiest, snappingest fish this side of the piranha, even if they took me nowhere near my backing. Anthony, my thirteen-year-old, got a dozen and a half one evening—on flies: and they taught him as much about fly rodding as bluegills had once taught me. We brought a batch of them home that night and we fried them like smelt, dipped in beaten eggs and rolled in bread crumbs, and they were delicious.

All in all, I was feeling very damned happy with myself—having caught *something;* having caught my first saltwater fish on flies; having surely caught more fish per hour than *anyone,* ever—until I thought of Lefty's tarpon, a photo I once saw of Mark Sosin with a huge fly-caught permit, and a movie of Lee Wulff whopping a couple-of-hundred-pound marlin on a fly rod.

Snappers!

Well, I might have said, had I been pressed, that I'd caught several hundred bluefish. They *were* bluefish.

* * *

I'd had great fun—which I always have when I fish—but as usual it really didn't add up to very much. I could even have fished for these bluefish after lunch without much of a twinge in my stomach.

Always prepared, I'd asked my daughter, Jennifer, to follow me around with a camera. She got one memorable photograph of me smiling and straining to release a bluefish approximately six inches long, seven to the pound, fly-caught. The sunset is gorgeous. My barrel belly is prominent. The fish doesn't show.

VERY MINOR TACTICS ON
AN ENGLISH CHALKSTREAM

An English chalkstream is a gentle, pastoral part of this frantic world. Limpid green and translucent, the river glides clear and steadily over flowing waterweed. Here and there a swallow or martin or finch dips and glides. Herefords graze in the lush meadow. Protected for centuries, guarded by riverkeeper and rule and club fiat, the water and its world are much like they were a thousand years ago. Yet on such gentle waters, within the frame of carefully fashioned codes, mighty dramas often transpire.

From a busy week in London, an American went one morning recently to the "Wilderness" section of the River Kennet in Berkshire, one of the noblest of the chalkstreams. The Kennet, carefully tended by the good riverkeeper Bernard, grows lusty trout to test the highest art of skilled fly fishers. John Goddard, who has taken three- and four-pound brown trout from these noble waters, usually passes the stern test. The American could not have had a better guide. And he had the company of Timothy Benn to advise him wisely about tactics.

The American had been to this river before. He had fished the Kennet several years earlier, for twelve hours. There were good trout in the Kennet—two- and three-pound browns—and he had seen many of them that day. You had to be careful to see the fish before the fish saw you, and the fish should be "on the fin," feeding. That was the code. You fished to the fish; you did not fish the water. And you fished only upstream, with a floating line. Often you had to kneel so that the trout would not see you, and the American marveled later that he had spent most of that day in the praying position, although, perhaps mistakenly, not for spiritual guidance. Often the casts had to be guided with deft skill through the maze of low branches, back branches, and high border weeds; the American only sometimes managed this but felt his flies lent a festive touch to the trees. And the trout spooked easily. The American had not gotten one of those large Kennet browns to move toward one of his flies.

But for two years he had dreamed of the river, and his dreams were mingled with the most cunning scheming. This time he was not without strategies. He had studied the minor tactics. He had learned the puddle cast. And he carried his lucky net.

But then, that morning, working hard and fishing to two or three good trout on the fin, he'd moved precisely no fish. He was not up to it. It was my youth, he thought in a paroxysm of shame, misspent worming and spinning. I am unworthy. And there is too little time to train the eye and hand for such noble work, let alone cleanse the soul.

The three had a pleasant lunch near the river, drank some wine, ate pâté, laughed, told tales, and then headed out again. Neil Patterson, a young friend who lived on the river and would meet them later, had left a map for the American indicating that in the upper region there were some "very interesting trout." It was good, the American thought, to know young men who knew interesting trout.

The wine had been cool and pleasant and the American had perhaps drunk a glass too much of it, which made three. He did not count as one of his very few virtues the ability to drink much wine or to remember the names of the wines he had drunk. They all sounded French. The afternoon was warm and he had eaten well and he had had that extra glass of wine, and he was feeling very content and hopeful when John Goddard spotted a steadily rising fish of about two pounds at the head of a broad pool. This proved to be a most interesting trout. Despite two slap casts, three linings, and an hour of more delicate work, the fish was still rising merrily to naturals with very slow, very deliberate rises. He is lunching at Simpson's, the American thought, and he has paid a pretty ten pounds sterling for the privilege and he will not be disturbed by the traffic on the Strand or the punk-rock crowds at the Lyceum. He is quite intent on the business at hand and knows precisely what he has ordered.

So the American was pleased when John Goddard called downstream, "When you've had enough of him, come up here. I've spotted an interesting fish." Timothy Benn, who had taken a fine two-pounder that morning, positioned himself upstream with a camera to record properly the confrontation of the American with this new interesting trout.

The fish was feeding in a one-foot eddy behind a knobby root on the opposite side of the river. The American knew that the fish would not move an inch from that spot any more than the Simpson's trout would be disturbed at his selective lunching. He knew that an exceptional cast was needed—upstream, with some particular loops of slack, in close to the bank—for the fly to catch the feeding lane and float into the trout's dining room without drag. A puddle cast.

After four short casts and another two that led to drag, the American was sure he could not manage this minor tactic. It was subtler fishing than he was used to, and he was not impressed with his ability to move Kennet trout. But he had not put it down. The occasional sip-rises in the eddy continued. The fish might be quite large.

And the American managed an able puddle cast beyond his wildest hopes and the fly floated a foot or two and went calmly into the trout's domain, and he heard someone whisper, "He'll come this time," and miracle of miracles, the trout did.

The trout rose, was hooked, made a low jump, came clear of the stump and then streaked downstream, its back bulging the surface, its force bending the bamboo rod sharply. A very good fish. Better than three pounds.

From that point on, the American was not sure why he acted the way he did. Perhaps it was that he had just read something about getting below a fish, which proved that fishermen should read fewer books. Perhaps it was the extra glass of wine. More likely it was pure panic.

The American bolted. He began highstepping downriver, busting, bursting the pastoral quiet of the chalkstream with his wild splashes. He heard one of his companions, in a high, incredulous, voice ask: "*Where* are you going?"

The trout, which had never witnessed a performance like this, and considered it extremely poor form, raced farther from the area in sheer embarrassment.

Then the American did something else he later could not explain. With the trout still green, he grasped for his lucky net.

The net was of the teardrop variety and had been bought in the Catskills and treasured for many years. The American carried it loose in his ArctiCreel, where it was safe from the brush. In fact, only a half hour earlier he had advised his English friends that this was a much more suitable net than the long-handled nets they carried, and that it could be carried in the creel, safe from the brush, out of harm's way, until needed.

The American grasped the handle of the net and wrestled it from his creel. In so doing, out came his fly box. This was his prized fly box, a Wheatley, the most expensive kind of Wheatley, with compartments on both sides, and he had filled it for this trip with some of his choicest flies—flies by Flick and Troth and Whitlock and Leiser.

The fly box twisted in the meshes of the tangled net bag, teetered on the rim while the American did a jig and a hop, midstream, then popped free and landed open on the limpid water of the Kennet and began to float serenely off to the left.

The trout was headed right.

The gentleman with the camera was reloading film at the precise moment the American had to choose between the fly box and the trout, so there is no visual record of the sudden swerve to the left, the deft netting of one fat Wheatley fly box; and since the trout had turned the bend, no one except the American saw the roll on the surface and the positive smirk as one very interesting trout rejoiced that on the other end of the line there had been such a raving maniac.

Later, the men gathered near the bridge on the main river and drank a bit more wine. Neil Patterson and another pleasant member of the club were with them now, and there was good talk and the spirited camaraderie uniquely possible along trout streams. Someone suggested that the Simpson's trout was merely one of Patterson's tethered pets, and someone else suggested that it was good the American's fly had pulled loose from the interesting trout because Bernard did not like his Kennet browns festooned like Christmas trees. The American was quietly satisfied that he would never have stooped quite so low as that.

Then John Goddard mentioned the big trout beneath the bridge and the American was invited to have a go at him. Not for me, he thought. Old Oscar—the not-to-be-caught behemoth brown. Not *that* fish—and not with *this* audience.

But the fish was high in the water, on the fin, taking the odd sedge a few feet under the bridge, and in a few moments, unable to resist, the American was tying on a Colorado King with shaky hands, squinting into the angular sun. And a few moments later he had made a truly classic puddle cast, holding the rod high and stopping the line short so that the current had three feet of slack to consume before the fly dragged.

The fly came down three inches from Old Oscar's nose. The chorus of onlookers, standing in a semicircle behind him, grew ominously silent. Old Oscar turned and floated down with the fly a few inches. The chorus audibly released breath, in a quiet whoosh.

Old Oscar took.

And the American struck, with no time to think of all the subtle minor tactics he had learned . . . and neatly snapped the fly off in the fish.

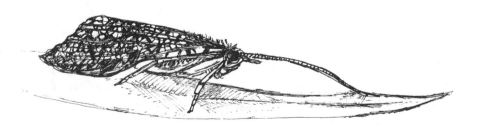

IN A FISHING HUT

In a fishing hut on the Benhams water of the River Kennet in Berkshire, I ate a sloppy cucumber sandwich, drank a mild white wine, and listened with the rest of the company gathered out of the storm as the stories began.

There was one about a lunatic who fished with bait and tied the line to his left big toe and got pulled in by a conger eel.

"I think someone is pulling our toe," said John Goddard, and he told a long, slow, very droll tale about a back cast that deftly hooked the ear of a Holstein cow, which then took off in high dudgeon across a muddy field, making the reel truly scream.

"They'll give you a great fight on light tackle," someone said.

It was warm in the fishing hut. The riverkeeper had started up a bright red fire in the cast-iron stove, I had caught my first Kennet brown that morning, and there was a profusion of food on the low center table and bottles of wine and thermos bottles of hot tea and coffee. From the open farmers' market in Newbury, Tim had bought fresh bright-yellow butter, rolls, cucumbers, a couple of different cheeses, a local pâté, and some sweet rolls—a feast. John had his usual pantry of delicacies. Hoagy and Kathy and Ross had their basket, and we were all sharing and drinking a little and bemoaning the fact that The Mayfly (important enough to be capitalized like that) had all but passed and the trout were surely glutted, and probably, anyway, it would be impossible to catch anything with such a sharp downstream wind in such a cold, pelting rain. Still, I had taken one—no matter that John had called: "What is it? A trout? Is that *really* a trout?"

When we came to the little wooden fishing hut, I had pointed out to Mari a few of The Mayfly spinners caught in spiderwebs at the edges of the windows. *Ephemera danica.* It is a big fly, only a bit smaller than our Green Drake, and often it itches and goads every fish in the river to feed on the surface. Some of the stories, which were by now mingling like the fresh pipe and cigar smoke in the tiny room, concerned the awesome spectacle of The Mayfly. Someone said he had seen eight regularly feeding fish in fixed positions in the lower end of the huge mill pool and had taken all eight of them, just like that, carefully, in order. Someone else had taken fifty-five pounds of brown trout one day during The Mayfly last year. Merely two days ago, Neil Patterson said, he could positively have *promised* me a dozen trout.

This did not trouble me overly. I have been there before. Aren't I always a couple of days late, a week early? Times too numerous to mention. And anyway, I had taken my first Kennet brown only that morning.

Someone suggested that perhaps the heavy winds would flush all the remaining spinners out of the bushes and branches. Then there might well be some real action later in the afternoon.

For a moment the little hut was lit with quiet excitement. The Mayfly might still be on! There in the little wooden hut, crammed with John and Neil and Tim and Mari and me and Hoagy and the riverkeeper and Kathy and Ross, crammed with stories and theories and past dreams and triumphs and recollections, anything seemed possible. Hope was a thing with a big white body and gossamer wings, and I noticed one or two such things over the dark cold water outside the window.

But there was some debate about what would and what would not happen, and the consensus of those who knew suggested that even *should* there be enough spinners left to interest the trout, and even *should* the wind flush them free and should they drop on the water, the downstream wind would make upstream dry-fly casting too difficult, the flies would be whisked off the water before the low-in-the-water trout could get to them, and anyway, the fish were glutted.

The logic of this position was undeniable, and I for one was in-clined to accept it. Anyway, the weather outside was truly putrid and the cucumber sandwiches with fresh butter were getting better and better. I had risen steadily to five of them.

Since no one was rushing outside and everyone was dipping a bit deeper into a corner or low in a chair, and it was cozily warm and the food was good and the quiet buzz-buzz of good talk was making me feel as comfortable as Winnie the Pooh, I did not mention that, outside, there was a little snowstorm—or at least some flurries—of Mayfly spinners, sent fluttering in the wind. I raised myself a bit to watch the water and followed two of them down through the main pool. They floated merrily, a cucumber sandwich to any hungry trout, and then they disappeared—undisturbed—into the lower riffle. There was nothing, really, to make me get up. I liked the talk, which in one quarter had shifted to fly rods—and I was now listening intently to talk of tapers and relative performances.

Then Hoagy asked if I'd like to see a few fly rods he had with him and I rose to that prospect very quickly. He fetched them from his car and they proved very much worth rising to. There was an odd glass Payne that felt like a hollow stalk of dried milkweed in my hand. There was one of Hoagy's own rods, and though he had made this a bit heavy—for his own use, as he liked them—and it was too heavy for me, the rod was clearly a superb tool and made with a master craftsman's skill. Then he took out an Everett Garrison made espe-cially for Everett Garrison. Hoagy said the old master had given it to him on the condition that it be used, not kept in a closet. Hoagy had so treated it. I said I wished I had his guts. I have four or five pieces of fine bamboo that don't regularly see water—out of fear, pure fear. Still, I'm not a collector and fishing is what rods are made for. I made a few brave resolutions, out loud, to use my own classic bamboo a bit more often—especially on water like the Kennet.

Afraid to try Hoagy's Garrison, I tried a piece of his smoked kip-per instead and then made myself another sandwich. I had had six butter-and-cucumber sandwiches, two butter-and-cheese, and three butter-and-pâté; now I tried a large butter-and-butter sandwich and found it exquisitely delicious. Mari frowned. I shrugged and told her quietly that the butter was really irresistible. She muttered something wise and glum about all food's being irresistible to me. I told her this was positively my last sandwich, and anyway, could she please be wise and concerned a bit later so I could hear about the fifty—or was it eighty?—big brook trout that Hoagy and some pals were currently catching in Labrador.

Before this story was resolved, Neil was somehow in the middle of a wild, interminable trip through France, headed for the Risle with a friend who mysteriously stopped at every available bar and collected pocketfuls of sugar.

Meanwhile, John Goddard—the master of the chalkstream—was telling how, on a trip to Norway, the host had forgotten to bring the packages of food and he had to provide fish for the entire party and resorted to an old poacher's trick of sending out into the lake a dozen flies attached to a hinged instrument that . . .

"And then a monstrous dog jumped out," said Neil, "and my friend plunged his hand into his pockets . . ."

"You're pulling my toe!"

"The butter is really superb."

" . . . one hundred and thirty-seven brook trout averaging . . ."

"Did the cow *really* . . ."

". . . and the dog lay down on the floor with all the sugar and licked his paws and smiled the most contented . . ."

The flurry of spinners had stopped and so had the wind. With great effort I rose to my feet and boldly suggested we try to fish again. Wasn't that a touch of sun? No, it was lightning, someone said. Didn't *anyone* want to fish? Not particularly, it seemed. I reached for a knife to cut myself a slab of straight butter, but Mari touched my hand wisely. So I went outside and in a few moments the others followed sluggishly.

Later, as I came around the bend of a carrier into a field of cows, I looked so intently at the ear of one of them that I failed to watch where I was stepping and stepped blithely into a mud sink. A lot of cows had stomped and relieved themselves there. It was quite soft and ucky. So I sank. I sank well down to my thighs and then sank a bit more down into the muck. Neil, who was guiding me, turned and said,

"What the hell are you doing?" He was standing on a hard mound of grass and seemed to be walking on top of the mud. "I didn't think such things really happened to you," he said. "I thought you made them up, that they were stories. Let me take your rod."

I gave it to him, glad it was not one of my prized bamboos, and continued to tread water in the mud for another minute or two. Something in my frantic motions made the nearby cow look intently at me and give a gigantic moo. Instantly, every other cow in the large field—there may have been a hundred of them—turned, shifted position, and eyed me intently.

Neil laughed.

The cows did not.

Later, back in the hut, I became one of the stories, and I tried to drown my embarrassment in one last cucumber-and-butter sandwich, but Mari said if I didn't eat so much, maybe I would not nearly die in the mud. There was talk that the "Wilderness" section of the Kennet had been laid fallow this year because last year I had festooned the fish with so many flies and they needed time to work them out. Neil began to recount, in some happy detail, my near demise in the mud, but I interrupted him and said that I had often heard of angling writers who walked on water but none, like him, who walked on mud.

THE LAST CHALKSTREAM IDYLL

There is a story by Morley Callaghan about a pleasant chap who took a job as an itinerant hangman because his travels led him to such interesting new places to fish. Callaghan is the huge Canadian writer who once beat up Hemingway in a Paris gym; he beat him so stoutly that the timekeeper, Scott Fitzgerald—astounded perhaps—let the round go on for several extra minutes. Hemingway never forgave either of them.

One dose of the British chalkstreams some years ago and I thought I'd lost my heart to them completely—and promptly allowed myself to become an entire subsidiary in the colonies of a British firm, with the caveat that I go to England once a year, in early June, in time for the famous Mayfly hatch.

I'd hole up with the accountants and the empire builders for a week and then head off to Berkshire and the haunting Kennet River. There, hosted by Brian Clarke, John Goddard, or Neil Patterson, I'd flutter indelicately around the river, quite unlike the ghostly Mayfly spinner. It was the choicest of fishing. Neil or Brian or John would husband me along the main stem or one of the carriers, eyes peeled for a rise or a fish "on the fin." It was gorgeous water—pellucid, trouty, mined with weed. They'd spot fish I couldn't have seen with a telescope, and then I'd creep into some ghastly uncomfortable position—on my knees in high grass, perhaps—and attempt to cast to the big brown. They were good fish: better than a pound, up to three or four.

The first year I caught none; nor the second; then one year it rained and I ate cucumber sandwiches in the tiny fishing hut all day and practically did not cast. Each time The Mayfly had been on the week before and *everyone* had taken fish. I shoulda been there. The weights were all carefully remembered—"one pound eight," "two pounds four," "three pounds six," "four pounds one." Then I got one, too small to have a weight, and lost one (with all my experts watching) that, on John's sharp "eye scale," went "better than four pounds two."

All that traipsing around in hip boots, waiting for a fish to show (or someone to show one to me), was less than kind and not at all comfortable. Choice as it might be, there were times when I longed for a good old egalitarian American river, where you can spend most of the day casting, not looking. And I had more than my share of disasters: losing that big fish amid the blistering silence of my audience; wading chest-deep, in my new Harris tweed jacket, into the muck, on which I thought, perhaps, I could walk. But by my fourth year I thought I knew my way around that territory.

I had two happy days on the Kennet that year. The Mayfly was off but a friendly little brown sedge was on. They'd dredged the river to get rid of the heavy weed growth, and though it wasn't as pretty, there were more fish and fish happened to be taking all day. Never one for figures, I can't quote you pound and ounce on them, but I must have taken seven or eight, the largest about three pounds, and I was deliciously smug about my performance.

Toward evening on my last day, I was fishing an upper reach that had just been dredged. The water was quite deep and a bit discolored from the soft soil, so I stayed on the high bank and cast comfortably to several rising fish. The two days had been immensely satisfying and without disaster; I'd taken most of the fish I hooked and felt I'd gotten to know the river better. When we walked down to the river from Neil's house, Neil had said that my success was a relief to everyone. It was surely a relief to me. I'd heard someone's wife, brought to the Kennet with some promise of seeing the American clown perform at this annual carnival, say: "I thought you said funny things happened when this bloke came here. I'm terribly disappointed." Well, you can't please everyone.

I felt quite content, standing on the rim of that mud mound, casting a little brown sedge to the circles. I looked out over the gentle Berkshire fields, at the pinkish sky along the horizon line, at the water as it slipped beneath an old wooden bridge, eddied, grew riffles, and spread out into this long flat pool, and then, suddenly, a truly large fish rose. I struck lightly, it thrashed at the surface, and then it bore upstream heavily. It was the largest fish I'd had on in the Kennet, better than four pounds, possibly five. From my height, I had the advantage on it and easily walked upstream and down, several times, to keep it above me. In ten minutes it tired and came close to the shore and I was positive it was a full five pounds. But how to net it? I was four or five feet above the surface of the water, no one was around, and I had no net with me.

I played the fish a bit more, until he turned sideways and quiet; then I lay full length on the soft dredged sod and put the rod on the ground beside me. I grasped the line, leaned as far over as I dared, and came eight or ten inches short of the fish. The 6X leader would scarcely allow me to raise it out of the water. What to do? The evening was growing late and misty and there were ten or twelve circles of rising fish in the pool. I wanted to catch another, perhaps two; I'd waited four years for a night like this. I even thought of breaking the leader off, but it would have been most ungracious to leave my fly in such a fish.

At last, not knowing how deep the water was, I decided to climb down the bank, digging my feet into the soft mud as I went. A lousy decision. I began to slip down the mud bank, couldn't stop myself, and went into the water, then went on down to the bottom of the river, which was six or seven feet deep there.

I have been dunked a couple of other times in my life, once in mud; I knew at once it could be treacherous, even fatal. So I forced myself up against the bank, got my head above water, screamed valiantly for help, and clawed at the mud wall. It didn't hold. No one came. I kept slipping back, gobs of mud in my hands, on my face, my hat off and sailing downstream, the fish gone now, mud dripping down my jacket, into my shirt, filling my hip boots. For a moment or two I was quite sure I was on my way to the Great Chalkstream in the Sky. Like Everyman, I wasn't ready.

The water and mud in my hip boots made them too heavy for me to kick, the mud kept tearing away as I clawed more and more desperately into it with my hands, and I slipped back under the water twice, gurgling and choking.

The disappointed wife would have gotten her money's worth.

I've often wondered whether the crowd of them would have been too doubled over with laughter to haul me out.

In the end, I must have levitated up that mud bank, out of fear or desperation, and when I got there, I lay full face on the ground, quietly, spitting out a bit of Kennet now and then, for a full five minutes. Then I checked my rod and headed downstream to tell Neil about all the fish that were still rising.

It's more than two years since that evening. I left England the next day, disengaged myself from that firm, and have not been back.

Recently, though, I found the photocopy of a letter Neil wrote to another friend, describing the event. He probably exaggerated when he says I looked like a water buffalo, fresh from a mud bath; and I'm sure he didn't *really* laugh for ten days—and if he did, deep down he'd have been truly sad if I'd become one with the Kennet; and I doubt if my "bum print" is worth preserving on his bathroom wall, where, still plastered with mud, I must have leaned my weary rump a moment.

I didn't please the wife during that last chalkstream idyll, but Neil seems to have gained a historic monument. He shows it to everyone. Lefty Kreh—who never falls in and has been zapping those Kennet browns and regaining the honor of the colonies—told me he had been shown that spot with great reverence. It ain't that important to me. It's just another place where I almost got hung.

THE METAMORPHOSIS

My friend Clyde awoke one morning from uneasy dreams to find himself transformed in the night into a gigantic brown trout. It was no joke. He looked around him, hoping to see his pleasant little one-room apartment where he had lived a hermetic life since his wife cashiered him. Its walls were papered with color photographs of rising trout and natural flies the size of grouse; each corner held three or four bamboo rods in aluminum tubes; the chests of drawers were crammed with blue-dun necks and flies and fly boxes and his thirteen Princess reels; the windowsills and bookcases were packed solid with hundreds of books and catalogs and magazines devoted to the sport to which he had devoted his life. They were not there. Neither were his hands, which were fins.

Instead, he was suspended in cold moving water under an old upturned maple stump. From the clarity and size of the water, he deduced he was in Montana, or perhaps Idaho. That was fine with Clyde. If he was going to be a trout, and he had often meditated on what it would be like to be a trout (so he could tell how they thought), he'd just as well be one in Montana and Idaho.

"Well, this love of fly fishing sure takes me places I otherwise wouldn't go," he thought.

And as soon as he thought this, he realized, since he was thinking, that he had resolved an age-old problem. If he, existing under that old tree stump, could think, he could analyze his own thoughts;

and since what was true for him would have to be true for all trout, he could learn what any trout thought. He was glad he had read Descartes and Kant before he went on the Halford binge.

Curiously, his esoteric studies had led him closer and closer to this point. Only the night before he had been sitting in the dimly lit room, sunk deep into his armchair in front of the lit fish tank in which swam Oscar, his pet brown. He had been staring intently, reciting a mantra, meditating, as he did every night for four hours, when, for a moment—no, it could not be true—Oscar had (at least he thought so) told him that Foolex dubbing was the ultimate solution to the body problem. "Not quill ribbing?" he had asked audibly. "Definitely not," said Oscar. "I like you so I'll give you the straight poop: Foolex is where it's at. Anyway, tomorrow it . . . oh, you'll find out."

And so he had.

He had a thousand questions and worked his way a bit upstream, where he saw a pretty spotted tail waving gently back and forth. The trout, a hen, about three pounds, shifted slightly as Clyde nudged her and eyed him suspiciously: it was still three weeks before spawning season and she was feeling none too frisky. He opened his mouth to ask her about Foolex bodies and careened back in the current. The henfish, named Trudy, thought he was a dumb cluck and that she ought to work her way quickly past the riffle into the upper pool. Maybe this bird's clock was wrong. She had a rotten headache and feared he might even attack her.

Clyde, ever watchful, immediately deduced from her defensiveness that communication among trout, like communication between fly fishermen and bocce players, was impossible. He'd have to answer his questions by himself. This is never easy, particularly not on an empty stomach. He had not eaten anything since the pepperoni sandwich fifteen hours earlier; and he was not dumb enough to think he could soon get another, since the Belle Deli was two thousand miles away.

There was a silver flash and Clyde turned and shot up after it, turning on it as it slowed and turned and lifted up in the current. But he was too late. A little twelve-inch rainbow had sped from behind a large rock and grasped the thing, and it was now struggling with ludicrous futility across stream, the silver object stuck in its lower jaw.

"Incredible!" Clyde thought. "How could I have been so dumb?" He had not seen the hooks; he had not distinguished between metal and true scales. If he who had studied Halford, Skues, Marinaro, and Schwiebert could not distinguish a C. P. Swing from a dace tartare, what hope had any of his speckled kin? He shivered with fear as he asked himself: "Are *all* trout this dumb?"

He worked his way back under the upturned stump, into the eddy, and sulked. This was a grim business. He noticed he was trembling with acute anxiety neurosis but could not yet accept that *all* trout were neurotic. He was positively starved now and would have risen to spinach, which he hated.

Bits and pieces of debris, empty nymph shucks, a couple of grubs swept into the eddy. He nosed them, bumped them, took them into his mouth, spit some of them out. By noon he had managed to nudge loose one half-dead stonefly nymph, *Pteronarcys californica;* he had nabbed one measly earthworm; and he had found a few cased caddises. Most food, he noted, came off the bottom; that's where it was at. The lure had come down from the surface; he should have known. He was learning something new every minute.

By now he had recognized that he was in the Big Hole River, below Divide; he was sure he had once fished the pool. Settled into that eddy under the stump, he now knew why he had not raised a fish here: the current swung the food down below the undercut bank, but his flies had been too high up in the water. The way to fish this run was almost directly downstream from his present position, casting parallel to the bank so the nymph would have a chance to ride low and slip down into the eddy.

He was trying to plot the physics of the thing, from below, and was getting dizzy, when he realized he could starve flat down to death if he didn't stop trying to be a trout fisherman and settle for being a trout. His stomach felt pinched and dry; his jaws ached to clamp down on a fresh stonefly nymph or, yes, a grasshopper. That's what he wanted. He suddenly had a mad letch for grasshoppers—and there was absolutely nothing he could do to get one. He was totally dependent upon chance. "A trout's lot," he thought, "is not a happy one."

Just then the surface rippled a bit, perhaps from a breeze, and a couple of yards upstream, he saw the telltale yellow body, kicking legs, and molded head of a grasshopper. It was August, and he knew the grasshoppers grew large around the Big Hole at that time of the year. It came at him quickly, he rose sharply to it, then stopped and fumed away with a smirk. "Not me. Uh-uh. A Dave's Hopper if I ever saw one. Not for this guy." And as he thought this, Trudy swept downstream past him, too quick for him to warn, and nabbed the thing in an abrupt little splash. Then she turned, swam up by him, seemed to shake her head and say, "How dumb a cluck can you be?"

So it *had* been the real thing. Nature was imitating art now. Oh, he could taste the succulent hopper.

Another splatted down, juicy and alive, and he rose again, paused, and it shot downstream in a rush. He'd never know about that one.

Oh, the existential torment of it! "And I thought deciding which artificial fly to use was hard!"

Two more hoppers, then a third splatted down. He passed up one, lost a fin-race with Trudy for the third. She was becoming a pill.

He could bear it no longer. He'd even eat a Nick's Crazylegs if it came down. Anything. Anything to be done with the torment, the veil of unknowing, the inscrutability, which was worse than the pain in his gut, as it always is.

And then he saw it.

It was a huge, preposterous, feathered thing with a big black hook curled up under it. Some joker with three thumbs had thought it looked like a grasshopper. The body was made of Foolex. How could Oscar possibly have thought that body anything other than insulting? Clyde's hook jaw fumed up in a wry smile; he wiggled his adipose fin. The fly came down over him and he watched it safely from his eddy. And it came down again. Then again. Twelve. Thirteen times. Trudy had moved twice in its direction. He could tell she was getting fairly neurotic about it.

Foolex? That body could not fool an imbecile. It *was* an insult!

Eighteen. Twenty times the monstrosity came over him. He was fuming now. How *dare* someone throw something like that at him! Had they no respect whatsoever? If that's all fishermen thought of him, what did it matter. He was bored and hungry and suffering from a severe case of angst and humiliation. Nothing mattered. It was a trout's life.

He rose quickly and surely now, fuming as the thing swept down past him on the thirty-third cast. He saw it hang in the surface eddy for a moment. He opened his mouth. Foolex? It infuriated him! It was the ultimate insult.

He lunged forward. And at the precise moment he knew exactly what trout see and why they strike, he stopped being a trout.

SALMO PSYCHOSIS

There came a time in my friend Clyde's life when the pressures of his addiction became more than a reasonable man could bear. So he sought professional help. He went to a doctor. The doctor specialized in diseases of the brain and nervous system afflicted by too much dwelling upon the trout. After one short session, the doctor found where Clyde's symptoms pointed inescapably: "Ja," he told me. "He's vun of dem. Dis Clyde all right ist eine trouptf nut."

The affliction is neither as new nor as rare as some people think. Some of those people who think it is rare are publishers, eighty-seven of whom rejected Dr. Helmut von Rainbogen's two-thousand-page book, *Salmo Psychosis: The Hidden Enemy*. Von Rainbogen's book catalogued 12,654,837 bona fide cases of *Salmo* psychosis, dating from the fourth century B.C. The publishers, though, said there was no market for the book, particularly because it had no sex scenes; they also thought there was too much emphasis on western *Salmo* psychosis, and that, in their view, from Madison Avenue, no one bought books west of the Mississippi unless they were about Zen or est or the lettuce boycott.

"Vhat vee have here," von Rainbogen told me in the waiting room when he came out with his arm around Clyde's shoulder, "ist eine truly classic case. Clyde Pfisht ist eine absolutely classic troupft nut." I tried to place his accent. It sounded like an Austro-Prussian-Croatian dialect by way of left field. He smiled benignly at Clyde, pretended to fly-cast an imaginary rod toward an imaginary river at the other end of his waiting room, and said, condescendingly, I thought, "Ja, ja, Herr Pfisht. Dot's vhat's on your mind, no?"

"Yeah, I'd rather be out pfishting than fritzing around with a loon like you," said Clyde, and I was again won over by my friend's candor.

While Dr. Rainbogen stroked his goatee and nodded vigorously, I scanned the waiting room. There were three aquarium tanks, filled with piranhas. On the walls were blown-up photographs of men and women shredded by sharks. Above the couch, there was a framed news clipping from Alaska describing an attack by killer rainbow trout on three Eskimo kids. Worse, in a plastic case there was a plastic eye into which was stuck the hook point of a Quill Gordon. But most shocking, when I looked closely, were the mottled backs of the piranhas and the bright red dots on the sharks: they were trout in savage bodies.

"It is dangerous, this pfly pfishting for the troupfts, no?" said the doctor.

I cannot repeat what Clyde said.

A week later I brought my friend back. He'd had a miserable week though I had done what I could to comfort him. I told him he'd enjoy his fly fishing more if he could keep it in proportion. I told him that the season was only a few months off—"Seventy-three days," he said—and he'd enjoy it much more this year.

"Don't be an idiot," he told me. "If this lunatic has his way, I'll never fish again. He's a deprogrammer—the kind they use for runaway kids. If he cures me, I'll have absolutely nothing to live for. I'm sane. I'm perfectly sane. I'm as sane as anyone."

Clyde did not in fact have all his marbles. He sometimes thought he was a trout. He divided the world into fly fishers and lunatics. He became manic during the hatch periods and depressive out of season. He had paranoid fits that his children wanted to roast marshmallows with his Payne rods. He accused the IRS of spoiling Opening Day for him each year. He haunted New York's garment district like a hog after truffles, searching for scrap pieces of fur to put into his dubbing blender. One or two of these and similar qualities you will find in your average basic fly fisher; together, as von Rainbogen has written, they're absolute evidence of *Salmo* psychosis.

After four long sessions, the doctor took me aside and said: "He vill not let go. He is holding tight to der primal gonnegtions." He looked at me intently and said: "He really likes this pfly pfishtng, no?"

"Maybe," I said. "Have you tried it?"

"Never, never," he said. "You do dis ding?"

I admitted that I had been known to do it.

"It is pfun, maybe?"

"Yeah, it's pfun."

"Hmmmm," said the doctor, stroking his goatee. "Der ist eine fine line, maybe, between genius and madness, no?"

Later that spring I was about to end a quiet early-May afternoon on the Beaverkill and was sitting on a rock smoking my pipe. It had been a pleasant, unhurried time—all I could want of a day's fishing. Some Hendricksons had shown about one o'clock, but no fish came to them. Then, about four, there was some deliberate feeding to the spinners. There were buds of green peppering the hillside and light waves of warmth in the air, and in the end I had taken four difficult trout on gossamer leader tippets. A pleasant spring day. Some difficult fishing. Some good stalking and casting. No disasters. A measure of success. Quite enough for me, thank you.

Through the trees, I suddenly saw two figures approaching from Schoolhouse Pool. Something about the way they walked and the loud sounds one of them made forced me to watch them. In a few moments they were near and I knew them.

One man was a walking Orvis catalog. His vest was crammed to overflowing, he carried two rods, a huge wooden net flapped behind him, and a smaller one was tucked into the belt of his waders. The mandatory fleece hatband was filled with fifty or sixty flies. He was gesticulating wildly, spreading his arms to show the size of something that he had perhaps lost or caught. And his voice was high-pitched, nearly insane, in a key I only hear along the Madison River when the salmonfly hatch is on.

The man was clean shaven and that three-dollar accent was gone, but it was surely Dr. Helmut von Rainbogen.

Clyde, usually the most talkative of companions astream, was stone silent.

"Big Hole . . . steelhead . . . Alaska . . . Muddler . . . no-hackle . . . thorax tie . . . up-eye . . . riffling hitch . . . pupae . . . 6X . . . sipping rise . . . Tricos . . . reach cast . . . flop cast . . ."

The words must have swarmed up out of the doctor's unconscious. I tried to think of how many troupft nuts he had disengaged from words like this. Now the words came back, all of them, and he was shouting them madly into Clyde's ear. He was one with the Great Collective Trout Unconscious.

"Elk-Hair Caddis . . . masking hatch . . . spinner fall . . . half hitch . . . no kill . . . Battenkill . . . nail knot . . . paradun . . . Rogue . . . spring creek . . . multiple hatch . . . saddle hackle . . ."

I knew the words but I could make no sense—if there was any— of how they were put together. The man sounded berserk.

I scrunched down in the bushes to let them pass.

As they did, I heard Clyde say: "But I'm bushed, Doc. Worn out. We've fished twenty-seven days in a row, twelve hours a day. I have a job. I have kids. I think I once had a wife."

Clyde, normally one of the swiftest men along a streambank, was falling behind. He did not hear something the quick doctor had said.

"What? No! No, I don't want to!" he shouted. "I know. I know I'm getting a fat fee . . ."

The doctor was around the bend now.

Clyde shouted: "But the book, Doc. Don't you think we ought to work on the book? No. We've done enough research. Doc! *Trout and Salvation* will be a best sell—"

And then they were both around the bend.

THE COMPLETE BOOK
OF FLY FISHING FOR TROUT

Introduction

I once swore I would never write a *complete* practical book. It's boastful and I'm not all that practical. I also once swore off cigars and hard likker. Anyway, I need the money and the fame won't hurt.

If you want to thank someone for the brevity of this book, thank my wife, who loathes fishing. Without her, I'd have written an epic.

Chapter 1: The Trout

Trout recommend themselves to fly fishermen because they eat flies. That they do not always eat flies, especially fake flies—and who can blame them?—is another good recommendation. Trout live in rivers and lakes, each different from the other. This differentness and the differentness of anglers, and the different tackle they manage to use, and the differentness of each trout, and other strange differentnesses too numerous to mention, makes fishing for trout wondrously different from eel fishing in the Hudson River. There is a well-known maxim in Aristotle's "Historia Animalium": If you've caught one eel, man, you've caught them all.

I once knew a man who talked to trout, but he found that they never talked back.

Chapter 2: Gear

In previous incarnations, trout fishermen were itinerant junk dealers who roamed from town to town with all their purchases and wares on their backs and hanging around their necks. I deduced this one day on the Beaverkill by looking closely at a fine specimen of the species and laughing so hard that, for some unaccountable reason, he threw a De-Liar at me. For most fly fishermen, more is better. As I grow older, less is best.

As a result, I no longer take with me along the streams: telescopes, binoculars, walkie-talkies, hand warmers, umbrellas, fly-tying equipment, extra rods, a two-week supply of Fig Newtons, ostrich eggs, extra waders, the last three selections from the Field & Stream Book Club, children under the age of thirty, or a portable television set.

Though the principle of simplicity is logical and well founded, I do not advise eliminating rod, reel, line, and flies.

Chapter 3: Basic Techniques

You cannot cast a fly until you have set up your equipment properly. This may seem too obvious to mention, unless you have tried to cast with your line strung through the keeper ring. I do not recommend this. Otherwise, follow your natural impulses. Only don't follow them too far.

Chapter 4: Stream Lore

The river is nothing like the city. It has its own laws and you must learn some of them before you will catch any trout on a fly. Bless it for not being like the city!

Chapter 5: Hatches

"A little learning is a dangerous thing," says Alexander Pope. "Drink deep, or taste not the Pierian spring."

On the other hand, Pope knew Latin, did not realize that there are thousands of bugs in American trout streams, and had not the faintest idea that a person drinking too deeply in entomology could go loony.

Pope also said: "True wit is Nature to advantage dressed"—another extremely valuable maxim for fly fishermen. Paraphrased, this means: Never go to a trout stream without a good supply of wit along, especially if it's dressed by Poul Jorgensen.

Hatch matching is a rapidly evolving art. Today we have no-hackle flies and no-wing spinners; tomorrow, the Emperor's New Fly.

Chapter 6: No-Hatches

When no flies are visibly hatching, you can quite safely assume— assuming your eyesight is adequate and if not you should have your eyes examined twice a year—that no flies are visibly hatching. "Heard melodies are sweet," says John Keats, "but those unheard are sweeter still." (That has no relevance, except that Keats once knew a girl whose father knew a man who was reputed once to have caught a trout; anyway, Keats developed the concept of "negative capability," which is a valuable capability for fly fishermen to develop.)

A trout cannot eat what he doesn't see, or what is not there; but he also cannot go to the 21 Club, though I'll bet he'd like to. If you can't figure out where the trout are, or what they're taking, try the nearest bar.

Chapter 7: Sunshine and Shade

Hamlet's statement "I am too much i' th' sun" is relevant here. None of us like to be examined too closely, especially if we have hives. Trout don't get hives but they're pathologically shy, wallflowers of an underwater sort. Frankly, they're pretty shady characters and very antisocial.

Chapter 8: Drag

If you saw a piece of steak moving unnaturally on your plate, would you eat it?

Chapter 9: Fly Tying

This is a very cunning activity, but I do not recommend your taking it up if you know Ted Niemeyer, Poul Jorgensen, Art Flick, René Harrop, Edson Leonard, Dave Whitlock, Harry Darbee, Walt Dette, Dick Talleur, Del Bedinotti, Helen Shaw, Dan Blanton, or some other individual with thirteen fingers and a good supply of blue-dun hackles who remembers you generously at Christmas.

Chapter 10: Playing and Netting Fish

If I have ever engaged in such activities, I've forgotten.

Chapter 11: Travel

I once knew a guy who spent $5,000 traveling to Scotland and staying at posh resorts on three of the best rivers in the country. He fished every day from daybreak until after dusk, until his arms were lead and he was willing to take up sleep as a sport. He did not catch a fish.

I don't catch any on West Eighty-fourth Street, either.

Chapter 12: The Literature of Angling

A couple of billion too many words have been written about fly fishing. I have contributed to this mess. Why are so many words written? Perhaps because they are read. Why are they read? Perhaps because fly fishermen fish too little. To pursue the argument further, we can stop all this damned pollution by fishing more, which I recommend.

Probably none of it will make you a better fly fisherman, any-way—and any novel by Hardy, Melville, Waugh, Dickens, Tolstoy, Dostoyevsky, Sterne, Proust, Joyce, Hemingway, Márquez, Faulkner, or Jane Austen is better worth your time. These will make you a wiser human being, which has a good chance of making you a wiser fly fisherman. But don't count on it.

Fly fishing has a long history. It is very long.

Epilogue

Many years ago I learned two lessons: If you destroy a trout river, it will not be there; if you kill a trout, it will no longer be in the river.

There is a corollary worth noting: If there are no rivers and no trout, there can be no fly fishing for trout.

And then I won't be able to make my fortune by writing *Son of the Complete Book of Fly Fishing for Trout.*

ADVENTURES IN THE FUR TRADE

Walking to and from my old office, I had to pass every day through New York City's fur district. This is an area roughly between Sixth and Seventh Avenues and Twenty-seventh through Thirtieth Streets; at least a lot of it is there, and some buildings—first through thirtieth floors—are wall-to-wall fur cutters, fur merchants, fur storage firms, fur designers, and fur wholesalers. The significance of this concentrated marketplace eluded me for more than four years.

But not even I can be that dumb that long.

One day last winter I passed a huge dump-bin in the middle of West Twenty-eighth Street; it was swarming with dump-bin scavengers. Thirty or forty people, men and women, were tearing at cardboard boxes filled with mink scraps. They were silent but intent about their business, and they were quite particular: they chose only the larger scraps, a foot or more in length. The rest of the stuff—slim cuttings of irregular size and shape—they simply threw back into the dump-bin or onto the street. In all, there must have been a ton of mink, mostly the smaller scraps that nobody wanted. It was everywhere.

I had been tying some small caddis flies and vaguely remembered a British friend who used mink for his wing material. So, nonchalantly, aloof from the serious picking, I picked up a few small cuttings, enough to tie a couple of dozen mink-wing caddis flies. Then I shook my head sadly at the hive of disreputable scavengers and headed home.

But in the night, while it poured, I dreamed of mink. I saw the dump-bin and the horde of silent vultures; but mostly I saw the scraps of mink that no one else had any use for. I woke early the next morning, forgot to shave, and rushed downtown an hour early, full of great expectations. I'd collect up a barrel of the stuff; I'd trade it for other materials; I'd swap it for flies; I'd sell it; I'd corner the mink market; I'd be rich; I'd retire to Montana.

But the dump-bin was gone and the efficient New York street-cleaning machines had left only a few scraps, which I picked out of the wet streets and stuffed surreptitiously into my pockets.

When you are unaware of a thing, you do not see it. I fished for years during leaf-roller "falls" before I saw them. And when I finally noticed those delicate green worms, I wondered how I had missed them for so long. They were everywhere: on the branches, on the leaves, dropping down to the surface of the water on spidery threads, on my rod, on my neck, on my vest, in my waders. How could I not have seen them?

I dreamed of mink and searched every morning for mink—and thus began my strange adventures in the fur trade.

Early and late I hunted fur.

One day I found a truck hauling out rabbits' feet—millions of them—and plucked a dozen out of the garbage and wedged them into my always crowded pockets. One night I found a small quantity of some exceptionally soft chinchilla cuttings, packed them up carefully, and sent them to Craig Mathews, the superb West Yellowstone tier. He tied me up a couple of mini-streamers that were bound to be lethal, and from then on I could not keep my nose out of the gutter. I'd shuffle down Twenty-eighth Street, tipping up garbage-pail tops, poking into green bags, walking off the curb and into alleyways. I found beaver cuttings, some mink, a bit of sable now and then, a couple of fox half-tails, some Australian opossum. One night I almost got hit by a truck backing up in the dark, and I must surely have been taken for one of New York's lunatic street people. Frankly, I didn't notice. And if I had, I wouldn't have cared.

I'd heard about road kills and the fine pelts that could be found on highways—from Eric Leiser's versatile groundhog to deer. But this was ridiculous. There was gold in the streets, just for the picking, and it was clean.

Off the stuff went to Craig and back came some of the most beautiful little mink caddis, No. 22, you've ever seen—and an enthusiastic letter saying that he'd take all I could find. We called the flies—in case you care—the Lyons-Mathews Seventh Avenue Specials. Not only my fortune but also my fame was assured.

My family, my business associates, and anyone else who saw me with all those fur scraps tumbling out of my pockets surely thought me mad. I was in ecstasy. I neglected my business and my friends; I ate lunch while walking and searching; I did not think trout, I thought chinchilla.

And then the flow stopped. For two weeks in January and early February, with snow and slush spoiling the streets, I found no more than a piece of rug and a hank of lamb's wool. Was the cutting season over? Should I go directly to the dealers? Somewhere out there, in the labyrinth of the fur district, was a fortune. Scrap fur—which must exist by the carload, which was being thrown out somewhere, by someone down there, every day—must have a yearly street value, if converted into flies, of at least $24 million.

I couldn't leave my business during the prime hours of the morning and afternoon, much as I longed to do so, so I enlisted the aid of my good friend Justin. Ah, Justin! Never was there a more passionate fly fisherman or friend. On a perfectly grizzly March afternoon, he called me from a pay phone in the street and said he'd found the mother lode. Our fortunes were made. The phone connection was poor so I told him to rush over and we'd huddle on it. Minutes later he was there, wet as a Labrador retriever. I dropped a mess of insignificant contracts and manuscripts in a heap on the floor and he gave me the dope: there was a scrap-fur broker, in fact a couple of them. He had been to a dozen cutters and dealers, and they all said they sold their scraps by the pound to a broker. Justin had found him, in a ground-floor, cement-floored room, surrounded by mountains of fur. "You never saw so much, Nick," he said, his voice rising. "There are bales of it, hundreds of them, up to the ceiling, all over."

So I raced out. It was three P.M., a Tuesday. Justin was right. Nutria, Polish nutria, mink, ermine, beaver, sable, chinchilla, five kinds of fox, Australian opossum—butt ends, tails, body fur, thin cuttings, fat cuttings, head pieces, belly slabs: you would not believe the amounts. It was a fly tier's Valhalla. And it was all dirt cheap. The broker filled a three-foot-high paper bag with Australian opossum and said, "Give me three bucks, make it two—you look like a nice guy." And Justin and I took all we could carry, enough to make fifty million flies, and hauled it all, struggling, both arms full, up the wet streets to my office. We were too excited—or exhausted—to talk.

Then I spent a couple of hours packing it up in cardboard crates and shipping it west, in trade for flies. In all, by the time the trout season opened, I'd spent dozens of hours hauling, packing, and shipping box after box of that stuff to tiers; and bits and pieces of it stuck to my clothes, spread out over the floor of my office, would not be extricated from the rug, nearly lost me an employee who shrieked when she saw a fox head in my pocket, and very nearly drove my little business into bankruptcy. Worse, we glutted the market and turned my little gold mine into a pig's ear. And I grew bored by it—oh, how bored I was by April after all the lugging and packing, with nutria coming out of my ears, after shipping all those dozens of cartons of fur cuttings. Justin was, too.

I might have continued my madness for months longer but the fates were with me: our lease was up and we had to move. Fortunately, we moved to the paper and printing district, where I have yet to find a use for the cardboard crates and boxes of paper scraps I pass every day.

It is months now and sometimes I get an itch to get my hand back into the fur trade. Now and again I'll get off the subway a few stations early, in my old stomping grounds, to check a few of my favorite haunts. They're still there: the garbage pails two doors from the corner of Seventh Avenue and Twenty-eighth Street where I found all the sable; the rutted corner of Seventh and Twenty-seventh, where I could *always* get a pocketful of chinchilla in the morning; the alleyway up Twenty-seventh where they dump the rabbits' feet. I still pick up a few choice scraps when I go, for old times' sake, but my heart isn't in it anymore. It's May, and I'm working a bit harder and longer, so I can take off the odd Friday and head for the mountains. I happen to prefer fish to fur.

But the gold's there, and Justin and I will tell you where it is—if you promise not to get us involved in the fur trade again.

THE LYONS ROACH

From the time I was a teenager, "Tap's Tips" has been one of my favorite columns. For H. G. Tapply is surely one of those rare human beings who can describe how to do a thing so you can really do it. Practical, sensible, and eminently clear, he yet has a voice of his own: he contributes to our store of usable knowledge and improves our fishing. He proves, month after month, that the "nuts and bolts" of fishing technology need never be mud—even if it takes a mixed metaphor to say so.

I had hoped, many years ago, to write a column called "Nick's Tricks." I wanted this more than I ever wanted to be an expert. I had a sincere desire, you see, to *help* people, not merely dazzle them.

But none of my tricks worked. Still, I had friends. So I asked for help. Good old Sparse said he had once tried to perfect a zipper for waders, so you could pee with your boots on. An eminently sane idea. But they leaked. He told me, too, how he had once often dropped his pipe into rivers but had invented a little string thingamajig that kept his pipe hung safely around his neck. Now when it dropped out of his mouth at the sight of a huge fish rising, it only plopped hot ashes into his waders.

My friend Clyde suggested helium-filled fly line, which floated in the air a few feet above the water and thus eliminated drag while dropping the fly (but not the leader) to the surface. Ingenious, I thought. But when I tried it out, an ash from my cigar touched the line and, *poof!* I watched helplessly as the largest trout I've ever seen rose to the free-floating fly and vanished forever while (and I've always wanted to say this) my reel smoked.

Barring a ready supply of tricks, I thought I might someday get my name on a new fly. Quietly, without fanfare, I perfected the Lyons Leafroller. This fly has two virtues: it catches fish and it can be tied by everyone, even cretins like me with three thumbs, two baseball fingers, and a pinky that stands at attention when the temperature drops below eighty degrees. Here's the recipe:

Lyons Leafroller

HEAD, BODY, TAIL: *One inch of chartreuse polypropylene*
THREAD: *Chartreuse*

What you do is this. First, rip off a one-inch slab of chartreuse poly (longer or shorter depending upon the size leaf rollers that drop in your area). Lay this directly along the top of the shank so that both ends hang loosely beyond the eye and curve of the hook. Then strap the thing to the hook somehow—a couple of run-of-the-mill knots or a good wad of chewing gum will do the trick nicely.

It's a lethal fly, pliant in the water, when the leaf rollers are dropping.

Unfortunately, they stopped dropping in my region four or five years ago, and although I gave several tying demonstrations, no one took much interest. No one seemed to care.

After that I lapsed into a fallow period, which often precedes the most creative days in my life. It lasted five years, four months, two days. It lasted until Vin Ringrose started to describe the pancora crab to me one day and the size trout it produced. I had seen photographs of such fish in Joe Brooks's *Trout Fishing:* ten-pounders only three or four years old.

Here at last was an enterprise worthy of my greatest efforts. I decided to start an importing firm with a Mr. Edward G. Zern called

Pancoras Unlimited. We would stock a hundred American rivers, from coast to coast, with these fat crustaceans. We would increase the average size of American trout from six inches to sixteen pounds. All this would be our service to the trout-fishing fraternity. Our cut could come from sales of the Swank Panc, a new fly I was perfecting and would have in mass production by the time fly fishermen across the country realized that Trikes were out and Pancs in.

Mr. Zern and I had incorporated as P.U., Inc., and were preparing to travel to Chile to snatch some seed pancoras when the U.S. Department of Agriculture got wind of the deal and threatened to leak it out that we used worms if we did not cease and desist—so we did.

Meanwhile, Mr. Zern copped out and began fishing in exotic watering holes around the world, abandoning stateside waters to me. Fame, that whore, had so far eluded me, but it would no more. I said my mantras and went into a trance for thirteen days. On the last day, the miracle occurred. I was perched on the kitchen floor muttering when a huge, juicy roach came out from under the refrigerator, nosed around near the stove, and then climbed up my waders (in which I always meditate), and slipped into my hand.

It was a thick and juicy roach, its hard brown back glistening brightly, its body packed with leftover protein. The cities across America were full of them. They could not be destroyed. Four appearances by the exterminator had not eliminated them from my kitchen. "Feisty little buggers," he told me. They thrived on garbage; they'd probably love pollution. The mayflies were vanishing; the caddis would probably be next. So I would promote the roach.

My mind was clear and cold now. There was an unlimited supply of these creatures in places where they were not wanted; and there was an unlimited need. They would make excellent trout food— crammed with protein and vegetable matter. *Blata orientalis.* Or maybe *Blatta orientalis lyons,* since I was about to raise them from ignominy to glory. And there was a moral issue. The cities had been squandering river water for the last hundred years: didn't they *owe* something in return?

I took four of the pretty little things upstate one weekend and dropped them into the riffle above Slate Rock Pool. They floated beautifully, which confirmed my hope that I could create a dry Lyons

Roach for dry states. And no sooner had they floated out of the riffle and into the pool then a stupendous brown trout boiled under one, took it, then came up again, smacking his lips for more.

Incredible. My fortune was assured. Did they have a Nobel Prize for this sort of thing?

I decided to proceed with caution. I wrote to fisheries management people and chambers of commerce across the country:

Dear Sirs:

I am able to supply an unlimited number of roaches to you for use as trout food. A few, stocked near blue-ribbon trout streams, will revolutionize your fishery. May I have your opinion?

"You should be locked up," one biologist wrote back.

"We run a clean town," said one little chamber of commerce in the Midwest. "No roaches."

I could not believe it. I had not one taker.

Worse, my letters caused alarm. Antiroach leagues sprang up across the country. Several nationally televised debates discussed whether the roach was sufficiently aesthetic—and unanimously said "No!" My college, which had been trying to sack me ever since I was caught teaching a class how to avoid drag instead of *The Importance of Being Earnest,* brought me up for charges under paragraph XXIV of the Higher Education Code, "Conduct Unbecoming." An organization called Love Your Roaches surfaced and called me a barbarian. And then Mr. Donald Zahner ended it. He threatened to reveal that I don't really live in New York City but on the Middle Fork in Idaho, and am a notorious live-sculpin fisherman, a ghost-catcher of lunkers for desk-bound honchos.

So there is no Lyons Roach today. I'd have told the tragic story sooner except that some rat, ordered to keep me mum, put Krazy Glue in my ChapStick.

THE LYONS SUPER-FLEX LEADER

I made the long detour every afternoon because of the snakes. There was a certain convocation of them sunning on the mounds of rocks near the river, and I climbed high above their territory to avoid them. They are mysterious fellows to me. I'd like them if I could, but I can't. They turn my backbone to mush.

The detour left me breathless but was worth the trek. For every afternoon about four o'clock, three in a row, I'd been treated to an astonishing sight: when the sun slanted from the west, you could see, below the short, shallow run, where the riffle flattened and the water deepened and grew dark, the pockmarks of a dozen good fish feeding, just at or perhaps just below the surface. And if you bent your head sideways, you could see, beneath the sun's glare on the water, that a few of the largest fish even moved into the thin broken water, where they seemed on the prowl, with their tails and dorsals extending above the surface.

Though there were some tiny flies in the air—a few blond caddis, a couple of different midget mayflies mostly—I raised not a fish during this spree to my dry flies, which was all one used on this water, on three successive afternoons of fishing.

Was it the particular glare of the sun at this time of day?

Were the fish taking nymphs swept down from the pool above?

Was I using the right pattern and did it cant on the water properly?

Was my leader too large—a 5X, which was the lightest I thought would hold such huge fish, and which did not trouble the same trout in the mornings, before the sun crested the hill and fell on this run? A fish or two turned toward my flies but none came to tea. And I'd taken four fine fish from this run during mornings of fine dry-fly fishing when a No. 16 Sulphur was on.

On the last afternoon, though, I felt incredibly smug because, in desperation, after years of intense experimentation, the difficulty of this pool had prompted me to a last massive effort to perfect my newest and most original innovation: the Lyons Super-Flex Leader. What it is, is this: two lengths of Tibetan braided leader, dyed with goat's urine, the uppermost exactly 39½ inches long, the lower 33¼ inches, with exactly 6.37 inches of rubber band inserted between them. I had tried 103 different rubber bands until I found one of precisely the right texture and dimensions (which I will reveal when my patent is approved, for a price), and finally found the perfect way to marry braid and rubber: with a Triple Overhand, Double-Loop, Over-and-Under Smitz Knot, which I created for the job.

The function of the Lyons Super-Flex Leader, as any idiot would know, is to serve as a shock absorber at the two most vulnerable moments: when a fish takes and when it makes a sudden move. I had tried rods with wet-noodle action to solve this problem but had finally determined that the rod should be stiffer, the leader noodlier—and stretchier. Now I could use 7X tippets with absolute confidence. I could fish No. 22 dry flies delicately. Twenty-two-inch browns would be cream puffs, if I ever found them. The Lyons Roach had failed to make me famous and rich, but this leader would change my life. I'd patent the idea. I'd get myself sent to Yugoslavia to test it. Millions of fly fishermen would pay me a royalty on each LSFL sold. I'd get on cable TV. I'd have a video made of myself.

The final stages of the Lyons Super-Flex Leader had taken me half the night to perfect. Determination of the exact length of leader, development of the Triple Overhand, Double-Loop, Over-and-Under Smitz Knot itself (a knot that takes only slightly less than three times the time needed to tie a Bimini Twist) were historical moments. I had knelt on the living room floor late into the night, using the tip section of my fly rod, trying to get the thing to turn over just right. By three-thirty A.M. it did—but I was too exhausted to make more than the one prototype.

So, armed with this, I'd made the long detour, and on my first cast with a No. 22 Cream Caddis at the end of a 7X tippet, the leader turned over gorgeously, I had a good rise, I struck, and I came up blank.

The lighter leader had worked brilliantly—but I'd missed the fish. Strange. I cast back into the pod of tails and dorsals and in seconds had another good rise, struck, and again came up blank. The Lyons Super-Flex Leader was too flexible to set the hook: that had to be the problem. The rubber band ought to be an inch shorter. Well, stream-side is no place to tie flies or Triple Overhand, Double-Loop, Over-and-Under Smitz Knots, so I'd have to improvise: strike harder.

Again I cast up into the run, watched the little golden dot alight and float a foot or two, then it too disappeared. I made a short, hard strike, again came up with a loose line, roll-cast the line out in a rushed, frustrated movement, could not see the fly, jerked it back hard, to bring the line off the water for another cast, and felt a sharp tug.

All fly fishermen feel a special satisfaction when they solve a difficult logistical equation on a river. Selecting the proper fly pattern and design, overcoming a stiff downstream wind, beating the drag built into twisted currents, solving a problem of approach, brings a flush of pride—and the proof is always in the catching. A slight, smug, self-satisfied smile comes to one's lips. Anything—even losing weight—is possible.

I smiled a slight, smug, self-satisfied smile. I had tried to solve this problem for three days. I might have solved it by swimming a Zonker through the pool, but that would have been like lowering the net in tennis. I'd stayed with the dry fly and my gargantuan powers of deduction had led me to the solution: the leader. I felt damned proud.

And it was a big fish, too—perhaps one of the alligators the river was known for.

Only it acted a bit oddly.

It did not go out in a heavy rush of power; it did not sulk; it did not come crashing out in a leap of exaltation and bravado. It sort of zigzagged.

This, I soon learned, was because it was not a trout.

Thirty yards out, right at the surface, I saw the writhing form of a snake, close to a thirty-incher, SSSSS-ing its way toward the opposite bank. The little golden speck that was the No. 22 Cream Caddis was attached to its middle, as if the fly had been dragged, quite wet, and foul-hooked the reptile.

I exerted as much pressure on it as I dared, and I am happy to report that the Lyons Super-Flex Leader worked beautifully: try as it might (and *I* might) the snake could not break the 7X tippet. I had created a brilliant innovation.

The constant pressure of the line and rod and the Lyons Super-Flex Leader drew the snake closer and closer. But now what to do? I was in the Rockies and I had no idea whether the snake was poisonous or not, and even if not, the closer it got the more I felt "zero at the bone." Not only could I hold an especially large catch, I now realized, but I could not uncatch it.

Closer and closer I played the snake. I gave it hard, short tugs, to bust the tippet, but the tippet would not break. I pointed the rod tip at the wretched thing and jerked, but the snake only turned and came toward me, so I promptly stopped jerking. Out it zigged and in I zagged it. Soon the twelve-foot two-and-a-half inch leader was to the tip of my rod and the snake much too close for comfort. I was sorely tempted to cut the leader where it joined the line but I didn't want to ruin my only LSFL, the prototype, and the only leader of any kind I had with me.

In desperation, I hoisted the reptile—wriggling and twisting—at rod's length and began a certain swinging, swaying motion that I thought might break it off at the tippet, launching it into space; but the 7X tippet held, and the snake kept dancing at the end of the yo-yo-like contraption, swinging closer to me on each backswing after each time I swung it out. I was furious at myself for being such a genius.

In the end, I swung it high and far, so the snake slapped down close to my feet, wriggled onto my hippers, made me dance a little jig until I stepped back into some sagebrush, and fell to a sitting position; when I saw the snake wriggle up my leg, I levitated and booted the leader harshly. Even then it did not break. But the braided butt must have rubbed against the rocks, for suddenly, as I tugged and high-stepped, it burst, and I kicked the snake into the water and galloped downstream, making a terrible commotion.

I'm still trying to construct another leader to the precise measurements I recorded that historic night, and I have high hopes for my invention. I still think I'm a genius and I still think the Lyons Super-Flex Leader will make me rich and famous—though I don't think I'll ever to able to recommend it for the fine art of wet-snake fishing.

NO-NAME BROOKS

Beaverkill, Battenkill, Willowemoc; Madison, Yellowstone, Big Hole, Snake; Deschutes, Feather, American—oh, and the Letort, the Brodheads, the Ausable, the Brule, and a hundred others. Magical names. Names peopled with layers of texture, story, history, legend—names associated in the minds of fly fishermen with particular men and fly patterns, with specific hatches like the Hendrickson, Michigan "caddis," salmonfly, *Caenis,* even riffle beetle larvae. They are names to which we make pilgrimages, rivers some men hold sacred. Often too many men hold them sacred at the same time.

But there are other trout waters, found East and West, down into North Carolina and certainly in Maine. These are the little unnamed brooks that rise from springs or ponds hidden far into the pockets of wilderness farthest from civilization. These are the bright creeks that flow clear and cold, dropping, always dropping in little waterfalls, white rushes, or slow, inevitable, downward glides, into larger streams, then into the major rivers—and also into my heart.

I know one in Montana, one in Massachusetts, several in New York State, a few in Colorado, another in Maine. Some of them have local names like Otter Run or Devil's Creek, but I rarely learn them. Usually I supply my own, for most often they appear as no more than the thinnest meandering line on maps winding back from the larger rivers like the veins of a leaf to places that are pure source. I have followed several of them this far, to the wild place, the still and steady

fountainhead of what is wild, the emblem of something pure coming
fresh into the world every moment. "We need the tonic of wildness,"
says Thoreau, "to wade sometimes in marshes where the bittern and
the meadow hen lurk, and hear the booming of the snipe; to smell
the whispering sedge where only some wilder and more solitary fowl
builds her nest, and the mink crawls with its belly close to the ground."
Such places are necessary. They are rarely found on "name" rivers.
The isolated creek is their source.

I do not hear the names of these creeks in my ears. They collect
no stories but those I have lived with them—and sometimes a few I
have heard from other initiates. They are not magical words but textured pictures in my brain. They are private places, so quiet that their
presence is often unknown even to those who live closest to them.

* * *

Bill Humphrey lived near one—a diminutive limestoner—for five years before he realized it held trout. He got the news from a friend, who one evening, astonished, had seen a local fish hawk coming out of the dusk with two gigantic trout. I have fished the river and taken only one small trout, but Bill, who fishes it regularly now, has had some surprising evenings there. It is an intimate, genial piece of water, which demands stealth and deft, short casts. You walk through farm fields, under barbed-wire fences. You talk with a good friend, watch the water, and never see another fisherman. Sometimes the water is merely a quick, short, shallow run, but now and then it opens into a pool with a hidden hole the size of a house for a bottom, or it cuts deeply under a bank. There are trout here, you know it—but you must be there at the right time, with the proper fly. For want of a better name—and I can think of none better—we call it Bill's Brook, and if it still withholds its charms a bit too often, we still have it to ourselves, and we still dream of finding two more leviathans, the size of your arm, in one of its deep holes. There is no rush; they will be there.

I was visiting some friends in Massachusetts several years ago, and knowing my passion, they suggested I slip away from the crowd at the house for a few hours and try the brook that runs through their property. "One old fellow catches some trout in it regularly," my host said, though, looking at the little creek, I had my doubts. It may have had a name but I have forgotten it.

I walked downstream a mile, fitted my smallest bamboo fly rod with a No. 4 line, a light leader, and a No. 18 Hairwing Royal Coachman. I could see that it was a deep, heavily overgrown creek, like the Fox in Upper Michigan, the prototype for Hemingway's "Big Two-Hearted River," but small, much smaller. The greenish water flowed over white-gray sand, turned in broad bends every fifty yards or so, swept under upturned roots, under willow branches, around a fallen log. There were little pockets, eddies, and holds everywhere—but no fish working or in sight against the light bottom. I worked my way slowly upstream, making short flicks of casts, happy to be off by myself and in the water. I vanished into the tangles and deadfalls, into the steady low sounds of the river. That I caught nothing in two swift hours of fishing troubled me not at all. I could not have spent an afternoon with better company than this brook.

I was approaching my friend's house, and about ready to quit, when a voice behind me said: "Won't get 'em that way, mister." I turned, nodded, and without further invitation he continued, and I knew at once that he must be the "old fellow" who caught trout regularly here. "Only way to catch 'em on flies in this crick is to use a small black nimp, like so. There's a couple big 'uns in there, though, and that's what I'm after with these minnies. Too easy with flies, specially that black nimp. Catch yourself a mess of good 'uns if you'll just turn around quiet and fish on back down the way you come, with a black nimp, like so."

It was worth a try. The man seemed privy to the inner conscience of the brook, a man not to be ignored. Anyway, I was in no hurry; small rivers purge my soul of fret and hurry.

But while I dug out my book of nymphs, I saw my adviser climb into the pool above me and plunk in one of his baits. Had he snookered me out of his hole?

In an hour, fishing slowly downstream with a weighted No. 18 nymph, fishing it into the runs, into the crevices and eddies, I took seven lovely brookies.

Little brooks hold such charm and surprise. Though many do not seem to have defined hatches, there may be a local pattern or two that imitate what the fish feed on regularly. Such creeks welcome experimentation.

I prefer the dry fly on such creeks. I like to wade wet, with only my sneakers, and feel the cold current against my legs. Fishing upstream, I disturb the fish ahead of me far less, and I am constantly moving into untouched water, closer and closer to the source. Often the water grows smaller, and the trees and shrubs along its banks wilder, more heavily overgrown. I once followed a little Colorado creek, above Steamboat Springs, for several miles—higher and higher, through tangles of berry bushes, thistle, above a series of waterfalls, past the last remnants of a road. I slipped to the side of the stream every time I could see a pool large enough to bear the cast; I fished below every waterfall. And the tiny brookies I found were the brightest I have ever seen—with dark mottled backs, almost pitch, and red and orange spots worthy of van Gogh's brightest palette.

I have found some startling fish in such creeks: seventeen- or eighteen-inch trout that turn suddenly for your fly with a drama—in such a tiny world—that shocks. Didn't I catch my first trout in such an unnamed Catskill creek—though by foul means? And I have found a leisurely pace, on such a stream in Montana, that was pure pleasure after the intensity of fishing several *name* rivers for a week. Far back on one of them, where a fallen spruce lay parallel to the surface of a small pool, I had to spend a half hour working my way into position to cast for a small rainbow rising just to the far side. I finally chose a No. 20 Blue Spinner on a 6X tippet and had to cast sidearm, into a pocket three feet wide, under the tree. That I did so, and caught the fish in such tight quarters, was a trophy for the memory.

There are practical reasons for fishing such small creeks, too. In the early season, when major rivers often bear the greatest pressure—and may even be unfishable because of heavy snow runoff—these tiny feeders may be rich lodes. Sometimes you'll find big river fish, which have escaped the turbulent flow; sometimes you'll find fly-fishing water when the main river will bear only rougher trade; almost always you'll find a touch of that wildness you thought was lost, nearer than you imagined.

No-name rivers. Bill's Brook; that Colorado creek; a place I once called Green Trout Brook—and a dozen others. These are private places, rarely stocked, rarely fished—places with the tonic of wildness, places that freshen my jaded eye with wonder.

DUSK

Sometime after the first full heat of summer falls, fishing shifts to the extremities of the day. Dawn and dusk are when the river is most alive, and there are times when a pool, even in the dead of summer, hosts a bacchanalia.

I used to fish the morning hours most frequently at this time of the season. I'd start while it was still dark and fish on into the first bright hours of midmorning. Often I'd fish a large nymph or streamer downstream in the chill of dawn, with the features of trees, hills, and farmhouses slowly emerging through the early-morning mists. There were big fish to be caught at such a time. I remember a huge brown slowly turning for a streamer as it raised up high in the currents below me on a Westchester County stream. The fish was twice, three times the size of any fish I'd taken from that river and much larger than any I'd ever seen taken from an eastern river. More fish and much bigger fish were on the prowl at that early hour, and often it was like fishing a different stream.

In July, with barely any light in the sky, I used to fish the broken water of the Esopus, with stonefly nymphs, for that fly hatches in abundance on that river, but always at night. The specific fly is the *Perla capitata*, perhaps half the size of the giant salmonfly out West, and using a smaller version of Charlie Brooks's stone, tied in the round, and Charlie's deep-nymphing technique, I often took three or four good rainbows.

But lately I've been drawn to the other end of the day. Perhaps it's the pleasure of being cooled and refreshed after a long, hot day of summer. Perhaps it's because the dry fly, at least for me, is so much more effective at that time—and the fly I always prefer to use. Or it may be that I'm growing shy of those early-morning jaunts and simply like that extra hour or two of sleep. But perhaps it's that something in the dusk stirs or touches something in me at this moment in my fishing life. Fishing can be like that: a matching of your rhythm to the rhythm of the kind of fishing you do. There are times when nothing but a raw float trip down a heavy Montana river will suit my needs, or fussing around with some terribly shy trout in a clear spring creek, or fishing a mountain feeder or a defined hatch on classic old Catskill water that I've gotten to know well. There are rhythms to a fly fisherman's year, to his life, to a day; there are rhythms to a cast, a drag-free float, and each section of each discrete river a fly fisherman ever fishes. Fly fishing thrums with harmonies.

Lately I have been powerfully attracted to the rhythms of dusk fishing. The sun begins to slant farther from the stream. Distances blur. A certain chill enters the air. Shadow and substance commingle. And sometimes, when you catch the river just right, a river that was a dead board all day is pocked crazy with a dozen rising fish.

I caught such moments twice on British chalkstreams. Both days had been long and lazy, with few fish visible and none "on the fin." With the local prescription of not casting other than to a visible or rising fish, my right arm had practically gone numb from disuse. Then the sun dropped below the Berkshire hills, that day on the Kennet, and suddenly the river was lit with a haunting gray light. I stood at the tail of a long deep run and in succession saw one, then two, then six or seven fish start to feed, their circles suddenly spreading out from the slate surface. I chose the nearest fish and it came at once to the little brown sedge. Then I took another, then a third. The river was hushed and there was no wind. The fish that had been so shy all day—a shyness that was more than what is called being selective; they were nearly dead—were now cream puffs. The same thing happened on the Test, after a terribly humbling day, when a Rusty Spinner fall made me think it was a different river—almost an overcrowded ghetto.

Such success is enough in itself to recommend dusk fishing. There are times of the year, times on a particular river, when the fish are simply most active—or *only* active—at dusk. Spinner falls, a hatch of big cream *Potamanthus,* half a dozen late-summer caddisfly hatches—often the only decent fishing of the day is when these evening hatches are on.

But there is something else: big fish.

Often they lose all caution when the sun is off the water, especially on western waters, where they feed less at night.

I'd gone with Don Kast, Les Ackerman, and a batch of guys to a private run on the Gallatin a couple of years ago, and we were all stretched out in various spots, fishing to a patch of water in which literally dozens of fish were working. There was no need to move; you worked your way into the place you wanted to be, and you could fish without moving a foot for an hour and not exhaust fish to cast to. I was with Don on a long flat glide, using a No. 18 red-bodied spinner, and he was catching a slew of fish while I watched and fumbled a bit and finally got the hang of the currents. We didn't get out of the water until after nine, and by then I'd had my fill of good fishing. We'd gotten no truly large fish, but it had been a perfectly splendid evening and a few rainbows went up to fifteen or sixteen inches.

When we got back to the car, one fellow was missing—and when he came up he was cursing like mad: he'd been fishing a huge sculpin imitation on a 1X leader, saturating it with fly dope and floating it into the heart of the heaviest current. Something had come up, taken the fly in a heavy swirl, turned a couple of times in the current, and then stormed downstream like a runaway train, breaking the line. The guy was in shock. He'd never hooked a fish that large.

"Serves you right, fishing for muskrats," said Les.

"Bring some cable next time," said Don.

I always think of such big fish when I fish at dusk: fish as big as a dog, coming out of black depths, to nab your largest fly. But it is the quality of the fishing that intrigues me most: the rapt, magical quality of that last hour or so before dark. The river seems more alive, the sense of time is suspended yet hurtling toward some peak moment. No matter that it now takes me six or seven tries, the fly held up to the vanishing light, my eyes squinting, to thread a hook; no matter that I can often only watch the general vicinity in which I've cast and cannot see the fly on the water. It's growing darker, second by second, the fish are working and may at any moment stop, and I fall into a hypnotic, even mystical state, astounded by remarkable happenings. On the East Branch of the Delaware one night, I suddenly looked up at the sky and saw a gigantic swarm of stoneflies, more than I'd ever seen in the East. The sky was thick with them and the birds were dipping and darting, and then I bent my head and looked at the surface of the water: everywhere in the riffles you could see the tooled turn of rainbows, porpoising, not leaping but turning in arcs, everywhere, wherever I looked, like martens or minks or something truly wild, come out only at a witching hour, and I simply stood and watched them, for twenty minutes, one with the mists, narcotic of riffles.

THE INTENSE FLY FISHERMAN

There was a time, some years ago, when I could fish with terrifying intensity. Give me a western lake and even the slenderest odds of hooking a ten-pound rainbow on a fly, and mules could not pull me from the water. From dark icy mornings until long after the sun bled beneath the sagebrush hills, I'd cast until my arm was numb and sun had baked the ridges of my right forefinger, wrist, and thumb a brilliant, blotched red.

I did this not once but dozens of times. I did it East and West, in Iceland and on British chalkstreams.

Sometimes I caught fish, sometimes I didn't. If I got some, I wanted more. If I got none, I had to hook a first before I left the water. If I got small fish, I wanted alligators. If I got a big one, one beyond my hugest hopes, I thought there might be another, even huger, down there. I lived merrily, mindlessly, uncomfortably on the fringe where fishing bleeds away into madness.

Such intensity led to fierce family fights and, much worse, I thought, botched fishing. The rush of blood heavy in my head, I raged around the waters, an indifferent caster, a diffident loner. I knew little about bugs and could not be bothered to learn. At its worst, I lost my love of new and remembered waters, my wonder at the quick dart of a trout for a fly, the fun of good fellowship and a common language. Only the intensity—dumb and manic—mattered. It positively wore me out.

I had forgotten why I came to rivers in the first place. I had forgotten the meaning of the Duke's gentle words, from *As You Like It:*

And this our life, exempt from public haunt,
Finds tongues in trees, books in the running brooks,
Sermons in stones, and good in everything.

There was, for a time, only the hot pursuit. But then, for whatever reasons, I swung to a far more leisurely frame of mind. I found I could stand passively behind a friend and chuckle as *his* fires raged out of control. Once, on a lazy little British chalkstream filled with wild browns anywhere from fingerlings to five-pounders, I spotted a fish rising just downstream of a river point topped with overhanging grasses. As the current zipped around the bend, swirled back behind the point, it brought a conveyor belt of easy food to the safe fish, which was dimpling steadily. Fingerling or five-pounder? I could not tell, though the protected lair suggested a smart, large fish.

Maples and willow on my side of the river made casts to that far bank quite impossible; there was enough current in the center to assure drag; and a cast above the point, from below, could only bring the fly whisking down past the trout's cafeteria. The rules of the river prohibited downstream fishing and that wouldn't have worked, anyway.

The one clear way to manage the classic little problem was to wade across the deep center current and cast to the fish from directly downstream. On a western river, with chest waders, I'd have done it even in my most leisurely, laid-back frame of mind. But I wore hip boots, practically the best suit of clothes I owned, and the only suit with me, and I'd caught a few fish already. So I sat down on a rock with my back against a maple and was content to watch.

After a few moments, my host came around the bend. He is a great enthusiast for fly fishing, a builder of business empires, a man not ever to retreat from a challenge.

"There's one, near the point, " he whispered loudly. "Oh, he's a good one. Oh, he's a very *verrrrry* good trout."

"I've been watching him," I said.

"Well have a go at him, Nick. Have a go at him. That's a *verrrrry* good trout."

"Not for me," I said. "Not today. He's all yours."

So my host got in and I leaned back against the tree to watch. He cast beautifully—a long line, hooking off to the right. But try as he might, he missed the corner by a foot, dropped his fly above and watched it sweep away from the eddy, picked up drag, got his fly caught in the willows behind him, came finally within inches of the eddy, and then stepped back and shook his head. The fish would not budge from that spot, not an inch. And my host *had* to catch it.

Sooner or later, I knew, probably sooner, he had to wade across the river in his hip boots. I felt quite smugly sure of this point.

He inched out toward the current and watched the water line rise on his boots. He cast again. Short. The angle was all wrong. He could not resist it, I thought. He *had* to have that fish. He was gut-hooked by that trout and could not possibly resist going after it.

And he couldn't.

A few minutes later the poor builder of business empires was sloshing helplessly across the river, soaking his Harris tweed jacket far above the pockets. And then, just as he got to the far side and prepared to cast backhanded up toward the fish, the trout stopped feeding for the day.

I was merciless toward him, for I had been there myself, many times: I had fished late into the night when my marriage hung on the slenderest of threads; I had waded into a pool in a jacket and leather shoes; I had walked through muck as treacherous as quicksand and waded on nights so dark an owl would have gotten lost.

But I was sad and envious, too. In my new contemplative height had I lost some of that marvelous passion that is also part of the sport? Of course I had. Fly fishing was never a purely contemplative recreation. There are times when, if you don't commit your full soul, if you don't put your blood into the pursuit, you might as well be playing a quiet game of cribbage before the fire. Isn't one of the prime reasons we venture out to *use* that intensity coiled within us?

Still, I was talking to Charlie Brooks about fish passion once and we agreed that certain symptoms of it could be lethal. I mentioned the guys on the Great Lakes who had died of salmon mania when wild weather came and they would not leave the water. He told me about a guy who'd arranged to float the Madison during the salmonfly hatch.

Ten minutes after the boat pushed off, the sport saw stoneflies every-where, and fish taking them. His casting grew wild, and with some help from a Montana gust of wind, he managed the unique distinc-tion of being probably the only man to hook himself with a Sofa Pil-low through the bottom lip and up into the flesh of the upper lip. Pinning his mouth shut. The guide wisely saw at once that this was a bad scene and announced that he was heading for the take out and would hustle the guy to a hospital.

There was a loud, determined noise from the sport. The guide thought he must be in great pain and rowed harder downstream. There was a louder, raucous, this time intelligible: "*Noooooooo!*" The man adamantly refused to leave the river; he *had* to finish the float.

"That's a real fisherman!" a friend said quietly, nodding approval, when I retold the story.

A *real* fisherman?

After eight hours on the water, the man had caught a dozen good trout but his face was distended beyond recognition, infected, and he was in a state of acute shock. The guide rushed him to Bozeman and doctors were barely able to save his life.

What intensity!

What lunacy.

IN A TACKLE CLOSET

The season has ended. There was not enough of it; there never is. Did I once actually write: "Fishing is nothing if not a pastime. It would be hell if I did it all the time." Now, in October, having fished too little again, still with the tug of angling in my veins, with good memories but somehow too few of them this year, with some dreams of meeting certain hatches I never met, I think I could do it every day, fish, most of the day, forever.

But this season is shot, and I am left only with those memories and speculations, some dreams that are never less than bright, and my tackle closet. It is tackle time, and I have skipped off by myself and hidden in my tackle closet, where I keep fussing around, touching, making lists, remembering.

The snake guide must be replaced on my No. 8 glass rod. Taking it down one afternoon at the pond, I pulled too hard, my hand slipped, and I ripped the thing off—and put the lower end of the guide an eighth of an inch into my index finger. Idiotic thing to do. The mark is still there. And also the mark, and sporadic sharp pains, on my heel, after that long day of wading with a torn sock.

I take out all the rods I used this year, about eight of them, old friends. There's the big No. 10 graphite I tried for the first time in the spring, on a small eastern trout pond. "Didn't know there were tarpon here," a man said, smiling, shaking his head. I had gotten the big weapon last winter and had wanted to try it out. A big, very powerful weapon. I used it with a shooting head, the first I had tried, on the pond, and I was astonished with what it could do. It heralded new worlds, a greater reach. So what if I didn't get to fish big western lakes or salt water with it this year. I had the thing now; I knew I could use it; I trusted graphite finally, years after everyone else, as always, after having seen two busted, four years ago, on mere back casts. It was light and it was remarkably powerful. My fish dreams were expanded by its presence in my closet. Tools beg for use, and I had added a new tool this year, one that augured possibilities.

Several glass rods had served me well: well-balanced journeymen of our time, modestly priced now, durable, pleasant to fish with. Not only could I not fault them: I realize, wiping them clean of some mud, that I had used them more frequently than any other rods this year. Cleaning one of the smaller rods, I remember that the last time I had used it, I told my companion John Taintor Foote's hilarious story "A Wedding Gift," in which the bridegroom sacrifices one wife for one legendary brook trout named Old Faithful. "That's nothing," said my friend, and he told me of an elderly gentleman we both knew, who, many years earlier, had taken his wife to the North Woods on *their* honeymoon. After they had been paddling for several hours, working hard because a three-day storm was predicted and the rains had already started, the guide called out that he had forgotten to tell them something: his shack had burned down. They'd all have to sleep in a tiny one-room cabin together.

My companion stopped.

"Is that the whole story?" I asked.

"Yep."

"Well, what happened after that?"

"Nothing happened, you dummy."

Then there are three rods, made of bamboo, and as I check windings and guides, wash cork handles lightly, look again at certain inscriptions, pen markings on them, I know that, as objects, I would never lose a speck of my affection for them. These are older than the others, two of them quite storied and priceless; touching them makes me shiver. Are they *better* tools? How would one judge "better"? More useful? More delicate? More durable? In some ways. At certain times. And they are certainly better to have *off* the stream; they cheer, thrill, delight me; the feel of them is the feel of something alive, vital, with something of the maker still in them. I worry about them, as I never worry about the others; I handle them like fine china; I remember threats to their health, the source of this nick and that scratch. I fish with them less lately but I love them as I have always loved bamboo. They are not snob-objects, not effete, not old-fashioned, not obsolete antiques. Each is the fruit of some one man's art, skill, imagination, patience, craft, and heart. Each is different. In a world where most things are the same, that alone is a lot. I admire them for themselves and for certain specific kinds of fishing they do best and I use them with a special pleasure and I want to protect them. Someday I want to make a piece of prose as useful and lovely as a fine bamboo fly rod.

There are some bad cracks in one floating fly line—happily one of my few last double-tapers; I'll cut off the bad end and see if I can make a shooting head from the rest. I want to learn a few new knots and splices this winter, and this five-year-old line will be my guinea pig. The other lines, like so much of the best modern equipment, have held up well; they need little care—only wiping down. I clip the last few inches off two, and build loops—which, stubbornly, I still prefer to nail knots: I've seen professionally tied nail knots pull out, and I find it easier to fasten a new leader to a loop.

The vest goes into the washing machine; the fifteen-year-old fish jacket goes to the tailor, for dry cleaning and sizing—it will last another fifteen if I can hide the ragged thing from my wife. The hat, which I prefer frumpy, remains scrunched in the corner of the closet. The nets do not need repair this year. The reels get a very light oiling and then go back into their chamois bags with their spare spools. The waders were new this year, and Phil gave me a new right rubber with aluminum cleats to replace the one I left in the mud; in a month or so, some wintery evening, I'll punch holes in the sides of the rubbers so I can run a shoelace through them and secure them to my ankles.

An old flashlight gets dumped. It's four years old, corroded. A few flies go out with some frayed leaders. I ship a fly box and some flies, which are serviceable, but not for me anymore, to a young friend who will be glad to give them a new life.

And then I turn to the flies.

Boxes and boxes of them.

Home-tied and store-bought; Whitlocks and Flicks and Greens and Bedinottis; some stoneflies Merrill tied for me and some striper flies Steve made in the Midwest and sent to me, which I haven't yet used; some Tapply hair bugs I had hoped to use in Maine this June (a June that vanished) or on Tap's lake; some of my good friend Thom Green's Leeches, which British friends called hairbrushes and which dozens of stillwater trout, in the East and abroad, could not resist this year; a Woolner mosquito larva; a score of Thom's Damn Greensels; delicate midges, outlandish Sofa Pillows, sleek little nymphs, and bushy Woolly Worms. I still have more than a dozen of Del Bedinotti's superb Hendricksons, thorax tie, which I'd got in a trade for an old Hardy Perfect reel, and a few funny Bitch Creek Specials and Girdlebugs from that Montana trip—was it really two years since I had been there?—and some of George Bodmer's Colorado Kings, which worked everywhere, and a last Boyle shrimp and two last Leiser Llamas.

I clip leader remnants from a few, fluff a few others, sort them, disengage some lamb's wool from a few barbs, put them in boxes and tuck them into their corner of the closet.

Then on the floor in a back corner of the closet, I find the little pharmaceutical box, with wire fasteners, that Flick used to send me a dozen Gray Fox Variants for Christmas last year. For all the madness the Christmas season brings to New York—with its mad crowds and madder buying sprees—I'd have it come twice as often if it came with such little boxes.

In the dark closet, in October, I finger it and put it on a shelf. Such a little box, filled with emblems of a craftsman's skill and heart, simple and elegant little delights and eminently useful in their day, made by hand at a time when most hands only turn knobs—such a little box, empty now, a bit crushed, found by chance in the dark corner of my fish closet in October, is the first harbinger of spring.

WINTER DREAMS WITH SPARSE

He walked into my life fifteen years ago, with his pink face and slight stoop, with his three-piece charcoal suit and quarter-inch-thick glasses, looking like an antique gnome or a tax collector. His first words to me were an angry growl. "You can't use it," he said. I didn't have the slightest idea who he was and told him so. "Alfred W. Miller is who, and if you think you're going to use my story 'Murder' in that blasted anthology of yours, you've got another think coming to you, buster." He liked to punctuate with "buster."

Interspersed with those growls were long, marvelous talks. perhaps in the great leather couch in his beloved Anglers' Club before a bright log fire, both our suits burning in a couple of places from hot cigar or pipe ashes. One minute he'd introduce me to a gigantic mutt named Mange, who could perform amazing feats with food and devour the refuse of his entire ambulance detachment in the mud and bivouacs of France in 1917, the next he'd be railing against salmon fishing, because when *he* caught a fish, sir, he wanted to know why the beggar took the fly. Sitting there, chuckling away, in danger of being burned to a crisp, we used to vow that someday we'd go winter camping together. He was tough enough to have done so, well into his eighties; I was the cream puff.

He had a thousand tales. A dozen times I heard him tell the long, rambling, hilarious "fly in the nose" story, about a friend who got a Fan-Wing Royal Coachman caught in the tip of his nose on a Sunday morning in Pennsylvania, and though he always carried a tackle box filled with a thousand gadgets, he could not find one with which to extricate himself; the story progressed to a diner, where a waitress was terrified by his odd nose-dress, and then to the sudden discovery that his car was on fire; then a rattlesnake somehow appeared mysteriously, and finally—an hour after he'd begun the tale—his friend tumbled down a hill and knocked the senior member of the Parkside Anglers Association nearly senseless—twice. He had tales about Mr. Hewitt, whom he had known well and loved and always called "Mister," and LaBranche, Roy Steenrod, and the Brooklyn Fly Fishers; he had serious reservations about Theodore Gordon because the man had abandoned his sick mother. Sparse's other nickname was Deac, from Deacon, for his moral uprightness.

He was adamant one June when I told him I had not yet been on the water. It was a disgrace. He growled and promptly hauled Mari and me off to the DeBruce Club on the Willowemoc. We fished a little together—he was a deft left-handed caster—and he showed me where LaBranche cast what he called the first dry fly on American waters. Then he said, "You've been working too hard. You need an uninterrupted couple of hours on the water to refresh yourself, bub. I'll entertain your missus." And he sat with Mari at the kitchen table in the Krum farmhouse and told her, in great detail, for four hours— the information being somewhat more than she wanted—about ballistics and maneuvers on the Mexican Border Patrol.

He was astonishingly precise about a great variety of gadgets and contraptions, some in common use, some of his own invention—like the zipper for chest waders and the attachment that kept you from dropping your pipe into the drink. No matter that the former leaked and when the pipe slipped it only dropped hot ashes down your waders.

I'd heard the "fly in the nose" story a dozen times and I was at the lunch table five years ago when Sparse began to tell it, faltered, and his great memory failed. I did not tell him to tell that story the last time I saw him, on his ninetieth birthday. Frail, shrunken, he had lost over eighty pounds. Hoagy Carmichael had rigged him a hat with a wire brace screwed into the cloth so that he could hold a pipe in place without using his hands and not incinerate himself; the old guy loved the idea of it. I wanted to hear Sparse tell one of the old tales once more and prodded him to tell me the "prune rod" story. He did so, as well as he'd ever told it—about his father's belief (when Sparse was eight years old) in the health-giving properties of prunes, the deal struck to eat twenty-five prunes for a nickel (with a limit of fifty per week), the rod eventually bought from the proceeds of this worthwhile activity—and then he produced the huge hickory club itself.

Like that hickory "prune" rod, brilliantly waxed and protected after eighty-two years, better than it had ever been or deserved to be, whatever Sparse touched became richer, finer. A friend's prose, a lunch at which he unfolded one of his inimitable stories, a day on the Willowemoc with him, a thousand lives he touched, a memory, an Anglers' Club *Bulletin* edited with his discerning eye, an event he'd lived or carefully researched—all were brighter, more memorable for his ministrations. He could make us laugh with a fantastic story about a fifty-pound brown trout that devoured pieces of bread soaked in Scotch and make us cry when we read "A Drink of Water." Nearly blind in one eye and with only 20 percent vision in the other, he was still the most meticulous proofreader I ever knew and always the firmest, most exacting critic. He saw more than any of us, remembered it precisely, and then crafted his words with choicest care. The trout were not taking, but a boy along on the trip "rose to chocolate bars all day long"; some of the finest fishing is in print; he always wanted to fish "not better but more." His counsel and encouragement to a hundred lesser writers, some quite famous, has yet to be chronicled properly, and his own prose remains a constant lesson.

The day after his first growl, he gave me "Murder" to use, and he kept giving for fifteen years—a score of unforgettable moments and a piece of his heart. With a roar like a werewolf, Sparse could not hide that he was really mostly a gentleman and a lamb. He practiced a code from another, nearly forgotten time, and it included strong doses of honor, steadfastness, loyalty, dignity, backbone, pride, the art of making truly careful sentences and the art of being a gentleman, and love.

He had been a reporter for the *Wall Street Journal* and then, until several years ago, a stockholder-relations counsel; he went to work every day, well into his eighties. In his last years, old age did its best to ravage him. The doctors rummaged around inside him and did their worst; at times he had tubes attached here and there and less than a full complement of parts. But most painful must have been the loss of his beautiful and astonishing memory. which no doubt had helped him become the debating champion of New York State long before the First World War. Hoagy, who saw him a couple of weeks shy of his ninety-first birthday, reported that the only gift he wanted was "the ticket out of here." He died on Veterans Day and would have liked that.

Everyone who knew Sparse will miss him sorely—not because he was always an easy man, which he wasn't, but because there is not a chance, buster, that we shall see your likes again. He imputed to the world of fly fishing, which he loved deeply, a sense of character and tradition and wit; he saw it as a human activity, full of wonder and excitement, far beyond the mere catching of fish—an activity that enlivened the heart and sparked the imagination. It had the power to bring out the best in men—and some of the worst. He told us about the stupidity of much high-pressured "sport" and the fun we might have on our fishless days. He was far more than what he'd admit to: "Merely a good reporter, bub." He was a superb writer, who will be read a hundred years from now, and a great-hearted, humorous, and perfectly remarkable man.

It is winter now and I delight to imagine us finally off someplace in the snow, sitting on a log, pufffing at pipes whose ashes sizzle and sink as they hit the snow. "Why don't you just tell me that 'fly in the nose' story one more time, old friend," I say. He grunts and chuckles and screws up his face, then says, "Well, it was an early Sunday morning in Pennsylvania, buster, and . . ." And my face keeps aching from laughter and I don't notice the cold, and finally, like some great chord, the senior member of the Parkside Anglers Association gets knocked nearly senseless for the second time.

SPLAT, SPLAT

It's winter now and the city is a mess. There are ruts of dirty ice and patches of gray slush everywhere. From my window I can see half a dozen people, hunched over and nearly hidden in their overcoats, walking briskly and breathing smoke. Wet snow flurries changed this afternoon to rain and sleet. This morning I got a letter from Craig Mathews in West Yellowstone and have read it over three times. He'd been midge fishing on the lower Madison and had taken three good rainbows; in the upper right-hand corner he always notes the weather: "clear, *very* cold, -32 degrees; heavy snows expected." I could be forced to pass up an opportunity to midge fish in that. I feel cozy in my living room, left to the bright fire, the splat of sleet and heavy raindrops against the panes, and my memories.

Mostly, I have been remembering a couple of weeks I spent in Montana last summer. As usual, I'd gone out bone tired and had holed up where I could be alone, except that my old friend Les Ackerman happened to be holed up there, too, which proved okay because he knew immediately what I wanted and bent his usual routine to those needs. Les doesn't look like a lunatic. From a distance you might take him to be your average fly fishing enthusiast. But he was in the ski troops during the war, and though he's ten years older than me, he could pass for ten younger. He fishes every day of the season and he fishes with astonishing vigor and passion. He's a fearless wader and a fright to try to follow. He cranked the engine down for the puffing likes of me and said, "I have all autumn; you're here for a week or so."

Mostly we explored nearby creeks and rivers for a few hours every morning. It was leisurely fishing, mostly; we were not particularly after big fish, though we raised a few; we were not after difficult fishing, though some of it was demanding. We fished the Gallatin a lot, which was nearby, and the Madison, which was a bit farther, and some odd little no-name brooks, some of which he'd fished before, some of which we both fished for the first time. We passed up several invitations to fish choice rivers a hundred, two hundred miles away, which I had come two thousand miles to fish.

It was late August. Bright afternoons trailed brisk mornings, the evenings had the first sweet sting of the fall, and grasshoppers were everywhere. We kicked them up in the high grasses, they splattered against the windshield; now and again—on a windy afternoon—they flipped into the river and we watched them sail downstream, kicking, in the current.

Early in the second week, when I wanted a bit more adventure, Les shoved me into one of his float tubes and we frog-kicked around a couple of local lakes. It was the first time I'd been in one of those contraptions and I enjoyed paddling backward, so close to the roof of the liquid world beneath me, watching the pelicans, Canada geese, mallards, and ospreys. Across the lake, over one of the broad meadows, a hawk was working in long gliding swoops. We saw a moose and a small herd of elk. On the surface of the lake I watched a plump mayfly wriggle from its nymphal shuck and hatch, plucked a few *Baetis* spinners out of the film, and trailed my hand and line slowly. I picked up a couple of modest browns the second time out and a chunky rainbow, like a bright silver football, the third.

It was a pleasant, restful time, with the kind of happy, leisurely rhythms that are addictive. If I could steal a month, six weeks of fishing every year, I thought, I could blissfully live in gray New York forever—no matter that we'd been mugged this year, rents were skyrocketing, business was too busy, and you didn't step on soil from one month to the next.

But as I sit in this warm room in the midst of winter, I'd as well be here as anywhere else right now. I have my books, my papers, and this antique Underwood Standard to peck at, and the sleet is splatting merrily against the windowpanes. And I have my memories.

Most, I remember the late afternoons on the Gallatin, after I'd done my serious fishing for the day, when I went with Mari down to the meadows.

Craggy bluffs rose on the opposite side of the river, and when the sun hit them, they glowed a tawny red. Mari had begun a series of watercolors, and the forms—looming and etched against the bright blue sky, the layers of the canyon built into Vs and almost abstract, divorced from their local meaning—satisfied her very much. Thoughts of the few hours ahead always satisfied me very much as we chose a motif for the day and pulled off the highway onto a dirt and rutted road heading toward the river.

When she had set out her paper, palette, brushes, and paints and had filled an olive jar with water from the river, I'd start to fuss with my tackle. I would set out my waders to dry on top of the car (they'd begun to leak) and rig up one of my longer fly rods. Then I'd tuck a half dozen flies into a Sucrets box, pop the thing into the top pocket of my shirt, and tramp off downriver.

I'd stay low on the bank and cast across and slightly upstream with a Sparrow, that marvelous nymph-what-have-you originated by Jack Gartside and nicely adapted by Don Kast, the fine tier and excellent Gallatin guide. If the water was deep, I'd cast a bit farther upstream, to get the fly down; when I found a shallow riffle, I'd cast across and downstream and let the fly swing in the current. The fly was fetching. Bright wild rainbows would suddenly tighten at the end of the line and jump briskly, flashes of wet silver.

When I'd gone a half mile or more downstream—the fishing leisurely and languid enough for me to pass up lots of good water on the opposite side of the river, which I couldn't reach from my shore— I'd stop, sit on the bank with my back against a jackleg fence, in the midst of gray sagebrush and lemon-yellow cinquefoil and Indian paintbrush, change my sunglasses for a pair that would let me see the eye of a fly, and smoke a cigar. I'd smoke it very slowly.

The daily late-afternoon gusts would have come up by then, and the slant of the sun sparkled the broken water in ten thousand diamonds of light. Was that a spurt of water near the midriver rock? A grasshopper would land on my khaki pants, I'd trap it, look at it carefully, and compare it favorably to my Jay-Dave's Hopper, and then chuck the kicking thing out into the current.

This was the time I liked best. I'd tie on a No. 10 hopper and head slowly upstream, watching the water for fish, for likely runs. I'd try the far current if I could reach it, or the riffle where two branches of the river came together, or the eddy behind the boulder two-thirds across. The hopper would roll over on the cast and slap down on the water with a pretty little *splat*. I'd see the electric flash of a dark form in the clear river, and there would be a spurt of water and a fish would be on. How many did I catch and turn back each day on that hour's slow walk upstream? Enough. More than enough. The fish seemed to be everywhere—along the far bank, in midcurrent, behind the boulders, where the riffles became pools. I'd even fished with a short line against the near bank, casting fifteen feet directly upstream, where grasses hung over the water and the river carved caverns under the sod, and I would watch the rainbows and browns bust up out from the dark, no more than three or four feet below me, and blast the fly. The biggest fish were there, right below me, where I'd always ignored them, and on consecutive afternoons I raised but did not hook a rainbow that left me trembling.

* * *

By eight on that last night we were ready to leave. The rush of the wind stopped. I watched the water closely while Mari put away the last of her supplies. The evening caddis hatch would start in a few moments; I'd fished it twice and had done very well with a little No. 16 Elk-Hair pattern. I'd pass that up tonight. Almost as an afterthought I caught a couple of grasshoppers in the sagebrush, tossed them in at the head of a run, and watched the two quick spurt-rises—*splat, splat*—like rain and sleet splashing against a living room window in the dead of winter.

from

Spring Creek

(1992)

THE FIGHT

From where I stood I did not always see the fly alight on the slate surface of the water, and now and then I'd pour myself another lemonade or fuss with my reel or line. I felt very contented. I had caught a couple of remarkable fish and that, thank you, had been quite enough. But I was facing the river and whenever I looked up I saw it and Herb and watched until whatever little drama was being played was done. I was looking up when I saw a fish rise twice, then—with a wake—drift off to the right. Then it came back and took four or five PMDs. Herb watched, tense now, waiting to cast. I wondered why he was waiting so long. Did he want the fish to get good and confident? It was clearly a very big fish, but there were a lot of big fish in this pool and it was quite impossible to tell from the delicate rise and the wake quite how large this one might be.

For a few moments the feeding stopped. Then I saw the slight bulge and dimple of the fish, about seventy-five feet out, to the right, and then I saw Herb's rapid cast.

I saw his bright yellow parachute alight four or five feet up from where the water had pinched a moment before. The cast, with only one false cast far to the left, had been exactly on target. The rumpled leader started to straighten, the fly moved ever so slowly on a current you could not see, and I felt my heart leaning out onto the water, straining after the fly—my breath slightly irregular—wanting to coax the fish into taking.

That moment was more than six years ago and memory, for me, about fishing, always mingles with fantasy and dream. But this memory is too sharply etched not to have been real.

I remember the long length of line going back and then forward, and then shooting to a distance of perhaps seventy feet. I remember the No. 17 Pale Morning Dun parachute alighting with a final little somersault of the leader and then picking up what there was of current and floating slowly downstream. I remember the expectation and the wait. And I remember with perfect clarity—when I run the entire scene out in my mind, in sequence—the slight pinch and bulge of the flat surface . . . and then the sudden, immense, electric rush of force.

The trout took Herb's fly lightly and did not move off unperturbed by the prick, like the books say. The fish zoomed off like a bonefish—hard and fast and far, in a straight line, like any wild thing held; and then, two hundred feet up the long pool, it leaped once, erupting, exploding, splattering the air with bubbles and silver splashes of water.

"Bigger than I thought," Herb said.

He stood up now, intent, looking upstream.

"Parachute?" I asked.

Herb nodded.

I worried about the size of his leader point and asked: "Six-X?"

He nodded again.

After the jump the fish settled down to doing what a truly big fish is supposed to do. It moved off heavily, steadily, heading for the uppermost part of the pool, where the river pinched through the last narrow sections of land and broadened and slowed.

The fish was clearly larger—by a great measure—than the two fish I'd taken. Quite how large it was I could not tell. The fish was now well into the backing, perhaps three hundred feet upstream, and all you could see was the long expanse of buckskin fly line and then the smaller white backing, and at the far end a steady surge of water, as if a foul-hooked muskrat or a beaver or an otter was burrowing just beneath the surface. There was simply no way that this fish would not break off.

Herb's shockgum leader was decisive. He'd surely lose the fish without it. For with all that line out, and the fish making sudden moves to the left or right, the 6X leader would surely otherwise have broken. But it did not. The fish veered off toward the far bank and the tippet held. The fish slashed at the surface and I thought that surely now it was gone; but the line was still taut when the commotion stopped. The great trout came up twice more—hugely, splattering water high, shaking, then crashing back down—with ninety feet of fly line and two hundred and eighty feet of backing between it and the fly rod, and the fish was still on, and heading still farther upstream, around the bend.

You could not begin to pressure such a fish on such tackle yet, but you could stay with it, subtly—lean into it, drop your rod tip when it jumped, lower the rod (as Vince Marinaro advised) when the fish ran, so the line came directly off a finely tuned reel, with less friction. With abrupt, deft, athletic movements, Herb managed it all.

But then I saw him fumble with his reel and lean forward awkwardly, his rod extended as far as he could extend it in front of him. Something had happened. Was the line tangled? Surely he'd lose the fish now.

The bottom of the pool here was muddy and pocked with muskrat holes. It would be treacherous to wade toward the fish, and to get out of the pool and walk up the brushy, irregular bank could be fatal to the fight in a dozen ways. No, he had to stay in the water, where he was, in that one spot, and he had to manage the fish from that fixed position where he stood. There were no other options, no other ways to save what was becoming a desperate situation.

I did not have to stay so far from the action so I had walked to a high bank upstream where I'd have a better chance to see the great trout. I trotted back now to see if I could help Herb with whatever problem he had. The problem was this: the fish had taken the last foot of backing and for a moment—fumbling with the reel, leaning forward—Herb was trying to reach out and secure another foot or two of line before the gigantic fish broke off, which surely it would do. The fish was at the very end of the backing and sort of wallowing there, not pressing forward, finally tired perhaps, after the run, the shaking, the acrobatics. The fish could not be pressured but perhaps it could be *urged,* and Herb leaned his rod back a bit, then dropped it and reeled, to regain another foot or so of line. But the line would not come back onto the spool; tied loosely, with a slip knot—the only carelessness in Herb's rig, or perhaps not—the line was circling the spool without coming back onto it. With the fish moving slightly toward him now, the line threatened to go slack.

Herb's fingers, fussing with the circling line, grew frantic for a moment.

Still leaning forward, he had to tighten the knot with his free fingers and coax line back onto the reel.

Well, that's it, I thought. A fly line and one hundred yards of backing hadn't been enough to hold this fish. If the great fish made a sudden move now, Herb would lose it for sure.

But despite the slack and the fumbling, the fish was still on.

Foot by foot Herb urged the gigantic thing back toward him, regaining half, then three-quarters of the backing as the fish turned and headed heavily, at an angle, downstream. There was no urgency in its movements now; the fish was subdued, worn, if not yet quite beaten. It could be led without being forced. The process—now done by inches—required immense patience.

Back on the high bank I kept my eyes flicking from fisherman to fish. In ten minutes the trout was back onto the reel and I knew that it would only take a few more minutes before Herb had it at his side and would be reaching down to release it. I'd seen him handle the endgame flawlessly dozens of times.

The fish was near the surface now, canted to one side slightly, not twenty feet from me, and I could look down and see it with absolute clarity. I can see it still, all these years later. The trout was a full foot longer than the two I'd caught, thicker by far, more than double their weight. And it was nearly beaten. I have seen larger trout come from lakes, on leaders the size of cables; steelhead are larger, even stronger; and this was fully the size of a dozen Atlantic salmon I'd seen. Why did this fish seem then—and why does it still seem—the most prodigious trout I'd ever seen? Surely the light tackle—not an affectation but a necessity for luring such a fish—and the relative size of the fish to this type of fishing played their roles. But a two-pound

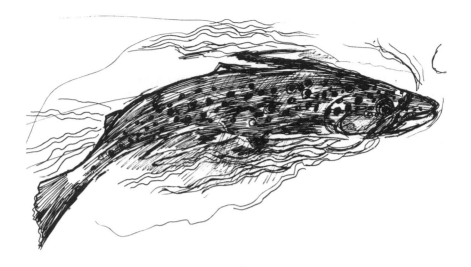

bluegill, even a giant of its species, is still only two pounds of blue-gill, a piker. This fish was a monster.

"It's heading toward the weeds," Herb said flatly. "Can't put more pressure on."

The big head came half up out of the water and shook once, and the leader held, and Herb coaxed it slightly, firmly, away from the weeds. I felt quite sure he'd keep the great trout out of the weedbed. I felt sure he'd take it now, with only thirty or forty feet of line out.

And then the fish went a couple of feet off to the right, into the region of the weeds, and was off—and I felt then, and feel now, years later, as you must feel reading this, as all of us feel at such moments— as if I'd lost a part of myself and would forever be searching for it.

Herb reeled in quickly, checked the end of his leader, and found that the No. 17 golden fly had neither broken off nor bent straight, but simply pulled free. "Didn't break him off," he said. He smiled, shook his head, and said mildly, "*That* was a very big fish, Nick."

Now, so long afterward, I can forgive him his insouciance: a man who could fight a fish so well and lose it with so little trauma had to have caught a dozen that size.

I'd have punched myself silly.

AT THE SECOND BEND POOL

The East Branch, skirting the base of the bench, thick with willows, cattails, and marsh, bore little resemblance to the West Branch or the main stem of Spring Creek. It was a moody, mysterious place. The water was thinner here, and there were fewer bends. In only a run or two, and usually only within inches of the far bank, could you expect to raise a fish on a fly that did not actually imitate a living insect. The fishing was more exacting and the entire attitude of the river here was different, and had a different effect on me.

Herb had not taken me to it for the first ten days, and of course there had been no reason to do so, for we had more than enough fishing elsewhere, especially when the Green Drakes were on. And there was less water here, barely enough for two people to fish comfortably. There was the huge pondlike pool in which we had both taken those large fish, the slick thin head where water from the river flattened and spread; three pools; and then a second huge pondlike pool. Above the second pond, the river grew even more mysterious and wild—and was extremely difficult to fish. I kept saving these East Branch headwaters for a more leisurely day. I kept thinking that some day I'd spend six or seven hours up there, track it to its source, wander a bit and perhaps fish a bit, and see what I could find. Meanwhile, whenever I went up the East Branch, I thought about those headwaters, even as the lower East Branch itself made me strangely contemplative.

One day I caught a marvelous hatch of PMDs where the river went into the first pond, then caddis and PMDs in the First Bend Pool, and more rising fish in the middle run. By eleven o'clock I'd taken nearly a dozen good trout, all big browns and one twenty-inch rainbow, and had had more than my fill. I'd fished very hard the day before and this burst of action—and success—had bled me of much of my usual ambition. So I decided to sit down on the pleasant inside rim of the Second Bend Pool and merely watch the water.

That great cluster of fish were in the deep hole—thirty or forty of them, in all age classes, and a couple of fish were rising steadily. But I put my rod down in the high grasses and got out a little black notebook I always carry in a vest pocket. Usually I'm too busy to write in it; usually when I'm on the water I want only to fish. But I had been fishing hard, every day for more than three weeks, and I had caught a lot of fish, and I rather wanted to write about those fish I'd found rising in the slick at the head of the pond. I'd had to cast across and slightly downstream to get them and that hour had been exceptionally pleasant. It was best to fish not as I usually did, when I could, but when the fishing would be best—and slowly I had been learning, because of the enormous number of opportunities at Spring Creek, when that best was. The morning had been a revelation; I had not known that the bigger fish, from the pond, would move up during a good PMD hatch, though it was logical that a good head of flies would bring them there. I noted that the first of them had risen at about ten forty-five, and promised myself I'd come back the next day to see if it was a daily event. I had seen fish move steadily upstream during a hatch, ever closer to the source of a hatch, several times; and I had also seen them, in the big flat, slip back downstream during a heavy hatch, taking flies lower and lower in the pool, using less and less energy and drifting back with the current. I never went to Spring Creek without seeing something new; it was so fecund, so full of chances, that I don't think even Herb had seen all of it, nor would anyone, ever.

A snout came up in the current of the Second Bend Pool but I decided not to pursue it.

I was scribbling rather quickly now.

Learning something new about angling always excites my brain—what would take a specific fish, why it was feeding, how to solve an individual angling problem. I'd done something right and I wanted to understand what. The general laws of angling never held for all situations but they always overlapped. You learned the parts of speech, one at a time, and then you tried to put them all together: not parts anymore, but speech.

There was a "speech" to the writing about fishing, too, and I'd thought hard about its many different languages. Literary friends told me that the great trick was not to use the technical language of fly fishing—the thorax spinners, the 7X leader tippets, the *Hexagenias* and Tricos and PMDs. These, they said, were the jargon of the sport and made it quite unavailable to the intelligent general reader, he who did not fish but read with care and discernment. I'm sure this is so. But the technical language is not the voice of the idiot savant except when it is used by an idiot savant. And I wasn't after a language of literature.

Just as I would not write down, I would not write up. What I was doing, I hoped, with as much skill and invisible artifice as I could muster—as little of the factitious, the posturing as possible—was to report on days afield, and the nature of my relationship to the sport, a relationship that included having, at various times, the keenest possible interest in the minutiae of fly fishing: not using the fancy or occult words, or the Latin, or the names of people and places to impress, but choosing, always, the fullest, most personal way to tell where I'd been. A Trico is a Trico is a Trico; it is not merely a small black fly, nor is it a rose.

I had tried, for more than twenty-five years, to find and to build a language that represented me—something with feeling but not sentimentality, a voice playful but not mannered, not down, not up, not safe, not different just to be different. Some clever populist once wrote to a fishing magazine complaining of the literary references in essays I wrote—to Yeats, Keats, Kafka, and Chaucer—as if these had been laid on with a trowel, with pretensions. He had deliberately misspelled every other word in his letter, feigning a superior ignorance, to defend something called the common man. But I read Yeats and Keats and Kafka in my twenties, on my own, and they changed my life. I wouldn't think of hiding them. They are as much my friends as Len and Mike and Doug; they are as much a part of my speech as Tricos and 7X tippets. Do we read books to get bland pap or mere information or clever nonsense, or to touch another human being? I want those who read me to touch me, to know me—for better or worse—not some studied mask I might put on. And this is the stew of me: Yeats and PMDs, wit that leavens and builds proportion, not sophisticated but (I hope) not dumb, a warm mulch that heats the postmodernist chill. I'd like the stew to be rich enough to catch some of the stillness, complexity, joy, fierce intensity, frustration, practicality, hilarity, fascination, satisfaction that I find in fly fishing. I'd like it to be fun, because fly fishing is fun—not ever so serious and self-conscious that I take it to be either a religion or a way of life, or a source of salvation. I like it passionately but I try to remember what Cézanne once said after a happy day of fishing: he'd had lots of fun, but it "doesn't lead far."

I'd like fish talk to exist not by itself, as a separate estate, but in relationship to scores of other languages that live in me, from art language to street talk to the voices of a thousand writers who echo in my head: not them, nor the echo of them, but something absolutely mine, as real a possession as a Sony Trinitron or a Winston rod or my grandfather's oak dining table.

Perhaps, I thought, sitting on the inside rim of the Second Bend Pool, I am not after trout at all; perhaps this is a ruse; perhaps, among my many ulterior motives, one is the discovery of a language. Or has writing about fishing, which cannot occur without first fishing, become quite as important to me as the act itself? "Wouldn't think of disassociating Fishing from Art," said the happy John Marin—"one and the same thing with me."

A trout shoves its snout up, my heart beats quicker, and I doubt all ulterior motives.

I would as well be here, beside this pool, right now, as anywhere in the universe. I have thought about such a place without knowing it existed. At times I have wished life as simple as this riverbank—the world a logical structure of bend, current, riffle, and pool, the drama already unfolding on the glassy surface, and me, here on the bank, my ass wet, armed with some simple lovely balanced tools and some knowledge, prepared to become part of it for a few moments.

A fish rises with a slight spreading circle; then another comes up, its snout rising from its world up into mine, of air; the drama begins. In a while I may choose to enter it, or I may not, for I have learned enough skills to play; I can cast beyond my shoelaces.

This is a contained, mostly understandable world, and in my nearly sixty years I have understood less rather than more of that other, outside world. Like Kafka, I sometimes seem to hop about bewildered among my fellow men—and they often regard me with deep suspicion. That larger world, away from rivers—and my little place in it—stuns me with its complexity: The old friend who last month looked me in the eye and lied. The other who stole from me. Incrementing details and details. People with Rolodexes for brains. "The beating down of the wise/And great Art beaten down" and down. That bewildering bear I have been—rife with contradictions. The demons in me that demand more of friends than they can ever give, and nothing; that want only solitude like this—and the rush and lights and edge of the cities; that like and crave and despise all "getting and spending."

Tolstoy speaks of an uncle who once told him, when he was a boy, to go into a corner and *not* think about a white bear. I have come to this riverbank, this rarest of corners of the universe, and of course cannot help but think of all that other jazz, and perhaps always will. Pascal says that the trouble with the Western world is that we don't know how to be content in an empty room. I am not content here—or anywhere. Nor, as I think of it at the Second Bend Pool, do I want to be content, like a cow or a holy man. I want to put boulders in the way; I don't want to flow without effort. I am restless—therefore I am. And here, now, it's best to get most of it out—like a good sneeze, god-blessed or not.

A muskrat surfaces in the slack shank of the bend, sees me just as I turn and see him—"Since things in motion sooner catch the eye/Than what not stirs"—and, in a lithe gray roll, porpoises and disappears. I follow his wake across the river, into the marsh, up out of the water and into a hole on the opposite bank; he never looks back.

There are more circles and snouts now. I may have been here half an hour or an hour or two hours and the world here feels quite safe from my possible predation. On the glassy surface, a couple of feet from my eyes, I see some flattened spent spinners, two mottled caddis, and half a dozen lovely Pale Morning Duns. I pick out one of the duns with my eye, one golden speck twenty-five feet out; it reflects the midday sun as it carries on the current and disappears in a rather full and satisfied pocking of the water. The trout here take the duns like that when they get going good. It's unnerving to see them do so. They are as vulnerable now as they'll ever be.

I tie on a parachute PMD, daub it with flotant, strip line off my reel, and make a first tentative cast. But my heart is not in it and the cast is too tentative. I have been thinking too much. The line lands heavily, well short of the nearest rise, and suddenly the pool is perfectly still, as if it contained not a minnow.

Well, I have been snubbed before, by trout and Diana Vreeland, and am sure these fish will come back. Anyway, my brain hasn't quite stopped nibbling on my concentration. And there is no place I'd rather be right now—not Paris, where the fishing is poor; not the beach, where you are asked to take off your clothes in public, put grease on your body, sit in the sand; not the great libraries or concert halls or even the museums I love. This valley feels like home to me right now—me, a city kid, descended from Russian city people, bent always, in a kind of hungry tropism, to space and clear water and open sky.

I would like to be here for weeks, even months, but I could not live all my life in trout country. I have other fish to fry and, difficult as that other world might be, I'd rather be in the thick of it, blasted by its terrors, than sit outside and snipe. If all the year were holidays, to sport would be as tedious as to work—and I have rarely found work tedious. And in the city I can stand before a Rembrandt self-portrait, a Velázquez, a Titian, a delicate Tiepolo, and be in some vital connection with the real thing: not some predigested version of it in a magazine, a reproduction in a book, part of a short course on television, but the real thing. Someone out this way, some years ago, called my Picasso a fraud and wondered how I could teach "Keats, Shelley, and all those weirdos." In my office, things other than trout rise, and some of them "lead far."

Why must I always compare them?

Why, when both are so important to me, must I hold one against the other?

Is it that they always bleed into each other and are never wholly separate?

Or that, looking always for one simple and direct view of this stew of a world, I am tugged in just a few too many directions?

The fish have started to feed again. There are two in the main current, slurping; one dimples in the slack water near the far bank; several are high enough in the water for their dorsals to poke through the slate surface.

I might have been trying for two hours to do something vaguely called "getting in touch with yourself and with nature," but now, with the fish rising freely, I have something specific to do and all that is irrelevant. If I have "gotten in touch" with anything it's the damp bank against which I've been leaning, the grasses soggy from spring seepage; mostly my elbow and ass, sopping wet, have been in touch.

I watch a teal with a string of five or six ducklings, like a tail, slip up out of the pool and around the bend. I see a couple of killdeer chicks, the size of golf balls, scurry into the underbrush.

The fish are going good now.

I check my fly, draw enough line from my reel, look at the simple happy scene before me, of five or six rising trout—and then calmly proceed to demonstrate I'm not just a dreamer.

ONE LAST TOUGH TROUT

For five or six years after my first halcyon visit to Spring Creek, I returned for several weeks or so, always in June and extending through the Fourth and on into the bright hot days of July. Three times the river, if that was possible, was more generous. We caught a gigantic Green Drake hatch one year that had us backing away, watching, before it was half over. Herb performed more of his prodigious feats, effortlessly, and I gradually became a steady, resourceful, more consistent spring creek fisherman.

Each year the nearby town held its Fourth of July celebration, with floats and a rodeo, firecrackers and flag waving. Herb and I never went. We stayed close to the river and what celebration we had related to the pursuit and capture of specific fish—days with their own pace, slow and full, with their own bold firecrackers.

"You really ought to come, you know," Mari said of the town celebration, telling us how unique it was—innocent and old and honest. "You and Herbert are old stick-in-the-muds."

Perhaps. But the fishing was too compelling to leave and even a slow day of fishing Spring Creek was more exciting and significant to me than just about anything else I might find in the civilized world, and rarer. When I got near Spring Creek I wanted to be fishing it.

New Junes came and we'd pack up tackle and art supplies and mostly a few plain clothes, and head west—starting at a crowded eastern airport, transferring at Denver, taking a smaller plane to an airport where I might well know three or four people of the few dozen that constituted its crowd, where Herb and Pat—with smiles—were always waiting. The years blurred. Had we caught that remarkable Green Drake hatch on the middle water three or four years ago? Which years did Al McClane come? Was it two years ago that I caught the fat rainbow in the Farrago Pool? Have I mixed some of those other years into that first, miraculous visit, when so much of my fishing life changed? Probably. I've probably done that. And why not? Spring Creek—all its years in one pot—has seemed to me an event separable from all other events in my life. It was always there. It was always a thing in my head, capable of being summoned at any time of the year, capable of sustaining and healing me. Surely it changed. The island in the Paranoid Pool might be smaller, the Great Horseshoe Bend might be cold one year. The pelicans—swooping in formation across a pool—might have skimmed a dozen fish out of the South End Pool. The Nursery might be even hotter than ever, but the flats above Farrago Pool had just as many wild, furtive, darting shadows over the light ocher bottom as it ever had, and I was as hard-pressed to catch them as before, and the channels might be different and the curlew might not stop on their migration from somewhere south up to Alaska, but the smell of mint at the Fish Trap was the same. Old green patches near broad oxbows showed that the river had clearly changed its course over the years, and would continue to do so, as silt accumulated at certain bends and eventually became solid. I never spotted that great fish I'd seen from the cliff again, nor any fish, ever again, in that run, and that goaded me every time I thought of that huge fish free rising. And Herb never failed to rag me about the apple trees growing near the Paranoid Pool.

One winter during those years Herb took ill, and I wondered (as he may have done) whether he would fish again. But he did—his cast as low and powerful and accurate as before, with perhaps only some greater reserve toward the longer treks,

Then a year ago I could not come in June; I traveled to other parts of the world for other purposes, grew heavier still and a little older and a little more tense, and finally arranged for an early-September visit instead, hooked to a business trip to Denver. The time was new for me and Herb had written that a particularly severe winter had taken a toll. Some spots, once good, were barren—skinned, perhaps, by that troop of pelicans we'd first seen two years earlier. Hatches had been sparse all year—with only a handful of Pale Morning Duns and no Green Drakes whatsoever. In September the hatches might be sparser still.

But I felt the same extraordinary sense of expectation as we climbed the first bench, rattled along the familiar dirt road, paused briefly at the last bench to look down at Herb's wealth of waters, that gorgeous blue ribbon laid out casually in the valley.

I noticed, that first day, that the carcass of the calf struck by lightning was little more than a spot now; it made me think of the passage of time since I had first visited Spring Creek, though still not of Alexander in his tent, Montaigne in his tower, and Saint Theresa in her wild lament. Perhaps fishermen live in a more temporal world. At least this one does, at least in his fishing life.

Along the river we found no Pale Morning Duns, few caddis, and only a modest Trico hatch the first few days. I fished poorly—casting hard, lining the fish, reverting to tics and glitches I thought I'd lost half a dozen years earlier. Several times Herb said, "I've never seen you do that before." I couldn't quite account for the regression. A bit more weight? A trying year? Business nibbling at my nervous system? An old friend and teacher who now teaches me how to hate, new ambiguities in a world speeding much too fast for an old fellow who still types on an Underwood Standard, Model S, vintage 1945?

I fished poorly and my chest grew tense and several times I had to switch from the demanding flat water to broken water, which was always far more generous.

Herb stayed in the car more, too.

I caught half a dozen truly fine fish during the week, often in spots that hadn't fished well before, and several on grasshoppers, banged rudely against the opposite shore of the West Branch bends.

On the last day I still felt restless, as if this river, which had for so many years been balm and salvation, was no longer capable of providing such munificence, perhaps because I had lost some of my innocent attachment to it or expected it to be more than it was, or perhaps simply because the world was, this year, much too much with me.

On the last morning I went out alone, with Mari, and decided to fish the East Branch. It was a gray day, with a chill and a few dashes of rain. There had been some *Baetis* on the water—a No. 20 dark-olive fly—and I thought of the jingle, 'The worse the weather, the better the *Baetis*." We'd seen a few up at the South End Pool the day before but only one fish had come up, twice, tentatively, and Herb and I had noted together that this was not precisely a feeding frenzy.

When Mari had set up her folding chair and had taken out the last of her sketchbooks, I kissed her, admonished her to keep warm, and headed off to the left. An hour later I could see the Second Bend Pool, which I had not fished for more than a year. You become attached to pools; something in their attitude or conformation draws forth something in you, or you find an objective correlative for something in you in it. Certain pools talk to you, others don't. Some pools are generous to a particular fisherman but resist all of a much more skillful angler's efforts.

I loved the Second Bend Pool.

I had always done well here.

I had been waiting all week to fish it.

As I approached it, I could see upriver forty or fifty yards, just below the bend itself, three fish rising steadily. The water came around the bend, flattened, and then pinched and came downhill toward me in a pitched gradient, a rush. The fish were in the flat water, lunching.

I crossed to the left, the inside, bank and waded slowly toward my spot. I didn't think my wading would disturb the fish because I was in the heavy water, but I moved methodically, shuffling, keeping my eyes on the spreading circles in the flat water above me.

The fish were happy—rising in that leisurely, steady way that suggests they've put aside all worries, are interested only in the bon-bons sliding toward their stations. I saw no flies in the air but in a backwater I scooped up Trico duns, Trico spinners, a couple of caddis—one tan, one mottled—and a few small dark olives, No. 20. There wasn't a profusion of any of them but one or more were providing an ample picnic for these trout.

When I reached my spot on the inside rim of the bend, I sat down. I was more and more impressed over the years by how sitting kept you lower than kneeling, and the trout in Spring Creek liked nothing less than a figure popping up from their accustomed shore-line, unless it was a white shirt. Then I pulled all the leader and some line through the tip-top, pulled twenty-five feet of line off the reel, and checked my fly. It was a mottled caddis with a little Z-lon tail, No. 16, tied by Craig Mathews, and I thought it would do as well to stalk with this as with anything else.

When I raised my arm and rod to cast, two fish went down and, for the next hour, never came back. A better fish, farther out, just at the edge of the far current and the flat water, kept poking its snout out; I pitched a first cast to it, the cast was pretty sound, and the fly came down right over the vortex of the fish's rise—and the fish, in-stead of taking, headed for left field.

"Just what I need today," I said just audibly.

Well, I'd had a fair shot at what looked like a very good fish and, as I'd done too often this past week, I'd messed it up royally. My rhythm was clearly still off. I'd been rushing around a lot this year again, in big gray cities, and had worked long hours the last weekend to get some piles of work done so I could make this trip, which I'd been looking forward to, sorely. On that first day with Herb, I'd put down half a dozen fish that were on Trico spinners; fishing directly upstream to them, I had overcast, lined them, missed their feeding lanes and rhythms, slapped the water—all. I figured that I could make up for all this nonsense on the second day, when I got my bearings. But the second day the Tricos didn't show. Nor did the caddis. Oh, I got a few good fish—one huge rainbow on a *Baetis;* three on hop-pers, fished boldly against some undercut banks; a couple on this little mottled caddis, when I saw a few fluttering near a bit of choppy water I knew had good fish. The river was all right. It had fewer hatches this year but its water and its trout were never healthier. Mostly, I was fishing like a klutz, missing easy as well as hard chances, and I could not seem to get a fix on why.

You look at yourself in hours like that, hard, and you look at your world. You begin to equate fly fishing with your emotional life and your business life, though I'm not at all sure there's any absolute connection. Still, you think some general jaundice in you is causing the yellow in the fishing and you think that fishing better will settle your nerves, or at least become evidence that you've solved the other matters. Maybe that's so. Fly fishing certainly presents itself to the mind at times as therapeutic and coherent and spiritual and capable of being affected by and affecting all else in one's life. Mostly, thinking all these heavy thoughts on the inside rim of the Second Bend Pool, I just wanted to be fishing a little better, with more care, and I felt jumpy, impatient, and the mix was very unsatisfactory.

I had begun this last day of my visit to Spring Creek by wrecking the First Bend Pool with four consecutive sloppy casts; I had pounded up a fish on a Humpy in an upstream riffle; I had tossed a grasshopper against a couple of banks without much enthusiasm; and then, as I watched rain clouds gather to the south, I'd promptly put down three good fish in the pool I'd been waiting a week to fish.

What to do?

I had a couple hours before lunch, and I could stretch these into three if I chose, if the fishing warranted. I'd also have the afternoon, if the rain held off, and early evening. There was plenty of time. There was no reason to feel rushed, though I did.

Perhaps I should walk upstream another half mile or so until I found some more feeding fish; I hadn't been to the headwaters this trip. Perhaps I should fish a hopper hard, match my mood, settle for that; the sun had vanished already but the wind would blow them around—and hoppers were always fun. I liked their rough-hewn quality, the slashing strikes they drew, the fact that they often pounded up very good fish in this river. They were often a satisfying antidote to the very difficult business of fishing a small dry fly on glass-flat water.

In ten minutes I started to get up, noticed that the better fish had begun to stick its head up again, and sat right back down. I continued to watch and he stuck it up above the surface a couple of times, regularly, every fourteen or fifteen seconds, rising in a tight pattern no wider than a square foot. I remembered Herb saying, years earlier, "That fish can be caught."

So I tried him again and this time managed to send five floats over him before he went down.

Perhaps he wasn't on the caddis.

When the trout came up again, fifteen minutes later, I tried first a Trico dun and then a Trico spinner. I was casting with a bit more of a snake in my line now and that enabled me to put the fly a full foot and a half above the snout, exactly where I wanted it, and to have it float two feet below the fish before the fly dragged and I began to ease it toward me. Lengthening my leader tippet by a foot helped, too.

But this tough old evil trout was not munching Tricos. And I soon found out that he didn't much care for the tan caddis, either, even when I changed my entire tippet again, making it still six inches longer. Was he being particularly snobby or did he simply have his own agenda and want to keep his skin?

And then I slapped the water a bit hard with the line and the fish made a terrific swirl and fuss at the surface and disappeared.

That did it, I thought. Gone. For the next week, minimum. I was ready for the hopper.

But for some reason I decided to wait, to play out this hand however long it took. I sat and fussed with my leader; I greased the braided butt slowly so that it would not spritz on the surface, and I tied on still a longer tippet, remaking the knot twice. I watched the place where the bend riffle became flat and I kept glancing down at the slack water near my inside perch, looking for new insects.

Sure enough, fifteen minutes later, the old fellow was back, pressing his snout up as boldly as ever, thumbing his nose at me. Or perhaps he just couldn't help eating, an itch I knew well. The sky was darker now, the wind chilly, and the worse weather made me think the *Baetis* might get stronger. So I rummaged in my busy vest and came up with a little tin box of No. 20 dark-olive Sparkle Duns. Well, that would round out everything I'd seen on the water, anyway.

On my first cast with the dark olive, the fly lit, floated a foot, came into the area in which the fish was feeding, hesitated, and then the snout came up, swirled—to my fly or a real one next to it?—I struck, and the fish bolted upstream in a manic rush. I raised the rod high, wound hard to get the fish on the reel, and then stood and high-stepped upstream as the fish headed around the bend and into the heavy run that led into it.

It was a long fight, with edgy moments as the fish went farther upriver, then sulked in the belly of the pool, then made—too late—a few runs below me. The 6X held, the fish began to tire. I backed toward my spot on the bank, sat down, and eased the great fish closer.

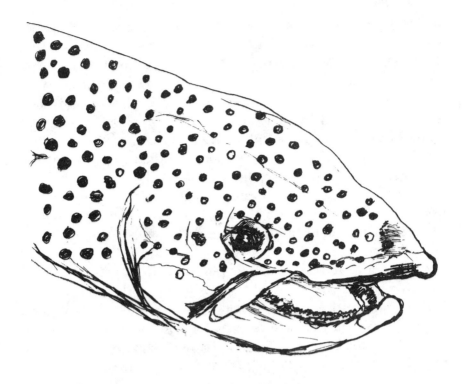

When he was in the water near my legs, and turned slightly on his side, I put my rod down quickly—in a clumsy, stupid movement—cupped both hands under the great fish, and scooped him onto the grass. Next to my rod, flapping feebly, the fish astounded me with his girth and length. He was a broad, heavy old fish, in perfect condition; his mouth showed no evidence that he had ever been hooked before. Then I had him back in the water, cupping his belly and holding his tail, and I watched the bright spots on his flanks disappear as he righted himself, and I saw the gills work hard and then regularly. After I'd taken my hands from him, he hung around in the slack shallow water for five minutes, as if he had some wise old comment he wanted to make to me—about perseverance or skill, perhaps even a fawning compliment to make me feel even more puffed up with myself—and then I touched his tail with the tip of my rod and he wavered off into the dark water below the bend and disappeared.

I breathed deeply and smiled and decided that the fish had been a rather nice old evil fellow after all, capable—with his sorcery—of changing a quivering pig's ear into a smug hero. Except for a touch of a shake, probably from the cold, I felt very calm and content.

There was still an hour or more to fish, and then I could fish in the afternoon and evening if I chose, but I clipped off the little mashed fly, wound my line in all the way onto the reel, and disjointed my rod.

When I looked up I saw that a couple of fish had started to rise again in the pool. One of them looked pretty good. I watched them for a few moments and then headed downriver.

Still more time has passed. I am not in the headwaters of Spring Creek but at my desk in a great gray city in the belly of winter. This year I will turn sixty and I have been thinking of time more than I like to admit, and of Camus's observation that at fifty each of us has the face he deserves.

Which face, I wonder—looking at the bewildered but lived-in face in the mirror—is that?

> *He is some twenty sev'ral men at least*
> *Each sev'ral hour,*

says George Herbert in "Giddiness," and I still find each of them in me, and other men, too. One of those twenty-odd men fishes—and still feels strange saying *Paraleptophlebia* among strangers. He fishes with a fly rod, mostly for trout, almost always, these days, with a fly that floats. All that seems a minor commitment in a world randomly destructuring itself. I don't know why this old fellow still loves to fish as much as he did when he was six and gigged his first trout on a Carlisle hook strapped to a willow branch, from a mountain brook, or, when at a grim boarding school, he was saved by fishing a sump called Ice Pond. But he does fish, and some new form of that particular life was defined and hammered into some permanence during those thirty-one days some years ago.

I find it quite wonderful, amid all the ambiguities and tensions of cities and business and the mystery of me, to have a sure and certain thing, like a spring creek, even in my mind, that never fails to bring such fun and serenity, that has filled my head with such indelible images: mornings in the Suburban at the South End Pool, waiting for the first flies to appear; Herb, working his magic and witchery, making impossible casts, long floats; Doug—fifty trout pocking the surface of the flat pool—*in extremis;* Gillian fishing hard in the freezing rain; McClane, now dead, upright in tropical clothes, nailing some big ones from the fast run; the smell of mint at the Fish Trap; apocalypse at the Paranoid—and apple trees; Herb trying to get the backing onto his reel, his great fish almost in, beaten, then gone; dreaming at the Second Bend Pool and in the headwaters; slapping grasshoppers against the West Branch bends; that great trout feeding in midwater as I stand on the cliff—the fish altogether catchable, *that once;* the sight of Mari as I come down the East Branch, close to her easel, then stepping back, pursuing some thing that might lead far; and my eye following a faint golden spot among other faint golden spots, far out on the pond, inching toward a spreading circle on a grizzly day, coming closer, and then, with a delicate rise, we're hooked.

A Flyfisher's World
(1996)

INTRODUCTION TO
A FLYFISHER'S WORLD

I am struck, as I move deeply into my sixties, by how much I still love to fly fish and to write about fly fishing, how grateful I am for the simple fun and happy intensity this passion has given me since that day, many years ago, when I saw a trout rise and had some brand of apocalyptic vision on Michigan's Au Sable River.

I had fished since before memory—with worm, frog, doughball, and spinning lure—but fly fishing, requiring such a galaxy of disciplines, was different; and from that day, despite all the complexities of my personal life and the much greater complexities of a world in volatile flux, fly fishing has always been in my head: quirky, maverick, green thoughts that shaped themselves into the kind of personal essays I've collected in this book. They came while I was strap-hanging in a New York subway almost as often as when I was on a river, while I was in business conferences, reading a book, waiting for a doctor, and even, a year ago, as I lay in a hospital bed, as I returned from a sour brush with death.

I have not deluded myself all these years into thinking that fly fishing was a religion, a "way of life," an activity more important than a thousand other human activities—neither growing a family, putting together a life in classrooms and offices, nor wars, tragic events in Bosnia or Africa or Russia or Asia, nor high art. It is merely a lovely, useless activity that, somehow, has become an axial line in my life, an anchor. I wanted desperately to write when I was young, and fishing, somehow, became a magnet for most of what I have had to say on *any* subject; I have found it one of the happiest parts of my life to write about this activity, to dream and imagine and recollect and theorize about fly fishing. It did not take me long, in my twenties, to discover that I was not Joyce, neither was I Faulkner. Tolstoy and Dickens were vaster than I knew, Kafka wiser; even a local columnist I thought thin had his special craft. In fly fishing I found a plot of land that was mine—small but not contemptible, capable of yielding a strange and amusing fruit or two, mostly beneath the world's notice, but always and inescapably my lot and something satisfying to write about. That it gave enough people pleasure to read what I'd done helped me to write more, and I am grateful to them as much as I am to rivers and fly rods.

This summer, in the West, as I've collected these essays, mostly of the past half-dozen years, I've noticed that more and more seem to be looking backward or to theory. Three-quarters of my life is behind me and so are most of my "firsts"—with tarpon, bluefish, pike, and other species but also, probably, with places. I've never been much of an explorer. I've always preferred intimacy to the exotic. Increasingly, I lean toward memory and reflection—perhaps because I am no longer bursting with energy, as I was in my manic youth. My fires are banked now: less flashy but probably hotter and certainly more concentrated. I fish more wisely; I have a keener sense of where fish will be and when they'll be up. I probably fall in less—and certainly I have reported on my pratfalls enough for this trip.

What's left?

Always to connect and to distill. Always to understand a bit more. The urgency of our senior years, if we rise to the challenge, is the urgency to find some "blessed rage for order," a desire to put things in their places. I doubt very much if "the best is yet to come," but we have more history than we had forty, twenty, or even ten years ago and that history can be very satisfying. We do not have to catch as many fish or fish quite so long and so hard each day; less counts for more. And as we extrude our history, the way spiders extrude their silky strands, we provide the traps in which to capture our future.

I fished a spring creek I knew well last week and came to a bend I'd fished fifty times before. It was a one- or two-fish bend, below a large lakelike expanse of the river, and it was a big-fish bend; I had twice hooked outsized browns here—one that ran me up to the lake and broke off in tangled roots, the other that I'd caught a year ago, twenty-seven inches' worth, on a hopper. I knew exactly where to position myself and where to look for fish. There was some nervous water in the small eddy and I thought I must have spooked the fish on my approach. So I sat down calmly, as I do more and more frequently, and changed my leader tippet from 6X to 5X. I checked the surgeon's knot I now use, tied on my favorite imitation of a Pale Morning Dun, the obvious *plat du jour* after two hours of proof, checked that knot too, turned back to the eddy, and made a crisp, low twenty-five-foot cast.

The fish took instantly and rocketed upstream. It swept past the willow roots at the outward bend, furrowed just beneath the surface, and then made a gigantic leap. Just as I thought. It was one of the alligators this river held—a truly gigantic brown—and I leaped from my seat as the fish leaped, prepared to chase it.

Then the fish leaped again. But this time its zeal sent it high on the bank, where it wriggled in some rose brambles and then flopped back into the river, my PMD in its lip.

That excitement—the odd admixture of the known and the new, of old skills leading me into deeper, unpredictable waters, of the electric rise and the hilarious, unimagined escape—keeps me coming back, and always will.

I am grateful to such moments—as I am grateful that, on a grizzly day in Michigan, forty years ago, I had my life nudged in a totally different direction simply by a trout's rise.

AU SABLE APOCALYPSE

Soon after we were married, my wife and I moved to Michigan—I to start graduate studies in Ann Arbor, Mari to study art at the Cranbrook Academy. We first lived in Pontiac—in the kitchen area of a huge, decaying mansion where it got so cold that first winter that a cup of coffee left on the table overnight froze solid. When our first son was born, we moved to Ann Arbor. Marrying, fathering, studying were each full-time occupations, and for more than a year I fished not at all. Soon afterward we had a second child, and for a while I was so preoccupied that I even stopped *thinking* about fishing.

But you cannot hide fire in the straw. When I passed my oral exams, I begged for a rest, and we all headed upcountry to the Au Sable River. I owned a white glass fly rod then and knew just enough about using it to avoid threading the line through the keeper ring. I practiced casting on basketball courts and ponds, and I had caught bluegills—though never a trout—on a fly. I had to face it: I was lousy with a fly rod and didn't think I could catch a fish with one. Mostly, I used a Mitchell spinning reel and a C. P. Swing—the ultimate in simplicity and killing power—for all occasions.

We found a cheap motel near Grayling, had a noisy family dinner, and in the morning I sneaked out about five A.M. and fished with my spinning outfit. It was late in April and quite cold. The water was a bit discolored, but clearing. I cast my spinner in against the famous "sweepers," into the heads of big bend pools, and by eight A.M. had taken five or six good browns. It had been a very pleasant morning and I'd enjoyed this new river very much, and it felt terrific being on the water again.

We had a leisurely breakfast, and I asked Mari what she would like to do. I'd taken some fish and wasn't in any particular fever to fish again—at least not for a few more hours. I could be generous.

There really wasn't much to do on a drizzly late-April day in Grayling with two infants, so we ended up taking a drive. It ended (as have so many since) on a bridge over a beautiful river. It was still chilly, so Mari stayed in the car with the kids. I said I'd be back in a few minutes.

The water had cleared a bit. It was a gorgeous section of the Au Sable, with deadfalls, overhanging willows, bright runs and riffles. You could see the bottom now, and I thought I saw several auburn shapes upstream by a large boulder. I can't swear to it, though. I often imagine fish.

Farther upstream, a fly fisher was wading out from the right bank, stripping line from his reel, watching the route of the current along the far bank. He had on a large streamer, and moments later he was casting it with great authority against the bank and fishing it downstream toward me. It was a pleasant, rhythmic sight, and I must have lost my sense of time before I heard Mari call out from our car parked beyond the bridge.

I thought she might be upset, but when I got to the car, she laughed and said I'd looked as if I was enjoying myself, the children were asleep, and she'd gotten into a good book, so why didn't I take out my rod and fish, which is what we'd come upstate to do.

In the trunk of the car, I saw the white fly rod lying to one side without a case, its Pflueger Medalist reel fastened to the handle. And I knew I had a plastic box full of flies in my canvas tackle bag. Why not? I'd caught some trout, the angler above the bridge looked as though he knew what he was doing, and the sight of the water already had made me itchy to get into my hip boots. So I rigged up, kissed Mari good-bye, skipped to the bridge to watch the fly fisher for a moment, then headed downstream a hundred yards.

For a half hour, I flailed away crudely, slapping the water behind me, ending my casts with big, flopping loops halfway to where I wanted them to be. Though I waded upstream, I remember casting across and downstream with a streamer, imitating the spin-fishing techniques I knew so well. But my casts were hopelessly short, and the harder I cast, the shorter they fell. The movements of the current that I had exploited well with my spinning rod now perplexed me as it ramrodded the bulky fly line and sent my fly scuttling in odd directions. I did not feel my fly was any threat whatsoever to trout.

Above me, I saw the fly fisher take two trout and release them. Then, at the bridge, he changed the spool on his reel, tied on a new fly, and began to fish upstream. I now was close enough to see that his fly floated. And I also was observant enough to notice there were now some pale yellowish flies coming up out of the water, a few fluttering just above it while others rode the current downstream.

I felt my hands tremble.

Clipping off my streamer, I rummaged through my fly box for a yellow fly. The best I could find was a battered Lady Beaverkill with a gray and yellow egg sac. I tied this onto the heavy leader I had been using. Leaving the river, I climbed back onto the bridge just in time to witness an event I had not seen before: a trout take a dry fly. My eye picked up the yellow fly the other angler had cast, and I watched it float a dozen feet, smoothly, pertly bounding up and down on the surface. Then, dramatically, it disappeared in a boil much like bluegills made when they took my flies. It was a decent brown, about thirteen inches, and he soon had it in his net, then returned it to the river.

Now my whole body started to tremble. Is that all there was to it? I fiercely wanted to try this, and when the angler waved to me that he was leaving the river, I scooted down the bank, took up a position near where he had been, and again began flailing away. Nothing. My casts slapped the water, and the fly dragged as soon as it landed. It was hopeless and, worse, frustrating beyond measure.

Finally, I breathed deeply, brought in my line and decided simply to watch. There were still a few flies floating about and an occasional rise. A bit below me and near the far bank, a series of rises caught my attention. They always were within a four-foot circle, and when I inched downriver, I could see a big brown lolling just beneath the surface.

There had been some sun, but it now was gone and the drizzle had started again. I was tempted to go back to the car and get my spinning rod, which would make short work of this trout, but instead I kept inching downstream until I was parallel to the fish. Then I crept toward it as far as I dared, then a little more, and cold water came over the tops of my hip boots. That didn't matter. I looked at the bedraggled Lady Beaverkill and my thick leader and decided I needed a lighter connection. I found some four-pound-test spinning line and tied it on with three or four overhand knots, since that knot and the clinch knot were all I knew.

On my fourth cast, the fish came a foot upstream and took the fly at the surface in a rush. I struck—and the knot broke.

It was a remarkable moment—electric, vivid, unforgettable—and eventually it changed my life.

I fished for an hour after that, using the heavy leader, fishing myself into a fast and hopeless frenzy. Of course, I raised nothing. By this time, the rain was quite hard, the water roiled, and after I had seen no flies or rises for ten minutes, I headed back to the car, soaked and shivering.

"You should have seen that fish come up," I started to say as I neared the car, then I stopped. The children were howling, and Mari—who had been alone with them in the car for hours—was crying bitterly.

It rained throughout our four-hour trip back to Ann Arbor, which was one of stony silences punctuated by muffled crying and the howls of infants, who could feel the tension. I had visions of a marriage slipping pertly downstream. I also kept seeing that trout rising and taking my Lady Beaverkill, and I dreamed of other trout in a world of which I had been given the briefest glimpse.

We soon moved back East and never again lived in places where coffee froze at night, or near enough, in my mind, to rivers. But now, years later, I have the same wife, and we've made our fish truces, and four children, who have grown and mostly do not fish, and I am still trying to get a full look at that world I glimpsed one rainy day on the Au Sable when a trout rose—with astonishing power and grace—to my fly, and changed my life forever.

SMALL FISH

"Wal, son," the Florida bass guide Bill Miller consoled a friend who had not taken a bass big enough to match his dreams, "just about everybody comes down here wanting to catch Bubba . . . but hardly nobody ever does."

We all want the big fish. We've traveled great distances to get to Lake Big Buster, and we don't want to settle for a couple of shrimpy bass, thank you. Little pickerel are just fine in the nearby farm pond, but you don't travel two thousand miles for them. When you pack your bags carefully and ready your equipment, you think big. A fifteen-pound bonefish this year. A hundred-pound tarpon. A trout over two feet. A thirty-pound salmon. Rainbows to knock your eye out. My friend Mort caught a fifty-pound Atlantic salmon in Norway last year, which is about as big as anyone, ever, would want a salmon—but what now can he possibly do for an encore?

Some people only like big fish. No travel fee is too large for the largest fish, no distance too far. They want to better their personal best and beat everyone else's biggest and best. They fish for records and for the "thrill of a lifetime."

No one would deliberately pursue small fish, though I have friends who consistently catch runts and minnows—and I am subject to such luck, too. We may not pursue them, but we all catch a lot more of them than we do the outsized freaks. Even when I traveled two thousand miles on a great bluegill trek, I was after alligator bluegill, fish that reputedly grew to three pounds or more. We caught fish larger than two pounds—which is a lot of bluegill, the largest I've ever caught—but they were bluegill and it just seemed as if it would have been more appropriate had we caught them a dozen miles from home.

Perhaps because the big fish is so rare, or so expensive to come by, and since I've always caught more than my share of midgets, I've made a happy peace with small fish. When I was seven and eight years old and a confirmed—and exclusive—bait fisherman, I several times had outlandishly large pickerel, bass, and trout take a small shiner, chub, or bluegill while I drew it back to the boat. Once a four-pound pickerel ambushed my five-inch shiner, and before it would let go I hoisted both fish into the boat.

But I love small fish not merely because they sometimes draw the dramatic strike from their bigger betters and because they're the best of baits, but because they remind us of other reasons to be on the water, reasons bigger than big fish.

Once Craig Mathews walked me far back into some swampy flats to beaver ponds that reputedly held huge brook trout. It was a long trek in but I had made such treks before with Craig, during which we usually found battalions of mosquitoes, lots of muck, and some-times three- and four-pound brown trout; so all the while I thought of three-pound brookies—which qualify as "tortugas"—with dark backs and bright rose marks and that softer, seemingly scaleless skin that felt like something from a dark wild place. The fish had dark backs and bright markings, but they topped out at five inches in length. Still, we laughed a lot and we couldn't catch enough of them; and we called them "tortugas" anyway . . . and maybe they were. Vince Marinaro once told me he liked bright little wild brookies best.

Several years ago I had spent a long and interesting day in the backcountry section of the lower Keys—fussing around, looking for bonefish, permit, perhaps a small tarpon or two. I was with John Graves, and it was a perfectly pleasant day, talking with a new friend, exploring a new kind of fishing for me, even practicing casts for a day with Jeffrey Cardenas, for big tarpon. We looked hard at some sand flats for bones and found only a small sand shark, which ignored us. We fished a section that reminded me of a river, where a falling tide swept off mangrove flats and out into the Gulf; and that might have been a barracuda that cut my line so neatly—or only a piece of coral. But we caught no fish, and the day wore on until we'd walked the boat through a long shallow stretch that sometimes held permit but today didn't—though, never having seen a permit, I wasn't at all sure I knew what I was looking for, or if I'd recognize anything whatsoever beneath the mottled glaze of sun on broken water.

At the end of the shallow passage, the water ran flush up against the corner of a mangrove island. "Now that's where I'd fish," I told John with a smile. Fish *had* to lie in the eddies where the ocean swept in under the mangroves, curling under them, buffeting exposed roots. Fish would be protected under the overhanging twisted branches, food would come to them on the conveyor belt of the tides, and we'd surely catch some now.

"They'll be small," John said, "probably mangrove snappers."

At the end of any long fishless day, any fish sounds all right, so I put on a Crazy Charlie meant for grander sport and chucked it a couple of feet out from the mangroves, letting the rush of water take the fly down and deep into the mysterious, dark, swirling heart of the overhanging trees. It felt like the wet-fly fishing I'd done after I'd shifted from worms. The line leaned away from me, grew taut; I released a few inches of line, gave the line a few short tugs so the fly would ride high and then drop back; and then I felt the pecking tugs of something alive. I repeated the cast a dozen times, and each time the fly would suck down into the maze of roots. Every cast would bring that pecking strike and a bright little mangrove snapper—the size of perch or bluegill, wriggling madly.

Small fish are not always so generous. A decade ago, a happy circumstance got me to Europe on business matters the same time as my twenty-fifth wedding anniversary. It was a happy trip, by sleeper from Paris to Aix, where we saw Cézanne's studio and his Mont Ste.-Victoire and some of his earliest work (which was so awkward it would give any young artist supreme courage to go on). And then we found a cheap *pension,* within sight of the blue Mediterranean. I had fished hard on my honeymoon, and fishing had not played well; and I only had one of those five-piece fly-rod outfits with me because a business colleague had given it to me; so I wasn't thinking of fishing. I had no intention to fish. And what would I fish for?

But by the third day, I'd had my fill of the topless beach and began to look more seriously at the water. It took me only a few minutes to spot some fishermen on the rocks. "I just might take a walk over in that direction," I told Mari.

"Have you found some fishing?" she asked without opening her eyes.

On the rocks I found three men fishing with long bamboo sticks, wispy line, tiny quill bobbers, and a bait so small I could not see it. They were fishing for tiny mullet, but the mullet were having none of whatever they offered. I watched for an hour, maybe longer. The three fishermen were as patient and committed as the fishermen on the Seine, who also catch no fish. My French was too rotten to extract precise advice about this refined fishery, but careful observation suggested that the mullet were taking a hatch of green weed.

In my new kit I found a few No. 18 flies, but they looked nothing like mullet food. So I clipped most of the grizzly hackle from a Griffith's Gnat, tore a piece of bright green yarn from the bottom of Mari's new twenty-fifth-anniversary sport jacket, wound the thread over the peacock herl, tied it off with itself, and left a quarter-inch strand for the tail of the new Lyons Mullet Weed Fly.

In the next two days I fished for nine hours, diligently. In that time, I saw one of my three brothers of the angle catch one silver fish, at least five inches long—which led to immense shouts of elation, louder than any I'd heard for hundred-pound tarpon. My score was exactly: eleven follows, two nips, one sore casting arm, several sun welts on my casting hand, no fish caught. It was the toughest fishing I'd ever done.

"You mean a big boy like you couldn't catch a tiny fish like that?" Mari said when she walked over and I showed her my fellow angler's catch.

I had no reply.

LARGEMOUTH MAGIC

Green-gray, chunky, with a gourmand's palate and beastly eating habits, the largemouth bass has probably given more pleasure to more people than any species other than its little cousin, the bluegill. I am addicted to the brute. I caught my first largemouth in my early teens, on a live sunfish, and they've never been far from my mind, even during some lengthy love affairs with trout.

They're not finicky or fussy or easily scared. They'll eat anything they can catch and get their big jaws around. They mean business when they strike but grow bored—as I do—with the ensuing fight. There is just no freshwater sight as heart-stopping as a truly big largemouth busting up for a hair bug on a muggy night, blasting the surface with the sheer weight and ferocity of its strike, sending a lathed fan of silver in every direction, hustling away like a spooked muskrat when the bass realizes it's been hooked.

I first caught largemouth at a summer camp in the Berkshires— first by mistake, while slowly hoisting out a three-inch bluegill, then on nightcrawlers and crayfish, then on minnows caught in a bread-baited jug, then on spinners, spinner-and-worm combinations, Jitter-bugs, Pikie Minnows, and finally on big deer-hair or molded-body bugs. The bugs were merely a plump turtle-shaped body with crisscrossed clumps of hair for the four legs. That's still the bug I use most, nearly half a century later.

When I found the fly rod, I never let it go. Even in those early days when I half-tossed, half-slammed a bug out on a level line—sticky from too much grease—I was hooked by the rise of a largemouth to a surface bug. You saw everything. The expectation—as the fly lit, twitched, wiggled, waited, stuttered, and rushed headlong toward you, almost independent of any movement you made—was thrilling. I could barely cast the big thing thirty feet, but when I got it out (and perhaps cheated by nudging the rowboat away from it a few more feet) its presence on the calm surface of the lake mesmerized me. Several times fish struck (and came off) while I looked away, dreamily, and I learned then, for all time, to rivet my eye to that little object on the surface and keep it there for dear life. And once I learned never to look away, I was hooked to the bug, felt its every movement, waited, every moment, for that explosion on the surface, that sudden eruption of calm, that stirring, heart-stopping moment when a great largemouth attacks a bug.

Besides, I liked the way the fishing was done. I didn't have to fish all day, to find fish in deep water, to use hardware of such weight (and number of hooks) that the fight was diminished. I liked an old rowboat that went at exactly the speed I propelled it; I liked the oars making their rhythmic sound against water and oarlock; I liked the constant sight of the shoreline with its myriad shapes and forms: eelgrass, lily pads, old rotted stumps, fallen trees or branches, jutting rocks, drop-offs, points, rocky flats, coves, islands, channels, overhanging brush or branches, and so much more. Here, you did not fish to a fish, as you did on the flats or for trout; you fished to a spot where a fish might be. Slowly you learned the spots, all of them, not from a book but in the most pragmatic way: you got strikes in certain places, none in others. You did not pitch a fly and let the current take it to a trout but cast to a stump or a patch of weed and then, by wiggle and pop, tried to induce a fish to come and play. It was great fun. It was leisurely—and dramatic.

My friend Mort and I went to the Thousand Islands section of the St. Lawrence River for smallmouths a number of times. We fished for them with live minnows in thirty-five feet of water, below ledge drop-offs. The largemouths were in certain defined channels, not far from the shallows where we caught northern pike, and when they took a plug or live shiner their bulldog fight was distinctive, powerful, memorable. They did not go in for the acrobatics the smallmouths did—angling away from the boat as they came up from the depths and then leaping once, twice, high and wriggling. We'd catch them—largemouth and smallmouth—an hour apart and then talk endlessly about their differences, about which we liked most. The largemouths were heavyweights, even the smallest of them—one-punch knockout artists—smashing the lure or bait, making their play hard, with bad intentions.

Technology came to bass fishing as it did to everything else, from typewriting to kitchen appliances, and it brought finer reels that didn't backlash, subtler and stronger and lighter rods in a wide variety of patterns, and a cornucopia of whiz-bang lures from spinnerbaits to plastic worms. I listened to their advocates sing their virtues, read about them, watched them work on video, and—at one time or another—tried them all. They caught fish. Often one of them caught largemouth when another worked not at all. Some caught them on the top, others in midwater, still others along the bottom. They were versatile, keyed to dozens of different fishing occasions, often highly effective, always capable of expanding our fishing options. But in the end they did not catch me. As we get older we make choices. We narrow our sporting options because we've found that one route simply gives us more pleasure than another. Isn't that why we're out there? For the quality of the pursuit, the discrete joys the hunt gives us?

I had lost my heart to the long rod, the fly rod. I liked its rhythms; I liked the fact that *I* had to work a bit harder, was more involved; I liked the lighter, more responsive flies and bugs it could cast; I liked the sight of a fly line floating out behind me and then reaching forward. I even liked casting less and being a bit more involved with each cast. And I found, every time I went out for bass, that it filled all my needs. I did not want or need to catch fish all day, every day; I could wait. I had quite enough fishing to try them when they could be caught on the top, at the extremities of the day. And on a long hot summer afternoon on a New England pond, I could take all the pleasure I wanted by easing a rowboat or canoe toward the edges of a weedy cove and casting in against the rim of the lily pads for the odd

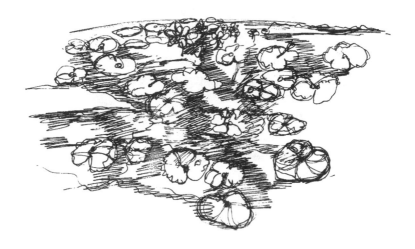

fish that had squirreled in for a midday rest, with half a hope that an
unlucky frog would come its way. I have taken a lot of bass from such
spots in the middle of the day, when even bait and deep-water fishermen are having lunch or readying their gear for the evening. If I'm
alone I may anchor the boat where I can fan out my casts for perhaps
sixty feet of that line that separates open water from the outer edges
of a large bed of lily pads. Some bass will be there, even at high noon.
I'm in no hurry. It's better than badminton or golf or a gin rickey in
the shade on shore. One fish for an afternoon of it will be plenty of
reward.

But mostly, the magic of largemouth fishing comes at dawn or
dusk, and not only then but the time just before and the hours well
after dusk. The pond is mysterious, moody, silent then. In the very
early morning, after a night on the prowl, big bass can be anywhere.
And they're looking for food. I've seen one blast the gently floating
plug a friend had left in the water while he untangled a backlash, an
hour before dawn; I've seen their streaks and bulges among the weeds;
I've had them storm a bug dozens of times, at any of a dozen different moments during a retrieve.

I like to get down to the dock by four o'clock, before there's
any light other than the moon's on the water. A loon calls; faintly, a
dog barks. The water, what I can see of it, is flat-calm and, in sum-

mer, light mist circles above it. I whisper to my friend. Neither of us wants to make the slightest unnecessary sound, even when we leave the car, a couple of hundred feet from the dock. We slip gear into the wooden rowboat, ease oars into their locks, untie the joining rope, and push off. I barely allow the oars to touch the water, just dip their tips gently against the surface. It does not require much more to propel the boat. Only a couple of dozen feet outside of the dock area, I bring the oars in and we both scan the dark waters for the best place to cast first. My friend is using a plug, I the long rod. He casts far out into the deep water, toward the center of the pond, claiming the bass will as well be there as anywhere, and I, from the bow, pull line off my inexpensive fly reel, false-cast twice, and cast toward the faint outline of the shore. I can see the shoreline brush, a few rocks, but not much more. On my third cast the water breaks and bursts, as if someone has thrown in a cherry bomb, and I feel the hard satisfying weight of a good bass. It does not make a long run, like a bonefish or a salmon; it jumps twice—hard, loudly, with a rude power, and then, against my stubby leader, comes toward me. It's about four pounds. I grasp its lower lip, extract the big hook of the bug, and slip it back into the water. Then my friend has one, a bit larger, on his four-inch jointed plug, and then another. And then we see the first lightening of the sky in the east and head for the other side of the lake, where we take another four fish before the sky brightens and everyone else's day begins.

Largemouth bass are on the prowl in the very early morning hours—and the more you can manage to avoid gentleman's or banker's hours, the better the fishing will be. If everyone gets to the lake "early," at, say, six o'clock, I'd get there at five o'clock or even four; there is no hour too early to fish for largemouth bass in the summer—and you will find it a different lake, to the eye and for the fishing.

Best, though, is dusk, those great hours when the heat begins to leave the day inchmeal and the lake and the fish gradually become more and more alive. I like to have an early dinner and be on the water about 7:30 in high summer. There will still be some activity on the lake but not that much that you can't find a quiet section where no one will go in for a late swim, where the faster-casting spinners and

bait-casters have been and gone. I like to row or paddle quietly, ten or fifteen feet farther out from the shoreline than I can comfortably cast. If I'm alone and the lake is calm, I'll often ship the oars and allow a slight breeze to take me along a shoreline, regulating direction by a brief pull on one oar or the other now and then. This is the time I love best. The sun is off the water, a sunset may still linger in the west, the evening calm has struck the water, and the cool air brings a strange mist to the surface. I can *feel* largemouths beginning to stir, beginning to look for their first meal of the evening.

I have with me the same order of tackle I used thirty-five years ago—as large and powerful a rod (in glass, graphite, or bamboo) as I have at hand, even a No. 11 or No. 12, even a tarpon rod. The fight is not my game; casting a heavy air-resistant bug *is*—and it requires a big tool. I use a simple reel with not much backing, for I've rarely had a largemouth run far; I use a weight-forward line (with perhaps two feet of the end cut off, which seems to help casting the heavy bug), a six-foot leader tapered to ten or twelve pounds; and I like a hair bug or a molded-body bug with a big cup, which will pop and throw a lathed wake when I tug the line to manipulate it.

I like progress. But I have found no reason to change—except perhaps the rod, since graphite is so much lighter and has exceptional power. And I'm still blithely content to fish a bug, on the top, where I make everything happen, where I can see it all happen.

I am astonished that more people don't fish for largemouth this way, that they rush around in high-powered boats with huge boxes of lures, that they plunk the lure out and draw it back with a grinding motion, that they need a lot to make them a little happy.

Lengthening my line, I double-haul and send a long cast out toward the fallen branches near the edge of the cove. The bug—that big four-legged one I love so much—lands a foot from the tangle of branches. With a lure I'd have to get it moving quickly or risk it sinking into the possible tangles of branches beneath the surface. But I can let the fly sit. And it does: settling itself from the long toss, rocking less and less, finally motionless. Now the game is all mine. First I twitch it twice, trying to keep it very close to where it fell—thinking that that must be the best spot of all, as near the branches as possible. I am all expectation. My eye is riveted to the bug. I leave the bug there for ten seconds, twenty seconds. Nothing happens. I give it a few abrupt tugs, which make the bug lean underwater a bit and then pop up. Then I leave it alone again, for forty seconds. I barely trust myself to blink. Then I rush it back toward me a foot or so in a steady tug, then pop it once or twice, then twitch it, then strip it back quickly.

I've had fish strike at every moment of such a retrieve: when the fly hit the water, when I was ready to yank the fly out to begin my next cast.

On my next cast I let the stationary bug sit, inches from a stump, for a full two or three minutes. I'm in absolutely no hurry. Then I twitch it slightly and let it sit some more. Then I twitch it again. There *has* to be a bass near that stump. That stump was made to harbor a big largemouth.

And so it does.

With a sucking in and out-rushing of water, a bruiser of a bass takes and bores deep, and then lifts up on sky hooks and rattles its sabers and falls back hard, with a heavy crash. Twice more it is up, into air, and several times it scurries off, with determined force. And then it comes in—five pounds' worth, green-bronze, thick as a loaf of bread.

There is no better freshwater fishing. There is no more delicious expectation than working a hair bug on the surface of a calm lake at dusk. There is no more excitement than the eruption, as if someone had thrown a pig or a garbage can into the water, when a largemouth takes. There is no day when I would pass up a chance at such largemouth magic.

RIVERBASS

Sometimes we judged the Ten Mile River wrong. We came for trout, but the season was too far advanced and we caught only bass. They were in the pockets and eddies behind the rocks that were now half out of the water. They came short to a bushy dry fly but slammed our streamers. They leapt higher and fought harder than trout, but they were not as pretty and we were always disappointed then to catch them.

Though we knew they were smallmouths, we called them river-bass. We had caught chunky largemouths in Lake Ellis, on plugs and live bait—big ones, up to eight pounds; these were sleeker fish, never as large, more durable fighters than their dogged kin in lakes, but they had neither the coloration nor the size to hook us then.

Still, they sure saved some long, slow days.

On warm afternoons in late spring, after six hours of hard and fruitless fly fishing for trout, we began to drop downriver to the slower, warmer water and spend the last two hours of our fishing day after smallmouths. In fact, after three or four whacks at it, we began to carry some primitive bass flies—bigger streamers, cork poppers, small hair frogs.

It was pleasant work: we'd cast a bug up into an eddy, into pocketwater, twitch and chug it a few times, let it drift briefly down-river, and then there would be a heavy pocking of the water and a bright green twisting fish would bust up out of the water and splat-ter liquid silver into the slants of sun. We might catch eight or ten or twenty of them; I don't remember. I was always an indifferent counter of the fish I caught, and I have still not developed much of a flair for it. We might raise one or two a bit larger than the others—say, a pound and a half. This was not delicate work; we used eight- or ten-pound tippets and rarely lost fish except when they threw the fly on a jump or the hook simply pulled out. A fish better than a pound was always a prize.

Later my roommate Mort and I fished the huge St. Lawrence River for smallmouth, though not with flies, and I had my first true sense of how powerful the larger members of the species could be. Fishing in water thirty-five feet deep, with live minnows, we caught smallmouths up to five pounds. They'd take with a dull, steady peck. We'd wait. We'd wait a little longer. Then we'd strike hard to counter the sway in the line, and then the line would angle up toward the surface. We'd watch them run away from the boat and higher in the water and then, suddenly, they'd leap—high, powerfully, rocketing out, big enough to send a chill through us.

Recently I've taken a second hard look at riverbass—in the lower Schoharie, the Ten Mile, the Housatonic. They're simply lots of fun, and people like Dave Whitlock, Harry Murray, and Bob Clouser are bringing smallmouth more and more into the mainstream—if there is one—of serious fly fishing. Clouser's Crayfish are brilliant concoctions—good enough to put into a Creole gumbo or the mouth of a three-pound riverbass.

I make special trips for smallmouth now, and as they did thirty years ago, they still save the day when I've gone for other species that just don't want to come out and play.

I like to start late and wade wet on a lazy late-June or early-July morning. I work my way upstream, looking for some of the deeper runs. There are no rises to search for. Every cast is prospecting: behind the big rock; in the dark run, like a seam, in the dead middle of the river; in the shadows under those low oak branches; in the tail, where the run widens, flattens, grows deeper. My arm is in continual motion. I cast, watch the yellow cork popper come toward me in the foam and chop of the river, twitch it, and flick it up, back, and down again. *There's* a likely spot, where a tree quarters the river and serves as a kind of wing dam. I swivel slightly and cast three times, each time a little farther along the heavy tree, always as close as I can manage.

I'm never really sure where the fish will be at midday. They always surprise me. I've found them in midwater, behind boulders where the water is most roiled, and along the shady shoreline. They seem to like water cooled by riffles and shade. But they'll move six feet for a popping bug, so I'm never sure where they've actually been lying.

Fly fishing for smallmouth bass in rivers is a rougher game than fly fishing for trout in rivers. You generally fish in larger, rougher water (though not always), with larger and rougher flies or bugs. You rarely see the fish. You rarely see the food they're taking. I'm sure there are many times when some reasonable brand of imitation is possible, especially for larger moths or mayflies. I've heard of such times, but I've never been on the river when smallmouth are rising steadily to a specific insect. Mostly there are four or five kinds of food that riverbass eat, and they eat such foods anytime they can find them. A frog struggling in the currents is always a choice morsel, and so is a crayfish. Any popping bug, of cork or hair, will imitate the former; and there are some excellent crayfish imitations: Bob Clouser's, which I like best, and several that are less subtle—chiefly the defined shape of the crayfish, and drawn backward in the water, like Clouser's—but often quite effective. Smallmouth will take other large insects on the surface, like grasshoppers and crickets; and like their big-mouth cousins, the larger ones will take voles and small field mice. Underwater they're always partial to any of a dozen smaller fish, including minnows, dace, sculpin, sucker fry, and the young of just about any other species in the river, and they'll take nymphs and always worms. So a whole variety of streamers works well—fluttered, darting, ambled, or even dead-drift. I prefer patterns with marabou and the Matuka-style streamers, including those with a strip of rabbit fur on top. Any of the Woolly Bugger patterns, which can be bait fish, leeches, or worms, are effective, too.

I've found riverbass slow at times but rarely uncatchable. Their clocks, I think, are less finely tuned to some hatching food than those of trout; they're greater opportunists—and I've found them to be so at the deadest hours of a summer day.

As these things go, with a large family of varying needs, you sometimes have to fish when you can, not when you'd prefer. A few years ago, for instance, I found myself at midday in Middlebury, Vermont, on a high-summer afternoon, with the sun bright and hot. My daughter was scheduled to graduate from a summer program that afternoon, and the entourage—some five or six of us—was wandering through this pretty New England town. My daughter and wife found a clothing store to entertain them; from a bridge in the center of the town, far above the water, I naturally found the Otter River.

From the height at which I saw it, it seemed a pretty river, so naturally I decided to take a closer look. Since I had a rod, reel, and some flies in the car—though no boots, no vest, and no net—I naturally decided I ought to take those, too. And naturally I needed a license.

The proprietor of the local shop, whose vested interest was surely in optimism, just shook his head and said there was no fishing this time of year in the Otter.

"No fish at all?"

"Too warm," he said.

Still, I bought the license and a couple of cork bugs and walked down to the edge of the water in my only pair of shoes and slacks. To make a decent back cast, I had to manipulate myself into the right position—and in doing so I noted that I had muddied my pants and that my shoes had taken some water.

The water was sixty or so feet across. I managed that just fine, putting the popper a foot from the opposite shore and about fifteen feet upstream. This was pleasant fishing. The bug came down a bit; I chugged it and let it hug the shoreline; then I began to bring it across the river, with fits and starts, always letting it drop downstream a bit, like a frog (I thought) struggling mightily to get across the stream.

It was a pretty scenario, and I was enjoying myself hugely, undisturbed by thoughts of catching a fish. Local genius is rarely wrong. But I was much happier casting than shopping.

And then, of course, I was rudely disturbed by a wake and a short strike—my heartbeat quickened—and then, on the next cast, by the fish itself, a plump fourteen-incher. After that, while townspeople, some half dozen of them, on the bridge looked at the strange creature up to his thighs in their river, I took four fat bronzebacks in less than an hour—one a bit smaller, several a couple of inches larger, which is a lot of smallmouth for a dog-day afternoon, or anytime.

I went to the graduation, with squooshy shoes and muddy, stained trousers, and a smile for the graduate. I just smiled and smiled, and several people said they could see how proud I was of her, and I was, but they were only half right.

SELECTIVE BLUES—AND STRIPED BASS

Bluefish (*Pomatomus saltatrix*), affectionately known as "choppers," are notorious slobs. They maketh the sea to stink of oily bunker when they've been feeding; friends pride themselves on being able to smell blues a mile away. Give them just about any sort of steak and they'll turn it to tartare in an instant. Over the years I've taken them on swimming and popping plugs, spoons, bucktail jigs, diamond jigs, drails, a dozen live and dead creatures, something called an "umbrella rig," can openers with hooks affixed, surgical tubing, and three or four sturdy styles of the feathered thing.

When they get a little blood on the brain, they'll generally make a sorry mess of anything you chuck at them. Still, I've had my odd times when they were what would pass for selective: evenings when they were thick in the surf yet would take only surface lures; nights when you had to retrieve a lure or fly just as fast as you could; mornings when—patrolling the shore in ones and twos—they showed an exclusive preference for a very thin, very chartreuse-green sand-eel imitation, wiggled ever so slowly. I'm not an expert on blues. I have gone to them these past ten years, now and then, to escape the tyranny of trout, to change pace drastically, to explore a part of the watery world I know too slenderly—the sea. It's bigger than any trout stream I've fished and has more places in it where the fish aren't; it also has bigger and more savage denizens than a trout stream, fish I understand not at all.

More often than not blues beat me quite as badly as most other gamefish do me in, though I've fished four or five times during blitzes from which I've walked away with fish still active, quite sated by the sheer volume of their eager strikes, their raw violence. They must be one of the strongest of all gamefish and among the most generous.

Last fall my friend Steve Fisher and his son David had me out a couple of times in Greenwich Bay, chiefly for stripers. They'd pick me up in front of my city apartment on warm fall mornings before the first light, weeks after I thought my season had ended for the year, and we'd head less than an hour out of the city. I had rather grown comfortable with midmorning starts for trout, when the western flies came, but these early-morning forays reminded me of my youth, of adventure, of how we often love fishing best when it breaks the bonds of the ordinary for us, the routine, the usual hours, the regularized life, when it puts us in touch with something a little more elemental, even for a brief while.

The Fishers' boat, a twenty-two-foot Winner called *Piscator,* isn't elemental; it's a sophisticated modern fishing machine with sonar and CB radio and twin motors and a john and a houseful of the best flies, rods, and reels for assaulting blues and stripers.

We assaulted the stripers with impunity, but they played hard to get. What those big fellows with stripes were doing, and when, was not clear to me. I had once taken them on the bottom, on diamond jigs, one after the other, but that wasn't our game today. I was sorely anxious to get a truly big one on a fly. Steve said he had gotten all of his stripers on a pale-blue popping bug so I tried one of those and did what he did, after my fashion, casting in against the breakwater and the exposed rocks, and generally doing what I would do with a slightly smaller bass bug. Steve did it all well. I enjoyed watching his popper drop near the breakwater and work its way back to the boat, sending out a V wave and a series of curls, plops, fits, and starts. I had taken my big tarpon rod, on some theory or other, and I liked the feel of the big stick and heavy line pulling against my arm and shoulders; I liked the deliberate and heavy rhythm of it, the long powerful cast and then the bug unfolding and dropping a bit better every half hour or so.

We got nothing.

"What am I doing wrong?" I asked.

"No one's doing anything wrong," said Steve.

"How do you know if the fish are there?"

"You don't," said Steve, "unless they roll or break the surface."

"Have you seen them here, right here?" I asked.

"Many times."

We fished quite hard on the strength of that history for several hours and neither of us had a follow or a touch. It was just like that sometimes. Yesterday—or was it last week?—there had been fish all around the breakwater; it was as good a place as any other to make a stand. Today, the deliberate, sturdy rhythm of my No. 11 tarpon rod began to saw into my back. I thought a chunk of me might just break off.

I switched to a Deceiver, let it sink a couple of feet, and then stripped it back. Sometimes I could see the fly a foot or so under the surface, sometimes not. I switched to a sand eel, on the theory that once, several years earlier, they had taken fish for me on Martha's Vineyard. The theory was poor medicine. I switched back to the Deceiver. David thought that as the light got brighter the stripers kept getting shyer. I'd heard that theory and it made sense; so I fished the Deceiver much deeper, where it would be darker. I was being very shrewd. And my shrewdness was rewarded. In a cove near some high grasses, on a White Deceiver, I finally caught one.

"How big is it?" asked David.

"Five or six pounds, I think," I said.

I was less than half right; it might have gone a fraction over two; I always like to be wrong the other way. But a little striper goes a long way. It has to.

So we turned our attention to blues, which were now doing terrible things to bunker in the harbor. What a sight! Acres of mossbunker skittering, leaping, charging at the surface, bringing the water to a wild boil. Some flew a foot or two into the air, in terror, to save their skins. Everywhere, in a great elemental massacre, there were desperate bunker, forced up against the surface by the blues. Half a dozen boats had blues on. This was a school of gorilla blues; they were in the fifteen- to seventeen-pound class. I'd have liked to be connected to one of those for a while. All those caught had been hooked on cut bunker.

There was now some serious and pointed talk about what was going on. Everyone had a theory about how these fish could and could not be taken. Steve said that blues never took flies when they had this much bunker available. This sounded sensible to me. I had read that they didn't even take whole live bunker when they were on this brand of orgy; I reported this theory, which nudged the discussion toward a concept of selective blues, but there were no takers. I also reported having read that they never took heads—which fell to the bottom and were later picked up and prized by stripers. I heard a faint chuckle or two. Steve thought they were selective to a good bloody midsection or tail section of bunker and that's what I saw my fellow anglers pitching out, overhand, and taking the big ones on. When the discussion finally drifted back to fly fishing, and I felt on firmer ground, someone wondered if there was a good Chunk of Bunker imitation or a Piece of Flesh fly that might turn the trick. Was this "fly" fishing or (as Conrad Voss Bark says) "artificial bait" fishing? Did it matter? Was it fun anyway? Was fun enough?

These were weighty questions for an autumn bluefish trip and I pondered them soberly as the sun came up, forgot them, and cast my biggest Deceiver almost fruitlessly into the churning water, catching two plump bunker on the fly, one even in the mouth.

For a moment, as I watched one of my bunker cut into three bloody portions—the fate of *Brevoortia tyrannus,* the Atlantic menhaden, familiarly called mossbunker, affectionately just bunker—a bunker's lot did not seem an especially easy one. If the blues or the bluefishermen didn't get you, the makers of cat food, chicken feed, fertilizer, fish paste, paint, or canned chum would.

In the end we caught no blues by any means, fair or foul, and by twelve o'clock, from a good deal too much of the elemental, I could barely stand and looked around eagerly for something with sugar to which I might rise, and found three chocolate donuts.

An hour later I wondered if I could walk up the stairs to my apartment or would have to get to my door on all fours.

Two afternoons later, Steve called and said they'd taken some people out that morning. The people had never fished for stripers or blues with a fly before and had even brought trout equipment. You know what happened but I'll tell you anyway: a striper on the first cast; blues all morning long—on cast after cast, a boatload of them; broken rods; chewed-up flies; shouting, excitement, no theories, busted reels.

All that elemental jazz.

WORLD OF THE SILVER KINGS

"How's your heart, Nick?" Jeffrey Cardenas wrote, and sent me a photograph of what a sixteen-foot hammerhead shark did with one bite to a one-hundred-and-fifty-pound tarpon: there was a head and half of a torso, and a lot of blood on the deck of the *Waterlight*.

My heart felt pretty good, and not so lost to those pretty little speckled things that I couldn't dream of at least one trip south for the great silver kings. So when an opening broke for two days in prime tarpon time with Jeffrey, I said, "Why not?"

I ordered a twelve-weight nine-foot-three graphite rod that was very fast and very powerful. Then I traded half a dozen reels I never used for a huge Fin-Nor with an intermediate line and six million yards of backing. I bought the strongest sunscreen I could find—to prevent more basal cell carcinomas, which had recently begun to pop out on my forehead like freckles—and scrounged sixty or seventy tarpon flies from friends and bought twice as many, and read Lefty and Dimock and all the articles on tarpon I could find in magazines going back ten years. And in the end I wasn't sure I really wanted this kind of fishing at all.

I'd never had a twelve–weight rod in my hand; I'd never caught a fish larger than twelve pounds on a fly; and I'd rather gotten to like tiny flies and tough trout lately. Four pounds of such tough trout would be more to my liking, I thought, than these silver monsters I understood not at all.

Still, I'd made the commitment and kept planning hard. I worked out everything with the greatest care. I even took a left-hand Fin-Nor, though I always reel with my right hand, thinking my right hand could hold the rod better. And day by day the letters came from friends who had tried tarpon fishing: "It's addictive." "You'll give up trout forever." "They're awesome, prehistoric fish!" "I envy you like mad."

Several weeks later I was back home, safe—my rod broken, the middle finger of my left hand scarred, bruises on my chest, my left arm, and rump, my nose and left arm scaling rudely from the sun, my head awash with dreams of big water and big tarpon.

And even now, many weeks later, scores of images keep porpoising in my brain, like great silver backs rhythmically rising from the sea and falling back.

I see the flats from Miami to Key West as the Jetstream J31 cruises low: so clear and calm I thought they were land, except for the sailboats and skiffs, like skittering caddis, on the flat surface of the thin water.

What a different game it is: standing on the prow of the *Waterlight*, which dips and rolls in the high winds, line coiled below me; Jeffrey high on the poling platform, eyes peeled to the horizon line, looking for dark-purple shapes beneath the surface or silver backs porpoising or nervous water. "One o'clock—about two hundred yards," he calls. "A big school. Large fish. And they're very happy"

I look and see nothing but the thousand refractions of light on the choppy green surface.

"Point your rod to where you think it is."

I point the rod.

"Farther right," he calls—a voice out of the wind, in my ear.

I point the rod to two-thirty.

"Farther. Yes. See them?"

I do.

"They're closing quickly. Make sure your line is ready. Keep them in sight. Here they come . . ."

Thinking back on those two days, I see the giant rays like magic carpets beneath the boat; the sudden appearance of a turtle's head, the size of a grapefruit; a happy tarpon's head out of the water, Cuban anchovies sprouting from its mouth; cormorants working down near the abandoned barge; pelicans diving thunderously; huge nurse sharks mating. Jeffrey says the nurse sharks gather near these islands and sometimes mate for as long as twelve hours, twisting and turning together, white belly high, tails thrashing, milt awash in the green seas.

I see Mari making watercolors on the brief sand beach of an island, us rushing from the permit flats as the rain clouds angle toward her.

I see the sheets of rain as we turn tail and race back to Key West, water blasting me from the boat's spray in choppy seas and from above, my eyes stinging from the salt, Mari smiling through it all like a kid on a roller coaster.

I see Jeffrey madly untangling the knot in my fly line, the second day, after the bright forty-pound tarpon took and began to leap with abandon, and Jeffrey untying it and the fish soon coming close under the pressure of the twelve-weight and Jeffrey shouting, "If he goes under the boat, take it around the front end," and the fish diving under, me following stupidly with the rod, the new twelve-weight busting cleanly with a bang, Jeffrey leaping in to get the tip section that came free when the fish was off, me seeing that photograph he'd sent me of half a tarpon, and then Jeffrey hoisting himself back on board and all of us laughing.

It was very different for me out on the flats. I saw and understood too little. I felt untutored for it. In that one moment when tarpon and poled boat began to intersect, I had moments to get my line in the air, double-haul, and place it quickly in the line of the huge fish. I got one cast, perhaps two. I got buck fever and crashed key casts, after Jeffrey had spent twenty minutes poling into position. I nearly put a fly into his neck when I cast at twelve o'clock. I cast too fast. I cast late. I forgot everything I'd read, everything I'd been told, everything I'd practiced the day before in a skiff in the backcountry with a friend. It was after we'd fished the backcountry that afternoon and practiced with the big twelve-weight that I tripped getting out of the boat—nervous before I was within thirty miles of a tarpon—and smashed my chest, my left arm, and my rump. Out on the flats I forgot the sunscreen I'd brought and only used the one fly that Jeffrey gave me.

I took a tarpon on my first cast the second day, jumped another, cast poorly much of the time, decently on occasion, and half began to think I understood something (though I didn't), and wondered if I could ever master this exhilarating sport.

The two days had started with a minute of high drama, and I may even have thought then that I understood a bit more than I could possibly understand.

We had no sooner arrived on the flats the first day than Jeffrey tied on a fly with a bright red head that had been hot the past week. He said to keep alert. I remember a sailfish captain telling me that a dozen years earlier, and my sitting in the big fighting chair for five hours—highly alert, dragging a rigged bait fruitlessly.

Not this time. Two minutes after we arrived, Jeffrey spotted silver backs, not eighty feet away. You couldn't miss them. My legs

turned to jelly. But I stripped out line, stepped onto the casting area, saw the ruffled water angling toward us, and seconds later they were at eleven o'clock, forty-five feet off to the left, and closing.

For three weeks I have been trying to get a truly clear picture of what happened next. All is awash in silver and confusion.

Seconds after I made my first cast ever to a tarpon, a huge fish—over one-hundred pounds—took the fly. I struck three or four times

hard (as I'd been instructed); the fish careened dead away from the boat and leapt once, thunderously, rising like some great silver missile, shaking, vibrating in the air, and then crashing back into the sea.

It was off the hook.

There were voices behind me, but my first thought was that I might get in another cast before this large school passed. The line was too far out to put it in the air, so I began to strip it—fishing it, as I always do when fish are near.

Another tarpon picked up the fly. I felt the sudden surge of power, reared back three or four times, and this time the fish was on. Up it went—bright silver and electric, quivering with life—and I bowed (or at least leaned enough) and the fish stayed hooked.

There is an old 1920s cartoon about a Mississippi fisherman hooked up to a truly gigantic catfish, with the legend "Fish, do I have you or do you have me?" With my tarpon I could not tell. The fish took line when it suited him; it leapt magnificently; at times it felt unbudgeable. It proved to be modest-sized—about seventy-five pounds—but it was more than enough fish for the likes of me, and while I fought it, Jeffrey taught me how to gain line, keep the fish from rolling, apply maximum pressure, and haul opposite the tug of the fish. Reeling hard with my unused left hand, I put a huge welt on my middle finger; I could barely lift my right arm. An hour later the fish turned sideways and the fight neared its end.

Those two days—my first on the flats—haunt me. My heart held— but I lost a piece of it to the world of the silver kings.

FRENCH PIKE

The fly fishing in Paris was extremely poor. I could find no trout in the Louvre; there were none in the Orangerie; only the Musée d'Orsay had one—in a Courbet. Nor were there any fishermen with their long rods along the Seine. I walked the quais and looked but saw only one fish in four or five miles: amid the floating debris, among the heavy shore weeds, a carp, belly-up.

I did find two shops, one of which was surely my kind of place. It was called La Maison de la Mouche, on the Île de St. Louis, and it was crammed with flies, rods, reels, and all the delicious parapher-nalia that drives us nuts. The proprietor spoke little English, and I speak less French. Our conversation amounted to a muttered "Ritz" and a "grand mouche" and a "cad-ese" and a couple of "cul de canards." I bought several of the latter, blond, in No. 18, which reminded me of some Pale Morning Duns I'd once seen, in another country. And later I packed them up carefully and sent them to my friend Herb, well west in that other country. I told him to run them by some large speckled friends we knew in a certain pool called Paranoid. I told Mari: "We've come to the wrong place. The fishing's lousy here."

Matters picked up considerably, though, when Pierre returned from Portugal.

He had been at the beach with his family, far from rods and flies and any chance to fish, and his frustration had swelled to a fine frenzy. He wanted to go out right away. At once. The next morning. We could fish the upper Seine; we could fish for carp below the Pont Neuf—at four in the morning; there was a small pike pond an hour from Paris; there was the chance of a helicopter ride to a chalkstream only fifteen minutes as a fast crow flies; there was a pond with big pike on the border of Normandy and Perche.

I looked at the big pike on the wall of Pierre's Left Bank apartment. It was a considerable fish, better than thirty pounds, and it had come out of the big-pike pond about which Pierre had spoken.

My friend pushed the chalkstream option; he said it had a good head of wild browns and had been fishing very well—the big mayfly was on. I'd never fished a French chalkstream and the idea appealed to me. But the pike on the wall, with the mouth of an alligator, had put the hex on me. I asked Pierre lightly if that was the largest fish to come from that pond. No, there had been forty-pounders, and one day the previous October he had seen something that suggested some were much larger. He had been on the lake alone, during bird-shooting season. Now and then he heard shots. After one cluster of blasts, a pheasant came rocketing out of the woods, fluttered, and fell to the surface.

"Don't tell me the rest," I said.

"It lay there on the surface, Neek . . ."

"I don't want to hear about it."

"It lay there for a few moments, and I watched its wings struggle, and then I had to turn the boat a bit and for a moment I couldn't see it."

"I don't believe this, Pierre. It didn't happen. Not a whole pheasant."

"I turned away and then there was a tremendous splash . . ."

"No!"

". . . and when I turned back, there were just . . ."

"No, Pierre!"

"On the surface, Neek . . ."

"Stop it!"

". . . there were only three feathers. Fifty pounds. Fifty pounds that pike was, min-e-mum."

The pond, leased by Pierre's friend Alex from a duke, is two hours from Paris, if you drive over one hundred miles per hour most of the way. We stopped for coffee and then for the makings of a sumptuous lunch, and made it in 121 minutes.

Wobbling slightly, bundling myself against the rain and chill, I allowed myself to be ghillied by rowboat to an embankment where the water dropped abruptly to fifteen or twenty feet. At least seven twenty-pounders—if I kept the various pike distinct in my mind— had come from that very spot. Even one of Alex's girlfriends, out for the first time, had caught one that size. Twenty pounds seemed the size at which serious counting began.

I could see this was a remote, modest-size pond, perhaps twenty acres, surrounded by forest, with weedbeds in the coves, some deep channels, and the embankment drop-offs. Alex leased it very cheaply, with a house and some incidental buildings, and since I'm restless and always looking for a "home," I considered that option and concluded that I could live in this place forever and write shaggy fish stories, especially if I could get a twenty-pounder every couple of days.

The three fish Alex and Pierre caught were one-quarter that size. I caught nothing but a running nose and a rather large, full branch, well beneath the twenty-pound class but of a much more complicated species. That and the rain did their best to discourage me. I thought briefly of the warm museums in Paris. Then Pierre hooked one a bit larger and handed me the rod. I told him I didn't need his pike—in the fullness of time I'd get one of my own, thank you. Alex caught another, and I had one flash at my lure and struck much too fast and hard. Then Pierre jumped one on a big popping plug, and I got out a fly rod and began to flail away. The rod was light—only a six-weight— and the bass bug, with wire tippet, was unwieldy. In the wind the rig jerked around spasmodically, and I could not help noting that my companions had stopped fishing; they were now low in the boat, head tucked into chest, arms in protective embrace, strong French words emerging rapidly from each pile of person.

In the candlelit camp building we built a fire, had charcoal-roasted steaks, country pâté, warm local bread, and a pleasant Beaujolais— and my spirits picked up considerably. Then we walked back to the lake, and in a steady rain, rowed to the opposite side.

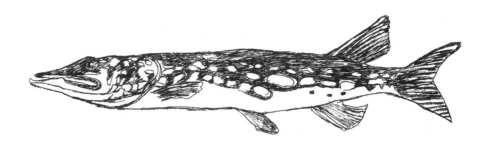

The water there was dotted with tiny rock islands, each fitted with one of the duke's duck-nesting structures. Each structure had a neat little metal ramp leading to the water. We saw one week-old duckling totter out to its ramp and then, wisely, have second thoughts and scurry back, for the pond looked very nervous where the ramp entered the water.

Though we did not have duckling or pheasant imitations, we fished near the ramps a couple of times, and Pierre had one good pike leap right over his big popping plug. He is one of the great fishermen—a former champion caster with several kinds of rods, a demon-pursuer of all the great gamefish. He once told me, "All I want to do, Neek, is fish. I want to fish for every species in every part of the world. I want to fish all the time, everywhere."

This is a sort of large commitment, and my little passions pale before it. Pierre also finds fish and eventually, late in the afternoon, when hope had almost metamorphosed into despair, he found one for me. "There, between the two weedbeds," he told me, and I cast the big frog bug in, chugged it, rushed it, let it wait, chugged it some more, and began to lift it out when my first pike struck—and missed.

"Back, back!" shouted Alex.

"Quick!" shouted Pierre.

I was quick and sure-handed, the bug bounced once, there was a heavy splash, I struck, I felt a heavy rush, and four minutes later I grasped my first pike behind the gills and lifted it into the boat. It may have been French but it sure looked like a northern to me.

The fish was shy of twenty pounds by about fifteen and could not have fit more than a couple of furry ducklings into its maw. But

I felt very happy about the outcome, got my picture taken a dozen times with the grizzly thing, then chucked it back.

The fishing in Paris is generally poor. Go for the museums, the food, the history, the culture, the ambience, the picturesque winding streets. Go if you want to try to regain your youth, even though you won't. The fishing isn't much, but if you know Pierre, you can do all right.

THE SNOBBISH BROWN TROUT

Salmon are larger and leap higher. Bass strike more savagely. Blue gill have the more generous heart. The fierce bluefish fights harder. And in various ways, at various times, the good case can be made for pike, bonefish, tarpon, striped bass, bonito, muskie, snook, barracuda, and a dozen other gamefish. On a given day, one might even be persuaded to vote for the fluke.

But I prefer trout. I like dark, mottled, and brilliantly rose-pocked native brookies from the headwaters of clear mountain streams; I like bright silver rainbows, with their honor stripe of crimson, in the brisk rapids below; and I like wild cutthroats, with their colors of mountain mosses and wild raspberries. But mostly I like the beautiful brown—sleek, dappled with crimson moles, its yellows the color of fresh butter. I love the wild brown trout beyond all other fish. But I love it not for its fighting ability nor even for its beauty.

I love the brown trout because it is shy to the point of being a wall (or shore) flower, but mostly because of its eating habits—habits so fastidious, so snobbish, that I'd probably abhor them in humans.

With infuriating finality, the thoroughgoing snob turns up its nose at what it refuses to eat, saying, "I would if I could, but, really, I simply cannot—not now." Nothing in the behavior of any fish, when coupled with its pleasure in taking food from the surface of the water, makes it more appealing to me.

Myself, I'm more like a bluefish. When I'm hungry I simply hunt out the oiliest fish, the nearest chum line. Even my wife, who is picky, will eat broccoli anytime, asparagus day or night—which, ironically, I won't eat, even when it is served in a gourmet restaurant. The brown trout eats what's served, but he's picky, temperamental; when he's living up to his best potential, he is a dainty picker of tiny morsels from the stream surface. The brown may have a brain the size of a pea but he knows what he wants for lunch and when he wants it, and when he wants it on the surface, the top of his world, I want to be there. Trying to figure out what he wants and when he wants it, though, I—who presumably have a much bigger brain—often fail miserably. Without the failure, I'd love the brown less.

When a brown trout wants a *Paraleptophlebia*—which is not a foot fungus but a mayfly—he wants a *Paraleptophlebia* and no substitute. He's got backbone and values. He'll only eat a *Paraleptophlebia* sandwich when *Paraleptophlebia* sandwiches are being served, and he'll come to the table only when summoned by the official dinner bell, not before, not after. Sometimes, being a very par-

ticular fellow, he'll prefer an immature *Paraleptophlebia;* sometimes
one that's just hatching; sometimes one that has fulfilled all of its
sexual obligations in this world and, wings spread-eagled on the surface, is quite spent and done in.

I have tasted *Paraleptophlebia* and have no sweet tooth for them,
not anytime, though a big *Ephemera guttulata* tastes a little like butter. A braver friend tried a giant stonefly (*Pteronarcys californica*) once,
then drank a glass of white wine, and said, "The wine's not quite right."
Each to his own, I suppose, though I've worried that if I can't taste
food like a brown trout, how can I learn to think like one?

What's the appeal of all this fussiness?

Simple. It makes a savage old bluefish like me think a bit more
when I pursue the fish, that's what. I haven't the slightest idea of why
a salmon takes a fly that looks like the British flag, and no one has
given me a convincing reason; the fish is up the river to spawn and
probably gets irritated or remembers some lunch it had a couple of
years earlier, but doesn't remember very exactly. It can't put a hand
out to touch it, so it takes it in its mouth. Big deal. A pike would as
well dine anytime on frog or perch or duckling or lizard as shiner.
When a fish takes my fly, more and more I want to know why—and,
frankly, though some people may think *me* a snob, more and more I
want to see him do so.

Part of the fun I have, of course, when I pursue wild brown trout,
especially in tap-clear water, is that I've got to figure out which of
the hundreds of possible mayflies or caddis or stoneflies a particular
fish is lunching on, and then offer him a reasonable facsimile thereof.
To find the right fake bug, I must think about the natural insect's color,
its size and shape, its attitude on the water, and how the bits and
pieces of fur, feather, and space age plastics can best be concocted
to represent them. The brown trout's brain may be the size of a pea,
but he's no dope. More than any fish that swims, he's determined to
save his skin. He'll rarely take a piece of food on the roof of his world
if it looks like a piece of grandma's old sweater—and he can spot an
inermis in the midst of his *Paraleptophlebia adoptivas* any day of
the week. The honorable brown trout in his middle years—before
he has become a toothy old cannibal that will eat any old living
thing that it can get its hooked jaws around—wants his plate of fake

Paraleptophlebia to look and act pretty much like a plate of real *Paraleptophlebia*.

I'm less fussy myself. I'm partial to smorgasbords and stews. Like the pike, I'll take liver instead of beef, chicken in lieu of duck, if that's what's available. I didn't choose my wife for her fussiness—nor my friends for their eating habits. It seems a curious criterion. But I like those of the brown trout. He's a thoroughgoing culinary snob, all right—and that makes all the difference.

HOW WE DO IT

In fly fishing, as in fashion or knitting or love or painting or eating a grapefruit or war, there are styles of behavior, ways we do it. It cannot be otherwise. Try as we will, we cannot escape who we are; style, say the French, *is* the man—or woman.

I've fished with some people whose fishing style was to work so hard at it that I grew tired watching them, and others for whom it was such a delicate aesthetic exercise that their fastidiousness made me think that fishing, for them, had descended into an art form. Some dress *up* for their fishing, some down. Some wear skin-tight waders, some wade wet. Some consider fly fishing a chance for "lifestyle" dressing, others wear only the drabbest, oldest clothes they can find. From dress to equipment to the doing itself, the ways we do it are wildly diverse.

And if for a moment we extend our range from fly fishing to any fishing, the divergent styles grow greater still.

Once, on Martha's Vineyard, I saw a fellow heave his bottom rig into a high surf positively wild with whitecaps; it was in fact one of the worst October storms in the history of the eastern seaboard and I could manage only ten minutes at a time out in the wind and cold. This fellow was quite mad. He'd rush up to the edge of the surf at a gallop, lean hard into his clumsy cast, and heave the thing no more than fifty feet. Then he'd scamper back to avoid the waves and a few moments later he'd furiously reel in, always with a full three feet of heavy weed at the end. It must have been as much torture to do as it was for me to watch. The guy simply believed: if you're in a warm car, you ain't fishing! His was a sad case of too much matter, no art— or common sense. He was related by temperament to that guy Charlie Brooks once told me about who fished an entire day with a Sofa Pillow pinning both his lips shut.

There is a saner commitment to hard fishing. Art Flick had his fly on the water more than anyone I've ever seen. Art was a vigorous, restless fisherman who liked nothing better than to fish a Gray Fox Variant in pocket water—pitching his fly here, then there, then up against a rock and into a broken-water run. He always caught fish.

Often the kind of water one fishes most regularly, or prefers to fish, determines the kind of fisherman one becomes. Art's Schoharie has a great deal of broken water and those runs and riffles and pockets were the sections he liked best; on other rivers, that's what he looked for. It matched his temperament. After a long slow morning on the Battenkill, fishing flat water, Art found a brisk patch of shallow riffles and, at midday—when no one catches fish on the Battenkill—tattooed the trout.

Vincent Marinaro, with whom I never fished, liked the limestone rivers of Pennsylvania—chiefly the Letort—and fished only to rising trout, which is the English way and the way of many people who fish the spring creeks of the West. Perhaps because it is so often associated with "refined" fishing on the English chalkstreams, where some anglers still do "dress up" for their fishing, in tweeds and ties, fishing only the dry fly and only to rising trout is often considered elitist. It isn't. There's no populist law that says we have to fish all ways any more than there's a law that says we have to fish one way. We fly fish—I hope—because it's fun; and we do it in ways that give us, individually, the most fun. Some people simply consider the rise of a trout to a surface fly an especially exciting experience, and casting to a specific target, requiring a specific fly, more challenging and fun.

Some of the best of these flat-water fishermen I've seen are John Goddard in England and H. G. Wellington in the United States. Both are superb casters, both fish only to rising fish, upstream, and with flies that imitate the insects on which the fish are feeding. Goddard has spectacular eyes, which are necessary to spot the form of a fish "on the fin" as well as actual rises—and I am intrigued that the kind of fishing one does prompts the development of certain skills: if you *have* to see fish first, you *must* develop the faculties with which to see them. Herb, who fishes the large open areas of the West, is a powerful caster; with the western wind, he must be so. Both can wait long periods of time, still as herons. Not for them a line constantly in motion, spooking every fish in the clearest of waters (where most of the fish's predators come from above, just like a fly line). Goddard once told me that the most valuable piece of equipment he owned was a portable chair; it folded into a kind of walking stick, then could be opened when he wanted to sit and watch. Herb finds even that height wrong. He'll sit on a bank for as long as necessary and then make one spectacular cast, eighty feet or more, low to the water, angling upriver away from the fish, hooking the leader so that the fly comes over the fish before the monofilament.

It stops my breath to watch them both. And at least some of the better fish they catch could not be caught without those finely honed and athletic skills, without a style keyed to their precise fishing needs.

Doug Swisher, the one day I fished with him, had his fly constantly on the water. We floated the Big Hole and he'd cast with left or right hand, switch hands as the line came downriver, juggle and jiggle the line on the water to get a better drag-free float, and invariably catch twice the number of fish that anyone else in our party was taking. He was like a boxer, attacking the river, and that aggressive, restless, hunting quality was the sure source of his success.

One fly fisherman casts fast and has his line constantly in motion, another waits. Ed Van Put, the Catskill master, casts so slow a line that I've sometimes wondered what keeps it in the air. But that cat-like quality about everything he does on the river makes him a great predator.

A memorable display of grace came from the late Al McClane. He'd just flown to Montana but his luggage had wandered off to left field. He came to the river in his traveling clothes, which included a light tropical shirt, designer shoes and slacks, and a straw hat. He borrowed a rod, walked downriver with me, and scoffed at my insistence that he had to crawl through the mud along this stretch if he wanted to catch fish. He stood straight upright, cast with a happy stylish care into some broken water, presented the fly where he wanted it to go, controlled it on the water, and took a number of fine fish on not very many casts.

Some fly fishers like to fish all the time; some (like me) must make a little go a long way.

Some wear pins, patches, and Stetson hats, designer vests and Austrian brogues; others settle for a baseball cap, a hip carryall, blue jeans, and torn sneakers.

Some talk a lot, some fish mum.

Some spout Latin, some know only size and color, some take the whole subject of bugs (wrongly) to be affectation.

Some fish a mile of water in a morning, some a hundred feet.

Some like a dozen friends spread out around them, some none.

It's a varied game.

As for me, who fishes too little and in a few too many places, I doubt that I'll ever develop one style. In fact, I sometimes think I have *no* style, indifferent as I am to what I wear, how I comport myself. I once sat at the same table as Diana Vreeland, then the doyen of high fashion. It was a corporate party, we were the last in, and there were only the two of us at the table. I tried several times to speak with her but she refused. She never once acknowledged my presence.

Invisible me likes to try to let the water dictate how I'll behave; I try to grow a bit more versatile and diverse; I learn a new trick or two; I generally dress drab, with what's at hand, with what can't be too easily ruined; generally I try not to make too great a fool of myself in front of trout or priestess of high fashion or friend. Unlike that surf caster, I lean toward that which is pleasure, not pain when I fish. I try to learn a bit more entomology because that deepens my understanding of what happens when I fish but—as my friend Gil Eisner said, on his fiftieth birthday—I try not to say *Paraleptophebia* when strangers are around or when it would sound pretentious.

If I catch a few fish now and then, that helps.

FLY FISHING FOR
ANYTHING, ANY WAY

The letter from Dermot Wilson began with this injunction: "When you're tired of catching snakes on the dry fly in Montana, it appears that you should come to England to perform similar miracles with eels."

There are those who think I have always been a closet eeler—and since there's some truth in this, I was all ears. I have practiced the fine art of Hudson River fence fishing and mastered some of its subtler minor tactics; and when my friend Joe Pisarro lived nearby we studied old maps of New York City to determine which manholes might sit innocently over choice glory holes for the eel. We wanted to write a book called *Masters on the Eel,* but Joe defected to Vermont, where they have more common pursuits, like trout and bass.

Then Dermot quoted this passage from *River Trout Fly Fishing,* a recent book by Peter Lapsley: "there are carriers and sidestreams on the River Test on which falls of spinners can be so heavy at certain times of year that the resident eels have been seen there, lying just beneath the surface and rising to the spent flies just as trout do."

One snake satisfied whatever curiosity I might have had in that regard—but eels! My head swarmed with possibilities.

I hastened to call my old friend Clyde, who has a natural interest in such matters. Twenty-five years ago he set out to catch every possible species of fish—game and not so game—on a fly, but I knew that he had taken only one eel, and that surely not on a dry fly. He had once drenched a battered Marabou Muddler in chicken blood for five days, added a couple of shakes of garlic salt and some Worcestershire sauce, and fished this behind four wraps of soft lead. He was fishing for channel cats and since he finally did not count the eel as fairly caught—it was a two-pounder, thirty-one inches—I don't count it either. There are limits—and Clyde had exceeded them.

"Eel on the dry fly?" he shouted.

"That's the story."

"On spinners?"

I confirmed that this was the report.

"On a chalkstream?"

"The Test itself."

"Astonishing!"

Clyde has done well for other species over the years and I had always listened with awe and envy to his litany of accomplishments:

Carp on his Mulberry Fly of crimson chenille;

Dace on a No. 32 Bread Crumb Special;

Sturgeon on a Duck-Gut Roller;

Piranha on a triple long-shank Finger Fly;

A small paddlefish on an Eelgrass Wiggler;

Mullet, on the Riviera, during his Twenty-fifth Wedding Anniversary trip, on his No. 28 Plankton Popper.

And the list goes on, including hacklehead and skate on his Cut Squid Fly from the pier at Sheepshead Bay in December and blowfish on a Clam Glob Red Tag anytime. He had so mastered the fine art of chub fishing with a fly that he could pluck one out of a pod of rainbows almost as quick, intentionally, as I always do not on purpose. No one could bring a flounder to a Blue Bloodworm Fly quicker than Clyde, and I'd put him against anyone for fluke with his Fake Stillborn Spearing.

There are people who still send their guppies to a local guppy-sitter when Clyde comes to dinner—and with good cause.

When one associates with such loonies, one is forced to think about what is and is not appropriate for fly rods. Since there is neither a pope of fly fishing nor a pontificating council of elders—well, there *are* a lot of plain pontificators, I guess—one is quite within one's rights to fish however one chooses. As they say: it's a free country.

Still, I've stopped using lead because, first, I once put a really lousy set in a lovely bamboo rod using the stuff and once got a tough knock in the head from a heavily leaded fly, poorly cast, which nearly caused a concussion.

As I think of it, that may be why Clyde is so weird. He used to use a lot of lead. He once told me that he'd socked himself silly one windy day with a Doughball Fly he'd made out of melted lead, mashed dough, honey, and peanut butter, permanently affixed with Krazy Glue but hollow near the head so that he could fill it with Alka-Seltzer, which trailed a little line of bubbles that must have simulated an emerging caddis better than Antron, for it was frequently taken by trout as it was raised to the surface. I guess I'd have reservations about that—about all smelly flies, all flies that are that heavy, all flies that require Alka-Seltzer fillings to work properly.

It may be sheer snobbishness on my part.

Still, I wouldn't want to say that something is *not* fly fishing just because it's not what I find myself doing anymore.

I guess it's all worth thinking about now and then, though I wish I didn't nod off during some of the better heated discussions. One guy insists that only dry flies are "moral"; a British friend called a Thom Green Leech I was pitching—with great success—into his reservoir a "hairbrush"; the British generally call all flies that don't imitate an actual insect—even when they're nifty fish-catchers—"lures." I once met a fellow who insisted that only flies No. 16 and smaller could bring him "grace"; many fly fishermen won't use lead; some use only flies that imitate a natural food—natural foods other than mice, leeches, grasshoppers, baby ducklings, salmon eggs, and the like; some use only floating lines or twenty-foot leaders. Someday it may be that you're not really *fly* fishing unless you use lighter-than-air flies that hover above the surface.

There are a lot of ways I *don't* fish anymore and I suppose I ought to have some profound theory about all this but what it all seems to come down to is this: I fish in a certain way because it satisfies my sense of what's fair play—for fish and fisherman; because it's a little more fulfilling to know why a fish takes a certain fly—especially when that's what he's feeding on; because I don't anymore have to catch every fish in the river but am reasonably content to get a couple of fish in a way I prefer to fish, when they can be caught that way—though this sometimes means fishless days; and chiefly because it's a lot of fun for me to fish in ways I've chosen to fish—more fun, in this hedonistic pastime, than other ways.

Frankly, Clyde seemed a little extreme to me and I worried that what might have been read as innovation was really some form of perversion.

The prospect of taking an eel on a dry fly made him positively delirious. He could not get it out of his head. I thought he'd gone nuts. He made ten phone calls to Dermot, at all hours, asking for absolute verification, hatch dates, the body color of these spinners, their size, whether poly or hackle points or fibers will make the better wing, how they will react to drag, the size tippet required. Dermot's letter to me was a masterful bit of understatement. "I didn't think anyone in the States," he began, "was a bigger nut than you."

I reminded Dermot that some respectable bulwarks of the American fly fishing establishment fished dry flies for catfish when the white fly was on the Susquehanna, and that many serious fly fishers over here considered the catfish-eel controversy six of one, half a dozen of the other.

In the end, Dermot has been persuaded—for Clyde is the most contagious of fly fishers. Dermot has forsaken France, New Zealand, Montana, Argentina, and all other chalkstreams and spate rivers in England for the prospect of some decent dry-fly fishing for eels on the Test come July; he's counting the days until Clyde arrives. Clyde is so excited I fear for his health.

Joe Pisarro is another story. He seems, safe in the lush hills of New England, to have forgotten the eel entirely and cannot be induced to travel anywhere for them.

I'd go but, frankly, my case is worse: I've discovered that in my advancing years I've become a species snob. I'm afraid this is just one more intriguing fly fishing opportunity that I can comfortably pass up.

Which doesn't mean I haven't asked Dermot and Clyde to call me on July ninth, the day they anticipate the spinner fall will start and the eels—like them—will go nuts.

GADGETS AND GIZMOS

Fishermen love to invent. We are forever tinkering with our flies, lures, boats, and boxes to make them more perfect. Thus the enduring popularity of "Tap's Tips," with its monthly stream of practical ways to manage our play more wisely. Thus the restless stream of new tools and materials, flies and fly boxes, gadgets and gizmos that turn up year after year, ever since someone discovered that you didn't have to fish merely for food, but could do so for fun.

Look at any recent fishing-tackle catalog, and the current extent of invention will startle you with its variety. The array for fly tying alone is amazing: a little metal frame that hooks onto your tying table, complete with a plastic bag for cuttings and scraps; wingburners for carefully cut mayfly wings; half-hitch tools, stackers, midge bobbins, dubbing teasers, new body and wing materials such as Antron and Sparkle Yarn, and enough clever devices to fill half a house.

From there we move on to lights for night fishing that attach to your shoulder or head or hang from your neck, new rod materials such as graphite or boron, rod-wrapping stands. Velcro tabs so line won't slip back onto your reel, miracle glues to attach anything to anything else, braided leaders, new lures made of new plastics, new fly coatings, upside-down hooks, pin-ons of all kinds, new vest designs, lighter wader materials, wader spats, and mittens without fingers. We have wading staffs that fold, stream cleats that hold, wading jackets that shed, rods that won't break, attachments to glasses that magnify, tubes that will float you anywhere, and videocassettes that will teach you anything. And of course, year after year, we get a perfectly bewildering array of new fly patterns that imitate everything from the stillborn hatch to the lowly leech.

It's a brave new world, indeed, that features such objects—and it's all bound to make your fishing life more comfortable and interesting, if you're not driven batty by the choices.

Of course, not all innovations survive. What was new yesterday—hailed as the ultimate breakthrough—may be extinct today. Look at a tackle catalog sixty or eighty years old and you'll find lancewood and hickory rods, silkworm gut, Senate "steel vine" rods, and pocket dry-fly vaporizers with rubber bulbs. There was once a "Walking Stick Rod" that, for some reason, was billed as having "not the least appearance of a Fishing-Rod." "Vaseline jelly" was once hailed as "a great advance on paraffin oil" for floating flies, and we don't see much "imported English Deer Fat" around anymore.

I don't know if the "Live Minnow Cage" caught fish. "The minnow is not harnessed, hooked nor mutilated—remains alive and active," its sponsors claimed, as they did also for their "Magnifying Glass Minnow Tube." We prefer plastic worms or crankbaits today. Nor have we much use for the "Patent Lever Fish Hook," which was "constructed on the principle of a lever, and the harder a fish pulls the stronger it holds him." That device as well as the "Celebrated Yankee Doodle or Sockdolager Fish Hook" have vanished, blown away by the winds of good sense. We have our own gadgets for lighting our way on the waters at night, and I'm pleased as punch (since I like to fish at night) that we no longer have to trifle with the "Ferguson Head Lamp," which burned "signal oil, or lard, or sperm oil mixed with kerosene."

Some of the wonderful old inventions were modified slowly over the years, and we couldn't do without them today. The Orvis perforated fly reel, which enabled the line to dry, is one such old standby; and dozens of flies, lures, boxes, and garments have endured a hundred years with only slight changes. They may well last another century, since they work.

Lots of people tinker with items for their own or their friends' use. The late Sparse Grey Hackle, an inveterate tinkerer, may have been the first to attach a jeweler's eyepiece to his glasses, the better to tie on small flies. A friend of Art Flick's makes a brass dry-fly oil container; I used one for years, until I discovered that my left shoulder drooped from the weight. Dave Whitlock snugs a piece of chartreuse fly line onto his leader—it makes a superb strike indicator. Charlie Brooks glues a needle into a simple felt-tip pen, which makes the pen a terrific tool for poking cement out of the eyes of flies— though it causes a bit of mischief when you use it to sign an expensive nonresident fishing license. My friend Justin Askins concocted a finely tooled device for me that was designed to help my bad eyes thread a No. 16 fly. But the aperture of the device is so small I can find the eye of the No. 16 fly more easily.

For myself, though I have nine thumbs, I make a nice little fly box from metal cough-drop boxes by gluing felt to the inside base and attaching some lamb's wool against the inside of the lid. It's simple, practical, and I consider myself quite brilliant to have come up with it. For years I've wanted to have my name on a fly, so I once invented a pigeon-quill dry fly, called the Lyons Quill. Unfortunately, it sank like a rock.

But that doesn't stop me from trying.

A FINE MADNESS

Another season won't begin for too long, and as an alleged balm for cabin fever I have been laying out on the dining room table my tens of thousands of trout flies. They are in half a hundred plastic boxes and metal cases of varying sizes and conformations; there's even a half-full shoe box. I surely don't need this number of flies. I could not use them if I fished every day for the rest of my life, which I can't. But I never have enough flies. I am mad for them.

With some delicacy, I pick bad ones out of the shoe box with my surgical tweezers and drop them into the wastebasket. Some that I bought twenty years ago—full of great expectations—I now do not think could catch a chub; some hooks are rusted; and a couple of dozen flies were mangled last summer. I set a Catskill Cahill next to a western Pale Morning Dun, tied parachute style, and check the proportions of each. I wonder where I fished that Adams with the sloppy tag of nylon still through its eye, or the mushed Hendrickson, or the Paradrake. These little bits of fur and feather are filled with stories—but they are first themselves.

Looking at all the flies, I begin to contemplate both my addiction to them and the odd meld of aesthetics and practicality that are the measure of this minor art form. In order to succeed, each of these thousands of steak tartares must gull a trout into thinking that it is worth the risk of its skin. This is not mere art for art's sake; the aesthetics of the trout fly concern life and death.

404 |

Do I need all these flies?

I have convinced myself that I do.

For these artifacts—made of fur, feathers, and various yarns, tied cunningly with thread onto a proper hook—imitate many of the several stages of the four or five hundred mayflies, caddisflies, and stoneflies that live in trout streams. And you need half a dozen of each. So I need several thousand or so, minimum. What would I do if I were three miles up the creek and didn't have a proper *infrequens* emerger? That isn't all. The trout's palate is of course more ecumenical, and I have at one time or another bought or made or borrowed imitations of sowbugs, scuds, inchworms, grasshoppers, leaf rollers, crickets, dragonflies, voles, damselflies, riffle beetle larvae, moths, caterpillars, leeches, frogs, worms, sculpins, slugs, blacknose dace, crawfish, salmon eggs, beetles, gnats, newts, jassids, ants (black and cinnamon), other trout (including their own and their neighbors' young), and dozens of other little creatures that, to their ultimate misfortune, satisfy the trout's sweet tooth.

Looking at all my flies on the dining room table—where I have now dumped them randomly in preparation for the massive reorganization—it is pleasant to think that because the trout's appetite is "selective," or at least keyed to a particular food served at a particular time (a sensible trout would question the propriety of grasshoppers, say, in early April), adds hugely to the fly fisherman's, and tier's,

challenge—and to my fine madness. Many of these flies I'll never use again because my prejudices mount and my preferences grow pickier each year. Imitations of bait—like salmon eggs and worms—just aren't my cup of tea anymore. Yet the selectivity of the trout requires a lot of options. We have to be prepared for the fact that if it is afternoon of a late-April day in the Catskills, a trout will probably want, almost exclusively, the mayfly *Ephemerella subvaria,* the Hendrickson. Trout would grow suspicious, as we would, if served a dish that did not look correct in color and form, whether Hendrickson or frog; I should be wary myself if my steak came to the table green.

To meet all the options, we need more and more flies.

We need to solve the great questions about what the trout sees from its unique position in the universe—so the tier, or buyer, of trout flies always tries to think like a trout. I try to do so now. I look at ten flies sideways and from beneath. I pop one into a glass of water and, holding it against the light, look slantways and up at it from below. In my youth, I once brought goggles to a bathtub, submerged myself, and viewed flies from the trout's angle. I learned nothing.

Since I am not a trout and haven't the foggiest idea of how they think—if in fact they do anything remotely resembling thinking—I know these issues will never be resolved except in the most abrupt and pragmatic terms: a trout will either accept the imitation as the real McCoy and try to eat it or offer the most ungracious of snubs. The trout is your ultimate arbiter and snob concerning the acceptability of the trout fly.

To help us whip this snob, we exploit all available resources trying to imitate some natural food on which the fish is snacking. The whole world of fur and feather offers itself to the fly tier's palette, in a cornucopia of colors and forms: turkey wing feathers, elk hair, coastal deer hair, specially bred blue-dun hackle, mink, sable, fox, woodchuck, rabbit, peccary, nutria, peacock, mallard, teal, grouse, and a couple of thousand others. Lately, a wide array of new synthetics have enriched the palette even more. This kind of stuff can be bought from special purveyors of fly-tying materials, or found in barnyards, fields, or along roadsides, in drugstores, or on ladies' counters. I have even found some of the finest bits of sable and fox in the gutters near New York City's garment district, my best luck coming on Twenty-seventh and Twenty-eighth Streets, between Sixth and Seventh Avenues, in the late afternoon.

As I look at my flies, one after the other, I see clearly that structure, design, pattern, shape, color, and a certain fishiness are all elements of the art of the trout fly. Like art, the genre has its schools—realism, impressionism, expressionism—as well as types that defy category. Over the years, I've found that realism has its limitations, for reality is not frozen in life, in art, or in trout streams. The best fly is often the one whose feathers—bruited by wind and moving water—look most alive. The best fly for a tumbling Catskill freestone river may be hopeless on a western spring creek. A fly that looks brilliant to the human eye—a Tiepolo of bright inventiveness—may to a trout look like moldy stew, or, worse, a bright concoction of alien furs and feathers.

Since anyone with the proper number of thumbs can tie a fly that will catch a trout, this is an egalitarian art. One of the finest modern fly tiers I know, Del Mazza, earns his living driving heavy earth-moving equipment; but the fly of his I'm holding to the light of the window suggests otherwise. Fly tying is also an ephemeral art, since most flies (if they aren't lost in trees or ear lobes) will collapse after catching half a dozen trout. But flies do survive and the art has its masters. I've owned at various times flies by the hermetical turn-of-the-century genius Theodore Gordon (whose flies now sell for $1,000 each); Preston Jennings, whose flies advanced the clean, classic, Catskill style; Harry Darbee and Walt Dette, two Catskill aces; René Harrop, the master of spring creek flies; Jay Buchner, whose grasshopper imitations are good enough to eat; and Al Caucci and Bob Nastasi, whose durable and deadly comparaduns have saved a lot of tough days on spring creeks. I've also owned flies by Art Flick, Al Troth, Dick Talleur. Larry Duckwall, Dave Whitlock, Poul Jorgensen, Ted Niemeyer, Del Bedinotti, Vince Marinaro, Frank Wentink, and scores of others.

Hold a Red Quill by Art Flick to the bright light of your dining room window, as I am doing now, next to one tied by a ruffian like me, and you will quickly see the difference. In the Flick fly, the tail comes straight off the shank of the hook to exactly the right length. The body is luminously tawny red, the duplicate of the natural. The lemon duck wings come briskly off the head, canted to provide just the right silhouette—not, like mine, the shape of some prehistoric insect. The hackle is of the finest blue dun. It glistens and glimmers in the light and seems to change color as I turn it; it seems brilliantly alive, like a great gem, tangy, like fine wine. It is able to ride high on the pocket water that Flick loved best to fish. I'd eat it myself if I could, though, sadly, I can't.

As I fuss and fiddle with my thousands of flies this afternoon—placing them in new boxes, in new arrangements, and culling the bad ones—I see clearly that the art of tying a trout fly begins with the gathering of the proper ingredients. It is the art of minute architectonics, the art of illusion, a meld of craft, vision, and imagination, whose chief goal is the simple one of gulling a trout whose brain is tiny.

That a trout with such a small brain often *won't* risk its skin for some of these brilliant flies is why I keep brooding about them this gray winter afternoon—scrutinizing them and quietly going mad.

CROWDS

They're wonderful, I suppose, if you're selling something—from snake oil to books to religion to hard rock. And you can't have a political rally for the best—or worst—of causes without them. They are the fodder and the clout of revolutions, the pulse and chorus of great sporting events, comfort and protection for all those who are afraid to act except in concert. But have you ever heard a serious fly fisher sing their glory?

There is a bit of moving water, a few trout rising, and you. That's where all value begins in fly fishing. A bit of moving water, a few rising trout, and ten people are a bad joke.

In the past ten years or so we've seen a huge increase in the number of fly fishers everywhere. A lot of folk refer to "The Movie" as the greatest ambassador—or shill—for the sport, and perhaps, if we forget what the book stood for, it has been that. There are lots more books today, too, some of which sell in numbers not previously imagined—while other decent ones vanish simply because there are too many titles vying for attention, crowding the magazine reviews, tackle stores, and patience of anglers.

Fly fishing is also the subject of more and more fashionable ads— and even I (surely the adult with the least possible style or interest in it) have been asked by companies like Ralph Lauren for tips on how the upper end of the fly-fishing world attires itself for sport; I could only laugh uncontrollably and send them elsewhere. Rods and reels and lines are more efficient. Flies are more cunning, making entry-level work more manageable. And a lot of time has been spent to dress the newcomer in a happy uniform (pink waders for new women fly fishers go too far). Schools proliferate and are often filled to capacity. Newspapers like the *New York Times* have run front-page articles on salmon fishing in Russia and the growing number of women fly fishers. The cable television shows take us everywhere and with careful editing can make us think it's heaven on that mosquito-ridden little island . . . and even major news/essay programs think it's all important enough to carry a "segment."

Fly fishing is everywhere—even where we could not have dreamed it would go: parodies—in the *Boston Globe* and the *New Yorker*—of fishing memoirs; and a recent article in a women's magazine showing a batch of young, ruggedly handsome male fly-fishing guides, who are possible "catches" for the young, bright, pretty women who read that rag.

Lots of folks who have loved fly fishing for many years, and have wanted to share it, suddenly discover that the indifferent neighbor now can't get enough of it. And the parameters continue to grow—with the emergence of great travel agencies that explore the world, finding new possibilities in New Zealand, the Pacific, Africa, Russia, and where-not else. "It looks like so much fun," a young friend told me recently. "Will you teach me?" I hesitated.

My friend Steven Meyers, in his *San Juan River Chronicle*, speaks of it as "a river in danger of being loved to death."

And there, on a specific river, is where the problem comes home hardest: will it bear all the love we want to crowd upon it?

Anyone who's fished for a substantial time—I'm beyond fifty years now—continues to feel that steady, inescapable erosion of waters known earlier.

I fished a river two hours from New York a hundred times in my childhood—a back section, meandering from a hillside under a train trestle, through a broad meadow, making a few sharp turns, and then sliding past a small town. It was a stream uniformly some sixty feet across, with deep water in all but a few spots, soft undercut banks, hundreds of deadfalls. It was never an easy river to fish, because the bordering trees threw a low canopy across it, you could only wade the edges, and it was always slightly discolored from its movements through farm country. But there were five miles of it that I fished, and it always stunned me with its surprises: once, the largest trout I've ever taken in the East—a five- or six-pound brown. Because the water wasn't easy to fish and because it had superb cover with the tangled branches of the deadfalls, the river produced a large number of outsized brooks and browns—and few people fished it after mid-April. I did a number of times and never caught a lot of fish—but I always caught or raised a few tortugas. I went back to it five years ago and found in the meadow no fewer than three or four hundred small houses, all looking pretty much the same. I haven't seen it since.

Mostly it has been the raw need (or greed) for some places to develop, or pollute, that has wrecked the waters I love—but increasingly it's the sheer number of fly fishers.

There is a bridge over a western river near where I used to park some years ago. The water was tough, heavy, but it held very good trout, and a lot of them. I fished it ten or fifteen times when I was the only person in sight, and then, as the years went on, I found other spots. One day recently I went back with Mari, who wanted to paint there, and my son Paul, with whom I wanted to share this exceptional sport, and I could barely control my rage—they thought I'd gone berserk or gotten bitten by a wasp—when I came over the hill and looked down to the bridge: there were no fewer than seventy or eighty cars there. I've never fished it since.

I can remember a dozen places—far back through weed, swamp, bramble patches—where a particular confluence of currents, a bend in the river, and a bottom dug out by the force of the flow combined to create a true "honey hole," a place bound to contain fish, a place that, time after time, *did* hold good fish.

If you fuss around rivers long enough, you find a lot of places like this, often just a bit farther from roads and access points than most folks care to go. You break through the tangle of brush one day by chance—after a dozen fruitless forays, searching—and discover a secret garden that rewards you with remarkable riches. You go back—the same thing. And then, as the entire river gets more pressure, you make the same unpleasant hour-long trek through the swamp that eats waders—get bitten by mosquitos, have your net catch on brush and thorns and then slam into your back, lose a box of your best flies and the whole contraption that holds clippers, fly dope, hemostat—and you find there are four lunatics there. They are fishing hard, wading in the wrong places, shouting over the sound of the water, spooking fish, and pounding the water to a fine frenzy. And you never have the heart to go back.

Or it's a spot to which you must wade through dangerous waters, for half an hour, and when you brave it this time and lift your head, you see that a Mackenzie boat has just lightly deposited two anglers exactly on the bar from which you have always fished.

Home waters become everyone's waters; a favorite spot becomes a public meeting place; and you feel tugged to hunt a receding *new,* or as several old friends have done, just stop. Give it up. Leave the field. One took up golf and loves it. "The crowds just got to be too much," he told me.

Some new people will come into the sport and drift away; a lot will stay. I wish I could see some change in sight—but I'm a Jeremiah about crowds. Look at Cairns Pool on the Beaverkill, Buffalo Ford on the Yellowstone, the traffic at Varney Bridge when Mr. Salmonfly has arrived—any of us could name a couple of dozen more.

The crowds will only increase, I'm afraid. We'll have to start thinking hard about some difficult, unpleasant options: exerting ourselves a lot more to avoid crowds, limiting access, finding or saving more water, and demanding of our new colleagues—before they enter a river—a bit more toilet training.

If you love fly fishing—as I do—we'll do all of the above, and more.

SPACE AGE STUFF

A rt Flick, who reduced the hundreds of fly patterns then available to a manageable handful, loved to tell the story about a fellow he met on the Schoharie, sitting on a rock with dozens of fly boxes laid out, bewildered as to which fly he should choose. He told Art he was searching for exactly the right fly—and really needed a computer. Art would tell the story, shake his head, laugh minimally, and then fix a true frown on his face; he said it was stupid to make a simple sport so complex. He caught plenty of fish on his few flies—in fact, mostly on his Gray Fox Variant, tied with light and dark ginger hackles, one good grizzly, the quill from a cream cock for the body, and a couple of ginger barbs for the tail.

Art still used a Dickerson bamboo fly rod when I first fished with him. He'd been a Dickerson dealer for years. But then he changed to a good glass rod—and he did so for the best of reasons: it was lighter and brisker, and he thought it cast better; it was, somehow, a simpler tool. I don't think Art had a special predilection for natural fly-tying materials; they were what he knew and he knew they would work. He said it was his Scots ancestry: he loved most what was economical, durable, and effective.

I'm just old enough to remember greasing HCH fly lines, stretching gut leader material, fishing with flies that had lovely names like Parmachene Belle and looked like Kandinskys, fussing with cheap bamboo heavy enough to wear out a quarterback's arm in half a day.

I still use an Underwood Standard, Model S, vintage 1945 typewriter. My four children and just about everyone else I know think me a dinosaur. But it's neither a point of honor nor an act of stupid fidelity to the antique. I just like the feel of the thing, the sound of it, the exact pressure needed to make it work, the faint ache in my shoulders when I've been pecking at it for most of a day. I've learned to *think* into the old machine, to fit the speeds of my brain and its mechanism together. And I haven't found a good reason to give it up yet, though each year the number of shops that can fix it or supply it with ribbons diminishes.

I'm probably terrified of computers, but for my needs my old Underwood serves just peachy. I've bought seven of them, with a couple of Remington Royals thrown in, and ribbons enough to last until I'm ninety-three.

I love bamboo deeply and often swore I'd never give it up. I like the look and feel of it, the craftsmanship of it, the special pleasure I take in holding something special in my hand, something made with skill, even art. I even like the purple poetry it draws from its fans. But when I tried some good glass—the kind Flick used—I liked it enough to prefer it on trips into tough terrain, like the boulders on New York's Ausable, chiefly because I'd have to worry less about it than about bamboo. I tried some early graphite and found it lumpy; worse, I saw a friend break a rod when coming forward with his cast. Bamboo was a pleasure and the best waters almost cried out for it—until, one summer, I fished a spring creek in the West and switched horses forever.

Here I had to cast quickly and hard. I had to use a minimal number of back casts. I often had to punch a line into the wind. I fished doggedly for a week with a wonderful old bamboo noodle, with intermediate windings. It was fine when I had a fish on but less than fine as a casting tool. This could well be my problem. In fact, it *was* my problem. But that's what we ship for when we fish: the arbitrary, the personal, the idiosyncratic. We want simply to do what will work best for us; we want always to make the fishing experience more pleasurable.

I don't think we go fishing to hold up the honor of the past— though the past is honorably part of the pleasure for many; but to me, suddenly, bamboo was not quite as useful or pleasant as a graphite rod I tried. Bamboo was heavier; it did not cast with as much authority as I wanted; I worried about it; apostasy be damned—I could cast better with graphite, and so I switched. I would have switched back to bamboo without hesitation—but I kept finding more and more reasons why I, at least, preferred this space age material that dinosaurs were supposed to loathe.

Then everywhere I looked there was more of the same. The new fly lines were more amiable to live with: they did not require greasing; they came in a variety of special tapers and coatings for special use; and each year they improved. Leaders, too. Even eyeglasses. Even waders. There were a dozen new variations on the vest, but the old one—like my Underwood Standard—served me so well that I didn't change. I felt no urgency to change, to be thoroughly modern. If anything, I'd always wanted to put a bit of sand in the mechanisms that hurtled us forward at such dizzying speeds before we had a chance to get used to one change or another.

In the realm of flies something quite subtle was taking place—something that offended a lot of old purists. A few tiers, like John Betts, began to work in synthetics alone; others, like Craig Mathews, began to blend them with natural fly-tying materials, using a bit of Z-lon for a tail while keeping elk hair for the wing.

The proof was in the fishing. I caught more fish with the new flies—well, with some of them; some, perhaps because I lacked trust in them, fished as poorly as they looked.

Some folks I know still use bamboo, and some will always use only natural fly-tying materials for their flies. Some even use only one fly—a Hairwing Royal Coachman, perhaps, an Adams, a Woolly Bugger, a bead-head nymph—and are not only as happy as clams but terrific catchers of fish. Fly fishing will always be lots of different stuff to different folk: a genial pastime about which the less said the better; a respite from other lives; a sojourn in pretty country; an adventure, pure and simple; a chance to be on the water with a few old friends; a place to work out what the poet John Engels calls "a coherent discipline"; a chance to play Huck Finn; a place to solve dilemmas; an opportunity for maniacal frustration; and much, much more. And why not? It's one of those areas where we can hang out the flag of our independence, our chance to carry one fly or 4,728. Fly fishing is neither "getting too technical" nor too complex. We can ignore high tech or embrace it—and we can pick and choose.

I guess it's more important to remember that intelligence, humanity, courtesy, skill, and heart exist whether one carries bamboo or cutting-edge graphite, and that the spirit with which we practice fly fishing means as much—even more—than the tools we use. And that reminds me somehow of what Sir Walter Raleigh said as he was prepared for the axman. Asked if he'd like the block to face the East, whence his soul would shortly travel, he replied, in his last words: "What matter how the head sit, if the heart be right."

WATER WATCHING

From infancy, I have been infatuated with water.

At five I could not be kept out of the creek behind my grandfather's hotel in Haines Falls, New York, a bright little brook that held newts, crayfish, dace, and the first trout I ever saw. Since I believed that those creatures had surely been put into the creek for no other reason but that I pursue them, I never went there without my eyes peeled for their presence. I could see them then in three ways—by color, shape, or movement—and it readily occurs to me that that's what I look for when I go to water to fish today, unless I am looking up, for birds or insects.

Barefoot, I learned to spot the backward-darting crayfish, the shape and color of the newt, the movement of the fish. And later, when I fished the pond from which the creek originated, I leaned far out of the old wooden rowboat, put my face flush up against the water, and peered deep into that other world with its mysterious wavering forms.

There is no science without careful observation and without it there is also only a primitive form of fishing. The best fishermen I have seen were constantly watching the water and I saw barely a tenth of what they saw and reported.

Water, of course, is an element of endless fascination to the child—whether the great force and life of the ocean beach, the movement of a river, the liquid strangeness of a pond, even a splashy bath.

Water has its own laws of gravity and biology and hydrology and when a barefoot freckle-faced kid looks at the beautiful suspended forms of perch and pumpkinseed and pickerel, he touches what animates all study and all outdoor sport: *he wants to understand.*

Why is the striped perch at precisely that depth? Why is the pickerel always so motionless? Why do the pumpkinseeds stay in groups, near the lily pads? Why don't the lily pads grow in that big hole in their midst, which is filled with a softer, grasslike plant that rises but a few feet off the bottom? Why? And why? And why again?

Ezra Pound, in *ABC of Reading,* tells the story of a postgraduate student, "equipped with honours and diplomas," who went to the great scientist Louis Agassiz for some "finishing touches." Agassiz showed him a small fish and asked him to describe it. The student observed that it was a sunfish. When Agassiz pressed him, the young man offered a textbook description of the creature, including its proper Latin name. Agassiz again told him to describe the fish and got a four-page essay, and then told the student really *to look* at the fish. Pound ends his anecdote: "At the end of three weeks the fish was in an advanced state of decomposition, but the student knew something about it."

Or, even wiser and more succinct, Agassiz's report: "I spent the summer traveling. I got halfway across my backyard."

Too many of us, I fear, rush to the water, make our play, and rush away.

Going faster, we see less.

Rushing, we miss everything except whether a fish chooses to lunch on something we've pitched in its general direction.

That's not enough—either for the basic skills needed to catch a few fish or for the function of teaching us something about our quarry and its world, something that will lead us to respect it more, protect it more wisely, and pursue our piscatorial pleasures with more understanding.

Some people, of course, start out with better eyes, keener instincts, more opportunities than most to observe a fishery. When I met the great river keeper Frank Sawyer I told him that what I admired most about his books was how much he'd seen and how helpful his observations were to me. He was a gentle, modest, white-haired man and told me quietly, even as Art Flick often told me, that his experience was limited to very little water. But, oh, how well they'd learned and how valuable their lessons have been to thousands of others. Spend the summer like Agassiz, with a hundred yards of your watery world, and tell me that he's wrong. Some narrow, deep, specific knowledge may be worlds better than that which the dilettante carries. Learn something (even almost *everything*) about the bugs, the pH, the speed of the water, the bait fish, the nearby terrestrials, the cover, the structures, the eddies, the slight bottom indentations, the monthly and diurnal cycles of your quarry, and so much more, and then tell me it is not worthwhile. Flick told me that the three years he did *not* fish but studied the bugs of his Schoharie were perhaps the most valuable of his entire fishing life.

Guides—either saltwater or on rivers and lakes—are on the water every day during the season—and even before and after. They *must* find fish; their livelihood depends upon it. I could no more pick a "happy"—and quite catchable—tarpon from a pod than I could a prize-winning music video from the jumble I used to see my children watching; but Jeffrey Cardenas can—and he can "read" a huge amount more to which I'm blind, too. John Goddard, with whom I fished on the River Kennet four or five times, stunned me with what he could see—from the slight bulge of water to the slightest variation in color that meant a fish to a bubble or two to what Skues called the "wink" of a fish nymphing in midwater. And Goddard stressed, too, how much the English code of *seeing* a fish before you fished for it demanded more careful sight and rewarded the angler by increasing, over the years, what he saw.

This does not happen randomly. It begins, as Lou Tabory is fond of noting for inshore saltwater fly fishing, with "time on the water"; only then can you know anything of importance about your quarry and his world. Being near the water more, watching it with more precise care, knowing what kinds of things to look for—from the flashes and changes in color beneath the water to the rips and breaks and currents on the surface to the birds above it—can be crucial. And you often see the oddest things. I swear I once saw water snakes rising to Pale Morning Duns—though Herb said I merely needed a strong drink.

Perhaps the most remarkable eyes I've seen at work are Al Troth's. I floated the Beaverhead with him some years ago and was astounded at the potency of his water watching. He saw everything, ten minutes before I could pick up the sight, even when he pointed precisely. At one heavy run there were "three rainbows and a brown, four to six pounds, nymphing." Frankly, I didn't believe him. I looked and saw only a rush of pale green water. So he took me halfway up a cliff, pointed more precisely, and there they were—and ten minutes later I raised the brown, which was about four and a half pounds.

Later that day, when the sun came in at a sharp angle, he took me to a side branch of the river and pointed to a spot where "four or five good fish" were rising steadily. I had double-strength Polaroids on but could only see the bright scar of the sun on the water. I'd have passed right over the spot. He told me to cast a certain length in a certain specific direction and I told him I didn't want to cast to what I couldn't see. Anyway, I didn't believe him. So he directed me on a long trek downstream about a quarter of a mile, then upstream through swampy terrain and tangled deadfalls, to the opposite side of the river. It was nearly eight o'clock when I got there and the mosquitoes had made my face a massive red lump.

And he was wrong.

There were not four or five good fish rising but eight or ten, and they were gorging themselves with large slurping rises. Either the sun had dropped or I was on the other side of the scar because I could see everything clearly now. Muttering to myself, "I shall always believe Al Troth's eyes. I shall always believe . . ." I tied on one of his Elk-Hair Caddises and began to tattoo the fish. And then I forgot the disciplined water watching that had gotten me to this spot because, as Mae West once said: "Too much of a good thing can be wonderful."

COUNTRY HARDWARE STORE

I stop by the window, not intending to buy, needing not a leader tippet on this bright spring day, merely tugged by the old promotional poster. It is a two-foot-long rainbow trout, grinning, brighter red than anything I've ever seen come from a river other than a rusted Prince Albert tobacco can. The old shop is in a town I've never driven through, in a forgotten backwater of the Catskills, and I am curious. That's all.

There's lots of great stuff in the window: a wicker creel, vintage 1940s; a Heddon bamboo fly rod, not quite straight, with a nondescript reel, filled with what is probably a braided level line, or some primitive taper, with a designation that dates back to my teens, HCH, HDH, one of those. There are some small silver spoons on a card, another card filled with panfish popping bugs, still another with crude wet flies, and yet another with dry flies in garish purples and pinks, with soft hackle and forgettable design—except for the McGinty, which still catches bluegill better than any other pattern, and sometimes even trout.

There are a couple of stuffed trout in the window, too—quite weather-worn, looking as if the cat got them, or moths, or just age—laid near a papier-mâché stump, on paper leaves. And there are some signs, announcing that live bait and licenses are available and that I should take a kid fishing. I tried the latter, with all my children, and mostly bored them silly.

This Catskill backwater is far from cities, shunned by tourists, because it is merely itself and has nothing to offer them, far even from rivers with great names; it's near lakes and ponds and creeks you've never heard of, a place where fly fishing still comfortably co-exists with spinning, bait-casting, minnow and worm fishing, even muskrat trapping—fly fishing of a 1940s stripe.

Standing on the rutted and pitted macadam sidewalk, looking down the short main street for my wife, who has found a little clothing shop in which to rummage, I am suddenly mad for this place. I remember its type and hunger for its bounties.

I figure that Mari will surely take half an hour or more to buy a pair of rough-and-ready socks and then will surely know where I am, and I open the door to the tackle and hardware store—which jangles a little bell—just for a quick look.

The inside is dark and shadowy, from bald bulbs under concave reflectors, widely spaced, and from far too many stacks of shoe boxes and shirts and sweaters and jackets, stacked to the ceilings wherever I look. It's better than I dreamed.

It is the place of my earliest youth, a cornucopia of discrete delights that come in little cardboard boxes with handwritten legends on them. I bought my first fishing tackle of any kind in such a shop, in Haines Falls, New York; it was a place that also carried candy, kites, cheap baseball mitts, shovels for sandboxes and snow, notepads, postcards, magazines, suntan lotion, aspirin, combs, toothbrushes, Vaseline, worms by the dozen, and what-not else. I bought a bamboo stick with a little ring on the tip, to which I attached a stout green cord, a red, green, and white bobber, and a snelled Eagle Claw hook. It all cost under three bucks.

Most of the fishing tackle here is old stuff—flies tagged onto willow-leaf spinners, big and little bass bugs on cards, green bait cans that latch onto your belt (for some reason with French words on them), nameless reels, metal and wooden nets in several shapes and sizes on up to gargantuan (which piques my interest), wicker creels, rubber boots, glass rods, a couple of cheap bamboo rods, minnow buckets, and lots of knives. I always like the knives. Everything is somehow mixed in with the hammers and tool kits, cosmetic staples, dry goods, three brands of cheap cigars, machine oil, rakes and shovels, guns, ammunition—an irresistible stew. To the side, as if they are too delicate for the heavier fare, are wooden trays filled with flies with names like Bumble Bee and Parmachene Belle and Silver Doctor. Once they caught plenty of trout. I imagine they probably will still do so when all our parachutes, paradrakes, thoraxes, no-hackles, and comparaduns are gone.

I correct myself immediately. No, our flies are very much here to stay. Those older ones are dinosaurs and won't come back.

These new patterns and designs, beyond fad and fancy, represent some astonishing developments in the past twenty-five years. People keep telling me that nothing changes, that there is very little true innovation, that people fished in the fifteenth century with no-hackles. But they're only slenderly correct. The splitting of tails, the building of the thorax, and the design of a fly without obtrusive hackle—architectonics that allow a fly to sit flat on the surface of a river—were minute but highly significant, not only forgotten but never really perfected. And that tinkering and perfecting, inchmeal, is what's been happening over the past quarter of a century, and it is still happening, and it has been a true revolution, taking us further and further from the wares of this simple and lovely country tackle and hardware store.

I think of a spring creek I know where few trout were caught except in the riffles on the older patterns and how much this shrewd innovation in fly design has made so much more possible. I live in uneasy relationship to technology, I think, standing there in the midst of my past; I still use an Underwood Standard typewriter—and it does what I need it to do, and I cannot imagine retiring it for something called a word processor. I am as wary of progress as the painter Edgar Degas, who, when he saw one of the first telephones, noted that it now meant that when someone rang a bell you had to come running.

"Anything I can help you with?" the proprietor asks. He is perhaps in his late sixties or early seventies, a simple man in a plaid shirt, neither interested in prodding me into what must be an infrequent sale nor able to lose one. He's just being helpful. He just wants to take a chance to talk.

"Lots of nice old things," I say. "But I'm mostly looking, I guess."

"Quite all right. Quite all right. Take your time. Nothing rushes much around here."

My eye fixes on the green worm box with its little circle of holes in its roof, and I remember wearing one very much like it on my belt and fishing for white perch in a reservoir near New York City, the box filled with night crawlers I'd plucked from lawns on a moist April night. I fished with a glass fly rod then and lobbed the worms out, ahead of a bobber. I used to grease the line, and it always stuck in the guides.

There really isn't much here that I need, or can use, and none of it really qualifies as "collectible," and I don't "collect" anyway—I just accumulate. But it makes me think of the past, when a dozen items would have attracted me, and it makes me think of a modern tackle shop, twenty miles from here, near a river with a famous name. That one has form-fitting waders and graphite fly rods and trays and trays of cunningly designed and tied flies; and it has racks of books, and on the walls there are handsome paintings; and there are splendid little fly boxes from Sweden, braided leaders from England and France, tippet material from Japan that lets us fish smaller and lighter to bigger and bigger fish, fly lines with clear nomenclature, which float and cast much more smoothly, and enough that is new and truly helpful for me to spend hours looking and touching and testing and buying.

I am mad for all this new stuff—especially if it isn't force-fed to me, if I can pick and choose, if it doesn't pinch those other parts of fly fishing that are full of mystery and surprise and drama and wit.

In the end I buy, for thirty-nine cents apiece, a dozen bass bugs made of cork, with feathered tails and rubber legs; some are quite small and will work well on a bluegill pond, I think; some will work on those alligator bass in that weedy Connecticut pond. They'll all catch fish. I can always use them.

Then I head out of this antique cave and into the bright light of a 1990s spring day.

Rather than walk toward Mari, I look back into the dark and musty shop. The old man has found himself a chair near the counter and is leaning back, reading a local newspaper. Then I look again at the two-foot-long rainbow trout in the window, still grinning at me.

"I thought I'd find you here," Mari says. "Buy out the whole store?"

"Only a piece of my childhood."

"Don't be maudlin."

The sun is very bright and I am feeling very maudlin, and I know I have no reason to go back into that old shop, but I finally admit that what I really bought were some bass bugs, which will work well in Connecticut.

IN THE CAR

Some of my most pleasant times on fishing trips have been in cars: driving with Les Ackerman the two hours from Big Sky to Island Park Reservoir, chattering without stop about business and being past fifty and fish; in the car with Thom Green, from Denver to Utah, where we intended to pursue rumors of goliath bluegill, listening to him talk about the structure of the earth, the geology of oil exploration; dozens of long trips with Mike Migel, hearing stories about a hundred of his crazy business deals—selling grass-making machines to the Arabs, leaching gold mines in Ghana, peddling cement to Nigeria. None of Mike's deals ever flew. The machines dried up, there was never, anywhere, enough gold, the cement ended at the bottom of a bay after a coup.

The stories went on for years, as we drove to the Catskills or the Connetquot or the Battenkill. Two new ones began before I'd heard the sad end of one I'd been following for two full fishing seasons. Deals came so close to a handshake, there even was a handshake, that I expected our forthcoming trip to the Ausable to be with a multimillionaire. And then they deconstructed. Every last one of them. We'd get into the car in front of my apartment and they'd start at once—interspersed with reports he or I had heard about the river we were going to fish, fish caught or lost ten or thirty years earlier, fly talk, rod talk, family talk, and then more elaborate business schemes and reports.

I loved the man and miss him and wish, somehow, one of those deals had flown, that he had not died dreaming that one last gold mine, with just another few days of search, would reveal its treasure, which Mike proclaimed—almost with his last words—to be there, absolutely.

We had lunch only a few times a year, rarely spoke on the phone, split when we fished; so those hundreds of hours in the close contained box of the speeding car, cigar smoke practically choking us, rocketing toward or from trout country, were (as I think back on those dozen or more years) the heart of our friendship.

And of my many trips with Mari, car time was always best—especially when I was at least an hour from the river, especially when I did not get lost and then come unglued.

We had driven from Bozeman toward the Big Hole, where we were invited to meet some new friends, Dick and Ann. I had left especially early so we could drive to the upper river, near Wise River, where I had once fished. I wanted to show Mari that gorgeous upper valley and then drop down to Glen and meet our friends at their place about one o'clock.

At eight-thirty we got off the main highway for coffee and, seeing a sign to Twin Bridges, decided we had time to take the long route, through Dillon. We were chattering blissfully, devouring every feature of the moving landscape. We passed through Twin Bridges about nine forty-five and I noted that there was a road nearby that led to our friends' ranch. I loved the Big Hole. I had had some spectacular days fishing it with Glenn West and Phil Wright. Perhaps we should call and come early. I'd trade a day of even happy sight-seeing for a day of fishing any time.

By one-thirty we'd been upriver and then down, and had barely gotten out of the car. We were already late. I looked at my scribbled notes and saw that Ann had indicated a road half a dozen miles from Glen as the back route to their place. So I got off the main highway, turned left then right onto what had to be old Route 1, and headed back toward Dillon. I looked carefully but found nothing that resembled the road she'd described. In fact, when I looked at the mileage gauge, I realized I'd driven eighteen miles already, not the six she'd indicated, so I backtracked, stopped at the Glen Post Office, and asked instructions.

The postmaster did not seem to have talked with anyone for the past six months. He was in no sweat to see me leave. He got out a map. He got out the telephone directory. He laid them on the counter. He had never heard of the road I'd mentioned. "It's only six miles away," I advised him. He had never heard of my friends, though they could not have been ten miles away.

Baffled, tense that I'd miss the afternoon Pale Morning Duns, I called Ann, verified my location, apologized for being so late, listened to my voice—disembodied now—promise to be there in fifteen minutes. It was two-thirty by now and we were clearly very close. "We're very close," I assured Mari. "Very close."

Mari told me, in her great wisdom, that I had been driving too fast and must have missed the road, so I went no more than thirty miles an hour for about ten miles, then picked it up to forty, then fifty-five, then sixty-five. There were no markers or signs on the road. I was now not even sure that we were on old Route 1.

Twenty-five miles down the road, my nerves began to race faster than the car and I listened to Mari's third sensible suggestion that we "ask someone."

I had been up and down this road now twice. I was on the verge of heading directly to Dillon and calling Dick and Ann and reporting a seizure, or something.

The only someone I could find was a fellow on a tractor. I jolted the car to a stop at the rim of a side ditch, jumped out, and asked the fellow where our mysterious road was. He shrugged and replied in Spanish. I told Mari I did not think we had gone clear to Mexico but that we were clearly too far and ought to head back to Glen for the third and last time, for one more try.

I raced back at seventy-five miles per hour, decided not to stop at the Glen Post Office again because the fellow might have me arrested for lunacy, and pulled alongside an old fellow in a pickup truck. "Is this old Route 1?" I asked, my body pulsing like mad, my foot ready to pounce on the pedal and be off, so we could at least catch a bit of the evening fishing.

"Wal, son," the man said slowly. "What's that you wanted to know?"

I repeated my question.

"I've been driving this road for fifty years," he said.

"Yes," I said.

"No. No, that's not right, son. It's fifty-seven years, exactly fifty-seven years come October since Martha and I came over from Townsend . . ."

"Yes."

". . . and I drove it every day for fifty-seven years. Most every day."

"Is it in fact Route 1?" I asked.

"It used to be the only road, of course, until the big superhighway was put in . . ."

"Yes."

". . . and I guess I drove it every day so I ought to know what it's called."

Ten minutes later he admitted it was Route 1, I raced back to Glen, barely speaking to Mari—who was the only person I could blame for all this, since she was laughing wildly now—got out, kicked the car, which might be responsible, went into the bar, got the exact mileage from a man I owe my life to, and sure enough found the road and arrived at Dick and Ann's at five-thirty, only four and a half hours late. On the way out that evening, I noted to Mari that it took us exactly thirteen minutes to reach Twin Bridges, where we'd been that morning. The fishing had been fair, the driving awful.

The car is not merely the source of good talk and torment, of course. Mari and I once drove with my friend Pierre from Paris to a pike pond near Normandy. It was a long, happy day—but a wet one; and in the evening, having started at five o'clock that morning, Pierre, who has boundless energy, said he wanted me to fish a small chalkstream an hour closer to the city. When we got there it was pouring like mad—steady and very hard. Mari said gently that she'd rather read than have the great honor of watching me catch my first French chalkstream trout. Pierre got out an old blanket and she put it over herself, covering all but her head. She seemed very warm and content as I looked back at her through the wet window.

Then Pierre and I marched a half mile through very wet three-foot-high grasses. I was exhausted from the long day and, without boots, wet to the skin, chest to toes—and cold. The sight of a couple of Green Drakes fluttering above the water and trying to avoid the cold raindrops perked me up a bit. So did the first little slap-rise I saw.

Twenty minutes later, fishing to that rise, I caught a happy little seven-incher, got photographed with my first French chalkstream trout, and fled back to the car. I had no itch to glorify or prolong my misery.

Mari was in the back seat, still huddled under the old blanket. She had put down her book.

"You . . . all . . . right?" I asked.

"Fine, fine," she said. "But back so soon? And I thought you boys loved to play in the rain. Isn't the fishing—"

"Had . . . enough," I said.

"Oh, dear. You're chattering," she said.

I grabbed a piece of the blanket for myself and my wife of thirty-five years sat up and hugged me tightly and in a few minutes I felt amiably warm. In a little while my teeth stopped knocking together, I felt no more chills, and was able to talk.

"All these fishing trips," I said. "All these years."

"Yes," she said. "Are you warmer now, dear?"

"Fine, fine," I said, and then feebly: "And I always thought it was so awful for you . . . back in the car."

ON A SMALL CREEK

In summer and early fall, when heat and sun have drawn down the great rivers to their best moments in the West and worst in the East, I like to explore little creeks. I like those boulder-strewn, pellucid fingers of water tumbling down a cove or dancing in curves through poplar and birch on a Catskill hillside—quick, bright rivers that look in high summer like the last places on earth in which we might find trout.

The trout are there. You can't often see them, and sometimes they'll only rise in the flat pools in the morning or on a buggy dusk. You can *feel* them, though, in the diminutive eddies where the water grows opaque, in the bubbling water under a dwarf water-fall, under that undercut bank, or in the dark hollow below the boulder.

In the East, the great rush and excitement of the Time of the Hatches is over. I've done my traveling, caught some trout, missed a big one. I've leavened the year with some pleasant bass-bugging—a lazy, intense three hours in a rowboat at dusk. Now, back in trout country for a few days, with other games to play on the long week-end—and a couple of people tugging at me, to get me to swim or wander with them—there is an hour and a half at the end of the afternoon, and I have slipped off by myself to conduct some private business beyond where the macadam has become a dusty dirt-and-rock road, and now has ended.

The water is not quite as I remember it from thirteen years earlier, but it is just as clear, a bit lower, with boulders I know and some I remember not at all. The birch stand is thicker, more mature; the willows, up at the bend beyond which I cannot see, hang lower to the river. There are a thousand bugs in the air, grasshoppers in the field I crossed to come to the river's edge, bees, crickets, no-see-ums, tiny off-white moths—but no mayflies, no caddis, not a fish rising.

I'd rarely seen a fish rise in this creek in the middle of the day—except one, regularly, a long time ago, in a pool a hundred yards beyond the stand of willows and the bend. It was a very large brown in a very shadowed eddy, and it was taking a smorgasbord of minuscule and elephantine insects. Tilting my head low, I could see the eddy laced with a thin embroidery of dust, beetles, grasshoppers, moths, and chironomids. The big fish, undisturbed all spring and summer beneath the beaver cuttings, had lost all caution and was spending a perfectly splendid afternoon picking daintily at this rich feast.

I hooked it on my first cast, with a foam beetle topped with a bit of white calftail.

It thrashed at the surface once—thunderously in that small space—headed for the crotch of the eddy and the maze of beaver cuttings. And that was that.

Today I have come in my usual high-summer uniform—khaki pants, a light long-sleeved khaki shirt with big chest pockets, a floppy khaki hat, high sneakers (the low ones fall off); no vest, no boots—only a small box of flies and a spool of 6X tippet material. I know this creek well and won't fish much. I might not cast at all. In fly fishing, I think, you get to a stage when your confidence about a few minor patterns grows complete.

It's cool here and the flowing water is cool around my ankles and calves, and the no-see-ums have stayed downriver. This is solo fishing. You don't want to share the few fishable pools or leapfrog with a partner; you don't particularly want to talk. The best of it is to have this happy, bouncing Papageno of a creek to yourself—to kick a bit of dried wood off into the grass, catch a grasshopper and chuck it into the far current near the boulder, learn a new bird or two, watch the water carefully, and perhaps sit on a log and read a book. Now and then you're waked by the whirring rise of grouse—or the quiet circle that marks a feeding trout . . . or a fallen leaf.

Papageno is a skinny, animated fellow Mozart found in himself along with the ogres and dragons. This unnamed creek reminds me of that happy fellow in *The Magic Flute,* who turns scowls to smiles and remains in the world along with the world's liars and poseurs.

I get to the willows without even rigging up, but this seems a true starting place, so I edge back to the woodline, pick a rock, and begin—as I have done a thousand times before—to thread line, tinker with leader, select and tie on a fly. It's a beetle with a tuft of char-treuse poly at the top. I've begun to prefer any specific imitation to an attractor. However loyal that Christmas tree of a Royal Coachman has been to me, I've retired mine. We were great friends once, but we've drifted apart. This trout fishing, I told myself a few years ago, has for me more and more come down to an imitation-of-a-specific-food business. It ain't snobbishness, I now remind myself. I've done all the rest of it and on a given day would no doubt do it again; and I've loved it all greatly. I've caught a whole lot of fish (though it always seems so stupid to brag). I don't have to catch a lot of fish anymore. I don't *need* to catch any fish. So when I go out—especially on a quiet, late-summer afternoon like this—I like to look more, understand a lot more, and fish when there's something to fish for. So I assure myself; and at the same time I know I am becoming too precious.

I turn the bend and walk a hundred yards without spotting fishable water. It's not deep enough here; the water ends too far from the banks (and cover) above me. But I peck my way upstream to the bend and eddy where, once, many years ago, a big trout made short shrift of me. There's no hurry. I've promised to be back at the cabin an hour from now.

The eddy is still there. The river hits a boulder straight on, then sweeps to the right, circumscribing a neat circle along the bank, laced with those fallen willow branches. The pool it forms might, even with this low water, be six or seven feet deep. The logical choice would be a quick-sinking nymph, perhaps one of those with a single- or even double-bead head. I could cast up into the riffle at the head of the

eddy, hold my rod high, and let that weighted fly slip into the belly of the pool, flash in the darkness, and then rise as it neared me, like a dozen aquatic foods rising to the surface to hatch. A streamer or Woolly Bugger would work, too.

But I sit down, watch the water, and think of big trout and beetles. I look up ten minutes or more later, and there's a skinny, lanky kid standing in the spot I'd left moments earlier. He holds a fly rod, wears a cheap green vest, carries an aluminum net behind him, in his belt, and wears a five-and-dime creel. He looks at the water hard, lifts a stone, then another, and then clips off what he'd been using and ties on a new leader and fly. He casts quickly, economically, then casts again, then roll-casts the line so that the fly lands near the tangle of branches. There is a heavy rise, a sharp strike, a short battle, and no more than a minute later he has the fish on a rock and is summarily bashing its head with another rock before gutting it and putting it into his creel.

I walk over and look at the fish—a brown, probably twenty inches' worth, about the size of the one I'd lost years earlier, brightly colored, with a bead-head nymph still in its mouth. The scene seemed to have been played out for me by a diabolic director.

"Well, that's four," the boy says with a touch of brio. "Enough for dinner and breakfast. Pool's yours if you want it." His hands are covered with blood and bits of guts; his shirt and pants, too.

I say I've just been looking, that I haven't fished and won't this afternoon. It all sounds hollow—or worse.

The boy looks at my graphite rod and Hardy reel, at me—sharply in the eye—smiles, and begins to turn.

He says, over his shoulder, "Yeah, I see." Before I can pontificate about killing trout or bemoan the loss of my own innocence, and while I try to stop shaking, he goes dancing down the little creek that had simply been a good place to spend a summer afternoon and catch breakfast.

SEASONS END

It's as easy for a fishing fanatic to let go of a season as it is to let go of a live electric wire. A week ago I tried. I patiently oiled my reels and tucked them into chamois bags, clipped old leader stubs from my flies and placed each fly slowly back into its proper plastic box, packed away my trout rods, looked at it all, sighed, and locked everything safely in my fish closet until spring. I had been to Montana. I had caught more trout than I deserved. I had my memories. There is a time to fish and a time to live like a normal, rational, civilized adult.

But before I could lose the closet key, Larry Madison insisted we fish a bass lake near his home in Connecticut. He reminded me that the bass were not shrimpy. I thought his offer over sensibly for three seconds. A last day in the country—to gird me for the long gray city winter—sounded harmless. Anyway, we'd be after bass and I'd long ago lost my heart to trout; there was no need to take any of this very seriously.

Larry did. He looked—walking ahead of me to the gray rowboat—loaded for bear. He carried a tiny spin-casting outfit, a baitcasting rig from which hung a five-inch swimming plug, and a gigantic glass fly rod he'd made himself, especially for big bass; it took a No. 10 or No. 11 fly line, he didn't remember which. I'd brought only a middling trout rod but I did not intend to fish intently; the day, after all, was an afterthought.

We took turns at the oars, the other casting in against the shore. It was a fishy little lake—maybe a mile around—with long gray trees fallen in from the shoreline, patches of lily pads and pickerelweed, beaver cuttings, stumps, marshes, and coves. The leaves of the maple, beech, and birch were umber, splashed with beige and red; an irregular V of wood ducks flew overhead. I could see no houses; there were no other boats. We had the lake to ourselves and might have been in Saskatchewan.

Before he'd made a dozen casts, Larry caught a two-pound bass on a bass bug of ridiculous size—perhaps three inches around. The bug was made of deer hair, dyed a dull orange, and had sprouts of hair at either end to make it look like a frog—a bullfrog, I thought—or maybe a duckling. Then he switched to the swimming plug, caught nothing, and then to the little spin-casting outfit and began to catch perch, one after the other, on a Mepps lure with a feather tail. We came to a spot where the stream entered—sluggish in mid-autumn—and he said there would be pickerel near the drop-off of the sand bar. There were. The man knew everything worth knowing. I caught one on a popping bug, retrieved as fast as I could, and then he caught four or five on a spinner and a plastic-minnow combination. He is a superb fly fisherman and I advised him that he had sunk very low, indeed, but I wouldn't tell. "Keep using that silly little rod," he said, "I'd rather keep catching fish." The pickerel were fourteen, maybe sixteen inches long. They'd take the lure in a lightning lunge and then, when we brought them in, squiggle like eels. I thought they'd be too bony to eat.

By five-thirty we'd fished three-quarters around the lake, had a fish box with twenty or so perch, pickerel, and that one bass sloshing around, and headed back toward the dock. The air was brisk. I started to tell Larry about Montana; he ignored Montana and said that this shore was good for truly big bass, six pounds or better, and that I ought to switch from my little toothpick now and fish with a real fly rod. "That redwood?" I asked. "If you want to catch a really big bass," he said. So I tried his rod, with that ridiculous hair bug, but at first drove it too hard and the line buckled and fell in heavy loops. "Let the rod do the work," he said. I allowed the fly line to come back more slowly and then let the bend of the huge rod push it forward. Miraculously, I got more distance, great accuracy; I could learn to love a contraption that let me do that.

We slipped slowly down the shore, Larry rowing now while I cast in against the deadfalls, the stumps, the lily pads. I grew curiously more intent about this bass business. My arm worked in slow rhythms, the heavy yellow line rolled out, and fifty or sixty feet in against the shore I'd watch the big hair bug alight and then pop and sputter as I lowered the rod tip and tugged the line with my left hand. The lake was perfectly still; reflections of autumn color doubled the ruddy palette of the place. I felt increasingly mesmerized, intense. I wished Larry would stop alarming me with stories about the big bass he'd caught at night in August; he said he could have promised me a couple of big fish then. There ought to have been a fish there, and there, and near that tree angling into the water. I forgot Montana. I worked the bug with more care, intently.

The trees were dark silhouettes against the ash of the sky; the autumn air was sharp. A bat buzzed us twice and disappeared. Another ten minutes and this second season would be over for me. I did not want to let go of it now. I'd had a perfectly pleasant few hours, in the best of company, but now I was properly stuck on the image of these alleged six-pounders.

And then, not fifty yards upshore from the dock, my bug landed near a lily pad, lay still for a moment, I twitched it twice, three times, and the lake burst up with a great rise and explosion of water and a largemouth bass half-rolled, half-jumped, its great green hump turning, the force of the thing heavy into the butt of the rod. I thought I'd been shot through with electric current. I thought someone had thrown in an anvil or a garbage can. And then it was over. The bug popped out of the water as sweetly as if it were a mayfly emerging from its nymphal shuck.

After a few moments I whispered, "What did I do wrong?"

"Not a thing. He slipped the hook is all. It happens. You look like you're in shock."

I couldn't even nod.

"That was a big bass—a very big bass," he said. "No. Don't cast again. He won't come back. Seasons end."

The great bass, its rise tremendous, its power still raising twitches and trembles in me during the long dark ride back to the city, would cook in my brain all winter.

A FIERCE PURSUIT BUT NOT A CIRCUS

I loved nothing better in my teens than the fierce games of half-court basketball with George and Stanley, Ira and Herb at Wingate Field in Brooklyn. Hacked on the arms and neck, eyes dazzled by the sun and motion and the bright pavement, sweat everywhere, picking a guy off on the metal pole that held the basket, bruising a knee, splitting a lip, we used every last scrap of energy when we drove to the hoop. We came not only to play but to win. We loved the intense competition, and we loved to win. In fact, we *had* to win, for there were so many people waiting to play the winner that if we lost a game we could wait until midnight to get back onto the court.

That was a long time ago, more than sixty pounds ago, but even now, when the closest I get to the neighborhood courts are the green benches safely outside the fence, I crave that competitive music. The stately strategies of baseball, the brute force of a pigskin war, the lithe speed and crushing power of a great middleweight championship: I never miss the chance to see a minute of it.

I also fly fish. I always fly fish with passion, often fiercely, often for many more hours at a stretch than ever I played half-court. So I am startled to discover the ferocity of my contempt for fishing derbies, fishing competitions, fishing tournaments (local and international), tagged fish worth fortunes, fishing games of all kinds. There was one aired this morning on a local cable television station, and I sat dumbfounded once again, as I have a dozen times before at such an image, of all these men zooming off in high-speed boats, nose up, zapping bass for a day, and then returning to the mob on shore, weighing in their catch in plastic bags, accepting the honors. Competing with my neighbor (or a stranger, or a hundred strangers) in the pursuit of gamefish offends me to the marrow, and I'm not sure why.

Is there a difference between the football star (who may love to play the game) being well paid for his tackling or tossing and a master bass fisherman earning a couple of hundred grand for a good year's work? Is a day out on a party boat fluke fishing spoiled because someone will win "high hook" in the pool? Does the presence of a $100 or $100,000 or $500,000 bluefish swimming blithely in Long Island Sound contaminate, in some way, my fly-rodding for blues or stripers along the shore, or anyone else's pleasure?

Frankly, I'd love to hook and land a fish larger even than my imagination could conjure; and some days, floating a western river, I'll get so caught up in the movement of a Mackenzie River boat and the shoreline and the transitoriness of the day that I'll fish monomaniacally, not wanting ever to stop, and friends will wonder if I've gone bats. On a given day, I can be a demon fisherman. On a given day, I can be a frighteningly intense pursuer of fish (usually the kind with spots, those that live in bright rivers). But I have never felt the faintest urge to compete while fishing, and have, in fact, stopped fishing when goaded into competing, or when I'd caught some fish and my partner hadn't. I've done that dozens of times. Even what's called "a little friendly competition" among fishermen interests me not at all. Let the golfers do it.

I find no connection between what those pro anglers do with their superbassboats and jumpsuits and starting guns and what I do when I drift down a weedy shoreline in an old wooden rowboat, Larry on the oars, me casting a big yellow hair bug methodically in against the deadfalls, lily pads, weedbeds, and coves. Maybe a bass will come for it, maybe one won't. Maybe the water will explode with a burst like a cherry bomb; maybe, when I twitch the line, expectantly, I'll just see the bug wiggle and blurp and wait. Maybe. Maybe the "maybes" help make it so enthralling. Or the fact that, with all the clocks in the world, what I do on that lake is at my own sweet pace, lazy or fierce, as I choose.

So long as the competitors release their fish safely, I can't see that much physical damage comes of their onslaught. In fact, some competitions raise money for conservation, which I'm for; and some build up our store of news about the fish we pursue, which is always welcome. But is that enough? As the tournaments grow in prominence and command more and more attention, as the winners become superstars and heroes and models, and the itch of the buck beats the itch to pursue, I keep wondering whether they're trading the quality of the sport for something quite extrinsic to it, whether they're fishing not for the inherent gifts of the activity but for those that come when the business of fishing is over—for winners sell more beer, more books, more subscriptions, more lures, and get well paid for all this.

I keep fearing that something I have always loved about fishing is being crowded out and lost. Bad money drives out the good; bad art drives out Cézanne; and I fear that the idea of these tournaments drives out an idea of fishing that is what first hooked most of us: the sheer love of the chase, coupled with our fascination with the technology of the sport, its gear and practice, the mysterious life of our quarry, the lush happiness of messing around near boats and water. Are we moving to a time when the pursuit of wild game will be a public spectacle or circus, not a private pursuit?

It just ain't why I go fly fishing.

For one thing, all that sounds too much like work. I may fish hard, but I never mistake it for what I do the rest of the time. I fish with Len or Larry or Bill or Sandy or Herb because I like to be with that person, or alone because I feel like simmering in my own juices that day. I may spend as much time looking at the mountain laurel and the rhododendron and the sun and the sunset as I do fishing, for I live where you see none of these things; or I may not, for I have come to fish and fly-fishing anchors my eye on water and the life in and around it, and anchors my imagination because the challenge of a fishing problem can be an exquisite kind of pleasure.

Pleasure, fun—that's partly, even mostly, why I fish. Any day on a river is better than a day off the river. I have had days on rivers (many times) when I have caught nothing, and days when the river gods could not have been more generous. Fishing can be easy or frustrating, dumb luck or a game of incisive skill; it is always unpredictable—

and the expectation matters. With fly fishing, I can take a plethora of pleasures even if I don't finally catch a fish: in having found and stalked a good trout, chosen the right fly, cast well and accurately, raised it, then possibly hooked but not caught it.

I can't tell someone who loves fishing competition that he doesn't or shouldn't love it. All pleasures are individual, and I don't doubt that he does love it, and that I'd be a smug mandarin to say, "You shouldn't."

But against all the promotion for his game, and others like it, I merely add my voice for something else: I keep coming back, never having got enough of it, because I like the company or the solitude or the chase, because some big fish got away, because I like the chance to use my fierce passions happily, because there are still many skills to learn, mysteries to untangle, because I don't have to win, because I don't have to go but want to go, because of the surprise, the delight, the fun.

I'd hate to go fly fishing if I *had* to catch fish—big ones and a lot of them.

I'd hate to make love, too, by the clock, for a prize, in a public place.

A PARLIAMENT OF SKILLS

In the beginning, I thought that when I could cast an honest thirty feet I'd be a fly fisher. And of course you cannot even begin to play until you can ante up a decent cast of that distance. In some places, under some circumstances, that one skill will get you your first fish— bluegill, bass, even trout, but it won't get you *all* the fish you want, not all the time.

Some of the fish you cannot catch will be another twenty, thirty, or fifty feet distant. Some will be feeding on insects or foods that, on or beneath the surface, haven't yet entered your consciousness. Latin aside, you won't even know the insects are there. Some fish may be feeding in sections of the river that require reach or slack casts, which you don't know exist, or some sophisticated manipulation of the line to avoid drag.

A dozen thwarting errors might have occurred before you're even ready to make your first cast: you might not have seen the bigger fish feeding to the left, nor known from a rise what food a fish might be taking; you might have put your quarry down by clumsy wading, by coming too close to the fish, by standing too tall; you might not have tied your knots with care, or selected the proper fly, or built a long enough leader, or positioned yourself properly to cast to the best advantage.

You might not have known your trout's behavior well enough, or the ecology or hydrology of moving water, or the entomology of the river. You might not have mastered the discrete angling skills needed to gull that particular trout, for it is the compelling fascination of fly fishing that we must constantly bring together many disparate skills and different faculties—even as a parliament does—and that some are learned rather quickly, even in schools and from books, and others require hundreds of hours of actual fishing.

Experience teaches—but only if we encourage it to do so. Without a wiser or more experienced hand nearby we're likely to repeat the same minute—but fatal—casting flaw *ad nauseam,* or miss the telltale wink of white that indicates a fish's mouth opening to take a nymph in four feet of water.

"Try casting from *here,*" the wiser head says, and you shift position, kneel, and the fly no longer drags, and the trout no longer takes you to be a threat. "Don't cast blindly," he says. "You won't be ready when the fish do rise, or you'll put them down."

Local experience can produce dazzling intimacy with a particular stretch of water, but there is another kind of knowledge that we ought to seek, too: the ability to fish *any* water, under almost any circumstances.

I was fishing a tough little run on the Beaverhead with Al Troth some years ago—well, it was tough for me. The water shot directly above me and the only suitable place to stand was a trifle to the left, directly downstream of the brisk, choppy run, with my left hand required for balance every now and then. I cast upstream and the current tugged the line, which then dragged the fly instantly. I S-ed the line and it still came down like a shot. I cast hard, stopped the line in the air, and let a whole section of it fall downstream; but the current was too strong, and this induced drag, too. What finally drew a strike, three-quarters of an hour later, was a very long, very supple leader tippet, perhaps thirty-five inches of it, that fell in a near bird's nest on the current and took a few seconds to straighten. Some years later, Lefty Kreh showed me a tower cast that would have worked—and had I asked, Al (who has all the skills) would have shown me what to do at once. I just didn't have the wit to manage that problem yet.

Golf, tennis, baseball, basketball, swimming, and every other sport require unique blends of skills—and some of them are similar, and all powers must exist more or less harmoniously for the thing to get done. Eye, stroke, timing, power—all must work together so that the result is so seamless we think it natural. "A line will take us hours maybe," Yeats says in "Adam's Curse," "yet if it does not seem a moment's thought / Our stitching and unstitching has been naught." That naturalness—in a poem, a golf stroke, the pursuit of a fish with a fly rod—is rarely earned without severe effort. And it's more than synchronized swimming, isn't it? It is the unique presence of the natural world in the equation, the live unpredictability of the fish and its world, the need to summon the too often forgotten skills of the predator, that makes fly fishing not a sport but a pursuit that engages our total selves.

In fly fishing, when one is learning, it all seems monstrously unnatural: line is always tangling; casts collapse; casts double back upon themselves; we're always a hand and a half short when we're tying knots; the fish fly before us in fright. We guess and we gamble. We're lucky when we succeed. We're clubfooted aliens striving for balletic grace. So we go to schools, read books and magazine articles, seek the help of wiser friends, add more and more time, more and more intensity to our efforts, stretch ourselves toward what we're sure we can be but cannot yet imagine. The confirmation, always, is when the trout takes the fly.

Only much later . . . when in some Zenlike fashion the rod becomes an extension of our arm; when we have tied a knot so often that we can almost do it blindfolded (the way we trained to dismantle and reassemble an M-1 rifle in basic training), using teeth and the feel of the tongue, then pressing the knot against a finger so that the loose strands stand at attention, to be cut; when the stutter flight of an insect instantly says "caddis" or the slow rise says "dun"; when the line is balanced to the rod; when we spot the fish quickly enough, identify its feeding preference, approach carefully to the exactly correct position, make an accurate reach cast (without lining the fish); when the fly is right, the hook properly sharpened; when the leader turns over beautifully and the fly floats with perfect naturalness along the feeding lane . . . it all comes together.

All those minute and differing skills, from the outposts of our existence, meet and find a single order. Eye, ear, foot, fingers—all are there, in concert. You have read the water right, chosen the proper fly, and cast from the proper position. The line has taken wing. The fish has seen the fly, risen, and been tricked. You struck with the deft hand of the young Arthur drawing forth the sword, and it all held.

It happens that way sometimes.

It happens for me more and more lately.

Trust me: it's worth the effort and the wait.

THE *THINGS* OF FLY FISHING

Now and again, after the controversies and the confusions, the remembrances of better rivers past, the good and necessary conservation talk, after the personalities and the skills and the beautiful places where you've been or want to go, after the myriad techniques and strategies, after the gossip and the news and the dreaming of adventures that might or might not occur next summer or in seven years, the new knots, the better tips, the words of it and the images of it and the act of fly fishing itself, I find enjoyment again in the simple things upon which all of fly fishing rests.

Take the dry fly.

There's something to admire for an hour, as it rests on the desk before me, balanced high on its hackles and firm tail, a classic Catskill tie. It took centuries for this fly to be born, from discrete, even minute, changes in its architectonics to the hackle, the winging, the body, the tail. Berners, Cotton, Ogden, Halford, and a dozen (maybe a hundred) others had a hand in it; genetic tinkering gave us that precise shade of blue dun; the great freestone rivers of the Catskills demanded a firm rather than soft tail, crisp rather than limp hackle; Theodore Gordon, Rube Cross, Preston Jennings, Art Flick (who tied this one), and others (known and unknown) fussed with the proportions; and then we got this Dun Variant, perky and brilliant and simple, and (to the right creatures) tasty as blueberry pie.

It took centuries, too, to build the rod and line that would cast such a fly properly—and such rods, dry-fly rods of bamboo, then glass, then graphite, led us to develop these other flies I now lay on the desk beside the first: an Elk-Hair Caddis and a Parachute Adams tied by Al Troth; a Sparkle Dun by Craig Mathews; A.K.'s Baetis; one of Dick Talleur's cut-wings (that goes slant on the table but will float exactly right); a Pale Morning Dun tied for me by Len Wright after Vince Marinaro's thorax-style, with a V at the bottom of the hackle so it will set itself on the film, allowing the body and wings to become visible to the trout, with Len's shrewd body segmentation and the body's precise shade of lemon-yellow chartreuse. I look at a grasshopper tied cunningly with bent turkey-wing legs, a deer-hair head, a yellow body, and at a magisterial Hendrickson, tied by Larry Duckwall, with its pale pink body, blue-dun hackle, and tight head.

The flies are minor monuments, and I touch them lightly and rearrange them, delighted with their ingenuity and with their diversity and with their possibilities. I have a couple of thousand of them in my boxes, and I take *almost* as much pleasure looking at them as in fishing them. But not quite. I'm not a collector but a user, and though I'm mad for them, I only recently allowed myself to be persuaded not to use the flies Art Flick gave me by the handful when we were on the water together. I may not be a collector, but I am a fly fisher who sometimes hoards.

We take special pleasure in all things made well—from a poem to a television set to a dry fly. We like the things in our life that are sweet and useful: color, shape, and form "beautiful" in ways we consider beautiful. And we like the precise taper and action of a rod—in whatever material we love most—such that it becomes an extension of arm and body rhythm. Over the years such tools are different extensions of different arms: how I once loved the soft and the slow; how I insist now on what is firm and fast. I recently lent my friend Knox, an experienced fly fisher, a rod that I had had specially made for me, and on a bonefish flat he found it too stiff to be used for more than half a dozen casts. I had asked the maker to fashion me a "telephone pole," and its authority and power give me great pleasure. With it I can cast more delicately than I can with the most delicate-seeming rods.

Nor is there, objectively, for everyone, the perfect reel, for each person will find most apt the certain sound of a click pawl, the muted hum of another, the absence of sound, the watchlike steadiness of the mechanisms as he turns the handle, its machined brilliance. Len Wright used only Perfects; another friend can afford to choose only Bogdans; I've been in love with my Princess for decades—but have betrayed her lately; and wise fly fishers love the Orvis, the Abel, the durable old Medalist, the Fin-Nor, and a dozen others.

In the beginning we find these *things* of angling bewildering. I once couldn't distinguish between some clunker glass and a Gillum; I scarcely knew the proper fly to choose, what to look for in a fly— and now there are hundreds of patterns and styles I loathe so much that I would drink bile before I'd tie one of them onto a leader.

Experience makes us finicky—but it teaches each of us differ- ently. I like downlocking reel seats to the exclusion of all others, except when a true fighting butt is absolutely needed; perhaps it's my poor casting, which causes line to wrap around even a slightly extended butt—but I eschew butts and rarely use even an uplocking seat.

I look for a certain strength and elasticity in my leaders, loose- ness in my boot-foot waders, and hundreds of hard-to-define quali- ties of fishiness in my flies. And the better nipper; there's less to love in a nipper—except when a poor one causes mischief.

Friends say I have betrayed some aesthetic god of fly fishing by abandoning bamboo—but I've found graphite lovable. Still, I've just acquired a bamboo rod from George Maurer that sings, and I may yet convert back, if partly.

I look for the things that are sweet and useful, and when I find them I become an ogler and a hoarder and even a proselytizer . . . until something happens that makes me change completely, and then I see differently and have different loyalties and prefer the opposite of what pleased me last year. "Do I contradict myself?" asks Whitman. "Very well then I contradict myself." And why not? This is not loyalty to a principle that, once seen clearly, might be worth a life or a life- time; this is the hedonist's search for that "thing" that will give a bit more pleasure on the water, that functions with greater ease, that brings together in a harmonious way the accumulated wisdom of great anglers and persuades because it works.

I never used a Suspender Midge until I sat beside John Goddard as he caught three large trout on his version of this fly—and now I won't go near the water without half a dozen of them. They're beautiful *things* to behold.

In the end, what *works* is what I find most beautiful in fly fishing, and often enough, what works does so because I believe in it and it extends from my discrete skills, at a particular moment in *my* evolution as a fly fisher.

Only at some last moment, on the water, does my attention shift from the lovely *things* of fly fishing to the pursuit, the challenge of the quarry, to the mysterious world of water that it inhabits. Then I want all of my *things*—my playthings and my tools and my weapons— to work seamlessly.

Sometimes, miraculously, they do.

FLY FISHING IN BED

For two weeks I lay on my back in the hospital bed, mostly awake and inert, without pain, life coming back into my veins through thin tubes that I knew could be made into splendid sand-eel or minnow imitations. Except for visits, I had not been in a hospital before. I had visited hospitals for births, and twice I had visited them to touch the dying shards of life. I did not especially relish the hospital's odd cross between Chekhov's Ward Six and a daytime soap with its admixture of lives impossible to save, degrees of madness and collapse and loss and pain, lives linked by disease. So I lived mostly in my thoughts, and these were about random moments of my life and whether my current position was the product of poor planning.

I thought a lot about fishing. I was not dying or delirious, nor was I terrified—like Hemingway's Nick Adams in "Now I Lay Me," who fishes every foot of a favorite river as a stay against fear, an exercise in reconstruction. Fishing memories came from times fifty-five years apart, from obscure to popular parts of the Catskills, from creeks fifty miles from New York City to Montana and Idaho and Iceland and England, from places where I'd merely fished for a day, passing through. I let the images appear as they would, a few at a time—some longer, some merely seconds; though I let them play themselves out in my mind, appearing by some happy free association, I found I could hold or dismiss them, too, and I found that they mingled with thoughts of my children and my wife and my little business and what I'd written and things I'd said or done.

There was plenty of time.

I was in no rush whatsoever.

For the first time in forty years, I had no place to go, no work I had to do. Quite selfishly, I had no one to think about but myself. I could take stock or imagine or remember or merely watch the gargoyle on the building out the window and across the street, which, when pigeons flocked to it, appeared to move. I wanted to understand what had happened to me, how I'd gotten here, my role in it. I wanted to walk out, after the operation, with a new plan. I'd had a nasty scare but had been lucky, and the illness had triggered a reset button. I'd been given a chance to head off in another direction, if that's what I chose.

Mostly I thought about fishing—the perch and pumpkinseeds I'd caught almost before memory, a bigmouth bass that wandered off

with the three-inch sunny I'd baited for it, a first trout, a ten-pound carp, smallmouth on popping bugs in the Ten Mile River, a first trout ticking a sunken fly on Michigan's Au Sable, a first trout on a dry fly, certain difficult or large or impossible trout, fish caught and fish lost. I thought about a dozen raw Opening Days on the East Branch of the Croton; trips to the St. Lawrence for smallmouth and pike; my first sight of the Rockies, of Henrys Lake, of the Madison River, of a spring creek. It had not been so vast and panoramic and adventuresome a fishing life as many, but I had made the most of what there was, and I had had other business to transact, which I took to be important.

A salmon suddenly took the Hairy Mary, riffle-hitched, at the end of my long line, V-ing its way across a flat slick on the Strengir section of the Grimsa. It was the only time I'd fished for salmon. The fish took in a rush, roiling the surface, and then raced for the far bank and leaped like a rocket. It was the largest fish I'd ever had on a fly rod, and I was sure I'd lose it. Up it leaped, and then again, suspended in the air, shaking. And then, at the end of the long line, two feet from the lip of the pool, it leaped again, and then rolled and slashed at the surface.

Surely it would leave the pool, head into the heavy rapids below, break off. But it turned and sped directly toward me, so I lost contact. I twitched in the hospital bed as I did so, and the arm with the intravenous tubes, my left, moved downward, imping a long stripping tug. And in a few moments we were connected again. While the fish hovered and shook its head, less than half a fly line from me, I got all the slack back onto the reel, raised the rod, and thought I might have a chance. I could see the fish clearly in the clear water—pushing its head down, shaking—and it was surely the largest salmon I'd had on that week, by double.

I kept a wide arc in my rod and pumped and urged the fish closer to me; it came inchmeal—and then it went upstream into heavy current, tired itself, and soon was at hand, bright silver in the auburn shallows, its great jaw hooked, sea lice on its upper flank, gills red and spastic, about eighteen pounds' worth.

I had gotten to this hospital bed through colossal stupidity. I had had what I misdiagnosed and misjudged as flu a full five or six days earlier—and I'd been rocky for several weeks before that. But I never got sick; I was the Lou Gehrig of publishing.

In my teens I'd always been able to hold my head underwater long after thirty competitors had come up for air. I drew liberally on raw will, rarely on good sense, and if challenged, took a few aspirin, slept a bit longer, and made perfectly clear to my body that I would have none of such foolishness. There was always more work to take on, more I *had* to do; there was always a bit more I should do for some good and proper reason. Then after four days of severe intestinal symptoms, chills like the *petit mal,* and increasing weakness, I found myself at a business lunch and took as a poor sign that I could not lift my fork.

And still I persisted, thinking another hour would turn me, until several days later I regained consciousness in an emergency ambulance, oxygen mask on my face, the faces of my wife and two of my children looking down at me with anguished fear—and I was fully dehydrated, yellow with jaundice, high-fevered, with a failing pulse and blood pressure headed south. I might have slipped into shock at any moment, they told me later. For the first time in my life I had not the slightest shred of will to protect myself. I could have danced away without a fight, merely closing my eyes, which wanted to close, and drifting back to where I'd been. I'd have felt no pain.

It was my unconsciousness of my predicament that troubled me most, later, when I lay there, letting whatever was in the tubes do the hard work, quiet the gall bladder that had broadcast such sour news to my liver, bile duct, and other parts of my body that would listen. I had worked too hard, thought too hard about everything and anything and anyone other than myself, and I'd nearly become nothing to anyone.

Many writers have been connecting their psychic lives to fly fishing lately, and the wits have popped out like crab grass and found fly-fishing psychobiography to be the fairest and funniest of games. But if you love and understand the simple magic of water and trout and wilderness and fly imitation, it is not at all far-fetched.

In the bed as I was waiting for the operation, my brain made trips, and the trips had flies in them: the raw strike of big bluefish to

a sand-eel fly Lou Tabory had given me; the generous curl on flat water when a parachute Pale Morning Dun slipped over the exact spot where a great trout had just risen; the lumbering bulldog force of a largemouth after it exploded under a hair bug; the rush of a pike and the quick take of mountain brookies; the railroad rush of that first tarpon, at daybreak in the Marquesas; the first sight of Hendricksons, after a long morning's wait with Mike Migel, now gone, on a gray May afternoon. What a glorious sight: the dead water suddenly covered with ten, twenty, then fifty slate-winged flies, like sailboats. Two trout cruising first a few feet from the head of the pool, then drifting back and taking fixed feeding positions. The flies disappearing in silent circles that could quicken the dullest pulse. It was the herald of a new season. The awakening of the dead earth. The return of life when life, in a winter of threats, had not always seemed sustainable.

And then I was home and had days yet to indulge myself in this sweet memory pie. I began to sort and tinker with my scores of fly boxes, and I began to think of my new season.

from

My Secret Fishing Life
(1999)

GOING AND COMING BACK

From those first days, at four or five, when I walked alone along the half-mile dirt trail from the hotel to the perch and pickerel lake, I felt that unique sensation of expectancy all fishermen feel when they head for water, always accompanied by a host of questions. Where on the big lake should I fish? Did I have the right hooks and enough of them? Had I forgotten my bobber, brought enough worms? Should I have left, as I'd planned, an hour earlier? Would I catch a pickerel even larger than the one I'd taken two weeks earlier?

And then, four hours later, returning from the lake, a pleasant tiredness in my muscles, my brain would wander very different paths—recalling, with the stark clarity of any recent disaster, the precise feel of that behemoth pickerel as it took the quarter-pound shiner I was hauling in, and the busting of the cheap bamboo stick that was my rod and then the busting of the line; recalling the oar I lost and spent twenty minutes retrieving when the wind came up; recalling another twenty minutes wrapping green cord around the part of the bamboo that had fractured and exploded. The rod had broken again, at the same spot, at the tug of a mere sunny, and, flustered, I'd dropped the worm box in the drink. And it began to rain thickly, and there was lightning that forced me off the lake, made me head briskly back to the hotel.

I'd caught some fish. I always caught some fish. I was born with some instinct for catching fish. But fishing was always a game that made you want more things to go right than wrong, where, at the right time, a lost fish could become a tragedy of the highest water. It's more so now, when I fly fish exclusively.

That same pattern repeats itself most of the times I go fishing—though the sensations have become marvelously more complex, even bewildering, and often enough related to other factors.

A friend who catches far more trout than most, all on the dry fly, says he never feels that the rich expectancy of a trip out is matched by any trip back, even after a pretty successful day. There are simply too many occasions for matters to go wrong on a trout stream: wind, rain, too much sun, no flies, a hitch in his casting, lost fish, high or low water, crowds camped at his favorite stretch, the fish simply not taking when he thought they should. His feelings almost always tilt, on trips back, toward what factors might have been better.

A literary friend, whom I did not know had the slightest interest in fly fishing, told me recently that he'd taken up the activity for about five years, to get away from his first wife. His trips out, he told me, were spectacular: the long day ahead of him, the prospect of wading to his thighs in a cool local river, the silence, the great peace that came for him on the water. He rarely caught a fish, and when he did it was irrelevant. But as soon as he stepped into the car to head home, he forgot the river, instantly and a strange feeling of terror and trepidation swept through him like the vapors of the Angel of Death. I said that must have been pretty scary and asked him if he still had any interest in fishing. No," he said, contemplatively. "I love my second wife and fishing reminds me of my first."

That all sounds pretty rotten, from whatever angle you look at it, but if you substitute a rugged, hectic life in a big corporation in a big gray city, and a middle-management job, you come to a place not too removed—at least as far as the fisherman is concerned.

Of course there are many of us, and I am now one of them, for whom a day on a trout river is so pleasant an event, such an amiable and engaging pastime, that it feels, both going and coming back, as comfortable as an old shoe. We go for the sheer joy of it, not to put notches on our rods. We go because no day on a trout stream lacks mystery, surprise, wonder, and suspense. We go for a glimpse of that most magical of sights—a spreading circle that is a rising trout. We see a world in that pocked surface. That spot becomes the condensed target for what we seek, the place at which—with all expectation—to cast our fly.

It's the same far and near, though I favor the shorter trip lately, even if it offers fewer and smaller fish. I like the immense surprise of catching a big fish in waters where you least expected it; I like to fish water I've fished a hundred times before, water that shares history with me, that I see in my head, going and coming back.

A friend knew a man who always paused at a bridge downstream from his parking spot on a remote New England river. He had seen, in his early fifties, what might have been the wavering tail of a truly gigantic brown trout, just twenty feet out, near the first abutment—though perhaps it was just weed, even a shadow. Still, each of the three or four times he fished the river every year, he stood quietly in the shadows and watched that three-foot patch of quieter water, just where the current glanced off the abutment and rushed toward the center of the run. The second year, in June, when the water was thinner and the sun at precisely the proper angle, he saw it with perfect clarity: a six- to eight-pound brown, perhaps twenty-six inches' worth, wavering, head upstream, high in the water, the largest trout he'd ever seen in an eastern river.

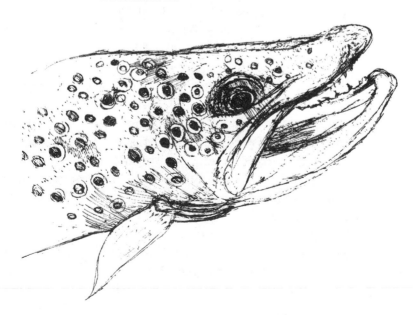

He was a knowledgeable fly fisher and quickly saw that little blue-winged olives were coming down and that the big trout was probably taking either the nymphs just below the surface or duns with an indiscernible rise on the surface.

He waded a few feet into the heavy current between his shore and the lightly riffled water below the abutment and made a few tentative casts that at once convinced him he couldn't manage this maneuver. If he cast directly to where the trout was or even slightly upstream, the current caught the belly of the line so quickly that the fly dragged at once. He couldn't mend the curve in the line upstream fast enough, and he could not get directly above or below the fish, where he could work the much more manageable seam of lesser current, because he could simply not wade through the heavy current.

Trips to that river from then on were filled with the hopes that he would see that fish and hook it. He ran through new strategies in his mind; he read chapters in books devoted to this exact issue. He even tried the river in the doggiest days of summer. But he could not always see the fish and he never raised it.

The fish was there for two years, then disappeared, then was back. After ten years of going to the spot, of dreaming of it and of its auspicious denizen, he realized that he could not even pretend he was looking at the same fish. Surely the original brown, old when he first saw it, was dead, and its spot was always taken by an especially good fish, perhaps the best in the whole river, because the lower corner of the abutment gave a king plenty of food and plenty of protection.

The man never grew bored of the great fish, even of not catching it. Another ten years went by; he retired, some painful arthritis led him to fish less. But he only thought more about his great fish— the first one and its successors melding into one, transcending themselves, becoming some kind of emblem. He knew he could take the fish on a spinning lure or bait or perhaps a bead-head streamer. He had no special aversion of such methods, but they were not for this fish. He thought about the fish when he went to the river and then he fished a little or a lot for it, and then he thought about it every time he packed up his gear and headed home. His only disappointment came not from failing to catch the fish but from failing to see it, thinking then that his fish might have headed downriver with the last heavy rain, that one of the local kids had taken it by climbing down the abutment and fishing for it on a short line, with a heavy sinker and a live minnow. He saw it last July, big as a submarine.

This spring he called my friend and said he'd never fish again; he had one of the really bad cancers, and it was doing its nasty work like a swarm of red ants. He'd told his wife to call my friend when it happened. He wanted to be cremated. He wanted my friend to drop his ashes from the upstream part of the bridge.

"That fish gave me so much pleasure over the years—thinking about it, watching for it, pitching a fly toward that abutment. Every time I went I simmered with hope, and if I saw it, I returned radiant—otherwise, full of happy questions." He paused for a moment. "We were really linked, you know."

My friend said he did know.

"And now, since I couldn't have him, he can have me."

MESSING ABOUT IN BOATS A LITTLE

More than a hundred pounds ago I rowed for the one-hundred-and-fifty-pound crew at the University of Pennsylvania. We trained hard, carried the narrow racing shell to the Schuylkill River, grasped the long oars with both hands, and then swung hard when the little coxswain rhythmically barked commands through his midget bullhorn. There were fumbles and fallings-back; there was disharmony. But after a few moments we began to propel the boat with astonishing speed. Our bodies rocked forward and back as if controlled by metronome or prayer, our oars dipped lightly and in perfect unison, we cut the surface so swiftly that I sometimes thought we were sailing inches above it.

After a moment, though, my arms began to tighten and I feared that what basketball skills I'd worked so hard to develop would be lost. Basketball was the game I loved most then, and played hardest, and since I'd already sacrificed my heart and grades for it, I gave up crew without looking back. Anyway, though I had always rowed, I had begun to realize that the competitive rowing was not at all like the kind I did in an old wooden or aluminum rowboat, on a lake, happily alternating left and right strokes to my own rhythm, with my fishing gear piled near the back seat.

For a while in my late teens (as the Water Rat tells the Mole in *The Wind in the Willows*) I thought: "There is *nothing*—absolutely nothing—half so much worth doing as simply messing about in boats."

They isolated me from the world of land and crowds and summer camp. They floated me. They gave me more mobility than feet and better access to the water that I was coming to love, that haunted my dreams. I liked nothing better in the evening than to take out a rowboat by myself on that Berkshire lake, head for a remote shoreline, and cast in toward the bank, when the lake was glassy, even covered with mist. And the rowboats were quite as comfortable as old shoes.

Canoes, at least for me, were for canoeing, but for fishing—even in my lithe athletic days—they were too tippy. I needed more solidity when I fished. I was never like those great fly casters in the Winslow Homer watercolors or the husband and wife (the wife with her baby in a papoose) I once watched on Martha's Vineyard. The two paddled their canoe out of Menemsha Harbor into the choppy bay without a moment's hesitation, to fish with flies for false albacore. It made my stomach shiver to watch them, especially when the man stood and began to throw a full eighty feet of line.

No, I prefer rowboats. I like their firm base, their responsiveness to both of my oars at once, the quickness with which I can turn them, the precise (modest) speed with which I move in them, so I miss nothing; and I love their reliable steadiness when I've found a proper cove. When the wind is down, they stay put. I can lean over and fuss with my big metal box crammed with bass and panfish bugs. I can turn the boat slightly, running it parallel to the shore, and have a firm platform from which to cast, a perfect angle to the shore. When I press the long heavy rods I use for bass—ten- or even eleven-weight—into motion and the heavy bug and line stretch out in front and then behind me, I don't want to think of the craft that floats me; I want to concern myself only with the business at hand—the varied shoreline, that angled stump, the deadfalls, the lily pads I'm working toward. I don't want my craft to tip when some great buster of a bigmouth black bass crashes up and takes the bug.

On the great rivers I've learned to enjoy the Mackenzie River boats—especially when I get to stand in the prow, rod at the ready, watching the shoreline that rushes past me and upriver. My great impulse is to cast and cast—a demon in me. I want to miss nothing. I want my fly on the water as much as possible. Down it travels into one eddy, along the dark shadow beneath the overhanging willows, into the strip of current that is the feeding lane, behind that boulder, back again at the eddy behind the boulder, as close to the rocky shoreline as possible. I manipulate the line so that the fly floats ten, fifteen, thirty feet, drag free. I back-cast once, maybe twice—no more. I bring the line up backhand, then down. I watch, always, the white or gray spot that is the fly as it slips downriver, drifting, dragging for a moment, drifting again, is taken suddenly by a fish that rises exactly where I expected it to be.

A good friend told me, when I floated the Beaverhead with him, that I cast far too much, that I should cast only to a rising fish, not to the good-looking water, of which there seemed no end. If I kept doing what I did, he said, I just wouldn't be ready when I actually saw my fish come up. He was right. Twice. But I'm restless. I fish from a Mackenzie boat far too little, and too many times there just aren't any fish coming up—though on the Beaverhead there are more than on most rivers, especially when Al Troth is rowing.

Having three thumbs, having graduated only recently from my beloved Underwood Standard, Model S, vintage 1945 typewriter to a 1950s Royal Standard, I do less well with motors of all kinds than I'd like. I wish it were otherwise. They seem like nifty ways to propel a boat in salt water or on huge lakes. A flats boat in the right hands is a fine friend, ideally suited to its chores. Motored boats of all kinds are splendid tools for getting you out there and then back. I've used them on the huge St. Lawrence River, when nothing else was possible, and on some larger New England lakes, but they always make me nervous. My friend Mort, who has messed about in boats for most of his life, likes them, but twice when I've been out with him we've been towed back by another boat when a motor wouldn't turn over. No, give me a rowboat and oars every time, especially when I'm alone, and give them to me on a small lake rather than on a river, please.

The last time I went off on a river by myself was less than a joy. We borrowed Vaughan's Avon raft, the pontoon-like structure with a wooden section where we sat, and a couple of oars. The bottom was rubber and when we tried to stand we felt like we were on a waterbed.

"Have you done this before?" asked Vaughan, and I told him I had and that I had once rowed one-hundred-and-fifty-pound crew. We were on the Madison and I realized only at the last moment, when I'd stopped boasting, that I had not come down this river by myself in fifteen years and fifty pounds. I wondered if the rubber could be punctured. If it could, would the raft sink? I looked out across the river, thick with whitecaps from the afternoon wind, and thought that perhaps there was a better trip I could take someplace, someday. And then we pushed off, a couple of trusting friends and I, and the current immediately assumed command.

It took less than a minute, no longer, for me to realize that I had absolutely no idea of what I was doing. The boat moved too quickly, the wind took us wherever it pleased. I nearly killed my rear passenger when I slammed the raft into a mess of protruding willows on the far side of a sharp turn, and at the end—none too soon—I over shot the take-out spot by two hundred yards. Some fun. It wasn't my kind of adventure.

Call me old, call me fat, call me chicken—but I love best a simple rowboat on a small lake of some ten to twenty acres. I love it because I'm in control, because it's steady, because it gives me the exact access I want to a kind of fishing, increasingly, that I love.

At my age I can't think that I'll ever graduate—or degenerate—into a lover of brassy bass boats or even high-powered flats boats. As they say, some of my best friends love them. But I don't give up old pleasures, old clothes, old typewriters, old loves, or old rowboats without a struggle. Maybe it's my way of throwing a bit of sand in the careening machinery of progress; but I suspect it's just that I've learned how happy I am messing around with what I know well, with what I'm comfortable. It's a challenge for a lot of us to be content.

THE JUDGE'S SWIM POND

Irregularly, it was half the length of a football field, give or take an end zone, and narrow enough even for me to cast across. The Judge had built it forty years earlier for his kids to swim in. He'd put in a wooden dock on stilts, some bluegills, and a handful of bass. Now and then a neighbor added the last few minnows from his minnow bucket or a pickerel or a small trout from a creek across the hill. The trout were never seen again. All else flourished, especially the largemouths.

In the fifteen years I drove upcountry to visit a close friend who lived nearby, I fished the Judge's swim pond a couple dozen times. I'd fallen in love with the long rod and poppers by then and always brought them along. We'd walk over from my friend's house after an early dinner on a hot summer evening with a fly rod each and a small plastic box with five or six poppers—panfish size to huge—and perhaps a few streamers and black leech patterns.

The pond was a complete, contained world—a cattail stand in the southern corner, a long bank with high grasses thick and snug to the shoreline, willows at the north end, the wooden dock that had buckled and leaned left, and a thirty-three-foot strip of shore, sandy and sloping, where the Judge's family, for generations, swam. I heard the pond was fifteen feet deep in the center, which explains why the fish wintered over. There was a shallow flat near the cattails where the bluegills spawned in June, and in the shade under the overhanging willows, you could often find a big largemouth in August.

We'd always fish in the evening, from seven-thirty or so right up until dark, and we liked the hottest of evenings best—the air thick with bugs, our shirts sweaty, the water flat, the fish eager for surface food. And we always caught fish—fat bluegills, unremarkable largemouths, pencil-thin pickerel that lunged at a leech or streamer, and now and then, when we least expected it, but most often when the sun was low and orange in the west, a largemouth that would break the surface as if a garbage can had been thrown in, a fish large enough to startle and make your heart pound, a glory fish, a hawg.

I loved the Judge's swim pond, perhaps because I came to know it so well, because it held such surprises, and because I shared it with a close friend. We chattered away as we walked to and from the pond,

but we never talked much while we fished. We'd fall into that happy familiar pattern that only the oldest and best friends have, when half sentences, intonations, single words tell whole stories, especially when whispered across a quiet pond at dusk.

And then the Judge, whom I'd never met, died and his property was sold, and shortly afterward something that parallels death happened: my old friend and I had one of those ugly fights that only old friends can have—friends who know each other so well they know how to hurt each other most. We were big boys and ought to have known better, but we didn't, and then we did those things that are impossible to forgive and we have not spoken in ten years and never will.

Often as the winter wanes and summer dreams begin, I think of the Judge's swim pond and those evenings when the water was flat and bugs danced on its surface, when sweat dripped from the rim of my old fishing hat, when a popper pitched out and negotiated in could bring the energetic tugs of a bluegill or the eruption of a bass that would open eyes anywhere. I think of the pond and of the friend I once had and of the simple good times we had together and now never will again.

THE 193 MINUTES

S ome wise fellow said in print that fishing was mostly expectation. We dream, we prepare, we tinker, we buy, we rearrange, we read, we go, and we wait; and what with the weather to delay us more and Al's cousin who needs to have his wind knots untangled every thirteen minutes, and an unexpected crowd at the Three Dollar Bridge, or last week's rainstorm, it's a wonder we ever get in enough fishing. Throughout it all, the planning and the doing, I have come to think that it's best done without clocks.

We do best when we simmer in our own juices, avoid the ticking clock—the handmaiden to our workday, and week, and year, to all programming, every deadline, all competition. We do best when we go slow and slower, when the going especially is caught up in its own time. And as we get older and wiser and surely more skillful, we can well expect our days to be more genial.

Last spring I was even busier than in most years; recently, I didn't have time to plan, or much time to fish. In May, on a half hour's notice, I rushed upcountry, satisfied that I had arranged all that needed arranging after the close of the last season. I had made good order of my thousands of flies, putting each group in its own box, finding a box for every fly. Pale Morning Duns—in sizes No. 16, No. 17, No. 18, thorax, parachute, and Sparkle Dun—went into one of a dozen thin European boxes I'd decided would change my fishing life. There was room for a dozen little Olives, too, and enough Tricos for an emergency morning. I did the same with a couple of thousand other flies, blissfully, and the long gray November afternoon vanished. Under my new scheme, all the flies I owned of a given kind or for one use would go into their own box, which would hold an essential eighty to one hundred flies.

Some reels needed cleaning; one needed a new line, and I bought the most expensive one I could find. I fastened some braided butts to three lines and built four ten-foot leaders to attach to the butts. My rods were all right, but the only waders I could squirm into at my new weight had holes here and there. I gave away some extra nets, flies by the half-hundred, even a rod. Then, to assure myself that I was not becoming a minimalist, I bought two new rods—fast, downlocking, the newest graphite. Great stuff. I didn't need them, but I had every expectation of fishing more than usual this year; after all, I was pretty close to retiring from some bulk of my work, I thought, and that, finally, would give me time to fish in some endless summer of bliss.

In mid-May my old friend Sandy called one Saturday morning around ten o'clock and said: "You sure write about it a lot and talk about it all the time but I don't see you doing much trout fishing lately, N." He calls me "N." I told him he was surely correct but that I had a mountain of papers on my desk. Instead of retiring, I'd sort of reversed my ground at the last minute and gone back into the harness more than full-time. There was more paper in my life than ever.

"The paper will wait," he said.

"It grows when I don't weed it. Anyway, I owe it to my stock-holders to work."

"I happen to be one of your stockholders, and it's a perfect day and I'd like some company."

It was in fact a very tempting, muggy day after a late cold spring; there had been no heavy rain in more than a week. I'd had a few recent reports, all good.

So I grabbed the nearest rod and reel from my fish closet, fetched out four or five boxes marked "East—Early," "Large Dries—Eastern," "East—Later," slipped my vest and hat off their hook and into a carry-all, and was downstairs waiting for Sandy in exactly seventeen minutes. He came four minutes later. We'd be back early but we'd have a few rejuvenative hours first.

I looked at my watch when we got to the river, then put it into the glove compartment. It was the most pleasant of mid-May afternoons—overcast, warm without summer heat, buggy; I'd have no need for clocks. There were a few insects around for most of the time we fished; I saw a couple of early Sulphurs and a half dozen March Browns within the first half hour. I used only big flies—mostly No. 10s and No. 12s—and it was a happy way to fish, flicking those high-floaters up into the head of little runs. I was happy that Sandy had gotten me out for the first time that year, and like Nick Adams in the Hemingway story, I wasn't going to rush my sensations. I fished slowly, and there was just the right amount of action. We leap-frogged or fished side by side, and Sandy caught most of the fish, which was all right.

Then I headed well upstream by myself, to a pool I knew that formed on the far side of the stream, beneath a small waterfall, against rock and a large bent hemlock. I had taken three fish, and it felt good to see the rise and feel the tug of decent fish against the curve of my rod. I was only upcountry for a day—a few hours really—and the fishing was superbly genial, restorative: exactly what I needed. There was a gentle quality to this eastern fishing that, stuck on the West, I'd forgotten for a few years: the bright rush of a freestone creek, the pocket water, the flats and ledge-pools and choppy runs, the intimacy, the clarity of the water, the wall of hemlock overhanging the far bank. I'd taken a few fish; that was enough.

    I approached the spot from well downstream. Planning carefully
not to disturb the little pool, I blithely cast thirty feet across the gray
stones. The line—my new line, not used before today, the caviar of
lines—got hooked in a flotsam branch. I walked upriver to unsnag it,
and then realized that I had not taken line back onto the reel. So it
was tucked under some rocks, tangled in the branch, wrapped around
one of my boots.

I probably should not have tried to roll-cast my way out of the problem in the first place, I thought, and certainly not three times, for now I saw clearly that the new line—dyed for me by Craig—was composed of a colossal bird's nest of knots, perhaps four or five related nests, twenty feet back, at my feet, around the branch. In fact, this was the mother of all knots, winding over, under, with little loops popping up here and there, with no beginning, no ending, no clear choice as to where to begin. I sat quietly on a rock, pecking away at it. I'd always fancied myself a pretty good knot unknotter.

But bad led to badder, tangle to worse tangle; more loops appeared, more routes seemed permanently blocked. From the edge of my vision, I saw a couple of those big juicy Sulphurs flutter over the hemlock pool and heard the splashy rise of a good fish. So I began to tug at the line and must now admit that I got very angry with it. The line simply refused to cooperate. I made some guttural sounds and then pulled it with both hands, hard as I could, to show I disapproved of the way my line was behaving. Then I took out my favorite serrated pocketknife and smoothly cut a fifteen-foot and a three-foot section out of the heart of my new fly line, tied all the loose ends together, clumsily, and tried to cast with the nasty knots. They caught in the guides, dropping my Sparkle-Dun Sulphur barely beyond my boots, then into the hemlocks. I took a step, tripped, felt water enter my waders where the patch pulled loose, and dropped the contents of one very carefully filled fly box, with all my "Eastern—Later" flies, into the drink. The flies popped out and floated downstream—sixty to seventy of them—and the box twirled in an eddy and disappeared. The sky was ashen now, and I fell light rain on my face.

On my brisk walk downstream, I tripped twice more, pulled my bad hip out, saw the foot of my reel snap off, felt flat on my new graphite rod, and cut my face on a locust branch.

"You look like you've had quite a time, N," Sandy said when I came up to him. He had a good fish on. He was humming. He often hums when he has a good fish on, when he's enjoying himself.

I was breathing a bit too hard to say anything, or to hum.

He'd gotten nine fish, more than enough, and I'd just had enough. "Maybe," he said quietly as we walked back, "you ought to do this more . . ."

". . . stockholders," I mumbled.

". . . often. You're out of . . ."

It rained heavily before we got back to the car, where I slowly disengaged myself from my wet vest, my half-full waders, my wet shirt and pants, and broke down what was not broken of my rod. I didn't tell Sandy about my new line. Or my reel. Or how much my hip hurt.

In another few minutes we were in the car and the windshield wipers were rhythmically beating their tattoo against the wet glass. I put my hand in my pocket and realized I'd left my favorite knife on a rock. I retrieved my watch and looked at it. This sorry business had taken exactly 193 minutes.

ON THE TOP

There is an unsubstantiated story about my old friend Darrel Martin that he deliberately traveled to Croatia during that country's awful internecine war of several years ago because he believed that the fishing pressure on the great trout rivers there would then only be light. Well, he had one of them to himself and was having quite a fine time when a stern fellow in uniform appeared on the other side of the river and lowered a Uzi slung from his shoulder. The two men from different worlds looked at each other for a long while without speaking, bewildered, each trying to understand the weird moment, and then Darrel waved his hand, smiled, and said in slow, halting English: "It's all . . . right. Don't . . . worry. I'm fishing . . . a . . . *dry* fly."

Darrel neither confirms nor denies the event, but his lips broaden amiably when he is asked about it, for he well knows that whether it actually happened or not is almost beside the point: the story contains an inescapable truth, that the dry fly is in fact considered by many serious fly fishers to be superior to any subsurface fly—morally, logically, socially, even (perhaps) mystically. Why this should be so is another question, for the assumption that a fly that floats can possibly contain such qualities is both deep-rooted and absurd.

I am certainly not scholar enough to tell when it all began, no doubt before Frederic Halford, who codified the matter, nor how it progressed to its exclusive and elitist stature; but so serious an observer of our fly-fishing mores as the late Mr. Edward G. Zern once told me of a man who had been accused by his long-suffering wife, with good cause, of loving fly fishing more than he loved her. He did not hesitate, but immediately responded, "Wet fly or dry fly?"

The first trout I ever saw revealed itself to me when it rose to the surface of a small creek, pocking the flat roof of that watery world below me, causing the spreading circle that still never fails to animate my heart rate. I have pondered the mysterious electricity of that sight for nearly sixty years—and other sights that produce different effects. I have seen, with the help of Al Troth's great eyes, huge trout nymphing on the Beaverhead, and with the help of Jeffrey Cardenas's great eyes, schools of permit—their dorsals like the unrigged masts of ships—on the Marquesas flats. These are great sights. These are spectacular fish to fish for. These are memorable fish to hook and to battle, though I did neither. And I have fished a nymph to feeding trout in a carrier two feet deep, attached to a chalkstream in England, where the stalking, the presentation, the exactitude of it all must be every bit as demanding as fishing a dry fly to a fussy old brown trout feeding, in a three-foot indentation of a bank, on *Tricorythodes* eddying there.

I can think of a thousand difficult underwater situations—enigmas within the inner architecture of rivers—only a few of which I've been angler enough to master, and dozens of opportunities I had and refused, not from any sense that I'd fish a dry fly or nothing but

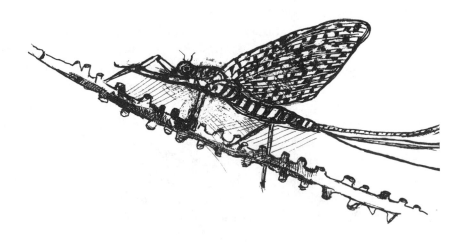

because they looked too hard. I scarcely think a dry fly superior to a wet fly, or he who fishes it either a better or purer or higher-minded angler.

But that spreading circle on the surface, the rise of a trout, or the explosion of a black bass after a bug, remains a mystery that perplexes and taunts me. And so does the nagging question of why I find myself fishing the dry fly almost exclusively lately, losing a lot of good fishing time in the process . . . and losing a lot more catching.

I have a sincere desire to be neither a snob nor a supposed snob. No doubt I am an incompleat angler by my increasing preference— though I don't dictate to my brothers of the angle nor for one moment think myself their better. If anything, I am less able, less versatile, less capable of fishing to all the fishing opportunities available to me, more restricted—and clearly I catch far fewer fish.

What was so haunting about that trout rising in the little Catskill creek—and all the other trout I've seen rise? The fish was coming from its mysterious element—the world of water, beneath the surface of pellucid water—and touching mine, the world of air. So long as it moved beneath the surface—and I had watched it do so for twenty minutes—it was separate from me, in its own world; but when it touched the surface it entered mine.

I fished for largemouth bass a lot in my teens, on a dark lake in the foothills of the Berkshire Mountains. I fished for them with plastic worms, Flatfish, spinning lures like the C. P. Swing and the Mepps, live sunfish, newts, and several surface plugs like the Crazy Crawler and the Jitterbug. I'll bet both of those surface plugs are still marvelously effective. I can see them clearly from the height of fifty years, chugging their way from the dark surface beneath the overhanging pines, across the flat surface at dusk. I learned to fish those surface plugs in the evenings, when the lake was as still as the wind, in against the shore, exactly the way I now fish a bass bug—letting the thing sit, jiggling, teasing it, stutter-starting it, then making it perform a dozen little dances as it swims toward me in the boat.

I am hard put to find much appeal in what so many of the great bass pros do on television, jabbering away as they do so: casting out and then retrieving an underwater lure with monotonous regularity. When a bass hit a surface plug then, and when one hits a bug for me now, I felt the same jolt of excitement—simultaneously to eye and brain and hand—charging through me.

And then I found in the dry fly much of what I had been searching for in fly fishing—the challenge of the exacting cast, the need to master drag and thus be in active control of my line at all times, the constant visual contact with the fly as it floated downstream, the variety of ways the trout might rise to my fly, the variety of instances that said we were connected. I cannot think of a better comment on the dry fly than Ted Leeson's observation that "the floating fly draws fishermen with an ineluctable gravity, and the source of this attraction is not difficult to locate. It originates with a flash, in the abrupt and certain take of a trout. Few moments in fishing hold the same immediacy and vividness as the rise to a floating fly, and none are endowed with the same satisfying sense of closure."

The only possible practical argument for using the dry fly more frequently is Lee Wulff's—that the dry fly fished on a floating line grants to the trout the sanctuary of its part of the river, allowing the connection to take place only at that place where air and water meet, and only at certain times. Of course this also means that you can fish with a floating fly only at those moments when the fish is likely to want its supper on the top, and we've all heard that more than 90 percent of a trout's diet is taken underwater. This confers upon the trout a lot of space and time free from we who pursue it—and it limits our fishing.

But while it may limit the time we can fruitfully fish, it also makes us a bit more observant, inevitably more interested in the entomology of the rivers we fish. I know of three superb dry-fly fishermen who fish only a few patterns, and those attractors like the Adams or Hairwing Royal Coachman. I know of several who once fished that way and have gradually begun to use some Latin, because the Delaware or the Madison began to yield them a few more fish when they learned which bugs were which.

Isn't one of the greatest pleasures of fly fishing that we can make it as simple or complex as we choose? And the choice, to fish an artificial fly that imitates an insect upon which a trout is feeding, to pitch our fly to a specific feeding fish—even as a straight-pool player must call his pocket, not merely bang away—is an honorable game, one that demands a bit more of us and therefore gives more. More and more I prefer that game myself.

I like the big bug that may imitate a frog or mouse or duckling or less determinate stew, resting near the lily pads at dusk, twitching a bit from its nervousness, then disappearing in a great washtub of a rise; I like the slashing strike of a rainbow that you can see lurching several feet through the heavy riffles on the Madison for your fake salmonfly; I like trout in a fixed feeding lane on a Catskill river, lunching on Hendricksons that float down on a cool gray late-April afternoon like little sailboats; and I cannot resist fishing to a shy trout on a river like the Firehole, the fish slipping gently along the far bank, below the grasses, perhaps thinking that its lips against the surface might betray it.

Mostly, and perhaps solely, I love to fish on the top because something in me responds to the rise, loves the experience of sight as much as touch, and more so because I must concentrate unblinkingly and intently—and because it's just so much fun.

NUMBERS CHANGE

There is a photograph of me taken in our backyard in Brooklyn nearly fifty years ago. I am wearing the man's felt hat that I always wore on fishing trips in my teens, holding a rod in my left hand, kneeling behind my wicker creel. On top of the creel are five small trout—silvery fish, impossible to tell if brook, brown, or rainbow, all stockers. On the ground in front of the creel are five of what we called "holdovers," fish that had been stocked a year or two earlier and had survived; there were no wild fish in the rivers we fished. The holdovers are fat browns, seventeen to nineteen inches in length, and even in the faded print their spots show sharply; we valued these much higher than the others, not merely for their size. The rod I am holding has a spinning reel at its base. This is serious business and I am not smiling.

Our state limit in the late 1940s was ten trout and "limiting out" was always our goal. We did it whenever we could. It provided a yardstick against which to measure our skill, and the day. Limiting out by eight in the morning was better than doing so by five in the afternoon. After we reached ten we stopped fishing and rooted for our pals. The limit was set by the state and we never questioned our right to take what we were allowed.

There are much larger catches in angling history—recorded with unquestioning pride in numbers. Consider these bloody portraits of Thomas Tod Stoddart, a popular nineteenth-century writer:

[Mr. Stoddart] was literally *clad* with salmon and sea-trout; his large hamper was full, and five or six strapped on his rod hanging across his shoulder and down his back, the perspiration streaming down his face and dripping off his beard and hair.

When told that he's killing himself with such a load, he says: "I'm doing this to let the beggars see that all fishers are not liars."
Or this:

His basket [a very large salmon one] was filled, aye, *crammed* with trout. The weight could not be less than a quarter of a hundredweight and nearly as many were lying on the bank, which he had begun to strap up on a strong cord. "Man," he says, "if I had not been out of bait, I could have killed as many more."

In our late teens, some of us began to throw fish back, heeding Lee Wulff's wise call that a gamefish was too valuable to be caught only once; we did this before it became popular and in the watersheds we fished our gesture was greeted with hoots and wry smiles. But keeping fewer fish did not mean we caught fewer. In fact, we caught more. Our skills had improved, our passion multiplied, and now our satisfaction came in numbers caught. "Sixty-two browns, fourteen to twenty-one inches," a friend boasted after a trip some years ago. Forty-eight, fifty-one, thirty-seven. Sometimes the numbers were physically impossible—did those friends cast, hook, land, and release a fish every sixty-seven seconds? Did their numbers include short strikes and inspection rises? As throwing back fish has taken on a moral height only slightly below sainthood, mendacity has grown like crabgrass.

I stopped killing most fish after I was part of a wholesale fish slaughter, with spinning rods, in my early twenties. Huge trout were in the spring-fed cove of a western lake and I caught twenty or thirty of them, big fish, bigger than any trout I'd then seen, and killed them all, hooking my thumb under the upper jaw and breaking their necks, to give to some local loggers who wanted them for a fish fry. By dark, my thumb was raw and bloody and I could not catch another. I'd had my fill of it, I felt guilty, and it had grown not only gruesome but boring. Some change began in me that evening at the lake—when the miracle of big fish and the numbers of them and the killing of them began to pall; but it was not merely a reaction or the taking on of a conscious ethic.

A dozen years ago I began to fish a pool that at first frustrated my best efforts. I had shifted most of my fishing to the fly rod and had learned it reasonably well, but not well enough for this tough river. I first fished this pool from the wrong position, with the wrong flies; I lined the fish, stood up and made the whole pool go dead for an hour, underestimated the head of wild fish it held. Once, standing, with the light at just the right angle to the water, I saw down into the deepest portion of the pool, just below the riffled bend, where the water slowed and broadened. Fluttering near the bottom like so

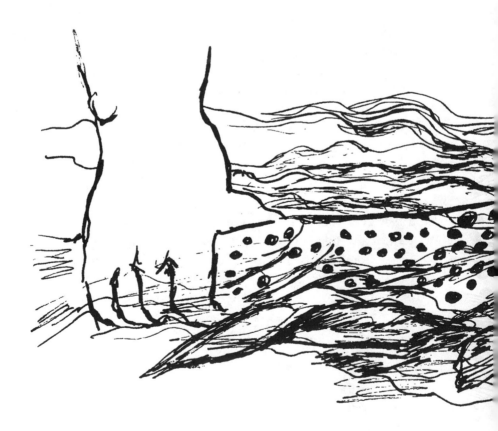

many frightened minnows in a pail were forty or fifty wild browns, from near-fingerlings to fish of twenty-four or more inches. They'd chosen this spot because the fecund riffle provided them with a maximum amount of food and the depth gave them protection from predatory birds, their worst enemies.

I didn't catch a fish the first year, caught a few by chance the second, and eventually became master of the pool. The key lay in matters that I learned by trial and hundreds of errors. I had to sit rather than crouch or kneel, which kept me low all of the time and comfortable enough to wait for precisely the right moment to cast; and there was indeed a right moment, determined by when a fish had last risen and how frequently it was coming up. I had to inch my way along the bank so that I came close enough to the fish that I could

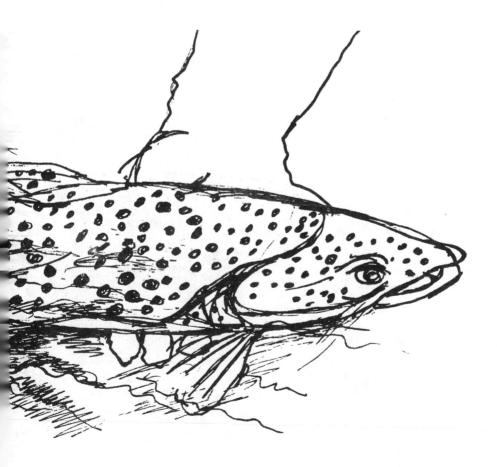

make the shortest possible cast—no more than twenty-five feet; I had regularly, at first, tried to cast forty-five feet or more, from below the pool, over braided currents, and over what I had learned were dozens of skittery trout. From my new position, and with a short low cast, I never lined the vast number of fish in the belly of the pool but fished directly to those in the bend-riffle. I lengthened my leader to twenty-two feet. I discovered that the trout would take no high-floating, Catskill-style dry flies but would come to emergers and those that, without underhackle, lay flat on the surface. Two or three patterns worked best and I depended upon them—but I had four or five others that alone proved fruitful at times.

I used a No. 4 rather than a No. 5 rod and line for this pool eventually, and brought a little net with a long handle so I could trap flies circling into the eddies near my feet without moving. If I did not stand to play a fish, despite all the splashing as I brought one to hand, another fish or two would begin to rise within ten minutes. And when all of this came together, I could take eight or nine large wild fish from this pool without budging.

Five summers ago I came to the pool one day about eleven o'clock, when I knew several mayflies and a small brown caddis would be on the water, shimmied into my familiar spot, and looked at the riffle. A fish was bulging in the current. I scooped up some insects, found a lot of Pale Morning Dun spinners, watched a bit longer, and then made my old short cast up into the riffle. On the third cast, the fish took. It proved a fine brown and after I released it I sat quietly, fluffing my fly, taking fresh line off the reel for my next cast. In ten minutes a new fish was up—did they issue meal tickets here?—and it took the first fly I pitched upstream, one of Craig Mathews's No. 18 Pale Morning Dun spinners, with bits of Z-lon for wings.

I knew this could be a remarkable day. I might break my record of nine fish at one sitting. There were flies everywhere now, even a few Green Drakes, and within a few minutes two more fish were feeding.

There is an old maxim that a fly fisherman should never leave a feeding fish—since you never know when you'll find this one, or a number of them, up again—and I did not leave the pool. But I also did not make another cast. I watched. What a deliciously pleasant sight—two, perhaps three good fish high in the water, dorsals out, wolfing down fly after fly. I was a long distance from those waterways close to the city, to which I'd trekked every spring in my teens, fishing overfished water, keeping everything I caught. We had *needed* those catches then, for our self-esteem, our competition with friends, an indefinable urge, always, for *more*. Now, plying a craft that had taken so much time to learn well, with subtler tackle, did I still have numbers on my brain—numbers that translated into a certain quantity of released fish in some state of exhaustion, even shock, with some immediate fallout from hook and fight? Was it enough to know that I *could* now take a half dozen or more trout from this once-difficult pool—if I so chose?

The flies slowed an hour later and then there was only one last fish up, taking everything, wantonly, a pushover. It had been a wondrous hour and, without making a conscious decision, I realized that I just did not want to stick a hook in any more fish that day; two, coupled with all I'd seen and learned, made a lovely, intense, successful morning.

Five years have passed and I've fished that honey hole a dozen times since. I like to kill an occasional trout now and then these days and to prepare my catch carefully and eat it. I'd forgotten the special pleasure of this whole process for too many years; in the right rivers, it hurts not at all to do this. But I never kill fish from this pool. I'm glad it's still there. I'm glad it's as fecund as it ever was. I'm glad it's always a bit different, and I find that those slight variations in its contours and the feeding patterns of the fish on a given day make it even more exciting to return to this place that I've mastered than I'd have expected.

I've always gone to rivers to catch fish, and I always will; that will remain my primary reason for going. Only the source of my pleasure—and the numbers—have changed.

ME, TOO

Not long after my old pal Clyde was informed that there was very big money to be made writing fly-fishing books, our longtime friendship almost headed south. His longer studies of the fishing neurosis, his extensive and esoteric notebooks, his postmodernist piscatorial poetry had sadly earned him only enough money to buy a couple of jars of salmon eggs. "My new concept," he told me, "is to tell the folks how to catch ten times what they're now catching on flies, of whatever species—and who knows more about catching fish than I do?—and make a small fortune."

He was surely right that, for forty-five years, he'd always caught ten or more times the number of fish I caught, and he knew, of course, that I ran a small publishing firm that published some fly-fishing books. He said that for a mere couple-of-hundred-thousand-dollar advance against future royalties, he could make me a huge fortune.

I told him I only wanted to be thin, not rich.

"But there are ten million fly fishers, all just waiting eagerly for my—"

"Happily there aren't ten million fly fishers," I told him soberly. "The number is extrapolated by the Internal Revenue Service from the bald fact that eight hundred and twenty-seven thousand four hundred and thirty-nine citizens declare on their federal income-tax returns that they earn at least a portion of their income by writing about fly fishing . . . or at least would like to do so." I told him that I got thousands of letters every year advising me that there were *fifty* million all-kinds-of fishermen and everyone of them would crave the proposed book. I told him that the best-selling fly-fishing book I'd published, thirty years ago, by some nifty students of the river, had sold a fraction of that number, and that the few books I'd written had sold a minuscule fraction of that fraction.

"But you don't know how explosive my concept is," Clyde said. "It will change fly fishing completely."

I sort of liked it the way it was but I merely muttered "If I had a quarter for every time I've heard . . ."

"Don't be cynical. My concept involves the architectonics of flies, the astrophysics of fly casting, the morphology of rivers; it blends in tides, retrieves, wading, advanced leader construction, rod repair, midstream lunches—all synthesized, brought into their cohesive and organic whole."

It sounded more like a drunken cook's smorgasbord, but I did not want to be mean to my old friend. In all the years I've edited books I'd seen a few of them march out into the world and conquer it, selling steadily and being genuinely helpful to a lot of fly fishers. And I'd seen a whole lot more descend into the darkness of oblivion on extended wings. I guess I'd survived as a publisher by being right a bit more than I was wrong, was all. I wasn't cynical, but I'd found that a bit of skepticism was the only way I could deal with the unending onslaught of proposals.

Over the years I'd had a number of proposals, such as Clyde's, that I simply could not afford, whatever their prospects. Only a few weeks earlier, I told him, a fellow had written me in broken English from Europe saying that he was pursuing a color theory—why fish were attracted to certain colors, and how they acted when they saw them—that was sure to revolutionize fishing. He said he needed only $25,000 a year for five or six years and he was sure to have the truly revolutionary results. Could I throw in a Pentium computer and life insurance for his family? I was sure to get back my bait with great interest since there were a hundred million fishermen in the world and I could have world rights . . .

Clyde said that color was not the key to fishing success. "Until we have the same optic structure and brain that fish do," he said, "we'll never know what they see. You were right to reject that proposal. But mine—"

"We've been friends for a great while," I said, remembering our childhood trips, the intensity with which we explored and fished then, the way Clyde ate worm sandwiches during one trip. "But I really don't think—"

"It's not a travel or mood book," he said, "like the one you once told me about—that fellow who wanted to fish all the way across the country . . ."

I remembered that proposal well. He was going to start in Virginia, with the first faint touch of spring, work his way up to the Poconos for the Quill Gordon, and then fish the Catskills, when the Hendricksons and March Browns were on. He'd fish the Hendricksons again, further north, then head for Michigan, following the major hatches so as to catch most of them; by early summer he'd be in Montana, where he could fish Pale Morning Duns, Brown Drakes, hoppers, Tricos, and then he'd push further west, to California, where he'd fish some of the spring creeks in the fall. He'd need a camper, of course, but could rent rather than buy that, and he wanted me to research the best local guides for him. "You can have the pleasure of lining up my itinerary," he told me. The trip could cost $23,786— he'd been very careful to keep costs down—and he'd want $50,000 for the writing, half on signing. He'd noted that one of the larger houses had paid $4.4 million for a *Gone with the Wind* spin-off a few months earlier. He was asking for a mere pittance.

"Me, too," I'd told him. "If you can find someone to fund such a trip, I'll go, too, and carry your rods."

I explained to Clyde my version of the economics of book publishing, and fly-fishing-book publishing in particular. I explained them at great length, using a pad to stress how difficult it was to make any money at it, how few people had been able to depend upon it for a living.

"So you think two hundred thousand is too much? Is that what you're telling me?"

"Yes," I said. "It's too much."

"How much isn't too much?" he asked. I mentioned a figure that made him snort.

"I couldn't pay my expenses for a week with that," he said.

I told him I understood, and that the book—to be done properly—would probably take him two years.

We were in my office and the phone rang. I told Clyde I'd have to take it—I was expecting a call from Kashmir, on a mahseer project—and turned from him. The call wasn't the one I was waiting for, but it was a proposal, and I repeated it, for Clyde's benefit. "Check out the rest of the Pacific for another Christmas Island?" I said. "Hire a seaplane? For three months? Four? Crew of three? Photographer?" Clyde was all ears. "Equipment? Of course. Yes. Clothing. Laptop computer?"

"Is he kidding?" whispered Clyde loudly.

I shook my head. No, this was serious. I was told about the magazine possibilities, the sale of information to travel agencies, outfitters, resort builders. I kept nodding. "Only two hundred and fifty thousand dollars? No. No, the figure doesn't scare me. Yes, a quarter of a million isn't a lot for such a pathbreaking voyage. I know. Yes. Well, no, I just don't think it's for us. Not today."

Clyde began to collect up his papers and shove them into the carryall he had brought. He kept shaking his head.

"Sounds like an interesting trip, actually. I guess I'd like to go on that one, too."

"Me, too," said Clyde. "But let's settle for a few bluegill in Ellis Pond, like the old days. I'd love that."

"Me, too."

HEAD WATERS

It is summer and when I turn on the faucet, despite the great drought upstate, water flows easily for as long as I like, ending its stop-and-start trip from wildness to what we call civilization. I watch for a moment, stunned by this rush of clear liquid I've seen ten thousand times before, then twist the faucet until the flow diminishes, trickles, and stops. The water may have begun on some remote hillside more than a hundred miles from my kitchen, but it has come more immediately from a city reservoir not a mile from my crowded apartment, or from one no more than a couple of dozen miles upcountry.

I once fished in such a nearby body of water, unceremoniously called "Reservoir 3," chiefly because my high school friend Bernie, in Brooklyn, had it on good authority that the Canadian exhibit at the old Madison Square Garden Sportsmen's Show dumped their Atlantic salmon and ouananiche there. Bernie, our savant of stockings, was never wrong. And we were all mad to catch ouananiche.

We had seen them at the show one February, when, in the midst of a frozen winter, we longed for spring and the rivers that were our salvation; the fish were long, brilliantly spotted, with a bright reddish hue. There was something magical, exotic, about their name. We had caught only silvery trout, fresh from a hatchery, and these creatures from the wilderness of Canada absolutely exuded wildness. Besides, the name sounded Indian and we all wished we had that blood, or imagined we did. We tried desperately, fruitlessly, with worms, live minnows, spinning lures, and finally flies to extract even one from Reservoir 3—and in the end we had to settle for messes of crappie.

If you follow the liquid trail beyond such reservoirs—usually north, often joined by canals, pipeways, sluices, or man-made rivers to other reservoirs—you will find that in each, successively, the water is colder, the fish more beautiful. Crappie, bluegill, and perch give way to pickerel, largemouth, then smallmouth bass, which in turn, at higher elevations, become brown and rainbow trout.

The reservoirs, man-made, can provide fine sport, and so can the various waterways between them. In one such river, fed by one reservoir and running only three miles into another, I did most of my early trout fishing. It did not feel particularly artificial to me. I was a city kid and almost all flowing water was manna then. Even now, after I have fished the great chalkstreams of England and the greater spring creeks of the West, I go back to this river—and I still find in it a chance to practice certain hard-won truths, to fish over fish that have winced at scores of flies and in water that remains as familiar to me as my living room. The trout then, mostly stocked a few weeks earlier— Bernie knew to the dozen how many had been put in—brought us excitement, especially when we took a larger brown, one held over from the previous season. But we caught no ouananiche.

Above the last reservoir something else happens: the water is colder, clearer, mysterious. In one headwaters creek I know, high in the Catskill Mountains, the gradient steep and the riffles thin, everything is untouched by civilization—or, rather, continues to retreat from what is civilized. There was logging there a hundred years ago. Telephone wires connect a remote wildlife manager's cabin to the nearest town. Now and again some kids walk in, leaving their bikes three miles below. The forest is thick here, and the deadfalls tangle beneath your feet; there's no way to make a living up that way. The river there is quick and cold, even in summer. It's wilderness all right—good as you'll find this side of Labrador.

In spring spate, the river rises ten feet and takes everything in its path; I can see its marks well into the woods. In high summer, like now, its flow oozes between exposed boulders and is clear as water from a tap. The place is overhung with hemlock, willow, and birch, so that the alley of the river is intimate, shady. I have walked up there, skipping from stone to stone when the summer heat is up, in sneakers, feeling the cool water up to my calves, looking for pockets, large enough to hold a trout or two, perhaps with cold seepage from a spring.

There are such pools and runs and undercut banks, and a dry fly pitched into them will bring a quick, eager spurt of water. These trout are not selective feeders; they are thoroughgoing opportunists and will take a Christmas tree of a Royal Coachman as quickly as they'll rise to a fallen ant or bug. Once I saw several large yellow stoneflies, *Perlas,* fluttering over one of the larger pools, switched to a No. 6 Stimulator, and caught a ten-incher, a prize in these small waters.

These are wild brook trout—five, six, sometimes eight inches, on rare occasions a foot long. They have flanks as smooth as an otter's skin, a dark mottled back, rose marks the color of wild strawberries, and striped fins. They wiggle like live jewels when you hoist them out of the water.

Greedy and wanton to their near extinction, vulnerable, full of an innocence and hunger that cannot protect itself, these fish are the ultimate emblems of piscatorial wildness, and it delights me to catch a dozen on barbless hooks and slip them swiftly back into their element. When I first climbed to the fountainhead of all city water and saw them, I stopped thinking of exotic Canadian fish and knew I had found a quiet place that satisfied my subtlest longings for that which was *not* civilized.

Little do those diminutive flashes of light and color know the fate, downriver, of the precious, pure liquid in which they flourish so unconsciously. Little do they care—so long as it is there, so long as the great cities do not drink them to extinction. They are beautiful rare creatures and they dance in my head, sustaining me, and I think of them even now, in the belly of a great gray city, during the dog days of summer, every time I turn on and turn off a faucet.

CONNECTIONS

A friend, a naturalist who has not fished since he was a teenager and won't, on "moral grounds," asked me recently if I *had* to fish to be close to nature. Wasn't it cruel? Wasn't it unnecessary? I said hastily that this was one reason why I went to rivers. "But there's so much to see and touch and understand," he argued. "Must you pursue fish, too?"

Though I have fished since before memory and have never needed a "reason," his questions itched me, and the more I thought about them the more I realized I don't really go to rivers to "connect" with the natural world; I go to catch fish. I go with tackle that I have assembled over a course of many years: a rod I bought only last year because of its space age power and lightness; an old reel I'd found at a country red-tag sale thirteen years ago that worked like a fine watch; some flies I'd tied, but many dozens more that I'd selected with great care, after years of studying the design and architecture of these constructs, trying to imagine what a trout would see, what would best gull it.

I go with old patched waders and a vest crammed with fly dope, tweezers, a thermometer, two nail clippers, extra leaders, tippets, magnifying glasses for my old eyes, my wide-brimmed hat to keep sun off my forehead pocked with scars from basal-cell carcinoma surgeries, and much else. I take leaders I built myself, with materials I finally settled upon after years of trial, with the best knots I could learn. I wear exactly the socks that do not rub my shin-bone skin and a brand of sunglasses I winnowed from ten choices. I go with skills of sight and casting I honed over more than fifty years of going to rivers, and I feel very connected to all of my gear and to the balance of it all—its fitness for the job.

And I have learned how to use it all. I now choose my flies not only to imitate insects I might find, but for the attitude of those flies on the water, especially what I think the trout would see. Over the years I have learned how to approach trout and position myself to best advantage. I learned on certain water to use a four-weight line rather than a five-weight, so it would touch the surface less invasively. If I knew the trout in a river I'd be fishing saw too many ospreys and

pelicans, I'd plan to make one false cast far to the right, over land, and then shoot the line once toward the fish I had located, trying not to cover it with line or leader.

I go to the river to catch trout. Everything I do depends upon that one fact. I am happy to think I am better skilled now than when I began, so many years ago. There may be sunsets, wildflowers galore, rainbows in the sky, good fellowship, good fishing, or lousy fishing; but what has drawn me here, the fulcrum of the entire equation, what will always draw me to water, is the simple prospect of catching a fish.

With luck—and some earned skill—the fly drifts a foot, two feet, and intersects with the fish's feeding lane. The fish that made the circle revealed itself to me individually, announced its intention to take lunch, is there, somewhere beneath the opaque, moving surface. I wait another second or two, then raise the fly smoothly into the air and cast again. This time, when the fly approaches the spot on the flowing surface where the trout rose, I feel the exquisite pleasure one feels when caught in any moment of suspense, of mystery: What will happen? There will be no "meaning" involved, only rejection or acceptance. The hesitation is palpable in the extreme and only later am I aware of how terrifyingly, blessedly concentrated I have been. The fly comes down to where the trout rose; the water pocks and bulges; I raise my rod slightly, and the fish and I are connected.

I need no more.

THE AGING FLY FISHER

As imperceptively as the growth of reason in a two-year-old, age comes to us all, even fly fishers.

At the latter end of the process you see it first in friends a dozen or more years older—how they don't move with the same speed they once did, when you suit up together, how they fuss with fly and leader a bit longer than you remember, as if cobwebs are covering their eyes or brain. You see it when their casts, for so many years smooth and accurate, drift inexplicably away from that rising trout you both stalked. You see it when they wilt before the day is three-quarters gone, as if a tank of gas were coming up empty, sputtering. You see it in the squint, the limp, the heavier breathing. You see it and call it "a bad week," "the extra thirteen pounds he put on this past winter," "a cold," "an ankle, mysteriously sprained." You don't believe it to be what it is—not for a minute—but you can't miss a telltale hint of the whole process.

I don't remember Charlie Brooks slowing down. I fished with him in his last years and he was always as vigorous and animated, in voice and movement, as ever. After a tough childhood during the Great Depression, years in the war, his body began to break up when he passed middle age—gall bladder, heart, this organ and that, bruised, failing. He'd always tell me, after a tough bout, that he never felt better; he told me he figured that if they took an organ a year from him he had enough parts left to carry him down the road quite far enough for his purposes. And then suddenly, in his early sixties, he died.

Everything has its cycle, I guess—a school year that begins in September and ends in late May or June, year after year, so that the student lives by its rhythm. And even after it had ended—after what seems an interminable number of years—it began again for me, when I taught in a college, for twenty-six years. The calendar year had its rhythm, too, beginning in the dead of winter and progressing to late fall, when all is sere, and then to the dead of winter again, when the world hibernates in cold and snow. The fishing season is more logical: April, with its great rebirth of earth and hopes, on through what my friend Palmer Baker happily calls "the sweet of the year," into the dog days of summer, and then the fleeting pleasures and surprises and melancholy of fall. The fishing season is the one my blood is chiefly keyed to—and I wouldn't have it otherwise.

All of these patterns are contained within the larger cycle of a life—for fishermen, a fishing life. We start, somehow, many of us, with some ineluctable tropism or tug toward water, toward a link with that bobber on a placid pond, the most electric object in our lives, its least movement telegraphed to our heart. At not many years younger than I was when I fished such a pond, my granddaughter has taken to asking, with great regularity, about everything from a noodle to a bus, "Wha zat?" It seems to be the emblem of something—the beginning of knowledge, perhaps. Surely it was that when I began to ask, as I watched the bobber and learned to decipher its faintest movement, when I looked to the ring on the water or the little splash made by a bluegill or small bass, when I saw the shadowy turn of something alive—eel, catfish, or perch—in the water's depths. "Wha zat?"—it led me to travel farther and farther afield, as I gained more independence and mobility; it led me to find new ways to fish, to understand more and more about my quarry, to "read" more and more into the great mystery that exists in that other world, beneath the surface. Perhaps the question led—it surely did for me—to fly fishing, for nothing could have seemed a more logical progression, based on hungers for more understanding as well as more challenges. In fly fishing I found all I wanted in fishing. And then other rhythms began, keyed to trout chiefly and to the foods they eat—from the first fumbling days with the clumsy long rod in my hands to halcyon days when I caught some of the largest and most difficult spring-creek trout imaginable. How many minuscule but telling questions led from the one day to the latest? And what fun I had at every turn.

For it is a happy progression, a seasoning of our timber, from bumbling to skill, from not knowing to knowing . . . but never all. Since fly fishing is—as Izaak Walton says—so much like the "Mathematicks" that it can never fully be learned, one's interest rarely falters, and mine hasn't. Nor does it with dozens of companions. I was with Len Wright the first time he went fly fishing for shad. I heard him say, as I heard him say on half a dozen new pieces of water, "What's the drill?" Then I watched him learn it by great concentration, and then, when he'd learned what someone else, more experienced, knew, he began to

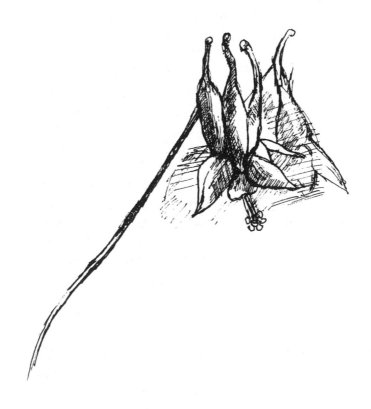

innovate. And he said it to me a dozen times, "Here's the drill," and I began to learn. That's part of aging, isn't it? Learning how to learn, assimilate, modify. It's not a bad route—and in fishing it doesn't seem to end.

Yes, it is easier to see aging in a friend than in oneself. From the slow changes to the abrupt, traumatic moments that punctuate our lives so dramatically and register their terrible changes, we see degenerating bone and muscle, the eyes that see less, the tightened residue of a stroke; they are not us and we read them better. Neither eye nor understanding really perceives what is happening to us until, mostly, it is reflected in someone else's comment or gesture, someone who helps us into a Mackenzie boat that we once could leap into, someone who offers to tie on a fly. Next, I thought, a few years ago, the man will want to help me pee.

Then, first, looking for it, I felt a certain dulling of what I heard, so that I didn't catch a friend's voice above the wind or a fly box slipping out of my pocket; and as I lost some hearing, I began to realize just how much it meant not to hear the whir of a swallow, the slurping rise of a trout; and I kept dropping clippers, knives, fly dope, and boxes, strewing fields with my smaller gear, not knowing I'd done so, losing it all forever. There came a time when I depended more and more upon my eyes—eyes that had read so much and learned to see the wink of a trout's mouth opening underwater—and then they began to fade, to see the world grayer, duller. When a gall bladder attack almost zapped me, and my limp proved to be an advanced dose of degenerative hip disease, I agreed with the maxim that growing old wasn't for sissies. There were reasons for all the tripping, for some of the new clumsiness I thought I'd lost forever. It's not that I don't like the genial optimism of Browning's "Grow old along with me / The best is yet to be," it's just that the hard facts mostly say otherwise.

But there are other changes—other choices—that come with age. We avoid water we know from forty years' hard experience to be dead. We choose the proper fly with less hesitation. We recognize the rise forms instinctively—instinctive after those forty years of looking—and false-cast ten times less than we once did, because we now know how to pitch a fly with a lot less of the old fuss and because a fly line in the air cannot possibly advance our cause with Mr. Brown Trout. We may wade less treacherous water but we read all water better. We may cast a shorter line but we know that coming much closer to a fish will give us a better chance. Because we know a few more of our limitations, and have those limitations, that doesn't mean for a moment that we can't look forward to even better—surely wiser—fishing in the years ahead.

Poised between what we can't and can do, still passionate about our fly fishing, though perhaps satisfied with a bit less, I find myself still asking the great question of my youth, with equal vigor and with ever new and undreamed answers: "Wha zat?"

FISHING, YEA, YEA

A *Wall Street Journal* article, filed from Ennis, Montana, reported that anti-fishing zealots had pelted with rocks the spot a fly fisher was fishing, then plastered his truck with their messages of nay. They want all fishing stopped—for bluegill, walleye, pike, carp, catfish, trout, the gentle bluefish, and Brother Crab—and the eating of them, too, of course.

There is now apparently a Crustacean Liberation Front to protect lobsters; and Mary Tyler Moore, the article reported, once offered $1,000 if a restaurateur would release a seventy-year-old, twelve-pound lobster (Rush Limbaugh offered $2,000 to eat it). That the fly fisherman eats less, if anything, of what he catches these days, means little here. We're talking about a charge of raw cruelty—and a fish struggling against the dangerous line or a hook in the lip is closer to the issue than the death we all owe, even lobsters.

Before I could smile twice and say, "Give me a break," I thought of several good friends who had abandoned their rods precisely because they no longer like the sight of that "live creature thrashing for its life." And I remembered a half dozen deer hunters I know who have stopped their sport (perhaps because the deer is closer to human size) and even a handful of bird shooters who have quit (in their case the most prevalent argument I've heard is that there are just too few grouse and woodcock left in their part of the world, their cover now malls or housing developments).

Fly fishers who throw fish back may seem more moral in this, but they merely have the opportunity to be more, practical than hunters. It's more morally defensible, if defenses are necessary, to fish for food than to fish for pleasure, I suppose, though innocent pleasure has never been much of a sin to my way of thinking; and some friends who kill only stocked fish claim—and they're probably right—that they are improving the gene pool. The best reason to return fish remains Lee Wulff's pragmatic assertion, increasingly true, that gamefish are too valuable to be caught once—which, if I were a moralist, would imply an even less defensible moral position: doing the bad thing with the fish over and over again.

But I'm not a moralist, just an aging fisherman who has caught all manner of fish in a number of different parts of the world for sixty years and has never once questioned either his "right" to do so or the

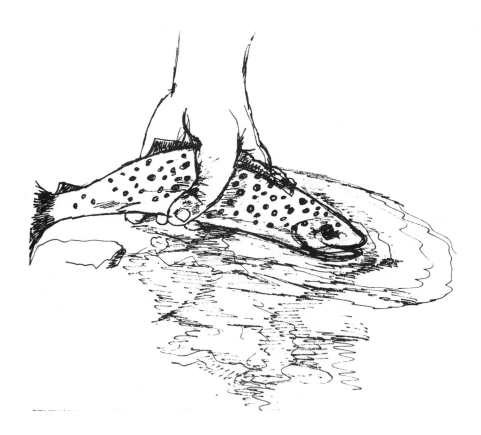

morality of fishing, and never will. I pursue fish because I like the mysterious challenge of gulling them to my fly, because I am enlivened by the intimate connection I then have to a wild creature, because I then like to bring them quickly to hand. I do so for my pleasure and recreation—which is a happy part of a full life—not for the fish's, and I am most concerned about their numbers and health not out of sentiment but mostly so that I can catch more fish, if I choose, and fish that are in better condition.

There, I've revealed myself as a hedonist of the first water: I pursue fish for my own selfish purposes and don't particularly fish for food, though I occasionally like to eat fish—and eating what you catch is a lost pleasure.

I am positive that my pleasure is no pleasure for Mr. Brown Trout. It may not feel with the same nervous system that we feel with; its mouth is not rimmed by the fleshy, sensitive lips we have; and it's cold-blooded, and only some human beings are such. But once hooked, a fish is definitely not comfortable. It would prefer to be near the bottom grubbing for crisp nymphs, rather than struggling against the restraining line, or still rising to those golden bon-bons floating above it.

The trout is not a human being and the repeated Disney-like, anthropomorphic assertions that a fish feels pain the way human beings feel pain are worse than simply misleading and spurious. They're downright dangerous. The anti-fishing and anti-hunting folk want fishermen to think in terms of human pain; but when Lord Byron in that infamous passage in *Don Juan* says that the "quaint, old, cruel coxcomb" Izaak Walton ought to have a hook in his gullet "and a small trout to pull it," he's sentimentalizing a fish's discomfort and severely undervaluing human pain, which civilization—with too many notable exceptions in our century—has generally tried to avoid since it stopped drawing and quartering, flaying, using the rack.

Consider the implications of this response Ed Zern received after a duck-hunting article of his appeared in *Audubon* magazine: "I hope you are shot in the gut," the nice bird-loving lady wrote, "and lie in a cold wet ditch and die slowly."

I don't enjoy watching any creature suffer—a mess of fish flopping on the bank or fish on a stringer, undulating listlessly, are unnecessary; I don't like to kill grasshoppers or any other wild creature slowly—except deer flies. I am the mortal enemy of Brother Deer Fly and kill every one I can, with impunity. After three of them have stabbed the tops of my hands, I grow to love the sweet crackling sound when I crunch them slowly.

Nature itself can seem pretty cruel. The heron will peck the back of a fish it cannot possibly lift from the water, leaving it disfigured, even disabled, for life. Lions begin to eat their prey while it is still alive. The gored lion dies slowly, abandoned by its pride, ravaged in the end by its mortal enemy, hyenas. A bluefish feeding frenzy is nature red in tooth and claw, but it is probably not, in the animal realm, cruelty at all, again an anthropomorphism. And fly fishermen, except when they become too profligate, wanton, in their pleasures, seem to me among the most innocent creatures in the universe.

My small contribution to the question of pain is the theory and practice of using the heaviest line, leader, rod, and hook possible. Ninety percent of my pleasure comes from hooking a fish. I don't find it more "sporting" to pussyfoot around with a fish until it's dead of exhaustion (or boredom), any more than I like the idea of a slow hangman. Get the fish in quickly and whack it abruptly on the head if you're going to eat it, or off the hook if you're not. This requires balance and judgment, which everything worthwhile requires: your equipment should not be too heavy to raise your quarry or your leader so light that it will ensure that you will festoon the fish's lip with your Pale Morning Dun, size 18, thorax tie. Since the trout has no hands to help it extract flies, its having "won" the contest by biting the too-light leader leaves it in worse shape than had it been caught by some-one with both hand and hemostat.

Though we will never convince a skeptic that there is relatively little pain for the fish in the fish's scheme of things, we aren't the worse for thinking about the issue now and then. I suspect that part of my addiction to fly fishing, after a childhood spent with worm and spinner, has to do with the fact that bait often gets taken into the belly, with the hook, and a fish cannot be disengaged without harm. My old friend Louis Rubin has argued, wittily, that bait-fishing is *more* moral because if a fish gets away at least it comes from the encounter with the tail of a worm, a bit of clam, for its efforts. But I guess that falls into the category of "fairness" to the fish rather than concern for

its possible pain. Fairness? We use space age rods, watchlike reels, imported leaders, an arsenal worthy of General Schwarzkopf, for a creature with no brain as we know it at all.

The poet John Gay, (disdaining nets, spears, trolling, and bait of all kinds), says, "Let me, less cruel, cast the feathered hook." I fish with a fly because it's more demanding for me, more intriguing in every way, and because it can be less cruel.

The world is full of a zillion sources of pain, from child molestation to genocidal wars to the medical problems of the folk next door, and one's own. And the tending of one's own house, the minding of one's own business, lost arts, are worth the worry far more than Disney anthropomorphism and, perhaps next, worry that cut plants may scream or rocks may cry. Don't those guys have anything better to do with their lives than save the carp and the lobster?

I love to think of generations of kids catching bluegill, as I did, with willow branches, stout cord, bobber, and worm, and those kids growing up to fish a fly to some pretty little brook trout or hundred-pound tarpon—and oh, cruel thought, would it cause great pain and suffering *to me* and a couple of million other folk to give up fishing forever.